The Business of the Roman Inquisition in the Early Modern Era

Established in 1542, the Roman Inquisition operated through a network of almost fifty tribunals to combat heretical and heterodox threats within the papal territories. Whilst its theological, institutional and political aspects have been well-studied, until now no sustained work has been undertaken to understand the financial basis upon which it operated. Yet – as *The Business of the Roman Inquisition in the Early Modern Era* shows – the fiscal autonomy enjoyed by each tribunal was a major factor in determining how the Inquisition operated. For, as the flow of cash from Rome declined, each tribunal was forced to rely upon its own assets and resources to fund its work, resulting in a situation whereby tribunals increasingly came to resemble businesses. As each tribunal was permitted to keep a substantial proportion of the fines and confiscations it levied, questions quickly arose regarding the economic considerations that may have motivated the Inquisition's actions. Dr Maifreda argues that the Inquisition, with the need to generate sufficient revenue to continue working, had a clear incentive to target wealthy groups within society who could afford to yield up substantial revenues. Furthermore, as secular authorities also began to rely upon a levy on these revenues, the financial considerations of decisions regarding heresy prosecutions become even greater. Based upon a wealth of hitherto neglected primary sources from the Vatican and local Italian archives, Dr Maifreda reveals the underlying financial structures that played a vital part in the operations of the Roman Inquisition. By exploring the system of incentives and pressures that guided the actions of inquisitors in their procedural processes and choice of victims, a much clearer understanding of the Roman Inquisition emerges. This book is an English translation of *I denari dell'inquisitore. Affari e giustizia di fede nell'Italia moderna* (Turin: Einaudi, 2014).

Germano Maifreda is Professor of Economic History at the Department of Historical Studies of the Università degli Studi di Milano, Italy.

Routledge Research in Early Modern History

In the same series:

Penury into Plenty
Dearth and the Making of Knowledge in Early Modern England
Ayesha Mukherjee

Violence and Emotions in Early Modern Europe
Edited by Susan Broomhall and Sarah Finn

India in the Italian Renaissance
Visions of a Contemporary Pagan World 1300–1600
Meera Juncu

The English Revolution and the Roots of Environmental Change: The Changing Concept of the Land in Early Modern England
George Yerby

Honourable Intentions? Violence and Virtue in Australian and Cape Colonies, c. 1750 to 1850
Edited by Penny Russell and Nigel Worden

Social Thought in England, 1480–1730: From Body Social to Worldly Wealth
A. L. Beier

Dynastic Colonialism: Gender, Materiality and the early modern House of Orange-Nassau
Susan Broomhall and Jacqueline van Gent

The Business of the Roman Inquisition in the Early Modern Era
Germano Maifreda

The Business of the Roman Inquisition in the Early Modern Era

Germano Maifreda

Translation by Loretta Valtz Mannucci

LONDON AND NEW YORK

First published 2017
by Routledge
2 Park Square, Milton Park, Abingdon, Oxon OX14 4RN

and by Routledge
711 Third Avenue, New York, NY 10017

Routledge is an imprint of the Taylor & Francis Group, an informa business

© 2017 Germano Maifreda

Originally published in Italian as *I denari dell'inquisitore. Affari e giustizia di fede nell'Italia moderna* (© 2014 Giulio Einaudi editore s.p.a., Torino).

The right of Germano Maifreda to be identified as authorof this work has been asserted in accordance with sections 77 and 78 of the Copyright, Designs and Patents Act 1988.

All rights reserved. No part of this book may be reprinted or reproduced or utilised in any form or by any electronic, mechanical, or other means, now known or hereafter invented, including photocopying and recording, or in any information storage or retrieval system, without permission in writing from the publishers.

Trademark notice: Product or corporate names may be trademarks or registered trademarks, and are used only for identification and explanation without intent to infringe.

British Library Cataloguing in Publication Data
A catalogue record for this book is available from the British Library

Library of Congress Cataloging in Publication Data
Names: Maifreda, Germano, author.
Title: The business of the Roman Inquisition in the early modern era / by Germano Maifreda.
Other titles: Denari dell'inquisitore. English
Description: New York : Routledge. |
Series: Routledge research in early modern history | Includes bibliographical references and index.
Identifiers: LCCN 2016036620 (print) | LCCN 2016047201 (ebook)
| ISBN 9781472480132 (alk. paper) | ISBN 9781315615905 (ebook)
Subjects: LCSH: Inquisition–Economic aspects--Italy.
Classification: LCC BX1713 .M2513 2016 (print) | LCC BX1713 (ebook)
| DDC 272/.20945–dc23
LC record available at https://lccn.loc.gov/2016036620

ISBN: 978-1-4724-8013-2 (hbk)
ISBN: 978-1-315-61590-5 (ebk)

Typeset in Sabon
by HWA Text and Data Management, London

Printed and bound by CPI Group (UK) Ltd, Croydon, CR0 4YY

Contents

List of tables vi
Acknowledgements vii
List of abbreviations viii

Introduction 1

PART I

The economy of the Holy Office 11

1 The financing of the inquisitorial system 13

2 Managing the courts of faith 54

3 Monetary penalties and the building of the inquisitorial machine 87

PART II

The Inquisition and economic life 137

4 "The citizen dies, the man remains": confiscation 139

5 A pervasive Inquisition 180

6 The inquisitor between land and finance 226

Epilogue 275
Index 286

Tables

1.1	Income of the local courts of the Holy Office in the year of 1748	22
1.2	Income and expenditures of the Congregation of the Holy Office	24
1.3	Years in which fixed incomes were assigned by popes or the Congregation of the Holy Office	29
2.1	Expenses of the Congregation of the Holy Office	66
2.2	Receipts and expenses of the local courts of the Holy Office in 1748	79
6.1	Income and expenditure of the Siena Inquisition	241

Acknowledgements

This is the revised edition of my 2014 book *I denari dell'inquisitore. Affari e giustizia di fede nell'Italia moderna* (Turin: Einaudi). My research would not have been possible without the warm collaboration of my colleagues in the Department of Historical Studies at the University of Milan, who took the anomalous incursion of an economic historian into a historiographical "country" presenting many difficult, or even uncharted, areas as an interesting venture. Grado Giovanni Merlo, then Chair of the Department, willingly read chapter drafts, sharing the thoughts and research of decades spent in the study of Europe in the late Middle Ages. Marina Benedetti, Elena Brambilla, Claudia di Filippo Bareggi and Susanna Peyronel Rambaldi, with their extensive knowledge of the complexities of religious heterodoxy and of the courts of faith, were always ready to discuss the questions and problems I found along my way.

Maria Luisa Betri, our present departmental chair, not only did me the honour of appointing me Vice-Chair of the Department: on the book's publication in Italian, she also encouraged me to revise the text with a view to publication in English. Professor Loretta Valtz Mannucci, herself a historian, has, as usual, proved to be much more than a translator, offering suggestions of content and form which have strengthened the text. Among the various colleagues in Rome, I am especially grateful to Gaetano Sabatini for his constant encouragement and his many stimulating theories; and to Marina Caffiero, Serena Di Nepi, Vittorio Frajese and the participants in the series of seminars *L'archivio e la storia. Temi e ricerche dall'Archivio della Congregazione per la dottrina della fede*, organized by the University of Rome La Sapienza and the Congregazione per la Dottrina della Fede, held in the Vatican City in 2012 and 2013; Monsignor Alejandro Cifres Giménez and Dr Daniel Ponziani took an interest in my research and, in a number of ways, made it easier to pursue. I have had the constant support of Loris De Lion and the suggestions of Edoardo Demo, Massimo Firpo, Sergio Luzzato, Mauro Perani, Giovanna Tonelli, Lucia Travaini, and Fabiana Veronese. Finally, I am especially grateful to Einaudi's Andrea Bosco, who first decided to publish the book in Italian; and for his suggestions for the text, as well as for having facilitated Routledge's acquisition of English rights. I am grateful to Max Novick for his editorial assistance. Of course, the responsibility for the results of that research, and for the various interpretations based upon it, are solely mine.

Abbreviations

ACCO	Archivio Centrale del Consiglio degli Orfanotrofi e Pio Albergo Trivulzio, Milan
ACDF	Archivio della Congregazione per la Dottrina della Fede, Vatican City
ASM	Archivio di Stato di Milano, Milan
ASV	Archivio Segreto Vaticano, Vatican City
ASVe	Archivio di Stato di Venezia, Venice
BAM	Biblioteca Ambrosiana, Milan
BAV	Biblioteca Apostolica Vaticana, Vatican City
Fc	Finanza confische
Mrm	The Medieval and Renaissance Manuscripts. Section I: The Roman Inquisition
Oec	Oeconomica
Si	Inquisizione di Siena
So	Sant'Officio
St.st.	Stanza storica
TCD	The Library of Trinity College, Dublin

Note

Punctuation and accents in selections from manuscripts or printed texts of the sixteenth–eighteenth centuries were modernized in the Italian edition of this volume, capital letters were suppressed, except for cases in which they appeared to be relevant in conveying emphasis or respect. Abbreviated words, both in Latin and in Italian, were spelt out and some obsolete spelling usages (especially plurals in *j* and *ij*) were modernized.

Introduction

Economics, declared Alfred Marshall, investigates the fate of humanity as it engages in "the ordinary business of life". So this book, setting out the story of the Roman Inquisition from the point of view of its economic management, casts an "ordinary" eye on an institution which today seems exceptional in a number of ways: the Congregation of the Sacred Roman and Universal Inquisition – or Holy Office – established in 1542 to direct the repression of heterodoxy, chiefly in the Italian peninsula, through an extended network of local courts.

But is it really important to study the conduct of the Inquisition through the magnifying lens of economics? Do we not risk trivializing its historic import, watering it down with a flood of colourless book-keeper's numbers? Before we can turn to our central theme, these legitimate questions need answering. A few brief examples will help us.

On 1 January 1749, Angelo Gattelli, Inquisitor of Vicenza, drew up the balance sheet of his court for the previous year. The following day he sent his accounts to Rome, together with a letter lamenting the difficult financial situation in which he had been obliged to operate for years. The Vicentine Holy Office had little income and, after more than six years in the post, Brother Gattelli had recently been obliged to pay a substantial accumulated debt out of his own pocket. In addition, the inquisitor reminded his superiors, the new year brought with it

> an imminent and large expense due to the necessity of imprisoning [...] Giovan Battista Carraro and Melchiorre Tanesco, both from [the town of] Bassano, who, inasmuch as extremely poor, as my Vicar in that town writes me, must fall upon the expenses of the Holy Office and be captured and transported here and kept – God knows for how long – and it will be a huge expense.

Vicenza's *Podestà* had already declared himself ready to proceed with the arrest of the accused: he required only the official "warrant of arrest". That would open a new and weighty item under expenses – and one which was all too likely to prove unsustainable. So Gattelli appealed "to the fondness and liberality of this Supreme" Congregation, closing his missive by pressing "the usual humble kiss upon the hem of the Sacred purple".[1]

It is unlikely that this brief document, which comes to us as a note attached to the accounts deposited in the Archive of the Congregation for the Doctrine of the Faith, would draw the curiosity of anyone researching the history of the Inquisition in search of compelling trials or vivid biographies of the judges and the accused. Gattelli is only one of the many inquisitors who carried out the thousands of formal trials – between 50,000 and 75,000, according to recent estimates compiled by Andrea Del Col – held on Italian soil in the period we are considering. The "extremely poor" Giovan Battista Carraro and Melchiorre Tanesco from Bassano del Grappa, mentioned so curtly in the letter, were only two of the many individuals – from 200,000 to 300,000 according to the estimate already cited – formally accused by the Roman Inquisition between the mid-sixteenth century and the end of the eighteenth.[2] The complaints of the friar inquisitor mix and consider the dramatic human situations and the murky exigencies of financial constraints that lie beneath the veil of bureaucratic indifference. The arrest, detention and trial of two poverty-stricken peasants would seem to concern him chiefly as a vexing occasion of personal expense. Yet, had this annoying drain upon his personal finances not existed, today we would not even have the stark evidence of these two that the printed names evoke.

Gattelli's report, though dictated by the "ordinary" need for money, can, indeed, help us bring to light a story which has fallen into total historical oblivion. In fact, the Venetian State Archives can give us a fairly broad picture of Carraro and Tanesco, who we learn were simple workers – one in a shop making felt hats and the other in a typographer's – denounced to the Inquisition by acquaintances for abuse of the sacraments, after they had practised, and taught, love spells using consecrated Hosts.[3]

Moving from a note attached to a balance sheet, the historian can glean many hints and broaden his research to other aspects of inquisitorial activity. The documents essential to protecting the economic interests of the states, the institutions and the single individuals involved, have all been preserved with great care and especially stringent criteria, and even the Holy Office itself archived them for centuries and used them to control the movement of its own accounts, to certify property ownership of real estate, to demonstrate the long-standing nature of incomes and privileges which it and its courts enjoyed. The same care was not always exercised with regard to trial documents, transcripts of testimony or of torture proceedings, sentences and abjurations: documents which, in the past, seemed both more difficult and less urgent to put in order, preserve, copy and transmit (and turned out to be, more difficult to save from the commitment to destruction moving both the heirs of the victims and the executioners, who had something to fear from history).[4]

The letter the Inquisitor of Vicenza wrote on 1 January 1749 opens a second order of considerations, reminding us that the Holy Office's activity was, to a significant degree, subject to the availability of funds. As we shall see, the Holy Office's courts, adhering to a model inherited from the Middle Ages, were financially autonomous and handled their assets in largely independent ways. The costs Gattelli sustained for the arrests and the prosecution of the case concerning the two poor workers would not have been covered by the annual allocation of funds or benefice settlements from the Holy See, as we might assume assimilating the structure of the Inquisition to that of present-day State administrations of justice. Apart from exceptional cases, the costs would have been covered with the income, revenues and patrimony which the Vicenza court had obtained or accumulated over the centuries. Should such resources have proven insufficient, as had been Gattelli's case in the previous years, the inquisitor himself was called upon to cover the debt, using his personal patrimony or that of his usual convent.

Day after day, the judges of the faith had, then, to keep an attentive eye upon the costs of their decisions to intervene. The investigations, the testimonies, the arrests, the imprisonment of the accused, the sentences pronounced and every other operation connected with the inquisitorial procedure ended up inevitably under a very attentive scrutiny of the relationship between the costs which would have to be met and the benefits which could be obtained. Accused who were prosperous had to sustain the expenses entailed in their imprisonment and thus contribute directly to the defence of religious orthodoxy; the prosecution of "very poor" culprits like Battista Carraro and Melchiorre Tanesco represented, instead, a total financial loss for the Vicentine Holy Office.

From the point of view of income, the inquisitors were required not only to administer the properties and the rents assigned to them, but to increase the resources at their disposition so as to strengthen the potentialities of their Office. This usually occurred through investments in real estate – managed directly by the inquisitors themselves with paid helpers, or entrusted to tenants or share-croppers – in public or bank bonds, in loans to individuals or communities or through the infliction of fines and the confiscation of property belonging to condemned individuals.

The day-to-day activities of the Inquisition, then, saw a close and historically critical joining together of the persecution of a mission – the protection of the integrity and purity of a dogmatic Catholic patrimony – and the careful administration of an economic enterprise which was a necessary prerequisite of the efficiency and continuity of this mission. We must not forget that what we may call the more clamorous actions of the Holy Office – actions which remain indelibly impressed upon documentary memory in the form of inquiries, arrests, interrogations, torture, condemnations, forced abjurations, imprisonments and the stake – all had their costs and often produced profits. "Prosecuting many cases, and giving satisfaction to the officials, ministers and servants of the Holy Office, cannot be done at all well with so little coming in", complained, for example, the Inquisitor of Bergamo, writing to Rome in the 1620s;[5] he was reminding his superiors that the efficient exercise of the *Officium fidei* required considerable resources and that, lacking these, his activity was exposed to the shifting and complex equilibriums which always develop throughout the history of humanity between practical limits and the possibility of action.

The Roman Inquisition of the early modern period was a complex organization, whose jurisdiction encompassed virtually the whole of Catholicism, though in practice it was exercised principally in continental Italian territory. Sicily and Sardinia were, in fact, under the jurisdiction of the Spanish Inquisition. At the head of the inquisitorial structure was the Congregation of the Holy Office, a commission established by Pope Paul III and made up of a varying number of cardinal inquisitors who met several times each week, sometimes in his presence, deciding the organization's general strategy. It was the "highest immoveable Mover" within the constellation of "local" or "peripheral" courts which, from the sixteenth through the eighteenth centuries, were in part continuations of courts established during the medieval period and in part *ex novo* structures.[6] The "Supreme" Congregation acted as an inquisitorial court of ultimate appeal, assuming the final decision in especially important or complex cases which had been originally brought before local courts; but it also acted autonomously, setting up investigations of its own, which it placed in the hands of a Commissioner of Judges nominated *ad hoc*. In all questions appertaining to the defence of the Catholic faith, the Roman commission communicated directly with the local inquisitors and the other religious and lay authorities involved in action regarding the justice of the faith: the apostolic nuncios; the bishops; the princes; and the highest officials of the republics, the governing and administrative structures of the states in which *Ancien régime* Italy was divided.

Even basic economic decisions were taken within the Roman Congregation, which governed the overall structure through a constant attention to territorial links and careful *ad hoc* intervention. As we shall see in the course of this book, local courts had ample margins of autonomy in managing their daily affairs, but were also required to illustrate and defend periodically the financial results of their administration. Rome, in turn, kept careful and constant watch over the economic decisions of its inquisitors. At the beginning of March, 1626, for example, the judge of faith in Mondovì (Cuneo) received this brief note:

> I inform your reverence that I have received the sentences and the abjurations of the Calvinists of Mompolieri [Montpellier]. I have already sent opportune orders to the Father Inquisitor in Saluzzo so that he sends you the necessary documents regarding Moisè Leonillo, Jew, imprisoned there. In furnishing the Inquisition with the movables, as he writes having partly done, I remind your reverence to be cautious in considering the need to provide and the revenues of this Inquisition, advising care to not incur debt.[7]

The letter bundles together the reference to some of the most important and fearful activities of the courts of faith – here the acts regarding the Huguenot bastion of Montpellier, besieged and conquered by the King of France, Louis XIII four years earlier, and the considerable Jewish presence in the seventeenth century Duchy of Savoy – with admonitions to be parsimonious in renewing the local court, occasioned by the fear that the Piedmontese inquisitor's accounts might fall into a negative balance.

A similar communication, sent from Rome the following year – this time directed to Novara – opened informing the inquisitor that the bishop had been invited to "advise the curates to abstain from absolving indifferently those who refuse to denounce heretics or suspects of heresy [...] as that absolution is privileged", and, immediately after, he adds "As for the payment which the Fathers of the *Grazie* in Milan and their substitutes must make to this Inquisition: since, as you write, the time set for payment has arrived, your reverence can oblige them to give satisfaction before the competent judge".[8] The defence of a fundamental and sensitive area of the repressive mechanism – the prohibition for parish priests to absolve in confession penitents suspected of heresy or of the protection of heretics was linked here – with no change of tone – to the brisk reiteration of practical business procedure. The Inquisitor in Novara was invited to take a defaulting debtor – a convent of his own order and an inquisitorial seat, as Milan's Santa Maria delle Grazie (containing the fresco of the *Last Supper* by Leonardo da Vinci) was – to court to ensure the continuity of the income of the court he himself presided.

It was the very organizational model of the Holy Office, established over the decades of the sixteenth century, which made the connection between judicial activity and the management of accounts fundamental. The Congregation of the Holy Office had its own accounts and its own specific sources of income. Without guaranteeing the economic health of the peripheral courts, it imposed limitation of expenses on the inquisitors, obliging them to dedicate time and energies to preserving – if not increasing – their incomes. So the inquisitor became a sort of entrepreneur: increasing his income he could exercise his function more efficiently and improve his living conditions and the quality of his service allowing income to dwindle, he would of necessity have to cut back his activities and find other funds, compromising his standard of living, his personal reputation and the efficacy of his battle against heresy. So we shall need to look carefully at the events and the overall repercussions of the Inquisition's administrative model, based on the budgetary autonomy of the individual peripheral courts and on the limited nature of the resources at their disposition. It is a model which certainly has important effects upon the administration, the efficiency and the operational continuity of the Holy Office during the centuries though, as important scholars have observed, it is still today almost wholly unexamined.[9]

The economic history of the early modern Inquisition does not, however, consist only in the story of the construction of its managerial model, nor yet in the analysis of the contingent repercussions of that model on the behaviour of individual inquisitors and the operations of the courts of faith. As we shall see in the course of this book, the ways in which the funds needed to make the machinery of the Holy Office function – starting with the fines of the condemned and the confiscation of their property – produced an incessant effort to build reputation and public consensus so as to maximize the efficiency of its activity in repressing heresy.

The question of property confiscation has recently produced important research, which has also examined anew the theological-juridical premises, as well as the collaborations and the controversies which developed between the Inquisition and the secular authorities in the day-to-day execution (and division) of tasks. These studies show us that, for the Holy Office, confiscations represented a noteworthy source of income – and of negotiations with local governments.[10]

Yet we shall also see here that, for the inquisitors, the confiscations and the other monetary penalties were far more than a source of funds. They were first of all an agile instrument for the enlargement of the power of justice of faith. They deprived individuals of all social groups of their material support and, shattering the hereditary transmission of estates of great prestige and visibility, set a tangible seal upon their own supremacy over some of the oldest and most highly revered social institutions of the *Ancien régime*: the permanence of the family name, the preservation of entailed properties and their intact transmission to the following generations. Confiscation procedures, further, provided inquisitors with the opportunity of securing information which had not emerged during the trial and, thus, enabled them to open new offensive procedures. We shall also see that fines constituted a crucial instrument of alliance and dialogue also (though not only) in terms of conflict between the ecclesiastical courts and the secular authorities, who were charged with the practical task of laying hands on the property to be confiscated. Once completed the phase of the inquisitorial trial – conducted by ecclesiastical authorities in a climate of nearly impenetrable secrecy – the justice of the faith burst into full social visibility at the moment of confiscation and conversed seriously with secular authorities, developing a common political language and a common policy of repression.

Finally, it is well to remember that, in the almost total loss of the documents produced by the courts of faith in the Italian peninsula, the documents compiled to enable fines to be collected can furnish a notable historic source for the study of the Inquisition as a whole. A few papers from the mid-1600s documenting the post-mortem confiscation of the property of two women – Anna Maria Pamolea and her maid, Margaritta Martignone – are all that allows us to know today that they were burnt at the stake in Milan for witchcraft in 1641, after more than four years of imprisonment in the convent of Santa Maria delle Grazie.[11] The simple list of their belongings, set down by duchy authorities the day after the execution, sheds a bit of light, however feeble, upon their stories. The young Anna Maria Madrillos, daughter of Hernández, Spanish chatelain of Mezzo, near Bellinzona, "married for love" by a certain Benedetto Pamolea, was subsequently left a widow with three children. Imprisoned by the Holy Office, she had entrusted the young Benedetto to a spinner who had brought silk to her to weave for some years. Thanks to the transcripts of the confiscation procedures held after her execution, we can hear, however formalized by the bureaucrat's pen, some of the words the spinner proffered in November, 1641:

> I knew the said Pamolea and also the said Margaritta, her servant, more or less any time these last four years, because a month before she went to prison in the Holy Office, I was giving her the silk to weave, being that I spin, only I consigned it to one of her servants – a certain Sabetta another servant of the moment – but this Margaritta I met only in prison, and while Anna Maria was in prison the father prior of the *Grazie* sent for me, and he told me to look after her house, and one of her sons called Benedetto, who even now I have at my own house.[12]

Spinner Francesco Ferrari's deposition reveals an unexpected permeability in the Inquisition's prisons, thanks to which the prisoner entrusted the prior of the Dominican convent with messages concerning the administration of her household and the care of her son. The same documents further clarify that, during the long years in which the mother defended herself in vain against the accusation of witchcraft, he was maintained with the sale of property belonging to Anna Maria and he was constantly supervised by the inquisitor. This personage, long before he had succeeded in condemning her to the stake had assumed power of attorney for the prisoner, taking possession, as well, of such estate documents as her defunct husband's will.[13] In this manner, the ecclesiastical judge could intervene in the duration and type of sale of the property belonging to the accused, playing a subtle role in the regulation of familial and relational dynamics. Understanding the ways in which a woman accused of witchcraft faced (to use Marshall's phrase) the "ordinary business of life", brings sharply into focus the inquisitor's unexpectedly pervasive role, stretching far beyond the traditional trial situation. Around the core relationship between judge and accused, a whole social space comes into view.

Notes

1 ACDF, So, St.st., LL5f, *Inquisizione di Vicenza*, Inquisitor Angelo Gattelli, Vicenza, January 2, 1749. With accounts for the year 1748 attached.
2 Overall estimates regarding the activities of the Holy Office from the fifteenth through the sixteenth centuries may be found in Del Col (2006), p. 779.
3 ASVe, *Senato, Deliberazioni Roma "expulsis papalistis"*, box 60 and 61, unnumbered papers; ACDF, *Decreta So*, 1748, seria quarta, June 12, 1748, c. 181r. My thanks to Fabiana Veronese for bringing these documents to my attention. We also find a brief reference to Angello Gatelli's activity in Veronese (2009–10), pp. 156–7.

4 For an initial survey of the history and the present conditions of the archival documents of the Roman Inquisition see: Del Col, Paolin (1991); Various authors (2000); Bonora (2008).
5 ACDF, So, St.st., GG3c, p. 66r, Bergamo, April 13, 1622.
6 For the evocative metaphor, see Simoncelli (1988), p. 9.
7 BAV, Barb. Lat. 6334, p. 55v, Rome, March 2, 1626.
8 BAV, Barb. Lat. 6335, p. 32r-v, Rome, February 6, 1627.
9 See Prosperi (1991); Tedeschi (1996); Prosperi (2003); Prosperi (2008); Benedetti (2008); Lavenia (2003, 2004, 2010); Del Col (2006), pp. 141 *et seg.*; Peyronel (2007). Merlo (2007), p. 28, has indicated the need to go through archival deposits which can shed light on the procedures regarding the confiscation of heretics' property systematically. It is emblematic that one of the most recent studies devoted to the Roman Inquisition (Black 2009) gave no attention at all to the economic aspects.
10 Lavenia (2004); Lavenia (2010).
11 ASM, *Finanze*, series *Confische* (hereafter Fc), box 2166, folder 1, sub-folder 3, transcript of interrogation opened on November 15, 1641, un-numbered papers. I have discussed the historiographic potentialities of the papers regarding confiscations in Maifreda (2006).
12 ASM, Fc, box 2166, folder 1, sub-folder 1, transcript of the interrogation which began on November 15, 1641, un-numbered papers.
13 "I have gone to a lot of expense" – affirmed spinner Francesco Ferrari – "and I have here all the stuff contained in the said inventory, except for what was sent to the said Mrs Anna Maria, which the said father inquisitor says he has taken into account. *Declares* I keep the boy in my house, and said father inquisitor had him consigned to me with the said stuff to keep him saying he had the will of his father, who was owner of everything and she [Anna Maria] was tutor [...] and the father inquisitor told me that everything belonged to said Pamoleo as appears in the will which he had" (ibid., pp. 4v–5r).

Bibliography

Benedetti, M. (2008) *Inquisitori lombardi del Duecento*, Rome: Edizioni di storia e letteratura.
Black, C. F. (2009) *The Italian Inquisition*, New Haven, CT and London: Yale University Press.
Bonora, E. (2008) 'L'archivio dell'Inquisizione e gli studi storici: primi bilanci e prospettive a dieci anni dall'apertura', *Rivista storica italiana* (120): 968–1002.
Del Col, A. (2006) *L'Inquisizione in Italia dal XII al XXI secolo*, Milan: Mondadori.
Del Col, A. and Paolin, G. (1991) (eds) *L'Inquisizione romana in Italia nell'età moderna. Archivi, problemi di metodo e nuove ricerche. Atti del seminario internazionale, Trieste, 18–20 maggio 1988,* Udine: Del Bianco.
Lavenia, V. (2000) 'I beni dell'eretico, i conti dell'inquisitore. Confische, Stati italiani, economia del sacro tribunale' in *L'inquisizione e gli storici: un cantiere aperto. Tavola rotonda nell'ambito della Conferenza annuale della ricerca (Roma, 24–25 giugno 1999)*, Rome: Accademia nazionale dei Lincei, 47–94.
Lavenia, V. (2003) 'Gli ebrei e il fisco dell'Inquisizione. Tributi, espropri e multe tra "500" e "600"', in *L'inquisizione e gli storici: un cantiere aperto. Tavola rotonda nell'ambito della Conferenza annuale della ricerca (Roma, 24–25 giugno 1999)*, Rome: Accademia nazionale dei Lincei, 325–56.

Lavenia, V. (2004) *L'infamia e il perdono. Tributi, pene e confessione nella teologia morale della prima età moderna*, Bologna: Il Mulino.
Lavenia, V. (2010) 'Struttura economica: Inquisizione romana', in A. Prosperi (ed.) *Dizionario storico dell'Inquisizione,* with the collaboration of V. Lavenia, J. Tedeschi, Pisa: Edizioni della Normale, vol. 3.
Maifreda, G. (2006) 'Culture popolari e culture dello scambio in età preindustriale. Idee per una ricerca', *Studi storici Luigi Simeoni* (56): 295–332.
Merlo, G. G. (2007) *Problemi documentari dell'Inquisizione medievale in Italia,* in S. Peyronel Rambaldi (2007), 19–30.
Peyronel Rambaldi, S. (2007) *Introduzione,* in Eadem (ed.) *I tribunali della fede. Continuità e discontinuità dal Medioevo all'età moderna,* Turin: Claudiana, 5–17.
Prosperi, A. (1991) 'Per una storia dell'Inquisizione romana' in Del Col and Paolin (1991), 27–64.
Prosperi, A. (2003) *L'inquisizione romana. Letture e ricerche*, Rome: Edizioni di storia e letteratura.
Prosperi, A. (2008) *Prefazione* in M. Benedetti (2008), pp. IX–XII.
Simoncelli, P. (1988) 'Inquisizione romana e Riforma in Italia', *Rivista storica italiana* (1): 5–125.
Tedeschi, J. (1996) 'New Light on the Organization of the Roman Inquisition', *Annali di storia moderna e contemporanea* (2): 265–74.
Various authors. (2000) *L'inquisizione e gli storici: un cantiere aperto. Tavola rotonda nell'ambito della Conferenza annuale della ricerca (Roma, 24–25 giugno 1999),* Rome: Accademia nazionale dei Lincei.
Various authors. (2003) *Le inquisizioni cristiane e gli ebrei. Tavola rotonda nell'ambito della Conferenza annuale della ricerca. Roma, 20–21 dicembre 2001,* Rome: Accademia nazionale dei Lincei.
Veronese, F. (2009–10) *"Terra di nessuno". Misto foro e conflitti tra Inquisizione e magistrature secolari nella Repubblica di Venezia (XVIII sec.),* Doctoral dissertation discussed in the 2009–2010 academic year, tutor G. del Torre, Venice: University Ca' Foscari.

Part I
The economy of the Holy Office

1 The financing of the inquisitorial system

Let us first try to understand how the Roman Inquisition was organized in the early modern era and what its functions in the Italian peninsula were; then we shall outline its general income at the height of its economic power: the mid-eighteenth century. In contrast with a view which presents the activities of the Holy Office as "in decline" in the 1700s, it was precisely in those years that the property of its courts and of the Roman Congregation itself reached their maximum development. The numerous historic-patrimonial résumés forwarded to Rome during the papacy of Benedict XIV as part of the contemporary renewed interest in the central and local administrative efficiency of the Papal State are revealing.

This rich retrospective – an exceptional source for the economic history of the Holy Office in the entire modern period – shows us that (apart from exceptional events) "the inquisitor's money" was ceaselessly piling up throughout the entire 1500s and 1600s. The sale of properties belonging to local courts, or to the central organ, was episodic: an event rigidly regulated by the Pope and by the cardinals of the Congregation and permitted only after scrupulous investigation of its circumstances and its timeliness.

We shall also have a look at the general strategy of those at the highest levels of the Catholic Church set up in the sixteenth century to provide for the material needs of the courts of faith and provide them with an ordinary income which made their operations financially independent. That strategy must be explained and interpreted in its pace and forms of implementation, clarifying in particular how it limited the prerogatives of the bishops – to whom, after all, the Council of Trent and the overall structures of the age of the Counter Reformation assigned a central ecclesiastical and political role in the seventeenth to eighteenth century. From this point of view, the Roman decision to assign patrimonial and beneficiary resources to the inquisitors (often transferring them from the bishops), showed the clear intention of making the repressive dimensions of ecclesiastical action equal to, if not indeed prevalent over, pastoral activity personified by diocesan vicars and the work of moral and cultural reinforcement of the regular clergy.

14 *The economy of the Holy Office*

The organization of a repressive structure

The 200 or so years between the creation of the Congregation of the Holy Office and the suppression of the Inquisition courts, which occurred almost everywhere in the latter half of the eighteenth century, saw developments of crucial importance for Italian religious, political, social and cultural history. The centres of heresy ignited throughout Italy with the arrival and re-elaboration of Evangelical-Reformed doctrines, had run out of energy during the latter half of the 1500s. Between the end of the sixteenth and the seventeenth centuries, the popes constantly extended the jurisdictional reach of the inquisitors, delineating the essential traits the courts of faith would present until their abolition in the final decades of the 1700s. It is just this solid structural, systemic, stability of the inquisitorial system in the early modern era – though with some partial reformulation of the objectives of repression from the late 1500s to the mid-1600s – which enables us to study the general operation over the long period examined in this book.

In the middle centuries of the early modern era heretics, apostates or the suspected practitioners of magic and diabolic witchcraft were not – as had been the case in previous centuries – the only figures to be placed under the jurisdiction of the Inquisition: A series of pontifical dispositions brought blasphemers, sodomites, bigamists, sympathizers of Judaism, astrologers, simoniacs, laymen who celebrated Mass without being ordained, men or women who "simulated holiness", individuals who ate forbidden foods, individuals who held or propagated popular superstitions, confessors who attempted to sexually seduce penitents during confession, scientists who denied the Truths of Faith, Quietists, Jansenists and various other "offenders" within the jurisdiction of the Inquisition. Intolerance towards Jews and Waldensians increased and controls and trials of members of the Greek Orthodox community began to appear. All this while, at the centre, the Congregation of the Holy Office – recognized as superior to the other Roman courts – imposed a unified procedure on local courts and intervened directly in the most important trials, transferring them to itself.

Further, Rome exerted tireless pressure upon secular authorities, limiting as far as it might any interference through the apostolic nuncios – diplomatic representatives of the Pope in the various states – sending, as well, its own *ad hoc* commissars into the various territories to expedite individual Inquisition cases considered to be especially important or delicate. Books were placed under progressive control and were subjected to censorship or to prohibition by the Congregation of the Index, which always acted in close contact with the Holy Office.

In this manner, the ever tighter grip of the Inquisition upon Italian society opened the way to the Counter Reformation and was one of its fundamental elements, aiming, as Giovanni Romeo puts it, to obtain:

> conformity to an orthodoxy that is much more than the holding of dogmas enunciated in the profession of faith, in as much as it excludes

behaviour, activities widely practiced, and long tolerated customs [...] A homogenous system of capillary control was set up in Italy, never before exercised in such a detailed manner; destined, in the intentions of those who planned it, to garrison the peninsula for all time.[1]

The Holy Office had deep historic roots, reaching back into the constitutional position of the Catholic Church within the Roman Empire when, as we know, Constantine declared it to be the official State Church, and Theodosius, subsequently, made it the sole Imperial Church.[2] This system, born in the late Roman era and later reaffirmed with the imperial Carolingian renaissance, led – with the universal obligation of infant baptism for Christians – to the rise of a judicial organization centred on the bishops, who became to all effects public magistrates operating as delegates of secular sovereigns. On the basis of both the Theodosian and Justinian Codes as well as the canons established by older general or ecumenical councils – which carried the full weight of laws in the Roman Empire and, after, in the Carolingian restoration – the bishops thus acquired jurisdiction which enabled them to conduct investigations and pronounce sentences upon both religious and secular individuals. The latter were liable to the judgement of bishops in cases regarding their civil situation, especially to baptism and matrimony.

Bishops were also competent with regard to the sin-crimes of apostasy, abandonment of the Christian faith (which regarded those judged guilty of diabolic magic and witchcraft due to having made a pact with the devil, as well as those guilty of schism and heresy [from the Greek *hàiresis*, meaning "choice"]) and all accusations directed at anyone who embraced concepts of faith judged erroneous and condemned by the councils which, in late antiquity, had accompanied the public affirmation of Christianity.

This transformation received its decisive imprint with the victory of the project of papal doctrinal and juridical supremacy pursued by popes like Gregory VII (1073–85) and Innocent III (1198–1216), who not only claimed the primacy of the Bishop of Rome over the Emperor in the nomination and deposition of feudal princes and bishops, but the power to govern hierarchically all of Western Christendom. This stance brought with it an increasing – though slow and difficult – process of centralization in the Pope's hands of jurisdiction over bishops and monasteries, as well as the confirmation of ecclesiastical benefices and the subdivision of dioceses.

The final result was the birth in Western Europe of a supranational structure of an ecclesiastic government and, more broadly, of an ecclesiology, culminating in the Roman Curia and thus in the college of cardinals. It was a structure, too, which, between the end of the twelfth and middle of the thirteenth centuries found a fundamental bulwark in a new organization of the *Officium fidei*: the *inquisitio haereticae pravitatis*, operating as a direct delegate of the Pope and through the members of the new Mendicant Orders: the Dominicans and the Franciscans. The restructuring and the re-enforcement of the old inquisitorial system centred on the bishops were made urgent – though within limits indicated by the more careful historians – by the contemporary spread of anti-simoniac, evangelical and pauperist movements, perceived by the ecclesiastical authorities as a threat and, often too hastily, accused of heresy.[3]

From the 1200s, inquisitors of faith delegated by the popes were usually appointed by the provincial Superiors of the Mendicant Orders. This evolution blocked (especially in the Mediterranean area) the possibility of direct structural collaboration between bishops and inquisitors, even though the bishops did retain autonomous powers allowing them to hold heresy trials. The papal-delegated Inquisition operated chiefly in the Italian peninsula, in Southern France and in Aragon. The bishop-centred church was still strong in areas along the Franco-German border and continued to act independently there in the prosecution of heresy, succeeding, in the fourteenth century, in introducing official controls on the activity of the orders as independent judges. In 1311, the *Multorum querela* decree issued by the Council of Vienne – convened in part due to the discovery of serious procedural and financial embezzlement by delegated papal inquisitors in Southern France – attempted to forbid the monks from prosecuting and judging heresy unless they belonged a diocesan college and had the bishop's approval.[4]

In the crucial period which the thirteenth century represented for the history of the Inquisition, Pope Innocent IV (1243–54), in line with the constant intent of establishing the supremacy of the papacy over Christianity as a whole, reaffirmed with the *Ad extirpanda* (1252) and the *Cum super inquisitione* edicts the various dispositions regarding heresy which had been established over time, setting up an "Italian model" of the inquisitorial office. This structure was based upon a fixed territorial organization and a practical procedure adaptable to the varying local and regional institutional realities, serving as the model for the subsequent territorial organization perfected by the Congregation of the Holy Office.

Innocent IV set up eight large districts – Lombardy and the Kingdom of Naples, entrusted to the Dominicans; the territory of Treviso, Romagna, Tuscany, the Marche, Umbria and Lazio, entrusted to the Franciscans – involving the provincial structures of the Mendicant Orders so that priors and provincial clergy worked systematically with the inquisitors, further weakening the terms of collaboration between the bishops and the inquisitors which had – however precariously – existed in preceding centuries.[5] During the Middle Ages, nomination of judges differed in the various districts but, in general, it remained in the hands of the provincial or general heads of the two Mendicant Orders, being confirmed thereafter by the popes. Only after 1542, with the creation of the Congregation of the Holy Office, did the appointment of judges of faith pass – although so gradually as to be complete only at the end of the century[6] – entirely into the hands of the Pope. Finally, between 1200 and 1300 – especially in Italy and Spain – a rich collection of manuscript inquisitorial manuals, written by the appointed papal judges themselves or by other theologians and jurists, piled up, progressively weaving together and fixing the procedures appropriate to "expediting" the trials of faith, transmitting them thereafter to the modern period.

Among these texts, two fourteenth-century works took on particular juridical and cultural importance: the famous *Directorium inquisitorum* written by the Inquisitor General of Aragon, Nicolás Eymerich, to which the Spanish jurist, Francisco Peña added an authoritative comment in the late 1500s; and the *De hereticis*, by Zanchino Ugolini, a fourteenth-century aide to the Franciscan inquisitors in Romagna, which Pius V had printed in Rome in 1568.[7]

Faced, in the opening decades of the sixteenth century, with the success of the Lutheran Reform in the German area and the growing diffusion of its ideas in Italy, the Roman Curia at first turned to the repressive intervention of the delegated territorial inquisitors (established in the districts set up in the Middle Ages), along with other figures: the bishops, the nuncios, present as ambassadors in the various Italian states, and, finally, the specific extraordinary Commissioners sent out on missions to Italian territories to take on cases of special importance or sensitivity. Between the fourteenth and fifteenth centuries, the Kingdoms of Sicily and Sardinia had passed into the jurisdiction of the Spanish Inquisition, which, however, failed in its attempt to extend that jurisdiction to the Kingdom of Naples. There, as a consequence of popular disorders protesting against the introduction of the inquisitors chosen by the Congregation of the Holy Office, an illegitimate arrangement was concocted: the Ordinaries continued to hold prioritary competence in the matter of heresy, while the vicars *pro tempore* of the Neapolitan Archbishop held the post of Commissioner Delegate coordinating the inquisitorial activities of the whole realm.

The State of Milan, which passed to the Spanish Crown in 1535, witnessed, in 1563, the failure of Philip II's attempt to introduce the Inquisition "as it is in Spain" due to the resistance of the Milanese aristocracy and the local clergy; the Roman Inquisition thus took definitive hold there. The only Italian State which saw no presence of inquisitorial courts in the early modern age was the Republic of Lucca, where, however, an "Office on religion" was instituted in 1545 which – like the "Sages for Heresy" in Venice – was a secular judiciary with competence on religious orthodoxy. In the early decades of the seventeenth century, the Holy Office's organization – which, in less than 60 years had become a central court free of restraint from any single State and capable of intervening and proceeding where it would even when the secular states involved were not in agreement – had taken on its definitive form. In continental Italy there were more than 40 peripheral inquisitorial seats, to which must be added the five courts of Besançon, Carcassonne, Toulouse, Cologne and Malta.

The activity of the Holy Office's courts, coupled with the extension to pontifical diplomatic personnel of options which might include vast inquisitorial powers – ranging beyond the traditional "visitation" to intervention in fiscal and beneficiary matters, to the conferring upon clergy of the power of absolution for "reserved" sins – inevitably curtailed the exercise of ordinary jurisdiction on the part of bishops in the repression of heresy. From the economic point of view, immediately after the Council of Trent, as we know, the Ordinaries were heavily penalized by its prohibition on accumulating incompatible benefices, with profound negative repercussions on their incomes.[8] In this chapter, I shall, however, try to show how the incomes of the episcopal revenues were reduced by papal order to provide for the maintenance of the Holy Office's peripheral courts. From this point of view the dislocation of the vast sixteenth- and seventeenth-century inquisitorial apparatus represented the culmination of the long-term Roman strategy aimed at limiting bishops' competence on heresy. So the imposition of regular annuities for the operation of the inquisitorial courts was an element of the more ample scope of Rome in the age of the Counter Reformation: it was intended to privilege the predisposition of coercive structures and disciplining control, in place of the pastoral regime of bishops and the self-government of the convent.

The redistribution of economic resources which the popes operated in favour of the Inquisition and to the detriment of the Dioceses in the 1500s and 1600s was an important phase – and one until now little studied – in the re-enforcement of Roman centralism between the first and second period of the early modern era. It combined with the predisposition towards an increasingly capillary control of the religious orders, to which the Holy See granted privileges, immunities and exemptions which, after Trent, were confirmed and sometimes enlarged. This element was also part of a strategy aimed at offsetting the powers the Council had conferred on the bishops, flanking them with members of old and new orders, considered less open to the pressures of the various local aristocracies and authorities.

The material and financial favour Rome displayed towards the inquisitorial courts after Trent should, then, be construed as having a number of different meanings, some of which were linked to the widespread penetration of Ordinaries in Catholic ecclesiastical institutions and the re-examination of the thesis of the centrality of the episcopal function in the decades which saw the impetuous rise of the Holy Office.[9] Considering the economy of the Inquisition from this point of view means touching one of the most sensitive points of the Counter Reformation and, even more broadly, contributing to the understanding of the process of concentration of ecclesiastical power in the hands of the popes – a key thread running through the whole story of the Catholic Church from the Middle Ages to the Contemporary era.[10]

A residue of the "murky centuries"?

One of the events which led to the creation of the Congregation of the Holy Office was the firm protest of the Governor of Spanish Milan, the Marquis of Vasto. Considering the zeal of the local inquisitor in combating the spread of Protestant doctrines to be insufficient, he called for a more energetic engagement on the part of the Roman Curia. On learning of this, in the Consistory held on July 15, 1541, Pope Paul III conferred upon cardinals Gian Pietro Carafa and Girolamo Aleandro "the universal supervision of the Inquisition", granting them the power to freely name, dispatch and coordinate the actions of new judges of faith in all Christianity.

This act initiated the transformation of the institutional structure of the medieval Inquisition. Confirmation swiftly followed with the emanation of the bull *Licet ab initio* (1542), in which the Pope conferred very ample judicial powers on a pre-existing commission of six cardinals (the "*Suprema*"), now nominated General Inquisitors. The centralization of the Holy Tribunal's activity – which occurred before the Council of Trent – consisted first of all in the faculty given the commission of cardinals to carry on their own, autonomous, investigations in the matter of heresy, ignoring any other ecclesiastical courts, any territorial borders or secular jurisdictions and whatever indulgences, privileges or exemptions might have been accorded in previous centuries to secular or religious subjects.[11]

Significantly, it was another event in Milan (since 1706 under the Austrian Habsburgs) which marked the end of the experience of the Roman courts of faith. Here, in 1775 – in the State which international diplomacy had for centuries considered "the gateway to Italy" – the first decree definitively suppressing the courts of the Inquisition in the peninsula was enacted.[12] The Austrian Chancellor, Kaunitz, had already made known to plenipotentiary governor Firmian in 1771 the firm Habsburg intention of "achieving, in the blandest and most placid of ways [...] the total suppression of the Office of the Inquisition", to the securing of which end he had discussed with Empress Maria Theresa:

> the serious disorders which had ensued, and might yet, however, affect the State by reason of such a bloody institution, which, being wholly contrary to, and incompatible with, the principles of a healthy Policy and the well regulated economy of States, as well as the opposite of the mild and beneficent maximums of religion and the well-known piety of Her Majesty herself, must no longer be allowed to exist and continue to exercise a jurisdiction improperly usurped from the bishops.[13]

Lucidly reading the multi-secular history of the Roman Inquisition as a basic element in the process of restriction of the role of the Ordinaries within the Catholic Church (a few lines later, in the same letter, the suppression was again justified as a means of "restoring all that authority to the Ordinaries which the constant decisions of the Councils and the Rules of real religious Discipline have always attributed to them"),[14] the highest Habsburg Officials moved to set aside the system of the courts of faith advancing considerations that were at once political, institutional and religious. Ideas in which we have no difficulty in discerning an underlying web of jurisdictional lore, strengthened by reference to the principle of the "well regulated economy of States", which saw in the patrimony accumulated by the Holy Office – as it did in that of other ecclesiastical entities on the road to suppression – a diversion of resources useful to the productive life of the country. Indeed, this policy found an immediate application in the invitation issued that same year to the *Podestas* of Mantua, Cremona, Pavia, Como and Lodi to inform themselves as to the properties held by Inquisition courts and their annual incomes which, after the suppression, would be assigned to local orphanages.[15]

In this, as in other moments in the abolition of the peripheral seats of the Inquisition during the late eighteenth century, the indignant opposition of the Roman Curia went unheeded. In vain, in 1774, Antonio Eugenio Visconti, apostolic nuncio in Vienna, presented the Empress with a richly elaborated history of the Inquisition from the time of the pontificate of Innocent III whose intent was, among other things, to refute the accusation of dishonest enrichment at the expense of the victims.[16] This was, over the centuries, a widespread accusation, at the basis of the *leyenda negra*, and had, already in the 1600s been reassumed by the Portuguese missionary, Antonio Vieira, who declared that Jesuit missionaries died for the faith, while inquisitors lived on the proceeds of the faith.[17] Visconti, on that occasion, exhorted the Empress, *in extremis*, to uphold an institution which:

> is not a political interest [...] not a temporal gain, not – in brief – dust and mud, as all the things of this world are. It is the purest gold, which admits no measure of impurity [...] that most precious treasure which constitutes the plenitude and the felicity of a State.

The nuncio continued, presenting arguments to which we shall return in the *Epilogue* of this book:

> The Holy Office seeks rather the emendation than the punishment of the guilty; the sins are hidden in rigorous secrecy, and the reputation of the guilty is protected; no one is imprisoned if the accusations are not proved and the trial not already instructed; the treasury plays its part against the culprit but, unlike other courts, still receives written proofs which diminish the crime and lessen the delinquent's guilt [...] The Inquisition's court absolves without punishment whosoever, being contrite, accuses himself spontaneously of his crime, as well as accepting the ingenuous confession rendered at the judge's first interrogation as a reason for lessening punishment; and when, finally, it is obliged to punish, this punishment is always gentle and discrete, and always governed by a spirit of fondness which yearns for amendment and not the loss of the sinner, whose death it does not desire, nor the spilling of blood; and if, sometimes it must relinquish him to the secular arm, it is the Church itself which intercedes for him and implores the secular judge to spare his life.[18]

Still, in the very days in which the Pope and his nuncios moved all the resources at their command to turn the Empress from her purposes, Kaunitz was prodding the Economic Council to conduct a rapid survey of Dominican holdings "too numerous and useless in Lombardy" and, further, to set in train "an exact statement of what each Inquisition possesses, as it is feared that, in the meantime, a part of the revenues may be transferred or lost". The chancellor's suspicions were based on the fact that, a few years earlier, "some fruitful capital had been realized by the inquisitor in Como without its further investment, with an almost manifest reduction of the patrimony of that Office". Inexorably, the following year, a dispatch from the Empress declared "the activity of the so-called Inquisitors of the Holy Office [...] introduced in the murky centuries" to be incompatible "with the original and inalterable rights of the principality and with the good order of the police". The "institution of the *Crocesignati*", already suppressed, was now declared by the Habsburgs to be "a relic of the times of ignorance, and party to an ill-conceived, sanguinary, zeal". It would be the destiny of the property and the incomes of the Lombard inquisitors to be transferred to the orphanages "that they may better furnish the bases of Christian education".[19]

At the moment in which – at least for an important part of the Italian population – the dramatic, centuries-long, experiment of the justice of faith drew to an end, sealed by the formal abolition of the Napoleonic Kingdom of Italy between 1805 and 1810, the theme of the financial management and the economic implications of the Inquisition was thus a protagonist in the institutional and political confrontation. And so it continued to be in the following decades, when, in the fervour of liberal polemics, voices like that of the economist Giuseppe Orano frequently proclaimed that "without prohibitive laws, the workers, the right of escheat, the privileges, the despotism, the Inquisition, the religious persecution – Spain, France and Italy would be today the richest countries in Europe".[20]

The question of the absolute economic burden of the Inquisition's structure – that of the supposed sterility of the patrimonies it accumulated; the charge of the enormity and the arbitrary nature of the fines and confiscations it inflicted; the question of the alleged negative fallout of the actions of the Holy Office on the economic realities of the peninsula and on its international outlook: to bring all these into open discussion together with other themes regarding the story of the Holy Office and Italian history as a whole, is one of the central aims of this book.

The patrimonial accumulation of the courts of faith

A general impression of the real economic positions attained by the Roman Inquisition, considered as a system made up of the Congregation of the Holy Office and a constellation of courts designated as "local" or "peripheral", can be derived from the annual incomes of the mid-eighteenth century, just before the beginning of the suppressions. Considering the peripheral courts for the sample year of 1748 – for which we have systematic documentation – the sum of such income is listed in decreasing order in Table 1.1.[21]

The incomes of the Inquisition courts fell into two large categories which, forcing a classic fiscal division, we might define as *ordinary* and *extraordinary*.

Table 1.1 Income of the local courts of the Holy Office in the year of 1748 (Roman scudi, rounded off to the unit)

Court	Order Dominican – D Franciscan – F	Income	Number of local vicariates
Casale Monferrato	D	649	24
Milan	D	553	91
Florence	F	515	121
Faenza	D	506	41
Vercelli	D	478	28
Turin	D	470	19
Novara	D	450	31
Saluzzo	D	436(*)	14
Piacenza	D	419	38
Bologna	D	410	17
Venice	D	394	3
Alessandria	D	391	24
Cremona	D	344	24
Genoa	D	344(**)	46
Asti	D	296	15
Ancona	D	279	29
Mantua	D	261	49
Brescia	D	254	34
Padua	F	228	6
Ferrara	D	218	22
Siena	F	215	122
Rimini	D	211	30
Pisa	F	184	65
Verona	D	178	46
Tortona	D	173	43
Aquileia and Concordia	F	165	7
Crema	D	162	Not indicated
Pavia	D	161	33
Bergamo	D	159	32
Perugia	D	149	66
Treviso	F	147	7
Como	D	142	24

Court	Order Dominican – D Franciscan – F	Income	Number of local vicariates
Parma	D	134	24
Mondovì	D	126	11
Vicenza	D	117	32
Capodistria	F	110	20
Modena	D	100	41
Fermo	D	80	26
Belluno	F	74	2
Spoleto	D	74	44
Gubbio	D	47	13
Ceneda and Conegliano	F	42	2
Adria and Rovigo	F	34	5
Zara	D	29	20
Reggio Emilia	D	23	46

Source: My own elaborations from ACDF, So, St.st., LL5e–LL5f. The figures expressed in different monies are presented in Roman scudi on the basis of a contemporary coefficient of monetary conversion deduced from the same documentation.

(*) This item is not very representative since, in 1748, the Inquisition in Saluzzo sold a vineyard worth about 222 scudi; its average ordinary entry of that period was about 130 scudi.

(**) In 1748, the Inquisition in Genoa was unable to collect any revenue due to the war. The figure that appears here is the result of my own estimate, based on the ordinary income of the Ligurian court, documented by the office in the same year. Since these figures included sums deriving from a share in the Banco San Giorgio with variable interest, I have calculated an average between the interest rates of 1739 and those of 1747, as indicated ibid.

Ordinary income was a sum of the *fixed component*, generally made up of monies paid annually by ecclesiastical benefices and pensions drawn from bishops' revenues – whose totals did not vary sensibly from year to year though they might suffer variations of some entity over decades or centuries – and the *variable component*, deriving from a plurality of payments guaranteed in some form which was relatively stable over time: these were mostly the result of the direct or indirect management of property and interests on loans or certificates of credit.

Extraordinary revenues were also made up of disparate items, whose common trait was to generate income for limited periods: confiscated property and fines levied on the condemned, contributions from other Inquisitions or from the Roman Congregation, monetary bequests, the sale of property or certificates, private gifts and similar windfalls. The brilliant economic situation of the Casale Monferrato Inquisition, for example (which outshone other offices with far more ample jurisdiction and older traditions) was not so much a result of the size of its ordinary, fixed, revenues – it enjoyed, from Paul V, three sinecures yielding a little over 200 ducats a year in the mid-eighteenth century – because of the amplitude of its variable extraordinary income. In fact, the inquisitors of Casale Monferrato directly managed the marketing of a part of the produce of the land they had accumulated over the centuries, earning almost double the value of beneficiary income with the sale of wheat and wine alone.[22]

The income of the Congregation of the Holy Office – for which I was unable to locate contemporary data – is not present in Table 1.1. We do, however, have some information about its income sources in the second half of the sixteenth century, which we will consider carefully later on, as well as a long series of sums received and paid out during the 1600s (see Table 1.2).

The Ministry in Rome had its most important sources of revenue in the estate and manufacturing activities of the Santa Maria in Conca, today part of the town of Latina lying between Borgo Montello and Borgo Le Ferriere. In 1564, Pope Pius IV had broken up an estate belonging to the San Nilo abbey, transferring Conca to the Apostolic Chamber. Two years later, with the apostolic letter *Dum inter archana*, Pius V transferred ownership to the Congregation and entrusted it to lessees – originally to Paolo, Francesco and Girolamo Odescalchi, merchants from Como, residing in Rome, who established themselves at this time in what is today Palazzo Falconieri.

Table 1.2 Income and expenditures of the Congregation of the Holy Office (Roman scudi, rounded off to the unit)

Year	Income	Expenses
1633	5,484	5,473
1634	8,221	8,729
1635	5,910	5,906
1636	11,337	12,390
1637	7,748	8,046
1638	6,082	7,002
1639	6,037	3,244
1640	4,993	6,888
1641	6,970	5,530
1642	8,514	5,609
1643	3,598	5,785
1644	8,776	5,834
1645	6,023	5,556
1646	6,590	7,318
1647	1,572	4,747
1648	8,149	5,284

Year	Income	Expenses
1649	3,856	5,467
1650	6,668	7,904
1651	23,274	6,915
1652	6,248	21,046
1653	7,528	6,186
1654	7,342	7,039
1655	7,400	7,424
1656	9,077	8,952
1657	9,555	7,401
1658	6,785	12,298
1659	10,280	10,664
1660	9,608	7,289
1661	19,973	18,084
1662	12,596	14,786
1663	7,152	7,552
1664	10,454	11,097
1665	11,319	6,513
1666	17,742	17,079
1667	10,786	7,937
1668	5,795	7,432
1669	5,115	7,620
1670	6,294	7,089
1671	4,725	9,381
1672	7,695	11,443
1673	3,723	8,795
1674	2,693	6,309
1675	6,784	5,606
1676	8,860	7,974
1677	7,339	7,694
1678	4,359	4,907
Average	7,978	8,243

Source: My own calculations based on ACDF, Register *'Entrata e uscita banco S, Offitio'*, *fuori Stanza storica*.

Monies saved from the previous year have been subtracted from the yearly income figure which appears here.

In 1578, the rents deriving from Conca came to 1,500 scudi each semester, and the sum increased over the following decades.[23] At the end of the 1500s, the Ministry had an iron works built in Conca. Finished in 1592, its operation depended on the tenants who farmed the property. The forge worked ferrous material from the island of Elba and used coal from some areas of Conca, from the zone around Neptune and the Campomorto holding, whose entire production was assigned to its exclusive use in 1631.

The marketing of Conca's iron products was entrusted to a network of "vendors" resident in various cities within the pontifical State and, like the agricultural production – chiefly wheat, forage and animals – benefited from the exemption from any tax or duty. These improvements allowed the Congregation of the Holy Office to increase the income from Conca greatly: the rent collected in 1637 came to almost 6,400 scudi a year; and even in periods in which the estate was managed directly, yearly income held to these levels for most of the 1600s. The average annual income overall for the Congregation between 1633 and 1678 rose to about 9,730 scudi – which falls to about 7,978 if (as in Table 1.2), savings carried over from the previous year are subtracted from the budget surplus.

The Conca estate tended to have a bad reputation, since it was situated in an area that was both dangerous and insalubrious. Vendors and procurers of provisions belonging to the estate had the status of licensees of the Holy Office and, therefore – in accordance with prerogatives acknowledged since 1595 and still confirmed by Benedict XIV in 1755 – the right to bear arms both within the confines of the estate and outside it. In the early 1600s, we can see this in a document in which Cardinal Camillo Borghese, among concessions to lessees, reaffirms their right to be armed as "Turks of all periods come through, and other persons [intent on] preying, and cause damages with violence, with great danger not only to the property, but even to the lives of the tenants".[24]

The Congregation of the Holy Office had full and exclusive jurisdiction over Conca, acting through judges specifically chosen for civil or criminal trials. It was precisely this special juridical structure which prompted many of those pursued by the ordinary judicial system to seek refuge in swampy areas like the Agro Pontino, where it was especially difficult to recruit labourers for the iron works as they could usually count upon tolerance on the part of local forces of order and a strong demand for workers. Though from the early 1700s the Holy Office began to forbid the more dangerous "fugitives" from seeking refuge in Conca – and, after 1826, civil and criminal cases regarding the estate and the iron works were entrusted to the more efficient figure of a governor appointed by the Congregation – the area was for a long period rife with social tensions and endemic criminality. During the nineteenth century, the conditions in the area showed no significant improvement and as late as 1902 – within a context of widespread violence – the shocking rape and murder of the young Maria Goretti occurred in Borgo Le Ferriere.[25]

As with any quantitative calculations concerning the "pre-statistical era", the figures presented in Tables 1.1 and 1.2 should be considered merely indicative. The inquisitors – who often, in peripheral courts, drew up their budgets themselves and, in any case, certified them, sending them on to Rome – applied varying accounting criteria: something which makes it impossible now to set up statistically rigorous synchronic or diachronic comparisons. Still, the data offered is a good basis for the evaluation of the overall income of the Holy Office courts in the final phase of their existence almost at the end of a pluri-secular process of patrimonial management. We shall be examining this process in this and in the next chapter.

The first thing to consider is the great variety of economic contexts in which the various courts found themselves: there were "rich" courts and "poor" courts – or rather, courts more or less provided with property and income. It is worth recalling that, in Bologna, the cost of the maintenance of a prisoner of the Inquisition on a daily diet which, however frugal, guaranteed survival, came to about 37 scudi in 1748.[26] We can, then, deduce that, within their annual income, the more unfortunate inquisitorial courts, though territorially extensive in jurisdiction, could only with difficulty take on the expense of a single destitute prisoner. Not even the wealthiest courts – many of which were in the hands of branches of the Dominican "family" could, if taken singly, boast yearly incomes comparable to those held by the foremost families of the Roman aristocracy. The patrimony of the Roman branch of the Chigi family, for example (whose value in the second half of the 1700s exceeded 2,400,000 scudi) earned several tens of thousands a year – an income far superior to that of the central and local courts of the Holy Office together.[27]

In the eighteenth century, both the Roman Congregation and the courts as a whole might, rather, boast an annual income comparable to that enjoyed by the great Benedictine monasteries of the Cassinese Congregation like Fara, in Rieti; Monreale, in Palermo; San Giovanni, in Parma; or Santo Spirito, in Pavia. So the patrimonies accumulated by the Roman Ministry and the local Inquisition courts over the centuries were not particularly striking, whether compared to the principal contemporary ecclesiastical or lay patrimonies or to the entire ecclesiastical patrimony just before the eighteenth-century suppressions; patrimonies of which constituted an undoubtedly secondary portion.[28]

The annual income of the individual Holy Office courts during the final decades in which they operated, though deriving in large part from real estate and investments accumulated from the sixteenth through the eighteenth centuries (including funds deriving from penal activities), cannot be simply assumed as an indication of the different levels of repressive capacity attained by the courts themselves in the centuries comprising the early modern period. The logic governing the economic behaviour of the Holy Office and, consequently, the patrimonial structure of its courts, is the result of a complex interplay between the decisions from above – taken by the Pope and the cardinals of the Supreme Congregation (which we shall examine in the first part of this book), and the management policies adopted by the inquisitors who were subject, as well, to local socioeconomic variables which I shall try to clarify further on.

28 *The economy of the Holy Office*

The monetary flow of the Congregation in the 1600s also shows that, in the phase in which its organizational and procedural patterns were stabilized, it held, in general, to criteria of good administration of its finances, emancipating itself from income directly resulting from its judicial activities thanks to the development of resources furnished by the Conca estate. The accounts examined indicate, in fact, a substantial balance between the Roman Ministry's income and its expenditure, with income increasingly based on revenue from real estate and manufactures. Where – as, for example, in 1639 – income strongly exceeded expenditure (6,037 scudi to 3,244), in the following year the Congregation allowed itself to spend more than it took in (6,888 scudi to 4,993). The same thing occurred when there was a strong negative imbalance: when, in the difficult year of 1647, with a meagre 1,572 scudi in income, the Roman Holy Office spent 4,747 scudi, it immediately compensated in 1648 – when its income reached 8,149 scudi – by spending only 5,284 scudi. The anomalous 23,274 scudi of 1651 depended upon the payment of credits accumulated by the Congregation with the Banco di Santo Spirito, which acted as its bank, and, above all, from the sale of hundreds of animals (66 oxen, 165 pigs, 32 horses, 32 buffalo, 144 goats), wheat, and several "rights" pertaining to the Conca estate, to a group headed by the tenant Filippo d'Aste for more than 10,000 scudi. Punctually, the next year we can see an equally exceptional total expenditure of 21,046 scudi due to the payment (for which no reasons are provided) of 15,000 scudi to Father Angelo Maria of Parma, attorney general of the Cassinese Congregation: a managerial operation, then, carefully considered and planned for several years. So, even taking into account that the annual budget of the Holy Office was not extravagant over the long period, the Congregation – should it have deemed this opportune – could have supported the local courts financially as well, supporting them with surplus funds in a much more substantial manner than will be observed.[29]

We may, finally, note that the overall sum of income – that is to say the wealth accumulated by the single Roman Inquisition courts – was not directly linked to the territorial extension of their jurisdiction, outlined in Table 1.1 by the number of local vicars each. There were courts with broad jurisdictions – like Perugia, Pisa, Siena and Modena – which had lower incomes than others (especially in the Duchy of Savoy) operating in territories that were smaller and equally populous. We should remember that the peripheral structures of the inquisitorial vicariates were set up during the 1500 and 1600s to bring the judges of faith – whose activities were originally urban – closer to the rural areas of interest, on the model established in the dioceses after the Council of Trent to allow the bishops to keep a more attentive eye on the efficient application of the decrees on ecclesiastical Reform.

The institution of the vicariates, whose seventeenth-century incumbents were appointed by the Congregation of the Holy Office (which chose from a group of candidates proposed by the local inquisitor), made the Inquisition's activity more capillary in the central and northern territories of the peninsula. The vicars were empowered to carry out investigations, collect denunciations and testimony and bring about reconciliations should culprits present themselves spontaneously, though final judgement and abjuration remained in the hands of titular inquisitors, usually resident in the nearest considerable town.

Today scholars agree that the Roman Ministry of the Inquisition – established in 1542 – began to exercise its task of coordination and supervision of the repression of heresy consistently only some fifteen years later. It was only in 1557 that the supreme inquisitors began to receive information and declarations from local courts and to promote judicial procedures on their own initiative, giving rise to trials and transferring the more complex, dubious or controversial cases to Rome. We may add that, after 1557, an equally extended period elapsed before the popes and the Congregation set up structured forms of financing for the inquisitorial courts – and they did so very cautiously even then (see Table 1.3).

In the latter part of the Middle Ages and in the very early modern era, the inquisitorial courts present in the Italian peninsula had carried on their activity without the support of fixed income in coins, turning to the convents of the Mendicant Orders for their material needs, or deriving funds from the fines imposed on the condemned or the confiscation of part or all of their property.

Table 1.3 Years in which fixed incomes were assigned by popes or the Congregation of the Holy Office

Court	Pope/institution and year
Adria and Rovigo	–
Alessandria	Gregory XIII (1579)
Ancona	Congregation of the Holy Office (n.i.); Innocent XII (XII) (n.i.); Paul V (1607)
Asti	Gregory XIII (1579)
Belluno	Congregation of the Holy Office (1580)
Bergamo	Gregory XIII (1579, 1581); Congregation of the Holy Office (1580)
Bologna	Pius V (1565)
Brescia	Pius V (1569); Gregory XIII (1579)
Capodistria	Gregory XIII (1580, 1584)
Casale Monferrato	Paul V (1606, 1610)
Ceneda and Conegliano	Pio V (1570); Clement VIII (1591)
Como	Clement VIII (1603); Congregation of the Holy Office (1607)
Crema	Paul V (1619); Alexander VII (1661); Innocent XII (1696)
Cremona	Pius V (1569)
Faenza	Pius V (1567, 1568); Gregory XIII (1572)

continued...

Table 1.3 continued...

Court	Pope/institution and year
Fermo	Alexander VII (1658)
Ferrara	–
Florence	Gregory XIII (1581); Urban VIII (1628)
Genua	Pius V (1569)
Gubbio	–
Mantua	Pius V (1566)
Milan	Sixtus V (1586)
Modena	–
Mondovì	Paul V (1619)
Novara	Pius V (1570, 1571, 1576)
Padua	Gregory XIII (1582), Alexander VII (1660)
Parma	Pius V (1569)
Pavia	Pius V (1569)
Perugia	Urban VIII (n.i.)
Piacenza	–
Pisa	Pius V (1566)
Reggio Emilia	–
Rimini	Congregation of the Holy Office (1580)
Saluzzo	Clement VIII (1599); Congregation of the Holy Office (1603)
Siena	Paul V (1608); Congregation of the Holy Office (n.i.)
Spoleto	Innocent XI (1685)
Tortona	Clement VIII (1592, 1602); Clement XI (1700) Congregation of the Holy Office (1580); Clement VIII (1593); Urban VIII (1631)
Treviso	Clement VIII (1594, 1596); Paul V (1606)
Turin	
Udine and Concordia	Gregory XIII (1578); Clement VIII (1591)
Venice	Pius IV (n.i.); Congregation of the Holy Office (1577); Gregory XIII (1579)
Vercelli	Pius V (1566, 1570); Sixtus V (1588); Urban VIII (1636)
Verona	Pius V (1569, 1570)
Vicenza	Gregory XIII (1578)
Zara	Congregation of the Holy Office (n.i)

Source: This table is based on my own elaboration of material in ACDF, So, St.st., LL5e–LL5f.

n.i.: date not indicated, or indicated incorrectly.

In the central decades of the sixteenth century, the alarm within the papal Curia at the spread of Reformed doctrines would – with its attendant push to reorganization leading to the creation of the Congregation of the Holy Office – need to urgently arrange fixed incomes for the inquisitors evident.

Table 1.3 shows, instead, that the peak of the Holy Office's repressive activity – which, between 1550 and 1570 led to the destruction of almost all the heretic groups throughout the peninsula – was paid for by the local courts, practically without any other sources of regular income. Further, the same figures tell us that, over the period, only ten popes actively promoted the assignment of fixed financial patrimony to Inquisition courts, usually proceeding, instead, in the rut of the long tradition of the haphazard accumulation of ecclesiastical benefices on which the whole structure of the secular and regular clergy was based in Italian territories. Direct interventions to similar ends originating with the Congregation of the Holy Office were equally sporadic: so much so that a significant number of courts never had any beneficiary income at any time during their existence. Some of these courts were in important places. Modena, for example – where the Inquisition was established in 1598, after Ferrara became part of the Papal State – received no ecclesiastical benefices from Rome or from Bishop Gaspare Silingardi (to whom the inquisitors had appealed directly); nor did they receive any subsidies from the d'Este Dukes.[30] Like other important localities in the Po valley, the Modena court remained without any fixed income for all of its bi-secular existence.

A number of popes who conferred the right of presentation to benefices on the courts of the Inquisition are included by historians among those whose pontificates were distinguished by a marked tendency to centralization and theocracy. These include the "inquisitor popes" Pius V and Sixtus V, the former universally renowned as champion of the orthodoxy of the faith and victor of Lepanto, the second as the organizer of the Church on centralist and absolutist lines; Gregory XIII, who built the great Jesuit *Collegium Romanum* and authorized the cult of Gregory VII – the first great promoter of papal supremacy; Clement VIII, who authorized the publication of the fundamental *Index* of forbidden books (1596) and whose pontificate represented "the passage from the incipient phase to governance and from the elaboration of rules to that of their application [...][entailing] the drastic degradation of the bishops and their subordination to Roman sovereignty";[31] Paul V, who completed the construction of Saint Peter's Basilica and canonized Gregory VII; Urban VIII, who compelled Galileo to abjure; and Innocent XI, who strongly attacked King Louis XIV of France on the concession of gratuities.

For all these popes, the assignment of fixed incomes to the Inquisition courts was a qualifying moment in a conscious policy of consolidation of papal supremacy within the institutions and the structuring of Catholicism in the early modern era. A conspicuous part of the revenues the popes or the Congregation of the Holy Office (which they headed) conferred upon the inquisitors in the sixteenth and seventeenth centuries inevitably curtailed the resources available to the dioceses and thus to the bishops.

Why did the highest authorities of the Catholic Church – though attributing political, religious and ecclesiastical priority to the Inquisition – fail throughout the entire Counter Reformation to provide the local courts rapidly with forms of fixed revenue ample enough to deal with the colossal challenges they were obliged to confront? Why did Rome face the problem of assigning fixed revenue benefices to its inquisitors only after the resolution of the sixteenth-century heretic emergency had been achieved? To suggest answers to these questions we need to see more clearly the forms of fixed revenue the peninsula's inquisitorial courts had.

The competition between bishops and inquisitors

Historians today agree that the papacy of Paul IV (Carafa) marked a fundamental break in the history of the early modern Inquisition. His election brought with it the definitive end of dialogue between the various positions within the Sacred College which had been – though ever more tenuously – still possible from 1550 to 1555, during the pontificates of Julius III and Marcellus II. With Paul IV, as Massimo Firpo observed, the "process of affirmation of the Roman Inquisition as the supreme normative, theological, pastoral, juridical and political exigency at the very top of the Church" was established irreversibly, making the Holy Office "far more than the council halls", a place in which "were laid the foundations of a Counter Reformation destined to go on for centuries – and, in many ways, continue even into our own time".[32]

As for the economic and organizational dimensions of the Inquisition, Paul IV immediately introduced important innovations. Already in 1556, personally presiding – as he would continue to do throughout his pontificate – weekly meetings of the *Sacro Collegio*, Carafa imposed absolute secrecy upon all those who participated in the Congregation's activities, from the lowliest of clerks upwards; violation was punished with excommunication *latae sententiae*. He further revoked a letter by Julius III, as well as every other similar disposition emitted by preceding popes and exonerating heretics within the Kingdom of Naples from the confiscation of their properties.[33] Nor did Paul neglect the delicate area of policy regarding the financing of the inquisitorial courts through minor benefices, where he established two important principles. In 1558, with a *Providence* – later confirmed by Pius V – he proclaimed that no Ordinary could intervene in the assigning of ecclesiastical benefices "vacant" by reason of heresy, whose destination was the prerogative of the Holy See.[34]

This provision came two years after the promulgation of the norm regarding the confiscation of property belonging to those condemned for crimes of faith (since the Middle Ages regulated by canon law) stipulating that henceforth ecclesiastical benefices were to be deemed vacant from the day on which, in the inquisitors' opinion, the crime of heresy had been committed. The retroactivity contemplated by this norm allowed the Pope to annul the assignment of benefices conferred in the past (even decades before the moment in which their titular cleric had been condemned as heretic) and bestow them at his pleasure.³⁵ Though inquisitorial practice in the 1500s shows cases in which benefices pertaining to clerics condemned for heresy were retained,³⁶ in the following decades the Holy Congregation exercised constant pressure on Ordinaries to dissuade them from allowing abjurors as well as adjudged heretics ("*abiuratos tanquam haereticos formales*)" to hold ecclesiastical office, immediately dispensing them where they had (as in Cremona and Reggio Emilia) been reintegrated by their bishops in their posts.³⁷

With this stroke the popes set the foundations of a "consistorialization" of minor ecclesiastical benefices before the Council of Trent had finished its deliberations,³⁸ forcing the medieval equilibrium in the matter of benefices for reasons of faith ("*fidei causa*") and broadening their own power to concede benefices to a virtually limitless degree.

Thus, in the 1600s, the assignment of benefices previously held by clergy considered guilty by the Holy Office was comfortably shifted to the men in the Roman Ministry who, indeed, in a number of localities did not hesitate to operate directly, assigning local benefices to the resident inquisitor without consulting the bishop. In the dioceses of Alessandria, for example, the seventeenth-century authorities were surprised to learn that a very small portion of the benefices had been awarded by the bishop with royal permission ("*placet*"), and even one of these few had been taken over by the local inquisitor without asking for royal permission (nor, of course, that of the bishop).³⁹

The *Suprema* might order the individual inquisitor to operate in conjunction with the local bishop as well, as it did with the judge of faith for Genoa, ordering him to substitute the benefice of the provostship of Saint George (which had hitherto been enjoyed by Father Giovan Maria Gondi, who had been found guilty of soliciting in the confessional in 1620) with another, more discretely situated outside of the city and having no duties with any responsibilities for the care of souls:

> and cause [the bishop], when some other ordinary benefice – or one without pastoral duties – is to be disposed of to confer it upon said father Giovan Maria who, relinquishing the provostship, may however be able to gratify another subject, certain that in so doing he is acting in a manner pleasing to the Holy Congregation.⁴⁰

This sort of operation indicates once again how, during the first years of the Holy Office the Fundamentalist faction within the upper reaches of the Roman hierarchy felt the need to lay out a very broad strategy of repression. This aimed first of all to block the spread of heresy within the Catholic Church itself, acting on the economic level to "consistorialize" as far as possible minor provisional benefices which fell under the jurisdiction of the cathedrals. In addition, drawn both by the conspicuous wealth produced by the episcopal revenues and the capillary network of provisions accruing to the canons holding ordinary benefices, it limited the rights of bishops to confer benefices and, indirectly, the rights of the local nobility who traditionally had a voice in such concessions in virtually all the states present in the peninsula.[41]

The examples of benefices linked to inquisitorial courts in the 1500–1600s in this model, saw on the one hand the Pope – or, less often, the Congregation which the Pope presided – and, on the other, the bishops attempting a more or less tenacious opposition. Bergamo was the city where, in 1550, Brother Michele Ghislieri secretly investigated the orthodoxy of Bishop Vittore Soranzo, drawing upon himself an armed attack which obliged him to take horse and flee his convent (though he took time to make sure the dossier for the prelate's trial was in safe hands before he left).

Once he had become Pope Pius V, Ghislieri must have recalled those moments when – as an eighteenth-century inquisitor from the dioceses of Bergamo wrote after having studied his archives, he became:

> the first of the Popes to bring together under the Holy Office ordinary benefices or incomes over the heads of the dioceses [...] having been an inquisitor and having learned from experience that without some modest income he could not sustain the Holy Office. Here too Saint Pius V wrote to the bishop [of Bergamo] of the time requesting him to free a few ordinary benefices so that they might be transferred to this Holy Office, but was unable to obtain any results during his pontificate.[42]

This diocese – an extraordinary case, and one which is to date the only one in all of Italy – after the return of Soranzo in 1554, was placed by the Holy Office under the administration of an external commission. Relations between the popes and the bishops must not have been comfortable even in the years that followed. Only the implacable determination of Gregory XIII, indeed, completed between 1579 and 1581 the consolidation of various clerkships and chaplaincies under the local Inquisition court. They formed the basis for its income for the next 200 years.[43]

In Bologna, too, the court's wealth was largely founded on the annual income of 200 gold scudi which Pius V had assigned in 1565, subtracting it from the episcopal patrimony, then under the tutelage of Cardinal Gabriele Paleotti.[44] The same thing happened in Brescia, where the inquisitors benefited amply from an analogous income thanks to the intervention of the same Pope – and where a long controversy ensued, concluded finally by Gregory XIII.[45] Ghislieri acted in the same way – always to the detriment of local dioceses – conferring hundreds of scudi in income on the Inquisition in Novara, unleashing litigation which was resolved only in 1587 "since the Father Inquisitor has gone to Rome".[46]

In 1582, 200 scudi from the patrimony of the local bishopric were ceded to the Inquisition in Padua by Gregory XIII – who ten years earlier had authorized the same operation for 150 scudi for Faenza, taking them from the bishopric of Imola: it was in Mantua, too, that Pius V had, already in 1566, made sure that the Inquisition was upheld by 100 gold scudi drawn from the episcopal patrimony.[47] The same thing happened in Pisa in the 1500s – 100 ducats from the episcopal holdings (again on the initiative of Pius V) – and in Tortona in the 1600s, by the hand of Urban VIII.[48]

Economic relations between inquisitor and bishop were no better in the Republic of Venice. In this city where the point of reference for the activity of the Holy Office was notoriously the Pontifical nuncio rather than the nominal inquisitor, the court was financed by three principal incomes: the patrimony of the bishopric of Verona; the patrimony of the nearby island of Torcello; and the vicarage of Cividate, in the Val Camonica.[49] After Gregory XIII had, in 1579, assigned a yearly income of 100 gold scudi to the Holy Office of the Serenissima to be paid *in perpetuo* from the episcopal patrimony of Torcello, the resident bishops of that island consistently evaded paying all of the sum required of them.[50]

We could compile a long list of similar instances of assignment by popes, or by the Congregation of the Holy Office, of benefices or incomes to local Inquisitions to the detriment of the resident bishop of the area, which were secured only after prolonged and difficult legal challenges and barely masked conflict. Pontifical letters of the late 1500s even went so far as to threaten with excommunication bishops failing to pay their inquisitor's income from episcopal revenues when it was due, and in full: as we can see in Gregory XIII's decree of 1572 assigning an income of 100 gold scudi to the Inquisition in Faenza at the expense of the Bishop of Imola.[51] In 1594, the Bishop of Vercelli went so far as to sequester the beneficiary incomes of the local Inquisition "on the pretext that he was obliged to rebuild anew a ruined church". Immediately called to order by the cardinals of the Roman Ministry, the following year this bishop renewed his conflict with the Holy Court alleging that he was carrying out ordinations inherent to the chaplainship of Saint Catherine, which had always been linked to the Holy Office (once again eliciting the immediate, harsh, reaction of Rome).[52]

Successful forms of episcopal evasion of financial support for the Inquisition may also be noted, for example, in Rovigo, where the Holy Office's only income was a benefice of 30 scudi wrested from the Bishop of Adria in 1594. After a vain attempt on the part of Sixtus V to impose the commutation of a bequest in favour of the local court and other attempts to garner lesser benefices, as late as 1638 "negotiations were opened with the bishop to settle an income on the well-padded prelate of Arquà; quite shortly the bargaining ran aground [*sic*]". The successful resistance put forward by the bishops throughout the seventeenth century cast the Inquisition's accounts in Rovigo constantly into the red so that, in the middle of the eighteenth century, annual debt still came to about four times as much as the annual income.[53]

This sort of resistance might occur within the pontifical State itself, Gubbio, where the Inquisition was established after the Duchy of Urbino had been annexed in 1631, never had any fixed income, though barely a year later Rome had begun to put pressure on the local bishop to provide a benefice.[54] In this case, the Congregation was forced to content itself with occasional forms of redistribution of the economic resources in favour of the Holy Office, for example, when it condoned periods of detention for a prisoner in the episcopal prisons in exchange for a sum in alms for religious establishments within the diocese, charging, however, the local inquisitor rather than the bishop with the distributive "disposition" of the sum.[55]

Another serious clash between a bishop and an inquisitor – and not only an economic one – developed in 1655 after Fabio Chigi, who had held the Imola bishopric, rose to the papacy, taking the name Alexander VII. Cardinal Giovanni Stefano Donghi, who succeeded Chigi in Imola, refused to pay the whole sum of the yearly pension assigned to the inquisitor in Faenza, citing a different interpretation of its effective monetary entity. In this document, he addressed the Pope "as Father and Proprietor of the Church of Imola and the Inquisition of Faenza".[56] The Pope delegated the solution of the dispute to the Congregation of the Holy Office. Hearing of this, the Bishop of Imola (as the inquisitor in Faenza, Vincenzo Paolini, reported to his superiors) "immediately fell into such a rage that, among much else, he declared that he recognized no one above him but the Pope and that he would be subject to the Holy Congregation only if he were a heretic, but that he was not so, with other things still which worried him [the inquisitor] to hear". The bishop's angry reaction, which reveals the numerous nuances of the relations between the two highest figures of justice in matters concerning the Catholic faith, makes clear how endemic the conflict present in various peninsula dioceses was. "The inquisitors", continued Father Paolini, "were unwilling to recognize computation of the benefice in local coin for fear of precluding later insistence upon receiving gold scudi through legal procedures, as they had already done in Malta, Mantua and elsewhere, or obliging them to pay its full equivalent".[57]

A thorough inquiry ensued, during which the episcopal archives and the records of the local court were closely scrutinized: it emerged that the Pope himself, when the bishop was there, had paid out curtailed income, just as Cardinal Donghi proposed to continue doing.[58] The case and conflict were resolved with a Decree of the Holy Office imposing payment in gold scudi upon the bishop, confirming the interpretation of the dispute favourable to the inquisitor. "I am, however, at the same time resigned to – and ready to obey – the orders given me", the bishop stiffly declared in a final letter to Rome on August 19, 1657.[59]

The acrimony displayed by the Bishop of Imola was justified on the financial level too, by the fact that the dioceses were doubly damaged by the assigning of benefices to the inquisitorial courts, which could not be subjected to any form of taxation. When this was attempted – as it was in Novara – Rome intervened immediately, warning the bishop:

> [we] Pray you to be most careful not to weigh [your diocese] with expenses that are superfluous and less necessary as regards the quality and the nature of the benefice and the place in which it is situated, because imposing heavy, unsustainable – and unnecessary – costs would all be damaging to the Inquisition, nor would observing such orders be obligatory.[60]

Furnishing the inquisitors with beneficiary incomes, the highest echelons of Catholicism not only compromised delicate and time-honoured equilibriums between ecclesiastical entities but they also redefined the relations between these institutions and secular governments. In the several different Italian states, these governments were the expression of aristocracies longing to enjoy the advantages of beneficiary incomes themselves and, at least formally, in a position to make any revenues deriving from such property subject to the "pleasure" ("*placet*", or "temporal possession") conferred by the Prince.[61]

Naturally the most complex case was that of the Republic of Venice, where the acquisitive strategy of the Roman Inquisition repeatedly provoked negative repercussions. In 1599, the authorities of the *Serenissima* prevented the Inquisitor of Udine from taking temporal possession of the benefices to which he was entitled: a situation which Rome declared itself for the moment powerless to alter, writing "let him do what he can". Pope Clement VIII intervened only a year later with the Venetian Ambassador in Rome when the judge of faith in Treviso encountered the same obstacle. Still, the difficulties did not come to an end; they became, indeed, more acute during Paul V's Interdiction. In 1605, the *podestà* of Bergamo obliged the local inquisitor to exhibit proof of temporal possession of his benefices for the last 40 years, while, in the following years his colleagues in Vicenza, Verona, Brescia, Crema and Adria were harassed in various ways by the Venetian government with contestations concerning the enjoyment of benefices or the participation in local taxes.[62]

Nonetheless, the relations between bishops and inquisitors in the era of the Counter Reformation were not driven solely by conflict. Besides the Kingdom of Naples where, due to the peculiar organization of the local Holy Office, an equilibrium necessarily the opposite of that prevailing in the Centre-North of the peninsula sprang up, examples of cooperation between bishops and judges of faith came into being where there were cases of flagrant misgovernment or flagrant lassitude on the part of local secular power.[63] A close community of action between bishop and judges of faith took shape, as well, in specific contexts – like the particularly well-studied case of the State of Milan in the era of Carlo Borromeo.

Already as a freshly elevated cardinal, Borromeo, nephew of Pius IV, from his very entry into the diocese in February of 1560, found himself easily assigned by his uncle the faculty of drawing income from all of the ecclesiastical benefices directly in the Pope's hands. In this fashion, and thanks to a papal letter of the following month ordering all ecclesiastical authorities secular and monastic to give every aid to Borromeo in the protection and management of the incomes pertaining to Milan's episcopal patrimony, the cardinal was able to strengthen his political and economic position and fear no possible interference from the Curia or resistance on the part of the chapter and clergy of the city. Finally, in the following year the Pope gave him the faculty of conferring all the ecclesiastical and secular pensions of the diocese, including that of the cathedral chapter, annulling any previous privilege or exemption.[64]

The singular amplitude and solidity of the resources available to the Cardinal Bishop of Milan, together with a favourable local and international political situation, easily obtained Philip II's approval – and furnishes us with a decisive basis for understanding the operation of the constant economic support afforded by the Holy Office's activities in Lombardy. This situation was reinforced by the spiritual bent of the cardinal who, leaving his diocese briefly at Pius V's bequest, acted personally as inquisitor in Mantua in 1568 and, acting through delegates, carried through to judgement the trials of more than a hundred individuals accused of witchcraft in Val Mesolcina, of whom seven were burnt at the stake.[65]

Carlo Borromeo acted most zealously, obtaining specific financing for the Milanese Holy Office without waiting for solicitation from Rome, he assigned an annual contribution of 200 scudi to be paid out of the income of the episcopal properties and, on the direct request of the Duke of Alburquerque, Governor of Milan, in 1572 assigned 3,000 lire to Father Angelo Zampi, Inquisitor of Milan, who almost certainly used the sum to cover the cost of new buildings at Santa Maria delle Grazie.[66] Nor should we forget that Milan enjoyed a statute of particular importance – and therefore a favoured economic regime – within the peninsula inquisitorial system. Philip II, in the attempt to raise up a secure wall blocking the spread of heresy within his domains, had attempted, in 1563, to introduce the Spanish Inquisition into Milan. When local resistance brought this project to naught, the sovereign offered his constant support to the activity of the Milanese Holy Office. Both through official ordinances aimed at impeding the entry of foreign, heretic, merchants into the State and by blocking the circulation of forbidden books, as well as with financial aid (as when, in 1568, he gave 400 scudi to Milan's court of faith). The popes also attributed a strategic function to Milan as barbican against the spread of heresy, conferring upon resident inquisitors of the Lombard capital a most ample de facto jurisdiction, since they were empowered to examine witnesses and intervene in cases before other courts within the state.[67]

The inquisitorial office in Milan was a sort of "collection point" and general supervisor of cases within an area politically and religiously strategic – that "gateway to Italy" – subject to the authority of the Spanish Crown and linked to an archdiocese both very extensive and institutionally varied, including the suffragan bishoprics of Alessandria, Tortona, Novara, Lodi, Cremona, Piacenza (in the Farnese duchy), Albenga and Ventimiglia (in the Republic of Genoa), Ivrea and Vercelli (part of the Savoy duchy), Alba (belonging to the Gonzaga), Ferrara (belong to the d'Este) and Bergamo and Brescia (which lay within the confines of the Republic of Venice).

To return to the overall situation of the Italian peninsula, it is clear that the enforced standardizing of religious financial procedures pursued by the Holy Office from the sixteenth to the eighteenth centuries drew conspicuous funds from the economic resources it removed from episcopal control – recurring to whatever means proved necessary, even to reserving final judgement to itself when a case proved especially controversial: "The Supreme Congregation habitually takes to itself and closes even civil cases which in any manner touch the interests of the Inquisition without any other court meddling in any way", the supreme inquisitors informed the Patriarch of Aquileia in the 1620s, on learning that this worthy intended to pass judgement on a dispute over revenues between the Inquisitor of Treviso and the city's bishop.[68]

At the same time, the economic conflicts gave Rome occasion to reaffirm the superior authority of the apostolic nuncios in matters affecting the Inquisition. The judge in Ceneda could, for example, be invited to inform the nuncio of Venice "exhaustively" concerning a dispute with the vicar of Colle San Martino over the payment of a pension "and let your reverence be entirely governed by his advice".[69]

Introducing, in addition to the jurisdictional competition between bishops and inquisitors – whose inevitable conflicts were mediated by the Suprema – an economic rivalry, the popes and the Congregation were not only enabled to secure precious means of sustenance for their courts of faith, but to maintain as well a moderate but continuing pressure on the various protagonists of diocesan ecclesiastical life. The ensuing climate is fully expressed in the words with which, as late as the mid-eighteenth century, the inquisitor in Treviso recalled the complicated early period of the inquisitors nominated in that city by the Holy Office after the judges of faith had been for centuries chosen locally by the superiors and enjoyed the material support of their home convent.

In that situation the Friar Minor Conventual, Felice Pranzini – who had been inquisitor in Pisa and, subsequently, in Padua and in Siena – found himself blocked economically by the resistance of the diocesan authorities: unyielding despite his presentation by the Cardinal of Santa Severina, Giulio Antonio Santori, who found himself obliged to provide support from Rome for several years, exerting pressure directly upon the bishop.[70] Several years went by before the Holy Office and diocesan authorities came to some sort of agreement even in Treviso as to the allocation of resources. A portion of the benefice of San Giovanni del Battesimo of that city amounting to 100 Venetian ducats assigned to the Inquisition by Clement VIII in 1590 was, in fact, harshly contested by the canons of Treviso, who "tried everything, and moved every stone in Venice as well as here in Treviso, to impede the Holy Office from enjoying possession". Only after a laborious accord – again, the result of mediations from Rome and "with letters from the Cardinal of Santa Severina" – was the Inquisition able to lay hands on the Treviso benefice – though only for fifteen years, after which it reverted to the canons.[71]

A risky management model

The launching of this irreversible process which set the Inquisition as the institutional hub of the normative, theological, ecclesiastical and political Roman system, produced "serious effects upon episcopal authority, the control of the clergy and ecclesiastical careers, as well as upon the relations with the secular authorities; the repression of any form of intellectual dissent and the circulation of ideas; the forms of devotion and cult; and even upon the very religious identity of Catholic Italy".[72]

In the new institutional structure produced by the definitive affirmation of regional states within the Italian peninsula – states, indeed, which increasingly exercised less influence on the equilibriums of a Europe well into the long era of absolute monarchies and national aspirations – the Supreme Congregation organized itself to over-arch political frontiers and intervene without limits, opening investigations and carrying out trials without regard to any office or authority. Within the Roman Curia conflict between Intransigents and Moderates – which the former won – rapidly led the supreme inquisitors to grasp "an extraordinary power" and to entrench the Congregation "stably in the system of ecclesiastical government".[73]

Striking examples of such power were the trial which Gian Pietro Carafa – the future Paul IV – conducted against Giovanni Morone, who had been nuncio, Bishop of Modena and Novara and President of the Council of Trent; the placing of such episcopal seats as that of Vittore Soranzo in Bergamo in the hands of a commissar, and the abrogation of the right of Superiors of the Mendicant Orders to appoint inquisitors. The Bishop of Cava dei Tirreni, Giovanni Tommaso Sanfelice, as well as Modena's Egidio Foscarini, and Pietro Antonio Di Capua and Giovan Francesco Verdura (the one Bishop of Otranto, the other of Cheronissos); the Ordinary of Veglia, Alberto Duimio – and the Ordinaries of Chioggia and of Capodistria (Giacomo Nacchianti and Pier Paolo Vergerio) were subpoenaed or arrested, tried and forced to reaffirm full orthodoxy or flee.[74]

All this came about while the faculty for the concession of secret abjurations regarding heresy – which the Council of Trent had clearly attributed to bishops as well – was reserved solely for the inquisitors in the papal bull of 1568 *In coena Domini* which, in this respect, definitively abrogated the Tridentine Canon.

With Sixtus V and Clement VIII the process of centralization of the papal hierocracy had reached a very advanced stage even within the Inquisition itself. So much so as to lead to a definitive demise of the canonical procedure which had for some 200 years directed inquisitors to operate in cooperation with the bishops and to discourage, instead, any autonomous episcopal activity in the matter of heresy.[75] Even in 1749, the Inquisitor of Capodistria was not without a reminiscent note of pride:

> The Supreme Pontif Paul III, indeed, in 1545, delegated in particular as Commissar and Apostolic Inquisitor our Father Annibale Grisoni of the Order of the Friars Minor Conventual to seek out the pernicious errors being spread forth against the truth of the faith by two bishops of this province – one called Pietro Paolo Vergerio, bishop of this city of Capodistria and the other, Gian Battista Vergerio, his brother and bishop of Pola, of whom the first fled and the second, exhumed and burnt the cadaver, the ashes were dispersed in the sea.[76]

The profound confrontation between bishops and inquisitors regarding the faith left a long tail of memories and favoured a historic process of self-identification of great importance in the cultural history of the Holy Office and in its central and peripheral organs.

Since, in the age of the Counter Reformation, the bishops were slowly established in residence and oriented their action to the pastoral governance of diocesan life, the centralization of the procedures concerning the justice of faith – together with complete papal control in the distribution of ecclesiastical benefices (affirmed even at the theological level by the Council of Trent) – produced important consequences. While, by assigning pensions deriving from episcopal patrimonies to sustain local inquisitors and granting them exemptions from taxation, the liquid resources available to bishops were curtailed, the assignment of ecclesiastical benefices to the peripheral seats of the Holy Office cut into the bishops' capacity to fully control the beneficiary system, depriving them of a structure many considered indispensable for the introduction into the dioceses of the material and moral improvements the Council's programme intended to achieve.

Significantly, in 1527, a protagonist of early sixteenth century religious and ecclesiastical change, Gian Matteo Giberti, had – well in advance of the Tridentine bishop resident in Verona – obtained the authority from Clement VII to oblige whosoever enjoyed secular and regular benefices to declare the same and to furnish documentation of the entire sum deriving from them. It was equally the case that Giovanni Morone, Bishop of Modena, considered the control of benefices crucial to his precocious and complex plan for the reorganization and moralization of the religious life of his diocese, intervening directly in all vacancies even when constrained to do so in direct opposition to the Duke: indeed, in 1542, he went so far as to take to himself all of the diocesan properties whose yearly rentals had proved impossible to collect, or which had been usurped de facto by their leaseholders.[77]

Just when the bishops' reforming impulse, set in motion by the Council of Trent, demanded a growing capacity to control diocesan incomes, the drawing off of benefice and pension resources in favour of the Inquisition represented an element of decisive affirmation of that institution's ecclesiological, repressive, orientation within local contexts. This is even more evident if we consider the fact that, in the first century of the Counter Reformation – as considerable research has shown – both the wealthiest and, even more evidently, the poorest dioceses found it impossible to set up the seminaries for the education of the clergy which were one of the reforms most strongly desired by the Council. The dioceses' financial difficulties were indeed such that, during the rest of the sixteenth and seventeenth centuries, the Council's decisions in this area were little more than words on paper – with the inevitable negative effects on the possibility of securing the results Council and synod deemed crucial: the cultural and moral education of the clergy, their capacity to administer the parishes, a higher overall standard of pastoral activity; in definitive, the same efficiency as the grand Tridentine "design" of social discipline binding the whole of Catholicism.[78]

Even more broadly, the advance of the inquisitorial attack in the field of battle for the control of the bishops' economic resources coincided with just that phase of the post-Tridentine period between the pontificates of Pius V and Paul V (that is, from 1566 to 1621), characterized by the bishops' attempts to apply the Council's decrees concerning the disciplinary reform of both the clergy and the faithful, the administrative reorganization of the dioceses entrusted to their care and the recovery of their jurisdictional competences regarding the other authorities, both secular and ecclesiastical. The inadequate pursuit of these objectives (or, indeed, the lack of even the attempt to pursue them) had, by the middle decades of the seventeenth century, seen the disappearance of any pretence to decisive jurisdictional and pastoral episcopal power. Though they did not prevail everywhere in the peninsula, situations of failure in the structures of diocesan administration in favour of other forms of ecclesiastical organization – among which a leading role was certainly assumed by the courts of faith[79] – were widespread.

In the latter half of the century, the problem of the liability pensions constituted for the episcopate would become increasingly urgent even in the eyes of the popes. The important memorandum written by Mariano Sozzini, an Oratorian from Siena, close collaborator of Cardinal Benedetto Odescalchi, who would become Pope Innocent XI, discussed at length, for example, "the heavy and intolerable pensions which are imposed upon the bishops", citing the dramatic evidence that "[due to the pensions] the unfortunate bishop cannot remind the poor that they are his children; cannot give any stipend to the worthy ministers for the government of the diocese: often he is tempted to commit indignities and, almost, to sell holy orders to find coinage and avoid the censure with which his dependents threaten him". "The bishop renders himself odious to the clergy and the people", concludes Sozzini, pointing out a problem to which we shall return, "what with imposing heavy taxes on materials that ought to be freely given or, at most, conceded with more modest evaluations".[80]

Yet when in February, 1677, a few months after his election to the papacy, Innocent XI published the constitution *Circumspecta Sedis apostolicae* with the intent of restraining and regulating the host of norms and procedures governing episcopal pensions and other benefices carrying with them the care of souls, he found himself faced with opposition in the college of cardinals and the Curia on the part of personalities who did not hesitate to attack him precisely on the grounds of the war on heresy. Among these were cardinals Francesco Albizzi (already in the forefront of the attack on Jansenism), and Pietro Ottoboni who, as Bishop of Brescia, had proceeded in 1650 to eliminate the quietist group of "pelagians" in Val Camonica.

Ottoboni, as secretary of the Congregation of the Holy Office, was one of the foremost promoters of the trial and condemnation of Miguel de Molinos and his *Spiritual Guide*, a text the Pope had shown signs of appreciating; in 1678, moreover, he cast doubts upon the Oratorian Pier Matteo Petrucci, Bishop of Jesi (whom Innocent XI had raised to the rank of cardinal the previous year as a challenge to his enemies), involving him in accusations concerning quietism. At the death of Innocent XI in 1689, it was Ottoboni who was elected to the papacy after a conclave which concluded its deliberations with extraordinary rapidity for the time: perhaps, as Claudio Donati has observed, as had been the case for Alexander VIII, because of "his position at the Holy Office and the ease with which, consequently, he might place even the members of the Sacred College who might smell slightly of quietism under accusation".

The election of the new Pope sanctioned a sharp change of tack in the government of the Church which, at the end of the 1680s became evident in the Pope's reaffirmation of a hegemonic role through the repressive use of the Inquisition and a doctrine emphasizing the centrality of the Roman Church, seen as the immutable theological and juridical organism, solidly based upon a body of doctrine and rights to be defended totally and without any exceptions.[81]

The widespread resistance carried forward by the bishops and those popes who were less willing to embrace a simply repressive ecclesiology – as well as that of other ecclesiastical institutions damaged by the process of transferal of ordinary, fixed, resources to the Holy Office, certainly contribute to explaining the slowness, the incomplete territorial extension and the limited financial entity of the properties and benefices assignments concluded between the sixteenth and seventeenth centuries in favour of the Roman Inquisition's peripheral courts. Yet even taking these retarding elements into consideration, we cannot help being surprised at the apparent inadequacy of the overall economic restructuring of the Inquisition carried out by the highest authorities of the Roman church not only in the period of anticlerical emergency in the 1500s, but in the 1600s as the situation settled down.

The failure to resolve the problem of the ordinary financing of the local Inquisitions in a general and coherent manner – whose indirect expression is the limited entity of their incomes – would appear to have contributed to limiting the efficiency and the forensic capacities of the courts of faith. "When the cases are in places near Naples", wrote the Archbishop of Naples' vicar and minister of the Holy Office in the viceroyalty, "it has often been considered necessary to send the fiscal officer with an advisor, and the master of Acts so as to obtain some diligence, yet this has not been done because it requires expense".[82] "Prosecuting so many cases and giving satisfaction to officials, ministers and servants of the office cannot be carried off well with so slender an income; and the upkeep of the prisons", echoed, as we already know, the inquisitor in Bergamo.[83] The fragility of the balancing of their yearly accounts seems to have hindered secure programming and an adequate performance in the activities of faith, exposing their interventions to delays and overall uncertainty.

The model of ordinary financing of the peripheral courts was doubly risky, both because the traditional system of benefices made their major source of income susceptible to the variable relations with the secular political authorities (to which in some states the actual enjoyment of the benefices was subordinated) and because that model made the fixed incomes of the Inquisition depend upon the administration of property which was in great part made up of agricultural land.

The devastating wave of the plague which overwhelmed the Italian economy and the society of Central Northern Italy around 1630, for example, also produced negative repercussions on the activities of the Inquisition, "as it proved impossible in that period" – as another inquisitor from the area around Bergamo wrote – "to collect fees, rent out land or remedy the complaints, due to the hardships and the confusion occasioned by the enormous Contagion".[84] The aftermath of war might be equally devastating for the efficiency of inquisitorial structures. In the middle of the 1700s, in the last, dramatic, phase of the War of the Austrian Succession, the rich agricultural property of the ancient abbey of Sant'Andrea in Sestri Ponente, assigned to the Inquisition by Pius V in 1560, was devastated by the passage of French, Spanish and German troops, with damages totalling 5,000 Roman scudi, for, as the inquisitor in Genoa wrote, "from the bells in the church down to the last nail in the houses, everything was carried away; moreover the fields and the habitations were laid waste". For three years – from 1746 to 1749 – the estate could not be leased out, with the loss of the yearly income of more than 200 scudi.

The economic repercussions of the dramatic situation were further amplified by the negative influences of the war on financial investments. In the 1600s, the Genoa Office of the Inquisition had purchased a share at variable interest in the Banco di San Giorgio which, as the inquisitor was well aware, "rises and falls according to the varying circumstances of war, famine, public necessity". In the first half of the 1700s, the income had varied from a maximum of about 784 Genoese lire in 1739 to a minimum of about 462 lire in 1747: between 1747 and 1749, due to the war, it had produced no income at all: "neither in notes [sic] nor in coin, so that this Inquisition finds itself without aid". Further, for four years it had not even been possible to draw the pension which the Holy Office in Genoa received from the *Camera ducale* – again "due to the war". It is easy to imagine how seriously this drastic scarcity of money hampered inquisitorial activism, especially since, as the same Ligurian judge wrote, "here we cannot hope for any support from benefactors: indeed, those signs of fondness which in other Inquisitions are seen on the occasion of the Christmas festivities here are notoriously wholly in disarray".[85]

The risky system of ordinary financing under which the peripheral courts operated could have been substituted, at least partially – or integrated with a direct reimbursment of individual inquisitorial expenditures – by the Roman Ministry or the Apostolic Chamber, the chief financial organ of pontifical administration (reorganized by Pius IV himself to restore efficiency and prestige). Certainly, such a move would have been advantageous in terms of overall procedural efficiency. Far from being bureaucratically inapplicable, it was lucidly envisioned by the Congregation where it was necessary to administer a complex reality like that of the Kingdom of Naples. The supreme inquisitors had no uncertainties in this regard when, in 1591, they wrote to the nuncio in Naples:

> As to payment for transport and their own expenses in carrying them [the criminals] here from Naples, there is no need for your Honour to incur any difficulty, not even should you receive other orders from the Chamber ministers, for undoubtedly the expenses of such prisoners will be made good not only to the Nuncio in Naples, but to all the other ministers of whatever other location in Italy and elsewhere they be sent; besides, we ourselves, cardinals, are in Rome to uphold the dignity, the authority, the faith, the things belonging to these who serve this Holy Roman and Universal Inquisition. And Your Honour must know this is nothing new, but – from the happy memory of Pope Julius III to the present day – the Nuncios pay on behalf of the Apostolic Chamber and in Chamber there is afterwards no problem of any kind. So you may freely convince yourself that you will be able to pay these and other expenses which you may need to deal with in the future in like occasions; for, doubt not, they shall be made good to you.[86]

The negative results of the failure to apply this simple accounting procedure are easily discerned in the discouraging tone of various inquisitors for the difficult material conditions in which they were sometimes obliged to operate. This emotional atmosphere makes itself clearly felt in a letter Pellegrino Galassi, the inquisitor in Ceneda, sent to the Congregation in 1711. After lamenting the frequent assignment to poverty-stricken inquisitorial posts ("I cannot discover why your excellency, on the occasion of inquisitorial vacancies has three times in Treviso, twice in Siena and once in Florence, passed over me and put forward others who either have never before served or who, compared to me, can be deemed nothing"), and the lack of help from Rome on occasion of indispensable repairs to buildings ("however loudly I have complained, I was never heard"), he adds:

> Having already served the Holy Tribunal for 24 years and having always obeyed you when they sent me from Siena to Rovigo, from Rovigo into Istria, from Istria to Belluno and then here – all trips which cast me into debt and took away all I had for each was more than 200 miles [...] – and all the while, when it rains, obliged to hop about from one room to another, now, with all truth, reverence and efficacy I make known to you that I must needs have bed covers and sheets, for I feel compassion when I see myself buried in rags; yet God will that I be consoled. Yet, most elevated princes, it is something to raise eyebrows to hear that many inquisitors, dying, leave spoils of thousands and thousands of scudi to fatten up the convents (which deserve little and take everything) and other inquisitors have not enough to live on: many have the means to keep a carriage and I have no way of buying myself a pair of shoes.[87]

How can we reconcile this unfortunate image of the Holy Office with what we know of its striking religious, political and symbolic power? Was the constant under-financing – at least in terms of ordinary fixed income – of the apparatus operating in Italian territory the fruit of a specific strategic choice or of the overall scarcity of resources? Why did the highest authorities of a church strenuously engaged in combating internal dissent – as well as in the affirmation of the priority of this battle within the society and secular institutions – fail to rapidly set up efficient forms of financing for their courts of faith? And what considerations can we draw from the fact that the destruction of the widespread centres of heresy in the peninsula was accomplished between 1550 and 1570 (in a fairly short time, then); and this without centrally providing the inquisitors with comfortable and secure incomes?

Notes

1. Romeo (2009) pp. 54 and 57.
2. Brambilla (2006) is an indispensable point of departure for a thorough, long term, examination of the Holy Office; see also Brambilla (2000). A recent study on the early period, with important considerations on the theme of heresy and on the episcopal courts, is Filoramo (2011).
3. Benedetti (2011) has convincingly sustained the impossibility of fixing a specific founding moment for the medieval Inquisition, proposing a model of "polycentric origin" which links the theoretic presuppositions expressed in papal bulls with a plurality of gradual legislative acts – papal, imperial and civil – as well as de facto situations in which the Mendicant Orders took part. On the "rise of the inquisitors" from the theocratic Roman project, see Merlo (2008), p. 16 and Merlo (2011), p. 146: "The anti-heretic repression is not a "negative" aspect; it is not an antibody produced by a threatened organism which must defend itself and defend the health of the faith entrusted to it […] The Inquisition, whether one likes it or not, descends from an ecclesiology and is one of its functional parts".
4. Brambilla (2006).
5. On the question of an "Italian model" of Inquisition emerging with Innocent IV, see Paolini (1994); this position is taken up by Del Col (2006).
6. As Dall'Olio (1993) shows.
7. Errera (2000).
8. The need to maintain the bureaucratic apparatus of the Curia and the Pontifical State did, however, oblige the popes to circumvent that prohibition through a pension system derived from the incomes of the monastic orders, those of the episcopal revenues and many minor benefices, as Fragnito (1997) ably argues.
9. The question is discussed in the fundamental Bonora (2007).
10. As the recent synthesis of Lill (2010) has persuasively argued.
11. Among the authors who establish a direct link between the Marquis of Vasto's protest and the birth of the Holy Office, we need mention only Prosperi (2003a) in particular, p. 53, and Romeo (2009).
12. Maria Theresa's decree established that, on the death of the inquisitors and vicars still operating in Austrian Lombardy, there would be no further appointments. The suppression of the Inquisition in the Duchy of Parma, though it preceded that in Lombardy by only a few years, ended up with a reintroduction in 1780 without, however, apparent consequences in terms of judicial action. In 1746, the Kingdom of Naples had already seen bishops forbidden to act in cases

brought by the Inquisition: see Romeo (2009), pp. 110–12. On the State of Milan as the "door of Italy" see Fernández Albaledejo (2005).
13 ASM, *Atti di governo, Culto parte antica*, box 2106, folder "1771/1775", Kauntiz to Firmian, Wien, August 22, 1771, p. 1r.
14 ASM, ibid., pp. 1r–v.
15 ASM, *Atti di governo, Culto parte antica*, box 2106, unnumbered folders, labelled "1771", "5 October 1771" and "26 October 1771"; see also Fumi (1910), pp. 174–7. Of this contribution, traces remain in ACCO, *Archivio dell'orfanotrofio maschile, Origine e dotazione. Aggregazione di corpi e istituti*, box 1, deeds of Notary Antonio Silvola, March 22, 1779, and September 19, 1782, with grants of the Holy Office of Milan and Como to the Milanese Orphanage of San Pietro in Gessate.
16 ASM, *Atti di governo, Culto parte antica*, box 2106, folder "1771/1775", "Copia di memoria sulla necessità, e convenienza di conservare nello Stato di Milano il tribunale dell'Inquisizione" ("Copy of the memorandum on the necessity and the opportunity of conserving the tribunal of the Inquisition in the State of Milan"), Antonio Eugenio Visconti to Maria Theresa, June 22, 1774.
17 As Prosperi (2003b) recalls; in particular on p. 17.
18 ASM, ibid.; the citations are drawn respectively from pp. 9v–10r and 5r–6r.
19 Kaunitz's letter is in ASM, ibid., Wien, June 14, 1774, p. 1r–v. The dispatch, dated Vienna, March 9, 1775, is in ACCO, *Orfanotrofio maschile*, box 1, folder 10, p. 1 r–v.
20 Orano (1865), p. 38. Emblematically, the Liberal condemnation of the economic damage caused by the Inquisition is accompanied in Italy during the nineteenth century with the attack on escheat; see Maifreda (2010); for the Habsburg reforms, Maifreda (2017).
21 In 1749, the Congregation's Assessor, Pier Girolamo Guglielmi, carried out a systematic study of the financial conditions of the local courts. The results are deposited in ACDF. At present, research has not yet discovered any other year for which the surviving documentation is as rich and systematic.
22 ACDF, So, St.st., LL5e, *Inquisizione di Casale*.
23 ACDF, Oec 15, p. 4r–v. In 1589 the renewal of a nine-year rental fixed a biannual payment of 1,625 scudi (ACDF, So, St.st., L3c, "*Instrumenta rogati dalla cancelleria del S. Ufficio*" ("Certified Agreement, Holy Office Chancellery"), pp. 316v–318r).
24 ASV, *Fondo Borghese*, series II, box 64–65, p. 278r, Rome, April 1, 1603.
25 See Lanciani (1912); Pagliaro (1991); Marino (2009). In 1874, the manor and the iron works, included in the disposal of church properties, were sold to the outgoing lessee, Count Achille Gori Mazzoleni.
26 ACDF, So, St.st., LL 5e, *Inquisizione di Bologna*.
27 See Teodori (2012), p. 205.
28 On ecclesiastic patrimonies in the 1550–1600s, see the figures provided by Stumpo (1986), in particular p. 274; on the period of the suppressions, it is useful to begin with Taccolini (1998).
29 ACDF, register "*Entrata e uscita banco S. Offitio*", *fuori Stanza storica*, pp. 18–19 and 109.
30 Biondi (1982), p. 171.
31 Frajese (2000), pp. 767 and 805.
32 Firpo (2010), pp. 949–50. The break with the past represented by Pope Paul IV had already been discussed by von Pastor (1944): "The terrible arms which the courts of the Roman Inquisition, reorganized by Paul IV, set up against heretics – prison, death and confiscation of the property of those condemned to the extreme penalty, had, until then, been employed in a fairly temperate and kind manner" (p. 479) – has been demonstrated on the basis of the *Decreta* by Seidel Menchi (2003), pp. 315ff.
33 See Seidel Menchi (2003), pp. 315–16.

34 BAV, Barb. Lat. 1370, p. 71r, September 29, 1558.
35 Ibid., pp. 70v–71r, June 17, 1556. The full text of the Decree, dated the following day, appears in Firpo and Marcatto (1998–2000), I, pp. 16–17.
36 See, for example, TCD, *The Medieval and Renaissance Manuscripts. Section I. The Roman Inquisition* (henceforth Mrm), ms. 1226, sentence of the Cremona Inquisition, December 19, 1581, concerning don Cesare Magarini, guilty of having been "in great friendship and familiarity – as he was also his disciple – of a heretic who died obstinate in opinions contrary to [those of] the Holy Roman Church", and was condemned to life imprisonment "excusing of its mercy the confiscation of thy property and leaving thee thy benefices" (pp. 411v–2r). Other cases in which the same inquisitor refrained from stripping condemned priests of their benefices (among which that of a Matteo Belotti, condemned to perpetual incarceration in a monastery on February 1, 1582: pp. 427v–8r) may be found ibid.
37 BAV, Barb. Lat. 1370, official letters, April 2 and May 1, 1578.
38 The reference is to the canonical distinction between a consistorial ecclesiastic benefice – that is, one conferred by the Pope (usually regarding cardinals and bishops) – and the non-consistorial (or "minor") benefice, habitually conferred by the bishops.
39 See Dell'Oro (2007).
40 See, for example, in BAV, Barb. Lat. 6336, p. 108r, Rome, April 29, 1628.
41 In the ample bibliography on this theme, fundamental texts include Bizzocchi (1987); Chittolini (1986, 1989); Del Torre (1992–3); Galasso (1992); Prosperi (1977); Zarri (1986).
42 ACDF, So, St.st., LL5e, *Inquisizione di Bergamo*.
43 Ibid., on the question of Soranzo, see Firpo (2006).
44 Pius V's bull indicated, in fact, 200 scudi "of gold in gold", while the bishops insisted that they would not pay the whole sum citing payments calculated in 15 paoli scudi (ACDF, So, St.st., LL5e, *Inquisizione di Bologna*).
45 ACDF, So, St.st., LL5e, *Inquisizione di Brescia*.
46 ACDF, So, St.st., LL5f, *Inquisizione di Novara*.
47 ACDF, So, St.st., LL5e, *Inquisizione di Faenza* e *Inquisizione di Mantova*; LL5f, *Inquisizione di Padova*.
48 ACDF, So, St.st., LL5f, *Inquisizione di Pisa* e *Inquisizione di Tortona*.
49 BAV, Vat. Lat. 10945, *Inquisitioni dello Stato, e loro entrate e gravezze*, pp. 162rff.
50 ACDF, So, St.st., LL5f, *Inquisizione di Venezia*. To the importance which an ample bibliography justly accords the strategic role of the apostolic nuncio in the inquisitorial activities in Venice we should add that this figure of the diplomatic inquisitor exercised an important mediation in the attribution and payment of the benefices assigned to the Holy Office's courts. "As for securing temporal possession from the Wardens, the Clergy and the Beneficiaries who have formerly been part of this Inquisition", the Roman Congregation wrote – for example – to the recently appointed Inquisitor in Vicenza in February of 1609; "[you are advised] to deal with Monsignor the bishop of the locality, and be careful not to prejudice the rights and immunities of the Holy Office and, in need, write to Monsignor Nuncio in Venice" (BAV, Vat. Lat. 10945, Rome, February 14, 1609).
51 ACDF, So, St.st., II2f, pp. 230r–231v. In the middle of the 1600s, the inquisitor in Faenza, during a dispute, reminded the local Ordinary that Gregory XIII "upon the instance advanced by the inquisitors, had pronounced interdiction on bishops who did not pay the terms owed" (ibid., p. 221r).
52 BAV, Barb. Lat., 1370, p.17r, official letters sent from Rome on March 5, 1594 and September 16, 1595. In the latter, the Congregation admonished the bishop "in no way interfere in what is due to this chaplain and should you have other

53 ACDF, So, St.st., LL5e, *Inquisizione di Adria e Rovigo*.
54 BAV, Borg. Lat. 558, p. 25r; ACDF, So, St.st., LL5e, *Inquisizione di Gubbio*.
55 BAV, Barb. Lat. 6334, p. 5v, Rome, January 5, 1626.
56 ACDF, So, St.st., II2f., pp. 221ff., 225r, 254r, 302r.
57 Here, too, the financial differences were due to the fact that the party which had to pay the pension, in this case the bishop, interpreted the total sum to be paid in scudi di Camera – that is local coinage; the Inquisition, instead, insisted that the pension be paid in gold scudi, or in coinage containing a comparable quantity of gold – a solution which would have brought them notable advantage.
58 "And this has been the usage of all the bishops and inquisitors, without any deviations, even by the Most Eminent Cardinal Chigi, elevated to the greatness of the papacy"; the certification of the episcopal chancellor follows (ACDF, ibid., p. 274v).
59 Ibid.
60 BAV, Barb. Lat. 1370, p. 18r–v, Rome, January 17, 1598.
61 See, among others, the case ably analysed by Giannini (2002).
62 BAV, Barb. Lat. 5195, pp. 14rff.
63 We find some examples in Fosi (2007).
64 The episode has been carefully reconstructed in Giannini (2002), pp. 213ff. Only a few months earlier, in August, 1559, the order given by Cardinal Ghislieri and the Cardinal Camerlengo, Guido Ascanio Sforza di Santa Fiora, to the bursar general (holding a double investiture, both ducal and apostolic) – charged with the seizure and the administration within the duchy of the property of vacant benefices and the declaration of Official Approval (*placet*) granted by the prince – to pay 500 scudi from episcopal incomes to the Inquisitor Giovan Battista Chiarini of Cremona "to build prisons and deal with the other concurrent needs of the Holy Inquisition in this city" (ibid., p. 211), had not been executed. In the 1576 Provincial Council, Borromeo made it definitively clear that the administration of vacant and minor benefices were of episcopal competence and that the Ordinary had the right to grant and confirm recipients according to the indications established by the Council of Trent: Dell'Oro (2007), p. 65.
65 See Del Col (2006), pp. 428–9 and 580–1.
66 ACDF, So, St.st., LL5e, *Inquisizione di Milano*. The payment of pensions, probably suspended after Borromeo's death in 1584, was made permanent by Sixtus V's bull of September 20, 1586. The grant of 3,000 lire – as the Inquisitor Ermenegildo Todeschini of Mantua wrote in the mid-eighteenth century on the basis of the Milan Holy Office Archive to which he had access – "was, we may believe, for the most part spent on the new construction work undertaken, as we can see no other visible signs". See his manuscript, *Storia della fondazione, ed origine della Santa Inquisizione di Milano*, deposited in ACDF, ibid., p. 6r. The working copy of this manuscript is at present conserved in BAM, O 223 sup.
67 This prerogative was attributed to the Congregation in 1630: see BAV, Borg. Lat. 558, p. 47r, October 30, 1610. On the general aspects see Maselli (1970); Giannini (2001); Borromeo (2007).
68 BAV, Barb. Lat. 6334, Rome, March 21, 1626, p. 66r. For other aspects of this controversy, see ibid., Rome, February 7, 1626, p. 30r; February 14, 1626, p. 39v.
69 BAV, Barb. Lat. 6334, Rome, September 5, 1626, p. 247r–v. Ceneda, today a neighbourhood within the town of Vittorio Veneto, was a township in its own right until Italian unification.
70 ACDF, So, St.st., LL5f., *Inquisizione di Treviso*. On the profile of Pranzini see Romeo (1990), pp. 169ff.; on Santori see Ricci (2002).

71 ACDF, So, St.st., LL5f, *Inquisizione di Treviso*. This is a particularly interesting case, since the cathedral chapters, exempt from episcopal jurisdiction (and routinely linked by blood to the most important local families), were often bodies in conflict with the Ordinary and thus reflect, in this case, preoccupations which were not, strictly speaking, "pastoral". It was they who managed the placement of numerous ecclesiastic benefices (whose wealth often attracted the Venetian nobility) see, for example, the case of Verona, discussed in Prosperi (2012). A similar case may be found in Lombardy where, in 1569, Pius V annexed the priory of San Calimero (formerly belonging to the Humiliates) to the Mensa of the Cathedral of Milan with the obligation of a payment of 100 gold scudi in gold to the Pavia Inquisition. In the course of the 1600s, the Milan chapter stopped paying the golden money in gold: "The appeals of the inquisitors to the Chapter were never heeded", concluded the Pavia inquisitor disconsolately writing to Rome in 1749: ACDF, So, St.st., LL5f., *Inquisizione di Pavia*.
72 Firpo (2010), p. 650.
73 Prosperi (2009), p. 134.
74 For this and other similar cases, see Del Col (2006), pp. 305ff.
75 An excellent discussion of this question may be found in Frajese (1999).
76 ACDF, So, St.st., LL5e, *Inquisizione di Capo d'Istria*. This document confirms the hypothesis – advanced by P. Stancovich in *Biografia degli uomini distinti dell'Istria* (tome 1, Gio. Marenigh Typographer, Trieste, 1828, pp. 297ff.) – that the Inquisition ordered the exhumation and post-mortem condemnation of Vergerio's brother, after his interment in the Capo d'Istria cathedral in 1548. Stancovich cites a letter from Girolamo Muzio to Gian Pietro Carafa, the future Paul IV, dated January 21, 1554, which declares: "As I know that Holy Mother Church is used to proceed against heretics, not only while they are in life, but even after their death [...] I cannot fail to write to you in this matter [... that] his [Pier Paolo's] brother, bishop of Pola, was of his school, since it is more than evident to all of Istria, though his name is not so widely broadcast, nor his infamy so notorious. He died in Capodistria before his brother was driven out, and died a Lutheran without the sacraments of penitence and extreme unction, with scorn for all the ceremonies and procedures of the Church: and he was interred in holy ground: and in a consecrated place those bones – enemies of all things sacred – still repose. I have remained silent on this until the present hour" (ibid., pp. 298–9).
77 See Prosperi (2012), p. 155; Peyronel Rambaldi (1979), pp. 136–9.
78 See the analysis of Comerford (2006).
79 The gap between the 1566–1621 phase and the one following, which lasted at least until the pontificate of Innocent XI (1676) has been discussed by Donati (1992).
80 The quotations are drawn from Donati (1986), pp. 723–4.
81 Ibid., p. 731.
82 BAV, Borg. Lat. 558, p. 132r, Naples, March 3, 1635.
83 ACDF, So, St.st., GG3c, p. 86r, Bergamo, April 13, 1622.
84 Ibid., sheet without number, Bergamo, December 8, 1632.
85 ACDF, So, St.st., LL5e, *Inquisizione di Genova*.
86 BAV, Barb. Lat. 1370, p. 215r, Rome, June 13, 1591. Three years earlier, the nuncio – having received the order from Rome to provide directly for the expense – had refused to anticipate charterage for the frigates carrying prisoners of the Holy office to Rome. On the reorganization of the Apostolic Chamber, between 1561 and 1564, see Giannini (2003), p. 23.
87 ACDF, So, St.st., GG 3d, Ceneda, December 10, 1711.

Bibliography

Benedetti, M. (2011) 'Gregorio IX: l'inquisizione, i frati e gli eretici', in *Gregorio IX e gli ordini mendicanti. Atti del XXXVIII Convegno internazionale. Assisi, 7–9 ottobre 2010*, Spoleto: Fondazione Centro italiano di studi sull'Alto medioevo, 293–323.
Biondi, A. (1982) *Umanisti, eretici, streghe. Saggi di storia moderna*, Modena: Comune di Modena.
Bizzocchi, R. (1987) *Chiesa e potere nella Toscana del Quattrocento*, Bologna: Il Mulino.
Bonora, E. (2007) *Giudicare i vescovi. La definizione dei poteri nella Chiesa postridentina*, Rome and Bari: Laterza.
Borromeo, A. (2007) 'The Crown and the Church in Spanish Italy in the Reigns of Philip II and Philip III', in T. J. Dandelet, J. A. Marino (eds) *Spain in Italy. Politics, Society, and Religion 1500–1700*, Leiden: Brill, 517–54.
Brambilla, E. (2000) *Alle origini del Sant'Uffizio. Penitenza, confessione e giustizia spirituale dal Medioevo al XVI secolo*, Bologna: Il Mulino.
Brambilla, E. (2006) *La giustizia intollerante. Inquisizione e tribunali confessionali in Europa (secoli IV–XVIII)*, Rome: Carocci.
Chittolini, G. (1986) 'Stati regionali e istituzioni ecclesiastiche nell'Italia centrosettentrionale del Quattrocento', in G. Chittolini and G. Miccoli (eds) *Storia d'Italia. Annali 9, La Chiesa e il potere politico dal Medioevo all'età contemporanea*, Turin: Einaudi, 149–93.
Chittolini, G. (1989) 'Note sulla politica ecclesiastica degli stati italiani nel secolo XV (Milan, Florence, Venice)' in J. P. Genet and B. Vincent (eds) *État et Église dans la genèse de l'État moderne* (Actes du colloque organisé par le Centre National de la Recherche Scientifique et la Casa de Velázquez, Madrid, 30 novembre et 1 décembre 1984), Madrid: CNRSCV, 195–208.
Comerford, K. M. (2006) *Reforming Priests and Parishes. Tuscan Dioceses in the First Century of Seminary Education*, Leiden and Boston: Brill.
Dall'Olio, G. (1993) 'I rapporti tra la Congregazione del Sant'Ufficio e gli inquisitori locali nei carteggi bolognesi (1573–1594)', *Rivista storica italiana* (1): 246–86.
Del Col, A. (2006) *L'Inquisizione in Italia dal XII al XXI secolo*, Milan: Mondadori.
Del Torre, G. (1992–3) 'Stato regionale e benefici ecclesiastici: vescovadi e canonicati nella terraferma veneziana all'inizio dell'età moderna', *Atti dell'Istituto veneto di scienze lettere e arti* (151): 1171–1236.
Dell'Oro, G. (2007) *Il Regio economato. Il controllo statale sul clero nella Lombardia asburgica e nei domini sabaudi*, Milan: FrancoAngeli.
Donati, C. (1986) 'La Chiesa di Roma tra Antico Regime e riforme settecentesche (1675–1760)', in G. Chittolini and G. Miccoli (eds) *Storia d'Italia. Annali 9. La Chiesa e il potere politico dal Medioevo all'età contemporanea*, Turin: Einaudi, 719–66.
Donati, C. (1992) 'Vescovi e diocesi d'Italia dall'età post-tridentina alla caduta dell'Antico Regime', in M. Rosa (ed.) *Clero e società nell'Italia moderna*, Rome and Bari: Laterza, 321–89.
Errera, A. (2000) *Processus in causa fidei. L'evoluzione dei manuali inquisitoriali nei secoli XVI–XVIII e il manuale inedito di un inquisitore perugino*, Bologna: Monduzzi.
Fernández Albaledejo, P. (2005) 'De "llave de Italia" a "corazón de la monarquía": Milán y la monarquía católica en el reinado de Felipe III', in P. Pissavino and G. Signorotto (eds) *Lombardia borromaica Lombardia spagnola. 1554–1659*, Rome: Bulzoni, 41–93.
Filoramo, G. (2011) *La croce e il potere. I cristiani da martiri a persecutori*, Rome and Bari: Laterza.

Firpo, M. (2006) *Vittore Soranzo vescovo ed eretico. Riforma della Chiesa e Inquisizione nell'Italia del Cinquecento*, Rome and Bari: Laterza.
Firpo, M. (2010) 'Da inquisitori a pontefici. Il Sant'Uffizio romano e la svolta del 1552', *Rivista storica italiana* (122): 911–50.
Firpo, M. and Marcatto, D. (1998–2000) (eds) *I processi inquisitoriali di Pietro Carnesecchi (1557–1568)*, 2 vols, Vatican City: Archivio segreto vaticano.
Fosi, I. (2007) *La giustizia del papa. Sudditi e tribunali nello Stato Pontificio in età moderna*, Rome and Bari: Laterza.
Fragnito, G. (1997) 'Vescovi e ordini religiosi in Italia all'indomani del Concilio', in C. Mozzarelli and D. Zardin (eds) *I tempi del Concilio. Religione, cultura e società nell'Europa tridentina*, Rome: Bulzoni, 13–25.
Franchini, G. (1693) *Bibliosofia e memorie letterarie di scrittori francescani conventuali ch'hanno scritto dopo l'anno 1585*, Modena: Eredi Soliani.
Frajese, V. (1999) 'Le licenze di lettura nel "600 tra vescovi ed inquisitori. Aspetti della politica dell'Indice dopo il 1596"', *Società e storia* (86): 767–818.
Frajese, V. (2000) 'Le licenze di lettura e la politica del Sant'Uffizio dopo l'Indice clementino', in *L'inquisizione e gli storici: un cantiere aperto. Tavola rotonda nell'ambito della Conferenza annuale della ricerca (Roma, 24–25 giugno 1999)*, Rome: Accademia Nazionale dei Lincei.179–220.
Fumi, L. (1910) 'L'Inquisizione romana e lo Stato di Milano. Saggio di ricerche nell'Archivio di Stato' *Archivio storico lombardo* (35, 36, 37): 5–124, 145–220, 285–414.
Galasso, G. (1992) *Il Regno di Napoli. Il Mezzogiorno angioino e aragonese (1266–1494)*, Turin: Utet.
Giannini, M. C. (2001) 'Fra autonomia politica e ortodossia religiosa: il tentativo di introdurre l'Inquisizione "al modo di Spagna" nello Stato di Milano (1558–1566)', *Società e storia* (91): 79–134.
Giannini, M. C. (2002) 'Una Chiesa senza arcivescovo. Identità e tensioni politiche nel governo ecclesiastico a Milano (1546–1560)', *Annali di storia moderna e contemporanea* (8): 171–222.
Giannini, M. C. (2003) *L'oro e la tiara. La costruzione dello spazio fiscale italiano della Santa sede 1560–1620*, Bologna: Il Mulino.
Lanciani, R. (1912) *Storia degli scavi di Roma e notizie intorno le collezioni romane di antichità*, vol. 4, Rome: Loescher & Co.
Lill, R. (2010) *Il potere dei papi dall'età moderna a oggi*, Rome and Bari: Laterza.
Maifreda, G. (2010) '*I beni dello straniero. Albinaggio, cittadinanza e diritti di proprietà nel Ducato di Milano (1535–1796)*' *Società e storia* (129): 489–530.
Maifreda, G. (2017) 'Immigrants: Asset or Threat? Foreigners, Property and the Right of Escheat in Enlightenment Milan', *Eighteenth-Century Life*, 41 (2), in press.
Marino, M. (2009) 'L'attività economica: la tenuta di Conca', in A. Cifres and M. Pizzo (eds) *Rari e preziosi. Documenti dell'età moderna e contemporanea dall'archivio del Sant'Uffizio*, Rome: Gangemi, 48–63.
Maselli, D. (1970) 'Per la storia religiosa dello Stato di Milano durante il dominio di Filippo II: l'eresia e la sua repressione dal 1555 al 1584', *Nuova rivista storica* (3–4): 318–73.
Merlo, G. G. (2008) *Inquisitori e Inquisizione nel Medioevo*, Bologna: Il Mulino.
Merlo, G. G. (2011) *Eretici del Medioevo. Temi e paradossi di storia e storiografia*, Brescia: Morcelliana.
Orano, G. (1865) *La libertà economica e la civiltà*, Turin: Tipografia G. Favale e C.
Pagliaro, M. C. (1991) *La tenuta e le ferriere di Conca nella valle dell'Astura. Aspetti e problemi. Secoli XVIII–XIX*, Rome: Tipolitografia Santa Lucia.

Paolini, L. (1994) 'L'eresia e l'Inquisizione. Per una complessiva riconsiderazione del problema', in G. Cavallo, C. Leonardi and E. Menestò (eds) *Lo spazio letterario del Medioevo. 1. Il Medioevo latino*, tome 2, *La circolazione del testo*, Rome: Salerno editrice, 361–405.

Peyronel Rambaldi, S. (1979) *Speranze e crisi nel Cinquecento modenese. Tensioni religiose e vita cittadina ai tempi di Giovanni Morone*, Milan: FrancoAngeli.

Poppi, A. (1992) *Cremonini e Galilei inquisiti a Padova nel 1604. Nuovi documenti d'archivio*, Padua: Antenore.

Prosperi, A. (1977) 'Le istituzioni ecclesiastiche e le idee religiose', *Il Rinascimento nelle corti padane*, Bari: De Donato, 125–63.

Prosperi, A. (2003a) *L'inquisizione romana. Letture e ricerche*, Rome: Edizioni di storia e letteratura.

Prosperi, A. (2003b) 'Inquisizioni cristiane ed ebrei', in *Le inquisizioni cristiane e gli ebrei. Tavola rotonda nell'ambito della Conferenza annuale della ricerca. Roma, 20–21 dicembre 2001*, Rome: Accademia nazionale dei Lincei., 7–28.

Prosperi, A. (2009) *Tribunali della coscienza. Inquisitori, confessori, missionari*, Turin: Einaudi.

Prosperi, A. (2012) *Tra evangelismo e Controriforma. Gian Matteo Giberti (1495–1543)*, Rome: Edizioni di storia e letteratura.

Ricci, S. (2002) *Il sommo inquisitore. Giulio Antonio Santori tra autobiografia e storia (1532–1602)*, Rome: Salerno editrice.

Romeo, G. (1990) *Inquisitori, esorcisti e streghe nell'Italia della Controriforma*, Florence: Sansoni.

Romeo, G. (2009) *L'Inquisizione nell'Italia moderna*, Rome and Bari: Laterza.

Seidel Menchi, S. (2003) *Origine e origini del Santo Uffizio dell'Inquisizione romana (1542–1559)*, in A. Borromeo (ed.) *L'Inquisizione. Atti del Simposio internazionale. Città del Vaticano, 29–31 ottobre 1998*, Vatican City: Biblioteca apostolica vaticana, 291–321.

Stancovich, P. (1828) *Biografia degli uomini distinti dell'Istria*, Trieste: presso Gio. Marenigh tipografo.

Stumpo, E. (1986) 'Il consolidamento della grande proprietà ecclesiastica nell'età della Controriforma', in G. Chittolini and G. Miccoli (eds) *Storia d'Italia. Annali 9. La Chiesa e il potere politico dal Medioevo all'età contemporanea*, Turin: Einaudi, 263–89.

Taccolini, M. (1998) *L'esenzione oltre il catasto. Beni ecclesiastici e politica fiscale dello Stato di Milano nell'età delle riforme*, Milan: Vita e pensiero.

Teodori, M. (2012) 'Non solo rendita. Tipologie gestionali e risultati economici in un feudo del Lazio nel Settecento', in M. Teodori and R. Vaccaro (eds) *Studi in onore di Angela Maria Bocci Girelli*, Milan: FrancoAngeli, 204–23.

Various authors. (2000) *L'inquisizione e gli storici: un cantiere aperto. Tavola rotonda nell'ambito della Conferenza annuale della ricerca (Roma, 24–25 giugno 1999)*, Rome: Accademia Nazionale dei Lincei.

Various authors. (2003) *Le inquisizioni cristiane e gli ebrei. Tavola rotonda nell'ambito della Conferenza annuale della ricerca. Roma, 20–21 dicembre 2001*, Rome: Accademia nazionale dei Lincei.

von Pastor, L. (1944) *Storia dei papi dalla fine del Medio Evo*, vol. 6, Rome: Desclée & Co.

Zarri, G. (1986) 'Le istituzioni ecclesiastiche nel ducato di Urbino nell'età di Federico da Montefeltro', in G. Chittolini, G. Cerboni Baiardi, P. Floriani (eds) *Federico di Montefeltro. Lo Stato, le arti, la cultura*, Rome: Bulzoni, 159–69.

2 Managing the courts of faith

Let us now look more closely at the mechanics of monetary circulation, solidity and financial compensation set in place within the Italian inquisitorial network from the 1500s through the 1600s. However much they present themselves as minute transactions, these incessant, capillary, monetary flows linking the centre to the periphery of the inquisitorial system – or, moving within the network of the courts of faith alone, eluding Rome – had the fundamental objective of guaranteeing the efficient and uniform operation of the Holy Court within the whole society and the multiplicity of its territorial components. The circular and overlapping financial techniques of the local inquisitors were, as we shall see, especially important in the Kingdom of Naples, where the justice of faith was organized in a manner which did not lend itself readily to the economic conduct discussed in Chapter 1.

We will next look at the local courts' managerial model, based on the capacity of the inquisitors to secure a positive balance of their yearly budgets and, should a deficit appear, fall back smoothly upon the direct financial support of the convents and the judges of faith themselves, required to make good the funds needed. This local mode of administration of the Inquisition's money might – as I shall attempt to demonstrate – bring with it fundamental repercussions on the overall operation of the justice of faith as, through the system of incentives to action which the final two sections of this chapter reconstructs, it might influence the way in which trials were conducted by the inquisitors.

Solidarity among inquisitors and its limits

As we have seen in Chapter 1, throughout the early modern period the most important source of ordinary, fixed, income for the courts of the Roman Inquisition was derived from benefices and pensions assigned by the popes and the Congregation. Often diverted from the dioceses and their multiple and delicate post-Tridentine activities, the benefice incomes – gradually attached themselves to the local seats of the Holy Office little, and that only from the final stages of the sixteenth-century anti-heretic emergency – extending only partially to the courts, were not enough to guarantee the general efficiency of the local inquisitorial system. Judges operating in smaller centres might, following the directives of the Congregation, enjoy support from wealthier courts: the Roman Ministry did, in fact, set up forms of obligatory solidarity among its courts with the intent of levelling the economic conditions within which the overall inquisitorial management operated so as to permit all of the judges of faith to maintain a minimum level of efficiency. With the sole exception of the Kingdom of Naples (whose Inquisition had a form of spurious financing due to its peculiar organizational characteristics), a network of monetary redistribution among judges of faith took form. These circuits of solidarity had real historic relevance, for not only did they bolster the situation of all the judges of faith, but, they also reaffirmed their common participation in a unified religious project, expressed in widely shared strategies and goals.

The circles of mutual solidarity among the local seats of the Roman Inquisition were based on the criterion of political-geographic contiguity. In these cases money almost always moved between inquisitors operating within the same state. From the second half of the fifteenth century at the latest, this criterion contributed significantly to consolidating a process of "statalization" in the placement and operation of the courts of faith in the Italian peninsula.

In the Middle Ages, the organization of the inquisitorial districts had developed within the context of the territorial divisions of the Mendicant Orders. Thus the inquisitors were normally distributed in cathedral cities or in localities where there were important Franciscan or Dominican houses, generally disregarding the political boundaries of the territorial states then in formation. At the end of the 1400s, with the gradual disintegration of the administrative divisions established in the thirteenth or fourteenth centuries, the numerous new inquisitorial seats were strategically placed within the State borders established by the Treaty of Lodi and remained substantially unchanged for the ensuing 40 years.

Before the founding of the Congregation of the Holy Office, this progressive tendency to restructure the jurisdiction of Holy Office courts following the new secular forms assumed by State structures, led to what Michael Tavuzzi called *State-Inquisitions*:[1] "Inquisitions within the state" whose political-strategic significance grew still larger during the anti-Lutheran emergency. When examining the religious orthodoxy of the individual reigning house, or of the highest governing organs – penalizing protection which might have been afforded heretics, or the excessive "permeability" of some frontiers – and exercising institutional pressure on principalities and republics to guarantee inquisitors full liberty of action became an absolute priority for the Holy Office, distributing courts and judges geo-politically showed itself to be a precious resource, and therefore a policy to be pursued tenaciously. We see this in the territorial distribution of new courts carried out between the mid-1500s and early 1600s, clearly shaped by the intent of redefining the reach of the justice of faith, following the remodelling of the political equilibriums and the institutional frontiers among the peninsular states.

In this progressive overlapping of the financial circuits of the Inquisition courts and the jurisdiction of territorial states, the Republic of Venice, from 1580, found its Inquisition paying 25 scudi *in perpetuo* to the Inquisition in Capodistria, and 28 to the Inquisition in Zara; Padua paid 15.50 scudi a year into Belluno's coffers, while, again from 1580, Bergamo received 50 scudi *in perpetuo* from Brescia. The same thing occurred in favour of the inquisitor in Parma, to the loss of his colleague in Piacenza, and to Casale Monferrato to the detriment of Mantua. In the Duchy of Savoy both the court in Mondovì and the court in Saluzzo enjoyed a pension of 25 scudi *in perpetuo* from the inquisitor in Asti. The Saluzzo Inquisition, instituted in 1555, was, in the sixteenth and seventeenth centuries, at the centre of a rapid series of beneficiary events: in 1599 three incomes of 25 scudi each were assigned to it: one to be paid by Turin, a second by Vercelli, and the third by Asti. In 1603, it was assigned an income twice as large – 50 scudi – to be paid by the Novara Inquisition. In the Papal State, Faenza paid annual pensions of 25 scudi to Rimini and Ancona, while Spoleto – in 1685, the last court to be established – received 20 scudi from Perugia. Florence, most of whose fixed income derived from the ancient and prestigious priory of San Pietro Scheraggio (repossessed from the archbishop by Gregory XIII) paid pensions to Siena and Pisa.[2]

The ministry in Rome did not limit itself to creating stable channels of finance between courts which were politically and territorially linked, but intervened, as well, in the financial decisions of its courts, obliging the more prosperous inquisitors to bestow more or less consistent funds upon their less fortunate colleagues. Such forms of extraordinary solidarity could extend beyond the political borders of states, accompanying and integrating the political-territorial logic which governed the assigning of perpetual pensions. Brescia's inquisitor might, for example, be ordered to transfer 50 scudi to his colleague in Crema, or to his colleague in Saluzzo: in the second instance he was also making good the failure of the Asti court to pay the pensions (and he was not spared the recommendation to "abstain for undertaking any not very necessary expenses").[3]

Or the cardinals of the Suprema could have their secretaries write to the inquisitor in Reggio Emilia that he was authorized to "pay the Bargello of the city the residue of the sum due for having brought Orazio Bacci to Rome [...] together with the 100 scudi forwarded from the Inquisition in Pavia, given by them to this Inquisition".[4] The Congregation could also oblige an inquisitor to cease insisting on payment of a sum owed to him, notifying, for example, the inquisitor in Saluzzo that Asti and Novara were not, at that moment, able to pay the pension owed to him ("yet Your Reverence will have to make the best of it, without further prodding of the above mentioned inquisitors").[5] In this manner all the operative sections of the system managed to function in some measure even when local financial crises arose.

Although, generally speaking, the managerial strategy employed by the Roman Inquisition in handling its financial resources was characterized by the intent of assuring that the funds needed to operate the repressive mechanisms came directly from the local seats themselves – or, at most, from donations exchanged between the individual inquisitors – an internal financial intervention might sometimes become a direct grant from Rome. This occurred more frequently in the second half of the 1500s, when local courts had not yet been given a stable basis. Still, in that period, gifts to the inquisitors from the Congregation were of little importance, especially in comparison to the frequent and consistent monetary grants it bestowed on external collaborators. Taking as an indicative period of observation the end of the 1580s, we can, in fact, see that, in 1578, the Suprema conferred 25 scudi on Prospero da Urbino, inquisitor in Siena and, in 1580, 100 scudi on Battista da Lugo, inquisitor in Cremona, while Dionigi da Costacciano, inquisitor in Florence, received 50; in 1584, Stefano da Calvisano, elected inquisitor in Casale, received 30 scudi, as did the inquisitor in Saluzzo in 1587; between 1589 and 1591 the judges of faith in Perugia, Vercelli and Tortona received, respectively, 45, 30 and 15 scudi.[6]

The real weight of such largesse should not be exaggerated: for example, the 15 scudi conferred on the judge of faith in Tortona are equal to the yearly tips bestowed on the Congregation's ushers at Christmas time. Still, it is the very modesty of these figures which brings home to us the degree in which the inquisitors confronted the period of the greatest repressive activity aimed at the Protestant heresy in financial conditions that were wholly inadequate to guarantee continuity and efficiency for the vast project of religious repression which they were called to support. Further, in the same years in which it bestowed these sporadic grants upon its local inquisitors, Rome intervened financially *in causis fidei* with sums as large – or, often, larger – than those conferred on judges of faith.

The oldest accounting information we have for the Congregation of the Holy Office regard the end of Pius IV's papacy when, in 1564, the overall monthly expenses of the ministry were slightly over 400 scudi. Half of this sum, "200 or more scudi", was made up of "monies paid to persons who are sent forth in the service of the Holy Office, and to others who have cause to come to Rome from other countries to bear testimony", to expenses, then, variously connected to inquisitorial and trial activities. The remaining 200 scudi were assigned to fixed expenses: wages of personnel; office material; maintenance of incarcerated prisoners without means; and rent of buildings housing the Supreme Court.[7] In the the years following the death of Paul IV on August 18, 1559; the people of Rome had revolted, burning down the Passeggiata di Ripetta court. The building which now houses the Holy Office in the Vatican City had not yet been purchased and restructured. It was Pius V who, in 1566–7, bought the *palazzo* of the heirs of Cardinal Lorenzo Pucci – built after 1514 near Saint Peter's in what was known as the Contrada degli Armeni – for 9,000 scudi. The expensive restructuring was completed only during the papacy of Sixtus V.[8]

The case of Naples

The practice of conferring occasional direct grants upon inquisitors, or, better, on prelates absolving functions of inquisitor, played an especially important role in the Kingdom of Naples. Under the authority of the Spanish Crown for a great part of the period covered by this study, it did not experience the Roman Inquisition operating through a system of peripheral courts comparable to that in the Centre-North of the peninsula. Attempts in 1510 and 1547 to place the State under the jurisdiction of the Spanish Inquisition were, in turn, defeated by the violent opposition of the local nobility and popular insurrection. In this setting, the activity of the Holy Office in the territories of Naples was assumed by the bishops, under the direction of the Bishop of the archdiocese and with the control of the apostolic nuncio, who, in inquisitorial questions, too, reported to Rome as well as to local, lay, authorities.[9]

In addition, the *pro tempore* substitutes of the Neapolitan archbishop – beginning with the Sicilian Scipione Rebiba, known as the Cardinal of Pisa – also became commissars, delegated semi-secretly to the coordination of anti-heretical repression, throughout the entire realm, though not officially assuming the title of inquisitor. The author of a secret report to the Suprema put it well:

> Neither because he [the Minister of the Holy Office, that is the bishop's substitute in Naples] has, at the present moment, notaries, fiscals, advisors, executors, prisons and archives, can it be declared that he has set up a court of the Inquisition, because this is not needed, to carry out the orders of the Holy Congregation – since all of the above-mentioned can rather call upon the minister of that same Holy Congregation than the Naples minister [...] and though by the common [person] he be called with name of general inquisitor, it is nonetheless an abuse [to so term him], and not appropriate to his institution and his authority.[10]

What, then, do the economic relations between the Roman Ministry and the Neapolitan territory look like in the context of this fluid institutional reality? The norm was the periodic concession of occasional grants by the Suprema, combined with authorizations to inflict monetary punishment and the assumption by Rome of the liquidation of the heaviest costs. When, for example, in 1618, the cardinal inquisitors had proof of the painful financial situation of the Bishop of Nocera Inferiore-Sarno deriving from activities linked to the Holy Office, they granted him the option of imposing a fine of 100 scudi on the Count of Carifi, who was on trial for heresy. In addition, they exhorted the prelate to "keep separate accounts for judicial activities", so also pointing out the managerial problems entailed in the exercise of a double function as diocesan Ordinary and as inquisitor.[11]

In the same years, the Bishop of Nocera Inferiore benefited from the notable gifts and the repeated concession of the right to impose monetary penalties: he took in 100 scudi in 1610; 270 scudi in 1615; and 250 scudi in 1620. This financial policy showed itself to be rather efficacious, as the particularly intense judicial activity within the diocese during the seventeenth century testifies.[12]

It is also worth noting that the bodies directing the inquisitorial activities in the southern areas of the Italian peninsula were also furnished – though somewhat delayed – with a modest fixed income. This was derived from some agricultural holdings in the territory belonging to Caserta, at Recale and Capodrise and confiscated property of the heretic Giovanni Leonardo Silvestro, given to the Church of the Annunciation in Marcianise. With a Supreme Congregation Decree of 1605, the patrimony was assigned to those officials of the Holy Office who were active in the Neapolitan area, yielding, in the mid-sixteenth century, some 50 ducats a year in rents.[13] This income was certainly inadequate to deal with the expenses the episcopal courts faced in pursuing the Inquisition's goals as an annual account in 1635 reports, 50 scudi barely covered the postal expenses of the Archbishop of Naples.[14] The ministers of the Neapolitan Holy Office had to continue forwarding their list of expenses to Rome which, without showing any urgency at all, from time to time sent back funds.[15] The self-financing solution recommended to the Neapolitan bishops by the Congregation remained, of necessity, the imposition of pecuniary punishment: fines were a form of "withdrawal" which, in the context of an ecclesiastical structure like that of the Italian South, was bound to have, once again, negative effects on diocesan economies. "Some sort of monetary subsidy for the affairs of the Holy Office in this city of Naples would indeed be very opportune, as experience has more than once shown", wrote Nuncio Alessandro Bichi in 1630 to the Roman Ministry, replying to a specific inquiry on the part of the cardinals "and securing them in monetary sentencing, such as the Ordinaries are imposing in their courts while easier or more certain levies do not present themselves, I believe would not be the case if it were not very well deliberated":

> Yet I must say that, as all of the church in the kingdom is poor, and obliged as well to furnish pensions – most of them almost in ruins or, at least, with damaged structures and perhaps all of them scarcely provided with the vessels necessary for divine services – and not having other subsidies, due to the prelates' scant possibilities, than the aforementioned fines (which are customarily applied to the aid or welfare of these same churches), there is the risk that, to gain a good end, another might be destroyed or enfeebled when such contributions should be taken in considerable measure from them.[16]

To overcome these difficulties, as well as the traditional hostility of local communities towards the courts of faith, the apostolic nuncio in Naples suggested the introduction of a hidden tax to sustain the local activities of the Holy Office. Calculating that the "pastoral churches" were about 140, and that each of them could furnish about 100 ducats in fines, Monsignor Bichi proposed a forfeiture relinquishing the basis of their economic conditions. This tax would procure more than 1,000 ducats annually, which would be secretly transferred to the Holy Office by the nuncio's office. By not taking the monetary penalties directly, this obligatory payment would not move the churches, wrote the apostolic nuncio, to find "grounds to feel annoyed and to bear this weight unwillingly". "I do not hesitate to declare myself persuaded", he concluded, "that the lower the imposed [percentage], the easier it will prove to collect and the less will it excite the curiosity to discover whom it may serve".[17]

The Roman Curia pursued this method of financing the Neapolitan Inquisition for some years. In 1635 it was still urging the Archbishop of Naples, Francesco Boncompagni, to send – as he indeed did – a complete list of the dioceses of the Kingdom, divided into "large" and "middling", prompting from that prelate the further opinion that it was opportune for the nuncio to collect the tax directly, since "through his commissars [...] he could do so without raising any clamour".[18] On the same occasion, the Neapolitan Ordinary also declared himself contrary to the Roman suggestion of claiming from the Spanish Crown what the papacy considered to be ancient beneficiary rights on the temporal powers in Naples – both for the difficulty of proving their existence with documents not open to question and because of the muddled intricacy of the relative judicial procedures. "And it would give the royal ministers the occasion to rake over the old pretentions: that the inquisitors were, in those times, simply monks, and commissars delegated in single instances", the archbishop then admonished, "on whom they conferred the royal *exequatur* – and not prelates residing in Naples in the form of an office, and so part of the family". Boncompagni therefore judged it necessary – as indeed subsequently occurred – not to reignite old differences with the secular powers, "In addition [to the fact that], the wider berth the Holy Office gives them, the more highly is it esteemed and independent".[19]

The political-economic stance assumed in that situation of a plurality of subjects who developed the activities of the Inquisition in the southern part of the peninsula was, then, one of maintaining a prudent approach and operating subtly, whether with regard to the authority of the state, or within the network of ecclesiastical institutions. So the highest reaches of the Catholic Church proceeded, in the case of the Kingdom of Naples too, in applying the usual mix of a modest sum in fixed income, occasional conferrals of monetary grants and pressure upon vicars and bishops to seek out directly within the local institutional and economic reality forms of financing which – as was the case with pecuniary punishments – by their very nature must necessarily be discontinuous. In this manner, an officer of the episcopal court of Molfetta found himself obliged to appear before the Suprema to collect 10 scudi in back wages.[20]

The Kingdom of Naples is, perhaps, the extreme example of the general financial strategy of the inquisitorial network established by the highest authorities of the Catholic Church between the sixteenth and the seventeenth centuries, based on a model of filling the coffers of the local courts which was in large measure unvaried throughout the peninsula. It prospected the fixed income – generally made up of beneficiary monies and/or pensions furnished by diocesan institutions or other inquisitorial courts – as guaranteeing a minimal operational basis for general activity without, however, a consistency which would allow inquisitors to count upon this sum alone to carry out their mission adequately and to broadly realize its ends.

The contributions to the staffing of the religious frontiers

The upper echelons of the Roman Inquisition did not limit themselves to carrying out only financial functions – direct or indirect, structural or occasional – for the activities of their courts. Above all, in the decades of most intense anti-Lutheran repression, they pursued a capillary action of informal economic support, to the benefit of individuals, institutes or initiatives they considered worthy of assistance. This type of intervention, especially with reference to the sixteenth and the early seventeenth centuries, is of special interest, for it tended to concentrate itself on the physical, ethnic and spiritual borders of the religious frontiers. And this in an epoch in which the missionary and propaganda techniques of the Roman Church were becoming progressively more subtle and numerous until they would consolidate, in the course of the 1600s, in organized forms coordinated by the new *Congregatio de Propaganda Fide*, established in 1622.

Though missionary activity did not fall under its direct jurisdiction, if not in the measure in which it was aimed at repressing heterodoxy and apostasy (or in the ambiguous case of the catechumenate of the Jews, which we will consider further on), the Holy Office occasionally participated in the promotion of initiatives to spread and consolidate the Catholic faith. Let us try now to identify some features of such intervention, even though it was conspicuously unsystematic. As far as may be ascertained in the surviving yearly accounts from the 1500–1600s, it had its most intense phase in the second half of the seventeenth century, when the slow application of the Tridentine canons and the still relatively scarce institutionalization of the "faith war" in frontier areas placed a high value on every form of support for those engaged in it, even if that support were only monetary.[21]

Unfortunately, in many cases, the vestigial surviving documentation dealing with occasional donations in coin made by the Holy Office permits us to advance only vague hypotheses on the objectives they meant to secure. Still confining our attention to the "long" 1580s, which we have just been looking at, to discover the entity of gifts occasionally conferred on local inquisitors, we can begin with the grant of 7.5 scudi in 1578 to a certain "Guglielmo Cuccho, an Englishman", who had been held in the Inquisition's Roman prisons, "so that he may transfer to Naples to do what he has been ordered [to do] by said Holy Office".[22]

This and other similar cases show a direct transferal of money from inquisitors to culprits, though this was rigidly forbidden by the decrees. Further investigation might, perhaps, make it clearer whether such contributions were intended to consent the execution of a punishment or – more probably – aid in the pursuit of investigation already underway, the celebration of new trials or the rewarding of collaborators or accusers. A famous precedent is the concession, in 1552, of a monthly stipend of 5 gold ducats to Pietro Manelfi "for excellent merits with the Holy Inquisition", after his memorandums led to the dismantling of the Anabaptist presence in Italy.[23] We do not, however, have any idea why, in the same year, the cardinals sent the Bishop of Toulon 200 gold scudi "so that he may carry out what we ordered of him with a [previous] note". Unknown, as well, the reason why two Minor Observant friars, Donato Molano and Francesco Sabin, were refunded the expenses incurred in a sojourn in Rome, or why, in 1580, a don Ferrante Guidi da Policastro was paid 100 scudi and a Reverend Federico Cefalotti 200 gold scudi "for services to the said Holy Office".

Some occasional Holy Office payments in coin made to individuals in the 1580s are, however, more clearly identifiable as forms of support specifically intended for informal – mostly foreign – collaborators. This is the case of that "Richard Listier, English" to whom, between 1585 and 1586, the Congregation, with official orders of payment, gave 6 scudi "for his support", another 12 scudi "as a bonus to the six assigned him and as moral support to go to and return from Naples on some of his duties" and, finally, 60 scudi "as alms and viaticum to go into France or in some other place according to the advice and counsel of the Reverend Father Darbisire [or Daubisire] of the Society of Jesus, and, as well, to pay some of his debts".[24] In some case, these forms of direct subsidy allow a glimpse of collaborations linked to specific trials: for example, the 25 scudi paid out in 1585 to a Camillo Dini da Lucignano (Arezzo) "for services carried out in the case of Francesco Merlani from Alessandria".[25]

These operations were the result of central decisions and were carried out with decrees formally issued by the cardinal inquisitors in the course of plenary meetings in the presence of the pope, whose documentation is, unfortunately, not more explicit than this.[26] The orders of payment were always signed by the Cardinal Depositary, a post that was held by especially prominent figures like Rodolfo Savelli and Giulio Antonio Santori. In any case, the personal aid furnished by the Holy Office was not always monetary, assuming instead structural forms which required the direct engagement of the leading figures of the Roman institution. For example, in 1626, the cardinal's nephew, Francesco Barberini, supreme inquisitor, put pressure upon the Apostolic Vice-Legate in Avignon to ensure he would provide funds to cover the needs of a priest from Geneva, who converted eight years earlier to Catholicism, as soon as a benefice attached to a church in the city became vacant.[27]

Donations intended for conversion campaigns or to strengthen processes of conversion to Catholicism already in course, were a special and frequent occasion of informal financial intervention by the Holy Office. This type of intervention is well exemplified by a project the Congregation pursued towards the end of the 1620s, when it decided to support two Genevan catechumens – Antonio Prodomino and his young brother, Urbano – who had travelled to Rome with an introduction from the Bishop of Geneva and from Brother Diego da Civitanova, provincial of the Capuchins in Chambéry. Prodomino went directly to the Roman court, where he abjured and, contextually, requested a grant in aid of 200 scudi, declaring that the sum would serve to buy back a building near Geneva occupied by a Calvinist "where [he] meant to introduce the practice of the Catholic religion and bring to it his mother and his sisters". The cardinals considered seriously the hypothesis of supporting this initiative. To begin with, they gave the brothers permission to go to Conegliano (Treviso) and there to stay in the palace of Count Nicolò Montalban, whose family vaunted a long tradition of welcome and support both moral and material for potential catechumens who intended to abandon the religion of their ancestors (especially those of Jewish origin). They then wrote to the Capuchin Provincial adjuring him to "diligently inform himself as to the quality and the connections of the heretic" who occupied the building which was Prodomino's property, as well as "the ease and the means of expropriating him, in the hope of introducing there the exercise of Religion, and bringing out of Geneva (when Antonio should be in residence there) his mother and sisters; and, in brief, if the business can be done successfully, whether there will be benefit to Religion, where, and with whom, one must deal, and to whom write, and if, with the sum of 100 or 200 scudi, the whole may be accomplished".[28] Even the inquisitor in Ceneda who had jurisdiction over Conegliano, was solicited with a letter carried by Prodomini himself to oversee the process of conversion of the two brothers and to supervise their education in the principles of Catholicism. The documentation available unfortunately does not allow us to discover whether the business in Geneva was really pursued by Rome in the years that followed.[29]

Another seventeenth-century example of the direct economic intervention of the Holy Office to favour the establishment of a process of conversion is constituted by an initiative undertaken by the supreme inquisitors through the Vicar General in Catanzaro. The cardinals decreed that 100 ducats deriving from the confiscation of cloth belonging to the brothers Girolamo and Giovan Tommaso Piterà, Calabrian shopkeepers condemned as "para-Jewish", be given to the women of the same family, evidently judging their course of conversion to be sincere, "having consideration of the danger for [their] honesty" which the abrupt pauperism of their family would entail.[30] It may be worth noting that this decision came after the trial of the Piteràs had been expedited by the Bishop of Catanzaro, with judiciary procedures on whose correctness Rome had expressed serious doubts.[31]

The Holy Office's occasional monetary grants in the difficult decades between the sixteenth and seventeenth centuries were often essential to a direct intervention of the Congregation in the social, geographic and religious reality in frontier areas. It would be interesting to understand why, in 1583, the Suprema granted a certain Giovanni Lopez from Ferrara (probably of Jewish origin), a loan of 12 scudi "for his services",[32] or gave 29 scudi to Daniele Leborat "from Losanna of Geneva, as alms so that he may maintain himself", refunding, as well, 42 scudi to some members of the clergy who had already advanced this sum to him.[33]

The financial intervention of the Roman Ministry in situations like that of the Valtellina and the lower Engadine where, from the middle of the 1500s, the movement for Reform had been particularly vigorous – and where some of the foremost Italian religious exiles had taken refuge – is especially striking, and clearer in its purpose.[34] Here the Suprema, on a series of occasions, paid out a total of 70 scudi to a "Bartholomeo Merliano Grisone" "to finance him", and similar sums to Valtellina clergymen, among whom don Giacomo Pusterla, don Francesco Intertioli, both of Sondrio, and Giovan Antonio Casolari of Bormio, preacher in Chiavenna once again "for (their) financing".[35] The first of these, the archpriest from Sondrio, Pusterla, a few years earlier had led the local opposition to the founding of a Raetian college by the Diet of Davos; driven from the valley, he had taken refuge first in Milan, then in Rome: Intertioli, curate of Torre and Giovan Antonio Casolari, Archpriest of Bormio, were among the driving forces of the contemporary process of application of the renewed Tridentine principles of the Valtellinese Catholic Church which took the form of selecting priests who were "appropriate" for pastoral positions, intervening in theological disputations, arbitrating and smoothing out public and private conflicts.[36]

Noteworthy sums were assigned, in the same final years of the sixteenth century, to a captain Antonio Arduino (300 scudi "in recognition of his strenuous efforts in the service of the Holy Faith in the territory of Grisone")[37] and to the Archpriest Giovanni Pietro Stoppani, responsible for San Vittore in Val Mesolcina (more than 300 scudi "for his aid and support"). After having first been Rector of the Helvetic college in Milan, Stoppani had been called to the valley by Carlo Borromeo to combat Reformed religious teaching, taking the place of the Archpriest Domenico Quattrini, condemned as head of the "witcheries" in the trials presided by the Archbishop of Milan in 1583. This significant form of intervention by the Roman Holy Office in the religiously fragmented area – subject to the various cantons of the Helvetic Confederation and the Three Grey Leagues – on the northern frontiers of the Duchy of Milan, are important markers of the extension of the repressive structure in an area formally outside the jurisdiction of the inquisitorial courts. When, then, the capitulation of 1639 definitively forbade the creation of Inquisition courts in the area of the Valtellina, the Conca di Bormio and Chiavenna, subject to Spain and religiously part of the dioceses of Milan and Como (as they were already forbidden for the areas of Lugano, Locarno and Mendrisio), the Congregation of the Holy Office already had other forms of indirect intervention (including the cultivation of sympathetic parish priests) in place for some time.[38]

More structured forms of economic support by the Roman Inquisition aimed at favouring and protecting paths to conversion were directed towards institutes created specifically to this end, first among which were the houses of the catechumens and the monasteries for converted women. Historians should look more closely at the forms of finance granted by the Holy Office to these fundamental organizations in the context of the conversion policies of the Catholic Church in the age of the Counter Reformation, also through new research dedicated to the economic aspects of the difficult relationship between the Inquisition and the Jews in the early modern period.

The Houses of the Catechumens and the Neophytes were, in fact, intended above all for the Jews, whose conversion to Christianity had a symbolic and apologetic value of particular importance for Rome. The most famous example was the House for Catechumens and Neophytes in Rome, founded by Paul III in 1543 after the *Cupientes* constitution of 1542 had set up ample privileges for those who should abandon their religion of birth; it saw almost 2,000 Jewish conversions from 1614 to 1797, compared to a little over 1,000 Muslim conversions. In any case, the houses were chiefly maintained at the expense of the Jewish communities within the Papal State. In 1554, Julius III had established an obligatory tax on the 115 synagogues then existent. When, in 1593, the Jewish population was expelled from all of the State territory, except Rome, Ancona and Avignon, the tax fell upon the Jewish "University" (Community) in Rome alone, for an overall sum of 1,500 scudi – reduced in 1604 to 800; 500 scudi a year were destined for the maintenance of the House for Catechumens and 300 for the monastery of converted women.[39]

To evaluate the significance and the weight of the occasional grants we have been looking at in the overall economy of the Congregation of the Holy Office, we can consider the pattern of outflow in the 1580s: in this case, once again, the figures should be considered purely indicative of relative size (Table 2.1).

The sums from time to time attributed to local courts – but, above all, to single organisms or individuals in varying degrees involved in the activities of the Holy Office in the second half of the sixteenth century – were undoubtedly significant both as regards to the overall expenditures of the Roman Ministry and in relation to its income, regarding which we have, unfortunately, discontinuous information: it amounts to about 1,720 scudi in 1578; 2,400 scudi in 1580; and 1,402 scudi in 1581.[40] The financial operations carried out by the highest ranks of the Roman Inquisition – which engaged a significant portion of the resources at the disposal of the Congregation in the years in which its courts were not yet generally provided with ordinary, fixed, income, was however only slightly devoted to subsidizing the work of the judges of faith.

In this respect, Rome was holding coherently to the long-standing policy aimed at encouraging the inquisitors to draw necessary funds from their activity in building direct beneficiary and patrimonial links with the territory in which they were situated, as well as from the results of their judicial activity (as we shall see in the chapters which follow).

Table 2.1 Expenses of the Congregation of the Holy Office (Roman scudi, rounded off to the unit)

Year	Paid
1578	2.611
1579	2.568
1580	3.724
...	...
1583 (*)	3.492
1584	3.126
1585	2.802
1586	4.416
1587 (**)	5.342
...	...
1589	7.004
1590	6.385
1591	6.089
...	...
1601	5.163

Sources: My own calculations, based on ACDF, Oec 15, 17, 18, 24. The figures expressed in different coinages are presented in Roman scudi on the basis of a contemporary coefficient of monetary conversion inferred from the same documents.

... - Unavailable data.

(*) Except for the month of January, for which there is no data.

(**) Except for the month of December, for which there is no data.

The inquisitor: "pen-pusher" or "entrepreneur"?

On August 12, 1705, Claudio Giugni, the Dominican prior of the San Bartolomeo convent in Bergamo, sent an angry letter to the Congregation of the Holy Office:

> With great surprise I observe that in this, our convent, the scandalous and obstinate segregation from the entire entourage of the [resident] Religious [figures] operated by the modern father inquisitor [Tommaso] Canossa from the first days of his arrival, as, wholly forgetting that his [behaviour] is contrary to the tenor of the Constitutions, contrary to the decrees, of this Holy Congregation; and contrary to the behaviour of his other predecessors; [he] has never shown himself at [conventual] meals, never in Chorus at the *Salve Regina* – from which no one is exempt – and he has barely let himself be seen at a few holy day vespers. In addition, he shows an erroneous presumption that he must per force enjoy unusual

and unheard of privileges, independently of his legitimate Superior, in earnest of which he has eaten meat for all of last Lent, without even deigning to request a dispensation of he who presided, in my place, over the Community; and, further, realizing it to be my resolute intention that, according to established usage, he should appear at least on one or two days a week in the common refectory in adherence to religious practice, rather [than comply] he is pleased to shop for food himself rather than submit to a single act of obedience or to humble himself to request the necessary permission.[41]

In the early modern period, the relations between the inquisitors and the convents of the orders to which they were attached for the exercise of their mansions, were sometimes difficult. On the one hand, the inquisitor benefited from a sort of special statute within the convent which guaranteed him specifically dedicated physical spaces and economic resources, on the other, he held an office in many ways outside of the control of the order's hierarchy, responding for the efficacy of his work directly to the Congregation of the Holy Office and, in an ultimate instance, to the Pope who, in the early modern age, was the stable source of nomination to the post. The obligation of secrecy and the freedom of action from which the inquisitor benefited, were difficult to reconcile with the more or less rigid and habitually practiced discipline which had regulated monastic and conventual life for centuries. The superior theological and juridical qualifications of many judges of faith, their frequent origins in foreign states where the mechanisms of rotation among the titular or various seats, their very territorial mobility, the aura of temerity and even of celebrity which might surround them as individuals and the sense of superiority they sometimes vaunted, did not fail to excite envy and diffidence in superiors and in other brothers.[42]

Even the availability of money and the discretion in its use which went with the Office of the Inquisitor might generate unrest within the monastic structures of the Mendicant Orders. The controversy which, in the early 1700s, separated the proud Inquisitor Canossa[43] and his Superior, gives us a few significant indications. On that occasion, Prior Giugni accused the judge of faith of having taken some money when the previous inquisitor died: Canossa attempted to excuse himself with the Suprema, declaring that the illicit action had, rather, been on the part of the prior. "In the examination he carried out concerning the goods of the deceased inquisitor, my predecessor", wrote Father Canossa to the supreme inquisitors, the Dominican Superior had "usurped this Inquisition of 100 scudi, as if they were coinage belonging personally to the dead inquisitor, who left 200 scudi at his death, 100 of which were noted by him in the receipt of his own property, and the other 100, as the father prior confesses in the report he made to this Podestà, [...] were not noted in the same receipt, and therefore belong to the Holy Office".[44] The 100 scudi left without receipt by his predecessor, Canossa argued, were not personal property – and thus due to the convent upon his death – and so belonged by right to the Inquisition. Father Giugni replied that, according to the Dominican constitution in force, the inquisitors must be considered "subject to the convent" and therefore the result of the "tally of the deceased brother", that is his individual properties, must remain at the disposal of the community "for the inquisitors, in so far as concerns their personal property, are unanimously equal to the other bothers, otherwise they would not be required to furnish any receipt at all to the prior".[45]

This is not the place to delve into the complex jurisprudence, weighty with local and particular privileges, that are part of the *spolia defunctorum* (chattels the dead) which for centuries governed the detailed matter of the disposition of property and, sometimes, the benefices, of clergy who died intestate (or without the capacity to make a will).[46] Still, this episode admirably brings to light an important managerial aspect of the activity of the Holy Office. The peripheral courts of the Inquisition were not offices staffed by dependent personnel working in physical premises organized by the central authority and having regular, specifically designated resources. The inquisitor was a regular member of the clergy who usually worked within the walls of convents of his order and at their expense, sometimes with the logistical and financial support of the Confraternities of Saint Peter Martyr, which had sprung up throughout the peninsula at the end of the Middle Ages.[47] In the first decades of the Congregation of the Holy Office, as we have seen, no fixed financial base, nor any regular "wage" were contemplated. Rome named the inquisitor and moved him from place to place: in principle, without assigning anything at all to cover ordinary, day-to-day expenses or defray the costs his activities might entail.

Though historians of the Inquisition long gave little importance to this development, the inquisitorial seats' managerial side settled into this pattern precisely from the Middle Ages to the early modern era. In the years in which the judges of faith were not yet coordinated and vigorously directed by the Roman Congregation, their continued symbiosis with the structures of the monastic and conventual orders set limits and conditions – including economic limitations – to their activities. These structures were entities with significant internal economic vitality. Besides enjoying a somewhat notably-sized patrimony, between the fifteenth and sixteenth centuries, convents might buy or manage both property and money. A notable example, materially and symbolically, is the Dominican convent of Saint Eustorgio in Milan, where Pietro da Verona, the patron of inquisitors (himself an inquisitor), had been buried since the 1200s and which, until 1559, was the seat of the court for Lombardy and the Genoese Marches.

In 1476, brother Bartolomeo da Cremona was authorized to exact payment of a 272 lire credit from a haberdasher and to purchase with this sum property to enjoy for life; and, in 1483, Father Bernardo Cattanei, a professor of theology, benefited from property of his own and sold, in his own right, a plot of land which he had received as a gift. Before leaving Milan to become an abbot in the diocese of Erlau, in Hungary, Bonaventura della Torre, authorized by his Provincial, bought, in 1499, a plot of land with building permission for 2,000 imperial lire and, at his death in Buda in 1516, left 1,300 florins and a house to his old Milanese convent. Giovan Pietro da Carnago, Procurator of the same convent of Saint Eustorgio and several times its prior, as well as Procurator and Lieutenant of the Provincial, was authorized in these same years to "dispose well of his property and its goods", and to keep some personal funds on hand; the order itself urged its fellow monks to pay their debts periodically.

In 1511, Silvestro Maggiolini da Prierio, many times prior of Santa Maria delle Grazie and inquisitor for Milan, Lodi and Piacenza, could keep money of his own in an account in the Banco di San Giorgio in Genoa; Tommaso Marliani, several times procurator of Saint Eustorgio, with the authorization of the Dominican general, bought himself a freehold in the second half of the 1400s, the order revoked his right to the personal use of a grain loft around which he had organized as a distinctly financial activity.[48]

It was in this fertile terrain of economic initiative, both large and small, by convent members that the "managerial" shape of the late medieval inquisitor took on the aspect it would have in the early modern era, when the judge of faith did begin to have sources of ordinary income previously lacking. Between the fifteenth and sixteenth centuries, the inquisitors were obliged to seek out and negotiate locally the funds they needed to carry out their activities. It was this practice of daily "contracting", carried out within the solid economic culture typical of the Franciscan tradition,[49] that cemented the already close relationship between the Inquisition and the orders which continued to be the basis of the Holy Office's structure even in the full sway of the early modern period.

An emblematic example is that of Matteo dell'Olmo, a friar from the Valtellina assigned to the convent of Saint Eustorgio, where he resided without interruption until his death, and was inquisitor for Lombardy and the Genoese March from 1487 to 1497. It was the Confraternity of San Pietro Martire – in whose premises within Sant'Eustorgio the Office of the Inquisition was housed – which paid the inquisitor's salary and covered the office's expenses. From the procedural point of view, as his account ledgers testify, Matteo dell'Olmo was decidedly more active than his predecessors, multiplying trips, transcription of interrogations, and trials. In 1490. he sent a certain Bernardone to the stake, ordering contextually the "description of his property" to the end of confiscation. The increase in expenditure of Olmo's management as compared to the previous period, provoked a conflict with the convent and the *scolares* of San Pietro Martire: in October of 1488, the inquisitor was forbidden to make use of the Confraternity's money without the authorization of the convent's prior and the Confraternity also appealed to the Holy See, sustaining that the inquisitor's jurisdiction did not extend to them and, therefore, Olmo had no right to use their money.[50]

So the model of the inquisitor which became dominant in the conventuary context of the late medieval period cannot simply be derived from that of the learned figure tormented by abstract dogmatic questions or the fierce prosecutor of heretical witches immune from quotidian banalities. The example offered by Matteo dell'Olmo's career show how the inquisitor might also appear to be a subtle financial mediator. In fact, his removal from the office of the judge of faith in May, 1497, was occasioned by Ludovico il Moro's decision to send him on mission to Pope Alexander VI in Rome, with predominantly economic ends in view: the cancellation of debts contracted with the Abbey at Chiaravalle near Milan, by Bianca Maria, the duke's mother; the exemption of the ducal Chamber of the difficulties in obtaining the payment of levy by first rank religious institutions, including the abbey of San Pietro in Cielo d'Oro in Pavia and the Church of Sant'Ambrogio in Vigevano; the problem of redefinition of the payment of ordinary duties on the part of State clergy, which required delicate financial elaboration to accommodate inflation; the abolition of Viscontean Decrees which prohibited the subjects of the duchy from appealing to the Curia directly for benefices and the assigning of benefices.

In recognition of the happy results of his mission and of his ties with the Duke of Milan, Olmo was named Bishop of Laodicea *in partibus infedelium*, but he did not abandon his inclination for economic activity. In 1499, the new ordinary, two years after having left his inquisitorial duties, participated, as financing partner, in a company buying and selling "mercantile things" – where he invested 900 imperial lire, rising to 2,400 in 1501, when the firm was reorganized with the new purpose of "dealing in silk-gold thread draperies", thus occupying an important place in one of the most vital sectors in the Lombard marketplace at the end of the fifteenth century. The notary public who served the firm was the same one who registered the ecclesiastical documents of the Milanese Dominican convents.[51]

This, too, was the intellectual and material heritage of the inquisitors, nominated by Rome and aided by beneficiary income acquired after the creation of the Congregation of the Holy Office. It was this heritage – never seriously questioned by the popes and the ministry itself – which guaranteed the judge of faith from ever becoming, administratively, a simple dependant of the Congregation of the Holy Office. He retained a fundamental prerogative: his right/duty to respond to the exercise of his functions personally, with his own resources if necessary; a condition strengthened by the complete affirmation of the individualistic and patrimonial conception of public office characteristic of the absolute State in the *Ancien régime*.[52]

Though the Office of the Inquisitor might not be purchased, sold or inherited and was, therefore, not fully venal, it did have a double nature. It was, on the one hand, an institutional position, regulated – from the administrative point of view – by increasingly stringent norms fixed in the course of the 1500s and the early 1600s by the Congregation. The Roman Ministry assigned the post and could revoke it at will. It had placed in a local court in the individual. Rome envisioned a personal, "entrepreneurial", assumption of the total local inquisitorial activity and, therefore, a direct investment of resources on his part and a continuous fusion of the inquisitor's money and the money of the office he managed. We can see this, for example, in what the Congregation wrote to the inquisitor in Tortona in 1626:

> Don Ottavio Cotta, recipient of the benefice of this Inquisition, has appealed for an order to liquidate his credit since it fell due at the last past [day of] San Martino, sustaining that Your Reverence has refused to pay [him], saying that it was his predecessor's; these, my illustrious Lords, have ordered me to write to your Reverence that you immediately procure he be satisfied, for this is a debt not to the inquisitor, but to the Inquisition; you shall, therefore, so act that this occurs without further delay, furnishing us with notice of its execution.[53]

Within the private conception of the jobs and the posts, a seventeenth-century judge in Tortona could refuse to pay a debt contracted by his predecessor, even though it was clearly part of the management of the Inquisition and not part of the private affairs of the inquisitor. The distinction between "inquisitor's debt" and "Inquisition debt" (and the corresponding credits of inquisitor and Inquisition) were, in this structure, far from evident: that was why the eighteenth-century inquisitor Canossa thought he could freely use part of his predecessor's money in conflict with another ecclesiastical institution which was convinced that this same right was its own.

The early modern inquisitors were members of orders and housed in the convents. The personal circulation of money fell therefore within regular discipline and might directly be of interest. We have seen that in the appeals for money regularly directed to Rome, judges of faith spelt out their malcontent writing, as the office holder in Ceneda did, "that dying many inquisitors, leave thousands and thousands of scudi to enrich the convents, which merit little and take everything, and other inquisitors have not enough to live".[54] Others, like the inquisitor in Vicenza, reminded the cardinals that "in the six years in which he has been in Vicenza serving this Suprema, to maintain this pious place he has stripped the small savings he had of 1,112 lire – which is, in fact, the present debt of this Holy Office":[55] a testimony to the blended flow, within the coffers of the local courts, of "the Inquisition's" money and "the inquisitor's", highlighting a problem which probably made itself more keenly felt where, in the eighteenth century, the judicial activities of the courts were infrequent in many localities and the operating costs hard to cover with the reparatory fines of the condemned.

All this, moreover, occurred within a general framework which, in the course of the early modern period, saw the religious orders multiply their presence throughout the territory to the point that historians talk of a "convent invasion" of Western Europe, in addition to a growth in the consistency of their real property and the establishing of efficient urban and rural credit networks.[56] Thus the convents which housed the inquisitors from the 1500s through the 1700s were sometimes very dynamic economic and social entities, constituting an opportunity for financial support for the judges of faith and, at the same time, a threat to their autonomy: two poles between which the judges of faith must navigate with care, lest he lose juridical dignity and besmirch the mission of the *officium fidei*.

In the complex equilibrium made up of the Inquisition accounts, the inquisitor's funds and resources and the structures of the Orders, we find one of the fundamental aspects of the Holy Office. From this interaction between convents and inquisitors, which burst periodically into heated controversy, broad consequences for the entire system of the Roman Inquisition were set in motion. The consolidation of the managerial profile, peculiar to the judges of faith in this historic moment, contributed decisively to the consolidation of a process of professionalization of the inquisitor which turned out to be much more efficient than what was happening to parish priests in the same post-Tridentine years.

If we assume that the Council of Trent, along with the great project of restoring morality and doctrinal competence among the parish clergy, strongly pursued the formation of a body of "pastoral workers" that was compact and well-educated, socially considerate and culturally cohesive[57] we must note that the project attained brilliant results precisely in the functional redefinition of the inquisitors of faith, for whom financial autonomy was a basic tenet.

The incentive system

Let us stay with Vittore Soranzo's diocese, put under the administration of a "special commissioner" by the Inquisition in the early 1550s, after its bishop had been jailed and tried for heresy. The Venetian Federico Cornaro, the first ordinary to hold the post with any continuity after Soranzo's death, entered Bergamo in 1561. He was a tenacious Reformer, strenuously engaged in applying Tridentine precepts – and, as suffragan of the Ambrosian diocese,[58] the Borromean Decrees – Cornaro, like Carlo Borromeo, acted in concert with the local Inquisition. Upon learning that, in 1569, Father Aurelio da Martinengo had collected 300 gold scudi, probably from a fine, the Ordinary cooperated with the judge of faith, having him build "a wall with some arches to hold up the episcopal garden", in exchange for terrain on which "to build an Inquisition and prison for the Office in the episcopal courtyard", promising to participate in the extra expenses incurred "and, afterwards, he would aid in the construction".[59] The agreement would permit the Bergamo Inquisition to build a place of its own in symbiosis with the episcopal residence at the height of the ant-Lutheran emergency. The finished project cost 403 gold scudi; "Master Paul of Bergamo, architect", remained creditor of the 103 scudi not at the moment available; he was probably the same Paolo Berlandis who, in 1575, designed the area of Porta Sant'Agostino, still today the eastern entry to the upper part of the city.

The money due to the architect was not paid by Father Aurelio nor by bishop Cornero, as the inquisitor, Nicolò da Brettinoro noted on assuming the post a few years later. This occurred, as he tells us:

both due to the departure of bishop Cornero and, as well, due to the poverty of this Inquisition. The afore mentioned master Paolo having persevered for many years afterwards in repeated appeals to the bishops, the inquisitors, and even to the most illustrious cardinal Borromeo, to be paid, finally turned to the secular forum and with the Rectors' sequestration has taken over the fruits of the Office held by [our] leasees. I, perceiving the situation to be irremediable, begged 24 scudi of the bishop and paid 50 gold scudi to the aforementioned builder, and with this have made him content for now.[60]

Faced with the sequestration of the income of the Holy Office (whose "poverty" was well known), and in the presence of the arrival in Bergamo of a bishop probably less inclined than his predecessor to act in rigid alignment with the courts of faith (he was, in fact, the theologian Girolamo Ragazzoni, who had previously been in Trento and would subsequently be apostolic nuncio in France),[61] the new judge of faith had to engage directly in covering the costs of a significant part of the undertakings of his predecessor. Still the inquisitor did not seem to be overly preoccupied by his passive accounts; indeed, he decided to do some more building himself. "Seeing the building to be quite comfortable, I made new agreements with him [Paolo] [...][who] assumed the obligation to wait a year for me. The builder tells me that he will engage to consign the whole construction of seven prison cells, with a small courtyard, in May [1583] for 400 gold scudi to his credit." "Here I shall not hide from you that this building is very necessary", concluded the new inquisitor, requesting the financial aid of Rome, "both due to the criminal cases and to that of the inquisitor, who has *no place to lay his head* ['*ubi caput reclinet*']".[62]

The expense Father Nicolò planned was a large one, as it regarded an office whose annual income came to about 300 scudi a year in 1582 – in a period when it was still possible to derive funds from the certification of the sentences (an activity that brought in more than 40 scudi) – and whose surplus for the same year was only 19 scudi.[63] So the inquisitor had taken on a project whose cost was more than the income of his court for the entire previous year: a delicate operation in a period in which the granting of monetary subsidies by the Roman Ministry was sporadic and which was, further, set within an already heavily indebted situation.

It is interesting to note that as important a professional as Paolo Bernardis, who had already held well-paid commissions in Bergamo, had no reservation in accepting the local Holy Office's project. And this was despite the fact that the fruits of that collaboration had been for so long impossible to lay hands upon, and not withstanding "the poverty of this Inquisition", whose income had already been sequestered. The architect "forgot", as well, that, in the past, neither the local Ordinary nor archbishop Borromeo had done anything to give him satisfaction. Despite all this, he considered the credit of the new inquisitor and the monastic reality in which he was imbedded to be adequate. So, evidently, he judged the two entities to be solidly linked since, among the ecclesiastical institutions to which he had turned in his attempts to get his bill paid after the inquisitor had refused, the convent was conspicuously absent. He was not mistaken in this: in 1622, when the judge of faith in Bergamo attempted to obtain money from Rome, he closed his letters "recommending this Inquisition, inquisitor, vicar and aid to the benignity of your most illustrious and most reverend lordship and of these most illustrious and most reverend Lords; and, in particular, the convent, which is creditor of a goodly sum of money as he has himself related".[64]

The facts we have just looked at are good examples of the unclear nature of the "business" administration of the inquisitorial courts in the early modern period. It contained elements of free initiative, expressed in the decisions of the inquisitor and his capacity for self-finance, linked to an institutional context within which the convent had a primary role. The *Book of Usages* ("*Liber usuum*") of the inquisitors in the area around Ferrara – constantly updated from 1533 to 1578 and analysed by Adriano Prosperi in an innovative study, which brings out the regular anticipation of expenses by the prior of the convent of San Domenico[65] – is an excellent testimony. The privatistic-patrimonial tenor of the management of the local seats of the Inquisition is, further, well exemplified by the books of the Inquisition in Siena, which show us the movements of its accounts over various decades from the seventeenth through the eighteenth centuries (see Chapter 6 of this book).[66] It should be noted that this type of record – as its head notes indicate – registered, for example in the case of Siena, "the income of the Inquisition [...] which shall come into the hands of the father" inquisitor and "all the expenses that be made in this holy Inquisition of Siena by the hands" of the treasurer.[67] So the figures we see did not constitute a merely figurative, "book-keeping" account of payments received or disbursed, but recorded the flow of real money entering – or exiting – the court's treasury. We can then deduce that the Siena inquisitor's accounts were constantly "in the red" during the 1660s and that the inquisitor habitually spent more than he was able to earn.

Regularly, at the moment in which he closed his accounts and sent them to Rome the titular official noted the negative balance of the year which had just ended, writing "and of this sum the father inquisitor remains in credit". The court's passivity – "debt of the Inquisition" and "credit of the inquisitor" – was listed as the first item of expenditure for the new year. On the basis of this mechanism, the inquisitor whose economic management had shown passivity for one or more years could hope to recover his credit only in so far as he managed to hold down expenses in the following years. If he was not able to bring about this accounting feat, the inquisitor himself – or his convent – would continue to vaunt a credit destined to grow over future years.

In an important effect of the ambiguous managerial conception of the local Inquisitional unit, the "inquisitor's credit" of a judge who died or left his post was still the court's business, even though it was not explicitly included in his successor's accounts. So when, for example, on June 2, 1688, Father Serafino Gottarelli da Castelbolognese took Modesto Paoletti's place in the Siena court, Poletti's "credit" was not carried forward.[68] The old inquisitor was still personally in credit with the court, and so with the Congregation, but at the same time, his credit was linked to the office he no longer held. In the same manner, when Father Serafino Gottarelli left the post of inquisitor in Siena in July, 1700, to become *Qualificatore* at the Congregation of the Holy Office, he left for Rome with more than 40 scudi still owed to him personally. From Rome, he appealed to his successor (and not to the treasurers of the Roman Ministry where he now worked). In the following months, Gottarelli wrote "he was still creditor of 19 scudi, 20 baiocchi, spent in buildings and windows and overlooked in presenting [his] accounts: thus bringing his credit to 60 scudi and 62 baiocchi, *to be made good by the Congregation*". His successor promptly added a note to his Sienese books: "Holding [now] the government of this Inquisition, Father Giovanni Pellegrino Sala, its vicar general, takes these expenses upon himself".[69] The direct consequence of the statutory elusivity of the local Inquisitional office was thus, first of all, the patrimonial and financial tangle of its relationship with the personal property of the inquisitor and/or his convent.

The perception which the judge of faith had of his role and of his own property in relation to the local seats of the Inquisition was, consequently, equally vague. In the course of a retrospective investigation of the situation in Bergamo conducted in 1625, the Congregation of the Holy Office ascertained that "in the accounts are listed many goods and account books for the Holy Office's use, of which no mention is made in subsequent inventories". This indicates that the inquisitors kept for themselves – probably in perfectly good faith – property acquired with the income of the Office and deemed by them to be their own.[70] The problems deriving from the confusion among the inquisitor's property, the local Inquisition's property and the property of the convents of the Orders, which characterize the management of the Holy Office during the whole early modern period, became fully visible only when the inquisitorial courts were suppressed in the late eighteenth century.

When, on March 13, 1779, after the death of the last Inquisitor of Milan, the official notary, Antonio Silvola, broke the seals on the rooms of the dissolved Inquisition at the convent of Santa Maria delle Grazie in the name of the Habsburgs, he was obliged to take a separate inventory of the furniture found in the judge's apartment. Part of it was included among the belongings of the convent, another part, "purchased with funds belonging personally to the deceased" was, at first, listed by the notary as due to "the same convent at the proper insistence of the religious prefects": a motivation later crossed out with a stroke of a pen and substituted with "[owed] to Religion", that is directly to the Order. Clothing and other personal effects of the deceased inquisitor were also considered as the property "of the Religious, as they explained to me".[71]

The Holy Office courts' spurious managerial model, making every inquisitor personally responsible for office accounts, might favour virtuous financial practices for two reasons: the first of these was that the inquisitor was required to contribute personally to cover any deficits his management might produce; the second was that it was extremely difficult for the judge of faith to recoup his "credit" if his direction produced repeated annual deficits. Only the extraordinary intervention of the Congregation with a direct subsidy, or the transferal of funds from other inquisitorial seats could heal a weak administration stably; this was, however, as we have seen, something that occurred quite slowly (and there was no guarantee, indeed, that it would necessarily occur or be adequate or regular if it did). However tortuous and potentially muddled this mechanism of accumulation and transmission of "the inquisitor's credit" appears in the eyes of our contemporary accountancy's rationality, it did, then, show a triple internal logic.

***

First of all, the mechanism of the "inquisitor's credit" obliged the inquisitors to be individually answerable for their management, with the intent of holding down excessive spending and discouraging a dissipation of resources (perhaps in illicit directions) – which would promptly translate into a deficit to be covered personally. Further, it tied the results (negative or positive) of each management to the court in which it was exercised, blocking the inconvenient renewal of the direct situation of debt between inquisitor and Congregation and, at the same time, making it more difficult for the judges to recover the sums "lent" to the Holy Office. Finally, the mechanism that compensated the Inquisition's negative accounts through the 'inquisitor's credit', postponing indefinitely the moment in which the credit itself must be liquidated, increased the real burden of the sanction which fell upon the inquisitors who engaged in an reckless financial policy without, however, formally becoming a monetary obligation.

What were the implications of the local managerial model based upon the "inquisitor's credit" – and thus on the direct financial responsibility of the individual judge of faith – in terms of the overall performance of the courts of the Roman Inquisition? We can realistically hypothesize that this model was an incentive for the inquisitors to act along three lines of conduct. First of all, it encouraged the inquisitors to consider carefully spending money and, ultimately, to hold down court expenses which might turn out to be:

a. unjustifiably out of proportion compared to the court's income; and
b. difficult to compensate in the account books with a corresponding sum received.

In principle, this sort of incentive might regard any item of the inquisitorial "firm's" expenses: from those linked to pure presentation – clothing, furnishings, hangings, tips to assistants to those most directly connected with investigating and judging. When, for example, the costs/opportunity of investigating, capturing, trying and imprisoning an accused were especially high – as might be the case if the individual was poor and thus insolvent, the inquisitor was likely to consider very seriously the results of an action destined to bring a notable increase in costs – beginning with the expense of feeding the accused during detention and so to increase the "inquisitor's credit as well."

To determine the degree in which this incentive did indeed effect the decisions of inquisitors, we would have to carry out research over a medium-to-long period on the few remaining archives of individual courts, looking into the socio-economic condition of each accused and seeking out hypotheses on the inclination of the judges of faith to prosecute specific professional or patrimonial categories. A study of this sort – which cannot be undertaken here – should, of course, assume a position on the old problem of the (hypothetic) different weight of heterodox religious culture within the various social and professional strata of the society of the *Ancien régime*, a question on which historians are not at all in agreement even today.[72]

***

The second incentive produced by the managerial structure of the inquisitorial court – in reality a particular case of the first incentive – led the inquisitor to avoid undertaking financially onerous cases when an equally satisfactory result might be obtained by other means. With regard to the final scope of the inquisitorial court – that is, the ordinary judicial procedure made up of an investigation aimed at bringing to light the guilt and the subsequent abjuration of the culprit – the judge of faith was clearly induced by the managerial structure of his office to favour a spontaneous presentation of the accused: the least expensive procedure in terms of material resources but, also, in terms of time and energy. The *sponte comparentes* – those individuals who came before the inquisitor to accuse themselves or to accuse their accomplices without being physically constrained to do so (often led to do so by confessors who could not absolve them through the sacraments) represented a significant financial saving for the inquisitor and Holy Office as a whole.

The voluntary presentation of the culprit allowed the inquisitors to retain possession of the resources necessary to continue with investigations, arrests, detentions, interrogations (and eventual torture), as well as to assure themselves *ex post* of the execution of the sentences: indispensable resources when following ordinary procedure. For this reason, too – though, of course, not only for this reason – voluntary presentations spread everywhere in the seventeenth and eighteenth centuries, accompanied by lessening numbers of ordinary procedures and a mitigation of the sentences inflicted by the inquisitors.[73] The process of "anti-Jewish specialization" which the Roman Inquisition took on with increasing emphasis between the 1600s and 1700s even provoked a not always theologically and canonically evident extension to Jews of the institution of "voluntary presentation" – with the benefit of summary procedures and milder sentences. Individuals of every social situation rapidly learnt how to benefit from the advantages which self-accusation before the Inquisition carried, manipulating ably the relative procedures, thanks, perhaps, in the case of Catholics, to the assistance of parish priests and confessors.[74]

Probably the prohibitions which, from the end of the seventeenth century, forbade the local courts to take in money from culprits during the various phases of ordinary procedure, also contributed to the growth of voluntary presentation from the 1600s through the 1700s. Already in 1578, the Congregation of the Holy Office severely forbade the inquisitors and their collaborators from making culprits pay for the interrogations to which they were subjected, or to writs or official acts produced in their accusation, "since the ministers are obliged because of their office to do all of these things without payment, contenting themselves with having the culprits pay for the examinations, the transcriptions and the other things that are done in their defence according to the tax or the usage of the bishopric in which the Inquisition has seat".[75] In 1626, a papal decree further established that the inquisitors must send all of the trial documents to the defendants free of charge and could not derive any sort of payment from them, as was already the case since 1600 for clergy who had taken vows of poverty.[76]

Regulations of this sort contributed to making the summary procedure deriving from voluntary presentation economically preferable to the judges of faith. It is worth noting in this respect that, at the end of the 1500s, the institutional taxes imposed on trials in his court by the Inquisitor of Bergamo included 67 items: a real price-list, whose application contributed significantly to filling the local Holy Office coffers. By 1595, the Inquisition's Ancona price-list – already in force for at least 25 years – was also highly articulated.[77]

***

The third type of stimulus deriving from the peculiar managerial organization of the Roman Inquisition's courts, was constituted by encouraging the inquisitors to recover their "credit" as soon as possible, for it was difficult to insist upon its payment and it would, in any case, be repaid without interest. One way of doing this was to reduce the annual expenses; a goal, however, difficult to pursue since the expenses of the inquisitorial courts were largely inelastic, consisting chiefly of the inquisitor's maintenance, the salaries of his collaborators, the costs of paper and correspondence, heating and the expenses of jailed prisoners. Comparing the income and the expenses of the Italian courts in the mid-eighteenth century, we find that annual accounts show a substantial parity, as well as a widespread need for the inquisitors to contribute personally to reach these yearly results for their seats (Table 2.2).

In the advanced phase of their existence – when, indeed, the mechanisms of progressive patrimonial accumulation operating in the preceding centuries ought to have ensured a discrete level of income as well as a consolidation of expenses – most of the local Inquisitions were spending annually more or less all of their income. Besides especially glaring cases, like those of Ferrara,

Table 2.2 Receipts and expenses of the local courts of the Holy Office in 1748 (Roman scudi, rounded off to the unit)

Court	Received	Spent
Casale Monferrato	649	641
Milan	553	587
Florence	515	544
Faenza	506	554
Vercelli	478	639
Turin	470	470
Novara	450	566
Saluzzo	436(*)	187
Piacenza	419	467
Bologna	410	402
Venice	394	374
Alessandria	391	462
Cremona	344	270
Genua	344(**)	n.p.
Asti	296	289
Ancona	279	374
Mantua	261	265
Brescia	254	211
Padua	228	310
Ferrara	218	352
Siena	215	148
Rimini	211	136
Pisa	184	185
Verona	178	332
Tortona	173	190
Aquileia and Concordia	165	204
Crema	162	n.p.
Pavia	161	160
Bergamo	159	195
Perugia	149	356
Treviso	147	147
Como	142	181
Parma	134	189
Mondovì	126	121

continued…

80 The economy of the Holy Office

Table 2.2 continued...

Court	Received	Spent
Vicenza	117	151
Capodistria	110	110
Modena	100	51
Adria and Rovigo	34	95
Fermo	80	86
Belluno	74	73
Spoleto	74	78
Gubbio	47	85
Ceneda and Conegliano	42	137
Zara	29	45
Reggio Emilia	23	84(***)

Sources: The table is based on ACDF, So, St.st., LL5e–LL5f. The figures expressed in other coinage are presented in Roman scudi on the basis of a contemporary translation coefficient derived from the same documents.

(*) See Table 1.1.

(**) See Table 1.1.

(***) In 1748, the court sustained extraordinary expenses due to the arrival of a new inquisitor as well as extensive construction work.

Perugia, Verona, Adria and Rovigo, we should note that the expenses listed in Table 2.2 do not include credits accumulated by the inquisitors during the current year or in previous years, showing, then, only the real expenditure which had occurred in the year concerned. So there are cases of courts which seem to be virtuous, but whose inquisitor and/or the host convent had conspicuous outstanding credits. In Rimini, Siena and Spoleto the "inquisitor's credit" came, respectively to about 100, 200 and 100 scudi. The previous year, in Turin, the judge of faith had paid about 65 Roman scudi of his own money; in Zara, triple the annual expenses listed for the court; in Vicenza, the Holy Office owed its judge nearly 150 scudi. In the worst financial situations – like that of the eighteenth-century Ferrara Inquisition, the "inquisitor's credit" combined with debts contracted towards third parties: in the mid-eighteenth century it was indebted for about 880 scudi, of which 100 had been furnished by its titular inquisitor.[78]

These difficulties certainly reduced the administrative efficiency of the justice of faith, especially where the inquisitors did not have significant real estate or funds to back up their budgets. Girolamo Antonio Faleri, Inquisitor of Belluno, added a brief résumé of his personal, unsatisfactory, judicial activity to the financial report which showed a passive annual balance – and the attendant obligation to make good almost 300 Venetian lire from his own pocket: "In the course of this year, I have not had the least occasion to call together this Holy Office, since this diocese is without any commerce and governed by the vigilant zeal of Monsignor Costa, a truly most worthy prelate". So the judge had registered only two "voluntary presentations": a young girl – Giacoma Butoli from Agordo "who, after having for a time doubted the actual, physical and true presence of the Most Holy person of Jesus Christ in the Eucharist, subsequently declared her soul to be positively convinced", and a young woman named Giovanna, "who, born and raised in her home town by parents infected with Calvin's heresy, asked to be received by the Holy Roman and Apostolic Church". The proceeding had been closed with two formal abjurations and salutary penances, conferring upon Giovanna "sufficient instruction in that which concerns our Holy faith". In the same period, the inquisitor in Pisa recalled the oldest territorial rivalry in Italy, lamenting the incomplete payment of a subsidy by the Father Vicar of Livorno, and, from it, drawing gloomy forecasts for the efficiency of his office:

> In truth, the miserable sum [sent me] would give me cause to complain about that Father Vicar who, being Tuscan, gives no thought to one who knows that the meagre income cannot keep and support him and his companion and aid in their need whosoever in their heart wishes to abandon Lutheranism or Calvinism, as has been the case of three girls, two of whom, thanks to God, have become Catholics, and been taken care of by me here, and the other sent there – as I had the honour of informing you – and of the other two, you will have documentation in the case [transcripts] sent you.[79]

In these documents, the preoccupation of the judges of faith with the widespread situation of debt among their courts is coupled with the indirect confirmation of the fact that the activity of conversion pursued by the Inquisition continued to be significant even well into the eighteenth century.

Given the managerial organization of the courts and the intrinsic limits of inquisitorial action, the most immediate solution available to the judges of faith and/or their convents to recover their credits – or at least to impede their overwhelming accumulation – was to inflict monetary punishment, fines and confiscation on culprits. That, indeed, was frequently inquisitorial practice, whose modes of application and multiple economic, social and cultural consequences must now be carefully described and discussed.

Notes

1 Tavuzzi (2007), pp. 20–9, quote from p. 25.
2 ACDF, So, St.st., LL5e–LL5f, *ad vocem*; BAV, Vat. Lat. 10945, p. 77r. and Borg. Lat. 558, pp. 30v, 43r.
3 BAV, Barb. Lat. 6334, p. 64r, Rome, March 14, 1626.

4   BAV, Barb. Lat. 6335, p. 96*v*, Rome, May 8, 1627.
5   BAV, Barb. Lat. 6334, p. 139*v*, Rome, May 23, 1626.
6   ACDF, Oec 15, 17 and 18. The sums were registered (dates not always indicated) in November, 1578; February, 1580; June, 1580, September, 1580; December, 1580; August 22, 1584; June 5, 1587; January 14, 1589; May 20, 1589; February, 1591; and August 29, 1591. Here I only follow the payments to inquisitors operating in the Italian peninsula. Payments in favour of the Inquisition in Malta were more conspicuous; among these, 100 scudi, given in April, 1579, to Monsignor Domenico Petrucci, Apostolic Protonotary and official inquisitor on the island, for travelling expenses and "to maintain his office"; 130 Neapolitan scudi and, later, between September, 1583 and November, 1584, 200 scudi to other inquisitors in Malta and then, again; 200 scudi in 1587 (ibid.).
7   ACDF, So, St.st., N3p, "Fragmenta pro officio Sanctae Inquisitionis", p. 24*r–v*.
8   See Ponziani (2008).
9   Romeo (1988); Del Col (2006), pp. 331ff.
10 BAV, Borg. Lat. 558, anonymous report, undated, p. 192*r*. The minster, continued, "has no sort of jurisdiction, if not when delegated for particular circumstances by the Holy Congregation, and his ministry consists simply in receiving the accusations and in forwarding them to Rome to await the orders to examine the witnesses and construct the trial" (ibid.).
11 BAV, Borg. Lat. 558, p. 133*r*, Rome, September 20, 1618; April 8, 1620; May 21, 1620. In 1604, Clement VIII also conferred donations upon the Bishop of Caserta "for the needs of the Holy Office" (ibid., p.192*v*).
12 Recently explored in Mazza (2009).
13 The relative decree was drawn up by the Neapolitan notary Giovanni Camillo Prezioso on January 24, 1606 (BAV, Borg. Lat. 558, p. 123*r–v*).
14 BAV, Borg. Lat. 558, p. 130*r*, Naples, March 6, 1635.
15 Ibid., p.124*r*, listing the "Expenses of the Ministers of the Holy Office in Naples of which, having sent notice to Rome, were paid"; information on 1609.
16 Ibid., p. 126*r–v*, Naples, January 8, 1630 replying to Rome, November 21, 1629.
17 Ibid.; other correspondence between Bichi and the Holy Office in BAV, Borg. Lat. 49, pp. 37*r*–52*v*, 161*v*–164*r*.
18 Ibid., p. 128*r*, Naples, February 3, 1635.
19 Ibid., p. 128*v*.
20 BAV, Barb. Lat. 6334, p. 2*v*, Rome, January 2, 1626.
21 The theme of the religious Orders' missions and their techniques of action and propaganda in concert with those of the courts of faith is treated extensively in Prosperi (2009); see also Pastore (2011).
22 ACDF, Oec 15, January 1578.
23 See Prosperi (2000), p. 434, note 64. The case of Manelfi was, of course, brought to the centre of historiographical discussion by Carlo Ginzburg (1970).
24 ACDF, Oec 17, pp. 98*r*, 101*r*, 107*r* (November 8 and December 24, 1585; February 5, 1586).
25 Ibid., p. 91*r*, sent on August 28, 1585.
26 Exploration of the texts of Congregation documents ordering payments – contained in the series *Decreta* of ACDF – have not turned up more precise information than that afforded by the registers of payment orders: see, for example, the hermetic reference to the need to send money to Riccardo Listier in ACDF So, *Decreta*, 019, p. 208*r*, February 5, 1580.
27 Ibid., Rome, April 18, 1626, p. 90*v*.
28 BAV, Barb. Lat. 6334, Rome, February 21, 1626, p. 45*r–v*. On Montalban's zeal see Tomasi and Tomasi (2012), pp. 37 and 141.
29 BAV, Barb. Lat. 6334, Rome, February 27, 1626, p. 46*r*.

30 Ibid., Rome, February 28, 1626, pp. 51r–52v.
31 Prosperi (2010), p. 164.
32 ACDF, Oec 15, August, 1578; November, 1578; April, 1580; October, 1580; Oec 17, February, 1583.
33 ACDF, Oec 17, January, 1585.
34 As Cantimori (2002), pp. 280ff., noted.
35 ACDF, Oec 17, March, 23; April 9, 15, 20; July 25; November 8, 1585.
36 See Masa (2011), pp. 153 and 187ff., which discovers a "network of solidarity" among some of the figures cited. For an overall view, see Mazzone (1991).
37 ACDF, Oec 18, p. 58r, October, 6 and December, 4, 1588; May 30, 1590.
38 On the religious complexity of this area and the limits of the process of religious consolidation, see di Filippo Bareggi (1999); di Filippo Bareggi (2006); Masa (2011), pp. 24, 55–9, 145–53.
39 Caffiero (2006), p. 161; Caffiero (2011).
40 ACDF, Oec 15, pp. 3rff. A more detailed analysis of Congregation entries and payments may be found in Chapter III.
41 ACDF, So, St.st., GG 3c.
42 The mobility of Observant Franciscans within specific circuits was another trait distinguishing them from the Monastics: see Fasoli (2011), pp. XV–XVI, for further bibliography.
43 A few months earlier, when he took up his post in Bergamo arriving from another state, Father Canossa had irritated the Venetian authorities, who had momentarily denied him the necessary permission to act within the territory of the republic. When Canossa decided to address a petition to the Serenissima's highest authorities, he received a brusque reply from the noble Soranzo: "is this the father inquisitor of Bergamo, Father Canossa, the one who has sent notice to the College? Who taught him to speak? Send notice? Go and learn miserable monk": see Veronese (2009–10), p. 113.
44 ACDF, So, St.st., GG3c, Bergamo, September 16, 1705.
45 Ibid., Bergamo, memory by Claudio Giugni to the Holy Office, unbodied.
46 A general impression of this complex body of *Ancien régime* procedures – which would repay more ample research – may be derived from the work of a Franciscan, Ferraris (1795), pp. 405–12. On the rules governing the properties in the Milanese case, see Dell'Oro (2007).
47 On these institutions, which we shall examine more closely further on, a preliminary bibliography might usefully include Gazzini (2004) and Zardin (2004).
48 See Fasoli (2011), pp. 242ff., *ad nomen*.
49 On this question Giovanni Todeschini's work is interesting; see, for example, Todeschini (2009).
50 Fasoli (2011), pp. 185ff.
51 Ibid., pp. 184–95.
52 I draw here on Comparato (1974), where a preliminary bibliography on this vast theme may be found.
53 BAV, Barb. Lat. 6334, Rome, January 10, 1626, p. 10v, the italics are mine.
54 ACDF, So, St.st., GG 3d, Ceneda, December 10, 1711.
55 ACDF, So, St.st., LL 5f, *Inquisizione di Vicenza,* Vicenza, January 2, 1749.
56 On the "invasion of the convents" see, for example, Henryot (2012), in particular, p. 294; on the dynamism of the convents' economy and their credit networks, see Perluss (2012).
57 For an application of the thesis of professionalization applied to post-Tridentine Italy, see De Boer (2006).
58 See Carlsmith (2003).
59 ACDF, So, St.St., GG3c, unnumbered sheets "Information of the debt and the causes of sequestration by the inquisitor of Bergamo".

60 Ibid.
61 See Bardelli da Nizza (1703), p. 448.
62 The quotation is from Mathew 8.20: "And Jesus replied: 'Foxes have their dens and the birds of the air have their nests, but the Son of Man has no place to lay his head'".
63 See ACDF, So, St.st., GG3c "Income of the Bergamo Holy Office for the year 1581" (in reality, the accounts furnish the expenditures from November 1581 through December 1582), unnumbered sheets. I use a rate of 1 to 7 in translating Venetian lire into Roman scudi of account, as this is explicitly contemplated by subsequent annual accounts (ibid., p. 152*r*). The figures are, therefore, to be considered as simply indicative.
64 Ibid., Bergamo, April 13. 1622.
65 Prosperi (2003), p. 129.
66 ACDF, Si, *Libro dell'entrata e dell'uscita del Sant'Officio*, from which I draw the information cited below.
67 Ibid., pp. 3*r*, 31*r*.
68 Ibid., p. 18*r*.
69 Ibid., p. 103*r*, the italics are mine.
70 ACDF, So, St.st., GG3c, unnumbered pages.
71 ASM, *Atti di governo, Culto parte antica,* box 2106, folder "20 marzo 1779", visit by the notary Antonio Siviola to the convent of Santa Maria delle Grazie, March 13, 1779, p. 4*r*.
72 Fundamental comments on this score may be found in Peyronel Rambaldi (2008).
73 Del Col (2006), pp. 768ff.
74 The progressive anti-Jewish specialization of the Roman Inquisition after the end of the anti-heretic phase, has been analysed by Caffiero (2011); the recourse of Jews to voluntary presentation is discussed in Caffiero (2012), pp. 143ff.
75 Communication sent to the Inquisitor of Venice on June 14, 1578: see BAV, Vat. Lat. 10945, p. 125*r*.
76 Ibid., p. 126*r*.
77 On Bergamo, see ACDF, So, St.st., GG3c, unnumbered sheets, "Copy of the taxes, of the sums paid by defendants tried by this Inquisition" sent to Rome on August 13, 1598, by Brother Pio da Lugo. Among other items, it included an obligatory tax of 14 lire for "any sentence", 7 lire "for any text in defence", 1 soldo for any obtained report", 6 soldi for "a trial transcript and of any provision [...] per sheet", 2 lire and 15 soldi "for a copy of any sentence", 7 lire for "the detention of any culprit in the city", 10 lire and 10 soldi for detention "in the countryside", 2 lire "surety for torture", 2 lire and 15 soldi "for any text in defence", 10 soldi "for every accusation [...] for any testimony, or accusing witness". The Ancona list may be found in ACDF, So, St.st., DD1e, p. 104*r–v*.
78 Information drawn from ACDF, So, St.st., LL5e–LL5f, *passim*.
79 ACDF, So, St.st., LL5e, *Inquisizione di Belluno*; LL5f, *Inquisizione di Pisa*.

Bibliography

Bardelli da Nizza, F. L. (1703) *Memorie dell'origine, fondazione, avanzamenti, successi ed uomini illustri in lettere, e in santità della Congregazione de' cherici [sic] regolari di S. Paolo chiamati volgarmente barnabiti*, tome I, Bologna: per Costantino Pisarri.

Caffiero, M. (2006) *I diritti degli ebrei. Le rivendicazioni della comunità romana alle soglie della Rivoluzione*, in M. Formica and A. Postigliola (eds) *Diversità e minoranze nel Settecento*, Rome: Edizioni di Storia e letteratura, 155–72.

Caffiero, M. (2011) *Forced Baptisms: Histories of Jews, Christians, and Converts in Papal Rome,* Berkeley and Los Angeles, CA: University of California Press.
Caffiero, M. (2012) *Legami pericolosi. Ebrei e cristiani tra eresia, libri proibiti e stregoneria,* Turin: Einaudi.
Cantimori, D. (2002) *Eretici italiani del Cinquecento e Prospettive di storia ereticale italiana del Cinquecento,* ed. by A. Prosperi, Turin: Einaudi (1st edn 1939).
Carlsmith, C. (2003) 'I vescovi e le scuole: la situazione a Bergamo nel "500"', in M. Sangalli (ed.), *Per il Cinquecento religioso italiano. Clero, cultura, società. Atti del convegno internazionale di studi, Siena, 27–30 giugno 2001,* Rome: Edizioni dell'Ateneo, vol. 1, 405–14.
Comparato, V. I. (1974) *Uffici e società a Napoli (1600–1647). Aspetti dell'ideologia del magistrato in età moderna,* Florence: Olschki.
De Boer, W. (2006) 'Professionalization and Clerical Identity: Notes on the Early Modern Catholic Priest', in W. Janse and B. Pitkin (eds) *The Formation of Clerical and Confessional Identities in Early Modern Europe,* Leiden and Boston: Brill, 369–77.
Del Col, A. (2006) *L'Inquisizione in Italia dal XII al XXI secolo,* Milan: Mondadori.
Dell'Oro, G. (2007) *Il Regio economato. Il controllo statale sul clero nella Lombardia asburgica e nei domini sabaudi,* Milan: FrancoAngeli.
di Filippo Bareggi, C. (1999) *Le frontiere religiose della Lombardia. Il rinnovamento cattolico nella zona ticinese e retica fra Cinque e Seicento,* Milan: Unicopli.
di Filippo Bareggi, C. (2006) 'Crinali alpini e passi, frontiere e confini linguistici, politici, religiosi fra "500" e "600": la Val Mesolcina', in C. Donati (ed.) *Alle frontiere della Lombardia. Politica, guerra e religione nell'età moderna,* Milan: FrancoAngeli, 41–70.
Fasoli, S. (2011) *Perseveranti nella regolare osservanza. I predicatori osservanti nel ducato di Milano (secc. XV–XVI),* Milan: Edizioni Biblioteca francescana.
Ferraris, L. (1795) *Promta biblioteca canonica, juridica, moralis, theologica necnon ascetica, polemica, rubricistica, historica,* tome VIII, Madrid: ex Typis et sumptibus regiae thypographorum et bibliopolarum societatis.
Gazzini, M. (2004) '"Fratres" e "milites" tra religione e politica. Le milizie di Gesù Cristo e della Vergine nel Duecento', *Archivio storico italiano* (1): 3–78.
Ginzburg, C. (1970) *I costituti di don Pietro Manelfi,* Florence-Chicago: Sansoni-Newberry Library.
Henryot, F. (2012) 'La quête francescaine aux XVIIe et XVIIIe siècles: théories et pratiques d'une économie de l'Evangile', in F Ammannati (ed.) *Religione e istituzioni religiose nell'economia europea 1000–1800,* Florence: Florence University Press, 293–305.
Masa, S. (2011) *Fra curati cattolici e ministri riformati. Nicolò Rusca e il rinnovamento tridentino in Valmalenco,* Sondrio: Fondazione Gruppo Credito Valtellinese.
Mazza, G. (2009) *Streghe, guaritori, istigatori. Casi di Inquisizione diocesana in età moderna,* Rome: Carocci.
Mazzone, U. (1991) '"Consolare quei poveri catholici": visitatori ecclesiastici in Valtellina tra "500" e "600"', in A. Pastore (ed.) *Riforma e società nei Grigioni. Valtellina e Valchiavenna tra "500" e "600",* Milan: FrancoAngeli, 129–57.
Pastore, A. (2011) 'Guerrieri della fede sulle Alpi. Missioni di frontiera (secoli XVI–XVIII)', in D. Dall'Olio, A. Malena and P. Scaramella (eds) *La fede degli italiani. Per Adriano Prosperi,* vol. 1, Pisa: Edizioni della Normale, 347–56.

Perluss, P. (2012) 'From alms to investments: Monastic credit structures in seventeenth and eighteenth century Paris', in F Ammannati (ed.), *Religione e istituzioni religiose nell'economia europea 1000–1800*, Florence: Florence University Press, 307–27.

Peyronel Rambaldi, S. (2008) Élites nobiliari in Italia di fronte alla Riforma protestante, in S. Levati and M. Meriggi (eds) *Con la ragione e col cuore. Studi dedicati a Carlo Capra*, Milan: FrancoAngeli, 89–116.

Ponziani, D. (2008) *Interessi architettonici: i palazzi dell'Inquisizione*, in A. Cifres and M. Pizzo (eds) *Rari e preziosi. Documenti dell'età contemporanea dell'Archivio del Sant'Uffizio*, Rome: Gangemi, 86–106.

Prosperi, A. (2000) *L'eresia del Libro Grande. Storia di Giorgio Siculo e della sua setta*, Milan: Feltrinelli.

Prosperi, A. (2003) *L'inquisizione romana. Letture e ricerche*, Rome: Edizioni di storia e letteratura.

Prosperi, A. (2009) *Tribunali della coscienza. Inquisitori, confessori, missionari*, Turin: Einaudi.

Prosperi, A. (2010) *L'Inquisizione romana e gli ebrei*, in Id., *Eresie e devozioni. La religione italiana in età moderna. II. Inquisitori, ebrei e streghe*, Rome: Edizioni di Storia e letteratura, 119–68.

Romeo, G. (1988) 'Una città, due Inquisizioni: l'anomalia del Sant'Ufficio a Napoli nel tardo Cinquecento', *Rivista di storia e letteratura religiose* (24): 42–67.

Tavuzzi, M. (2007) *Renaissance Inquisitors. Dominican Inquisitors and Inquisitorial Districts in Northern Italy 1474–1527*, Leiden and Boston: Brill.

Todeschini, G. (2009) *Franciscan Wealth. From Voluntary Poverty to Market Society*, Saint Bonaventure, New York: Saint Bonaventure University.

Tomasi, G. and Tomasi, S. (2012) *Ebrei nel Veneto orientale. Conegliano, Ceneda e insediamenti minori*, Florence: Giuntina.

Veronese, F. (2009–10) *"Terra di nessuno". Misto foro e conflitti tra Inquisizione e magistrature secolari nella Repubblica di Venezia (XVIII sec.)*, Doctoral dissertation examined in the 2009–2010 academic year, tutor G. del Torre, Venice: University Ca' Foscari.

Zardin, D. (2004) 'Tra Chiesa e società "laica": le confraternite in epoca moderna', *Annali di storia moderna e contemporanea*, (10): 529–45.

3 Monetary penalties and the building of the inquisitorial machine

From the Middle Ages the judges of faith imposed monetary penalties upon the condemned, sometimes in exchange for a lighter physical or spiritual punishment. The imposition of fines and other forms of monetary penalties, along with the total or partial confiscation of property of heretics and its transferal to the inquisitors – who usually then assigned it to uses which were not a part of traditional of ecclesiastical usage – constitutes an exceptional innovation in the history of the Church and of medieval society. Indeed, in the thirteenth century, the inquisitors appointed by the popes inaugurated a process of accumulation of wealth (personal property and real estate) which differed from the classic typology of ecclesiastical income: that is, bequests and donations, payment for services performed by the clergy, and taxes or tithes.

Stripping the condemned of the right to property, appropriating that property on the basis of canon law and reinvesting this wealth in the battle against heterodoxy, the Inquisition innovated the forms of material destination for pecuniary ecclesiastical income – traditionally destined to supporting the needs of the clergy, to financing educational and charitable activities (including teaching), to sustaining charitable institutions dedicated to the sick and the poor. "The administration of the forms of investment and income – according to the documentation we have" Lorenzo Paolini has concluded, "seems often dictated by the logic of mere profit and, indeed, exhibits signs of abuses, misappropriation and extortions which will prompt the papacy to intervene with severity". The medieval inquisitor seems to be personally "implicated in economic and financial activities to a degree sometimes so frenetic that we must suspect he has forgotten or neglected his natural juridical/pastoral function as defender of the faith".[1]

We have already seen how, from the thirteenth to the fourteenth century, the figure of the judge of faith gradually took on a fully economic and financial subjectivity which, in the modern period, became a norm. In this chapter we shall explore the role of monetary penalties – and especially of "faith" fines – in consolidating the economic administration of the Holy Office and the "entrepreneurial" role of the inquisitors in the 1500s and 1600s. After that, we will take a closer look at the confiscation system, an area whose importance is decisive not only in defining the tempo and the modalities of the Roman Inquisition's patrimonial formation, but also in understanding the way in which some sophisticated tools for the creation and maintenance of consensus within *Ancien régime* society operated.

"To ease the penuries this inquisition finds itself in as far as business"

Confiscation, fines, the monetizing of physical and spiritual punishment, were inflicted throughout their history on the eve of the contemporary era by Mediterranean courts of faith both inquisitorial and episcopal. And this was the case despite the fact that such punishment was particularly dangerous for the public image of the courts, since it immediately prompted popular suspicion that the trials themselves had been held for the sole purpose of monetary profit.

In France, where the bishops were freer from papal control than in Italy and where the Ordinaries organized a series of provincial councils aimed at limiting the power and the procedural authority of the inquisitors, there was already in the 1240s an open scandal due to fines, with flagrant cases of embezzlement. Still, the consequent measures adopted by the councils of Narbonne (1243), Béziers (1246), Valence (1248) and Albi (1254), were indecisive, shifting – as regards to fines – between prohibition and a renewal of concessions without expressing any solid set of rules for this delicate matter.[2] In the first half of the 1300s, in a period in which the activities of the Holy Tribunal had slowed down, some 50 Italian inquisitors were investigated and tried in the Marches of Treviso, in the provinces of Lombardy, in Tuscany and in the Marches of Ancona for abuses in their economic administration. Ottobono de' Razzi, Bishop of Padua, headed a delegation to the Roman Curia soliciting action to punish abuses on the part of inquisitors in various localities in the Veneto and the Friuli; the subsequent investigation ordered by Boniface VIII concluded, in January 1303, with the Pope's decision to remove the minor friars from the office of inquisitors in Padua and Vicenza and to send the preachers instead, though only a few years later, Clement V found himself obliged to institute new investigations. The apostolic nuncio, instead, ascertained, in 1333, that the last four Tuscan inquisitors had overstated their expenses and taken funds for fines which had nothing to do with the Office of Faith. In the nearly two years of his service, the Franciscan friar, Mino from San Quirico, had accumulated embezzled funds of 560 Florins in occult payments and 1,600 in unwarranted or inexistent expenses, living blithely in luxury even after he had been called to Avignon to justify himself and to refund his ill-gotten gains.[3]

These and other investigations – like the one involving Friar Guido da Vicenza, future Bishop of Ferrara (of whom it was publicly said had bought his post for 100 florins after having trafficked with usurers), were ordered by the popes and their local representatives as controls of the correct management of the many abundant funds (*"multa et magna pecunia"*) received by inquisitors in the preceding decades. Attempts to ascertain the legitimacy of the confiscation of heretic property and the use of the money deriving from their sale included the request – not always heeded – to exhibit the books registering payments and expenses as well as annual accounts. As Marina Benedetti's studies delineate, the results of these investigations show that, in the late Middle Ages the judges of faith did not have a cultural and mental outlook in which book-keeping found a natural place; their object was not to keep expenses equal to income – they worried, rather, about securing income. The official economic controls set up by the Roman authorities and religious superiors were not applied in daily reality. It should also be noted that at the accounting and financial level, practical relations were already much stronger, during the 1200s and 1300s and, between inquisitors and the religious Orders than with Rome and the papacy – both at the level of logistic services which were not susceptible of monetization furnished by the convent and as reimbursements or grants to the inquisitors – continued, according to a model which we have already seen, into the early modern era.[4]

In some measure unlike confiscation – which required complex procedures in its execution, involving a number of subjects and institutions – fines remained, in the late Middle Ages and the early modern period, an arbitrary prerogative of the inquisitor. During the sixteenth century, with the explosion of the anti-Lutheran emergency, fines had ended up within the administrative territory of the courts of faith and the system of incentives it developed. The risks involved in placing such a controversial penal instrument in the hands of the inquisitors was perceived already in the sixteenth century – first of all by the bishops. In 1567, the Ordinary in Asti pointed out to Duke Emanuele Filiberto di Savoia, who had decided to favour the extension of the Roman Inquisitorial network within his territories, that the ideal inquisitor should be "a learned person and circumspect, with his prosecutors and his secretaries salaried honestly at the expense of culprits and, above all, should not proceed through avarice for the confiscation of property".[5]

On its part, the Congregation of the Holy Office itself, once the mid-sixteenth century emergency had ended, began to send out firm recommendations like the one directed in the 1620s to the deputy inquisitor in Malta, Monsignor Nicolò Herrera:

> Of confiscations and monetary punishments, as your lordship will be yourself little convinced [of them], so act that, when some shall be inflicted of which it is known, this be done merely as punishment for culprits and not for any other interest: like [an act] which has as its scope not the good of the court, or of the ministers, but only the service of God and the conservation of the Holy Catholic faith.[6]

In the harshest moments of the war against the Reformed Evangelical heresy, which local Inquisition courts confronted almost without ordinary fixed income, it had, however, been precisely the Roman Ministry which urged the inquisitors to draw financial support directly from their repressive activities. Indeed, in Rome itself we find cases like that of the wealthy aristocratic Neapolitan, Pompeo delli Monti, executed in June, 1566, who was spared the canonical death by fire at the stake on payment of 5,000 scudi, being, instead, allowed prior decapitation *in ponte* (that is, in the open area between the bridge and Castel Sant'Angelo).[7]

The frequent choice of monetary punishment in the mid-1500s depended first of all upon the inquisitors' need to build appropriate housing for their activities – court sessions, torture, archives, cells for prisoners – which they were obliged to provide using economic resources that they had acquired on their own. While in the late Middle Ages friars delegated to an Office of Faith (*"Officium fidei"*) had usually carried out their task with the support of structures assigned them by the convents or in episcopal palaces, in the fifteenth and sixteenth centuries they began to use a separate, dedicated, location (*"domus Inquisitionis"*) explicitly constructed to serve inquisitorial procedures from the incarceration of culprits to the application of torture and the conservation of the precious archives which permitted the regular, systematic, pursuit of the war against heresy.

The inquisitors of Bologna, for example, built their own prisons between 1452 and 1482, while in Parma and Reggio Emilia the inquisitors built a new house reserved for their offices and including two prisons in 1509. Still, it was only after the middle of the 1500s that building projects specifically intended to house the Inquisition (*"ad usum Inquisitionis"*) – and make its presence a permanent given of daily life – became systematic: among early results were the monumental convents of Santa Maria delle Grazie in Milan (whose refectory da Vinci would fresco with *The Last Supper*) and, in Bologna, the San Domenico complex, which would be further enlarged during the 1600s.[8]

Where the scanty surviving documentation allows us to explore the basic economics of the building policy of the Roman inquisitorial staff in the 1500s and 1600s, it is not difficult to discern a direct link to the contemporary importance of monetary penalties on the part of local judges of faith. In the case of Modena, which became the inquisitorial seat for the d'Este duchy after Ferrara had passed into papal hands in 1598, this link is direct and evident. Once the offices were settled in the ancient vicariate of the convent of San Domenico (and this not without friction between the convent's prior and the inquisitor on the use of a number of "spaces"), the first judge, Giovanni da Montefalcone, described his lodgings unequivocally: "As for the belongings of our office, there is naught but a single cell in the dormitory with the other brothers, with a pallet – bedstead and litter – without sheets and covers, and bare of any other religious comfort". His successor, Arcangelo Calbetti da Recanati, after having begun a series of trials of followers of Judaism for dissuasion to baptism, possession of forbidden books and unwarranted contacts with Christians – and monetized a long series of punishments especially regarding Jewish culprits – was able, in 1607, to build "a new edifice for the Inquisition". This included a grand staircase with two ramps, each displaying 27 tiled steps, prison cells, offices for the notary and the custodian, a private, three-room, apartment for the inquisitor, consulting rooms and torture room. In these same years, the inquisitor in Reggio Emilia drew dozens of gold ducats from the censorship, or "correction" of Jewish books.[9]

On its part, the Congregation of the Holy Office, insisting on the rigid economic policy we have seen, stimulated the inquisitors to finance or restructure their seats using the income from monetary punishments. "As for the construction of prisons", the Congregation of the Holy Office wrote, to the inquisitor in Venice in 1579, "it is up to you, and to those gentlemen [probably the secular authorities] to do the best possible with spending the money there is, and on other occasions fix numerous other pecuniary punishments sufficient to complete the work, for from here we see, at present, no aid we can give".[10]

"My illustrious Lords understand the ruin which menaces the home of this Inquisition", Rome wrote to the inquisitor in Pavia some 50 years later:

> and desiring that there be remedy as soon as possible, has ordered your reverence to send us assurance from the architects of the State of the site and of the expense necessary to restore it; send this, however, immediately here and, at the same time, inform [us] whether there are trials which permit you to impose some pecuniary punishment, or some condemned whose imprisonment might be commuted into fines (though this does not seem possible to realize in the case of the person of which you have written).[11]

The following year, the Inquisition in Casale Monferrato was urged to draw the funds needed to "build the archives and the little loggia [...] as well as modernize the stairs of this Holy Office [...] spending money from fines conceded to date [...] always if no further debt be incurred".[12] In the 1560s, the cardinal inquisitors assigned fines like those (varying from 100 to 500 scudi) inflicted for the possession or sale of forbidden books or upon certain printers, among whom were Giulio Bolano degli Accolti and Venturino Tramezzino,[13] to religious seats, to which they further turned over a rich fine of 1,000 scudi each, inflicted on Matteo and Paolo Luppari, two gentlemen of Bologna – brothers condemned to perpetual confinement – to "buy or build a seat in which you and the other penitents of the Holy Office may be confined". It is highly probable that these payments contributed to the construction of the Inquisition complex in Bologna which we have already mentioned, completed in 1569 and still standing today as part of the convent of San Domenico.[14]

An exemplary financial chronicle of the construction of the Milan Inquisition's physical plant in the early 1600s, compiled by an eighteenth-century Milanese judge of faith on the basis of material in his archives, vividly spreads before us the contemporary blend of monetary punishments, occasional grants in aid, and debt, which the local seats of the Holy Office were obliged to manage if they were to deal successfully with that difficult phase in their definitive establishment throughout the territory of the Italian peninsula:

The greatest expense in the construction of the Holy Office [in Milan] was, however, incurred in 1608 and the following years, in which the chambers of the inquisitor and the ministers were raised up as they are today, and the loggia over the portico – or cloister in the courtyard of the convent – and the detention cells and rooms situated above this loggia; which edification – as Book one, Construction, attached by the inquisitor himself [shows] – cost 51,077 lire, 17 soldi. In two years Rome sent 2,300 gold scudi in 3 instalments and other 487 Roman scudi, 4 baiocchi – which are the 500 scudi sent by the holy Congregation translated into that sum for the commodity of the banks (which sum according to the exchange of the times amounted to 17,622, 16 soldi). Further, the money from 11 condemnations, to the sum of 11,976 lire, was employed. There was a gift of alms for 76 lire. Besides these, the depositary of the holy Congregation lent [a total of] 27,625 lire, 19 soldi in various occasions, so that the Holy Office took on this debt for the Construction. Indeed, in 1610, the Father inquisitor Seghizio, in the accounts sent to Rome listed a large debt for Construction: that is, 28,970 lire, 16 soldi, which total we can clearly see exceeds the above mentioned 51,077:17, which we cannot understand if not for other work necessary to construction, like that of carpenters or smithies. [...] As to payment of this debt, however accomplished, we find no other mention. [...] In 1629 [...] the altar was built, and a chapel, so that prisoners might hear holy mass without taking them to a church. In the same year, by order of the holy Congregation, dated 6 October, a wall which previous inquisitors had begun to raise so that prisoners could not talk among themselves, was continued. In 1666 the noble marble stairway which guards the convent door and leads to the loggia and the entry hall of the Holy Office was built [...] The hall where abjurations are pronounced and the chapter of the gentlemen Forty Knights *Crocesegnati* meet, we suppose built by the Father Inquisitor Deodato Gentile, a Genovese, before 1600 (that is by 1592) and this because its ceiling was painted by Ottavio Semini, a famous Genovese artist of those times.[15]

The notable effort dedicated to the construction of the Inquisition courts, together with the growth of a bureaucratic bent which multiplied the salaries for collaborators, was without doubt a very strong incentive to seek out new sources of income. It was probably not by chance that the period between the sixteenth and the seventeenth centuries, when the uprooting of heresy had been completed and, at the same time, new financial exigencies came to the fore, saw the appearance of new objects of persecution. Among these were witchcraft, magic practices, swearing, imprecations and transgression of prohibitions imposed upon the Jews, crimes for which, given the decline in heresy trials, stiff pecuniary punishments made it possible to continue to bolster income. These were also years in which the Roman Inquisition saw important increases not only in the costs of construction of its local courts, but in those of its own central administration. In the Congregation's offices in Rome, the salaries of the most important dependants in the 1570s were still 23 scudi a month for the assessor, 15 for the fiscal solicitor, a little over 8 for the secretary, 15 for the notary and 23 scudi for the prison guard. Between 1587 and 1588, the monthly salary of the assessor went from 23 to 40 scudi, while the fiscal solicitor saw his pay rise from 15 to 20 scudi and the salary of the notary – which had already risen from 15 to 27 in the period from 1583–6 – went to 34 scudi in 1590; in addition, from 1588 the figure of the Vice-Commissioner of the Holy Office grew up within the Roman Ministry, enjoying a monthly salary of 35 scudi. Finally, the monthly salary of the secretary rose, in 1590, to 10 scudi.

In January, 1591 – as it continued to do periodically in the years that followed – the Congregation gave "extraordinary gratuities" to all of its dependents: 70 scudi to the assessor, general commissioner and consultant, 60 to the fiscal solicitor, 30 to the notary, 15 to the courier and 10 to the official surgeon. In the same period, the monthly expenses for food for each individual imprisoned by the Roman Holy Office continued without change to be 4 scudi.[16]

The physical and bureaucratic stabilization of the Italian inquisitorial network came about, then, largely within a mixed situation of self-finance and support by the Congregation: a situation which, except for exceptional cases, did not allow the judges to proceed with construction without displacing resources from ordinary activities. The supreme inquisitors were quick to realize the need to establish a centre of command for the sixteenth and seventeenth century process creating physical plant and managerial structures, establishing rules requiring that the construction of buildings destined for the use of the Inquisition be undertaken only after obtaining a specific authorization; they even resorted from time to time to the threatening attempt to make bishops responsible for building expenses.[17] Authorization from Rome was required, as well, to use the income from fines to pay the salaries of prison guards, doctors, notaries, apothecaries and other specific collaborators.[18]

Despite these attempts to discipline the impetuous growth of the fixed costs of the inquisitorial apparatus in the late 1500s, it is quite likely that the local courts were heavily in debt with the Congregation itself – or with the artisans and professionals engaged in construction – making it necessary for both the inquisitors and the convents to increase their contributions to the courts they directed or housed. This, in turn – over a period which, in some cases, might even stretch to decades – almost automatically produced new monetary punishments or other similar provisions, like the posting of bonds in the case of the temporary release of incriminated individuals. The 500 ducat fine for "breaking surety" imposed upon a certain Pietro Agnolo, a Neapolitan doctor who had, evidently, fled, was thus destined in 1598 to the enlargement and the repair of the episcopal prisons assigned to the Holy Office: "having particular care that the funds not be diverted to other use", the supreme inquisitors admonished the Bishop of Caserta, who at the time was minister of the Holy Office in the realm.[19]

Funds of this sort were not everywhere available to guarantee the construction of adequate housing: the Rimini Inquisition, stably active from 1550, saw the construction of prisons of its own only in 1636, after it had been obliged for many years – as had also been the case in Fermo – to imprison and torture culprits in the episcopal palace.[20] In Cremona, instead, the city intervened, taking on in 1609 the obligation to pay "simply through its own liberality" the annual sum of 20 scudi requested by the local convent of San Domenico – which evidently was itself not very generous towards the Inquisition – to concede certain shops to be transformed into "prisons where witches may be held".[21] Still, in most cases, the direct link between the construction of buildings that were appropriate for setting up the inquisitorial offices and inflicting monetary punishment on the condemned was real and it was fixed firmly in the memory of the judges of faith. We find testimony, for example, in the mid-eighteenth-century memoir of an inquisitor from Perugia:

> From 1631, with the inquisitor [Francesco] Galassino, construction began on this palace of the Holy Office, with the chambers of the inquisitor, the vicar, the chancellor and the lay brother, with the prison cells – which in preceding years the Holy Office did not have and kept prisoners in secular prisons. For the costs of this construction, 7,828 scudi were furnished and these were in part obtained by commuting corporal punishments, even of life imprisonment, in monetary punishments for imprisoned culprits, by order of the Supreme, in part through fines from the episcopal Curia to this Inquisition, in part as grants in charity from the three fraternities of San Domenico, San Francesco [and] Sant'Agostino of this city, [who were] obliged by a decree of Urban VIII, and in part through other alms.[22]

Secular governments and courts also drew profit from the fines imposed by the inquisitors. In the Duchy of Savoy, from 1585 a decree of Gregory XIII declared that half of the fines inflicted on those selling forbidden books within the State should go to the Duke's chamber; this privilege was renewed in the early years of the 1600s.[23] As we shall see more clearly further on, the distribution between princes and ecclesiastical authorities of the income from monetary penalties inflicted by the Inquisition took on a decisive role in some Italian states even in the procedures regarding the confiscation of property belonging to those condemned for heresy. Indeed, the sharing out of funds deriving from monetary penalties represented one of the fundamental terms of dialogue and incentive for reciprocal collaboration between the secular and the ecclesiastical spheres within a common strategy of repression of dissent that had taken shape in *Ancien régime* Catholic societies.

The imposition – and the eventual sharing out – of Inquisition fines was made easier by the fact that such fines were a particularly flexible instrument of repressive intervention, whose application could be multiplied and spread over time as a "corrective", punishing in particular those who committed minor infractions. Indeed, fines were often levied by inquisitors as a form of punishment in cases where the terms of a sentence already pronounced had not been respected: the inquisitor in Tortona, for example, could oblige a certain Sebastiano Chiodo to pay a fine of 100 scudi each time he violated the Holy Office prohibition by medicating "the supposed bewitched".[24] The versatility of fines was enhanced, too, by the fact that the inquisitors, in establishing lists of punishable transgressions, were not obliged to fix the entity of the fine which might be incurred by any single crime: the monetary punishment might, then, vary at discretion, conveying the idea of an ample penal range aimed at discouraging minor transgressions.[25]

The degree to which recourse to monetary punishment was regulated by the inclinations of the individual inquisitors – on whose score doubts and open protest were beginning to accumulate – led the Supreme to undertake the regulation of fines and reparations. In 1587, taking advantage of a controversial case of commutation in Siena, it forbade local courts the transformation of physical penalties into monetary one, making all decisions of this sort the preserve of cardinals.[26] Subsequently, in the last years of the century, Rome emitted several decrees ordering – as it wrote to all the inquisitors within the Venetian republic in September, 1597 – to "abstain from pecuniary penalties […] with judgement expedite the end of trials in said Dominion by abjuration as well as by monetary punishment".[27] At the same time, orders like that sent to the Inquisition in Genoa in 1590, imposed the application of the monetary penalties for cases of blasphemy to religious entities, including convents housing inquisitors.[28]

So, as the sixteenth century unfolded, the levying of monetary punishments by local inquisitors was progressively subjected to the approval of Rome. Yet the very constancy of pressure upon local inquisitors to secure the permission of the Congregation – and to not keep the fines for themselves, but distribute them to religious entities[29] – makes it clear that this policy was not always respected. In the seventeenth century, Rome was still expressing "the dissatisfaction in all senses, and in particular for the scarce repute of the Holy Office" with which the popes received notice that the inquisitors imposed and required payment of monetary punishments.[30] The imposition of fines and the monetizing of punishment, then, was a long-lasting practice among inquisitors, enduring even after the sixteenth-century prohibitions. Indeed, for some types of sin-crime Congregation prohibitions were less attentive. Blasphemy, a matter for the Holy Office in cases which were heretical in nature, was often punished in pecuniary form according to the canons of Lateran Council V (1512–17), which made such a sanction easy. In its Session IX, with the *Bulla reformationis curiae*, it provided that blasphemous laity, if noble, should be punished in the first instance with a fine of 15 ducats and a second instance with 50 ducats to be put towards to upkeep of Saint Peter's Basilica. In the event of a third episode, Lateranense V prescribed the loss of the condition of nobility. For the "ignoble", or "plebian" blasphemer, the prescribed penalty was incarceration (which might even be for life) or condemnation to the gallows. Even the Jews continued well into the eighteenth century to be subjected to monetary penalties by the inquisitors, often only for having spoken to – or eaten with – Christian women.[31]

For cases requiring the authorization of Rome – that is, where the Suprema judged extraordinary circumstances might justify this symbolically dangerous practice – the procedure was to emit Decrees of Derogation. Though there might occasionally be contingencies prompting inquisitors to commute penal sentences into monetary ones – as in the case of soldiers freed for a fee to return to service in the time of war or prisoners suffering from some illnesses[32] – derogation was commonly prompted by the need to redress persistently passive local accounts. When, for example, in August of 1626, Galeazzo Canevesi and Giulio Cesare Croce, prisoners of the Milan Inquisition, requested the transformation of their sentence, the Suprema conceded it, explicitly instructing that the 600 scudi paid be destined "to relieving the needs of this [Milan] Inquisition".[33]

Rome might further act as collector, redistributing money deriving from the commutation of physical punishment to other inquisitions which found themselves in difficulty "to ease the penuries in which your reverence writes this Inquisition finds itself as to business ['*hacienda*']" – as the supreme inquisitors subsequently caused their scribe to write to the Milan inquisitor – "these my Lords have decided to assign you 500 scudi to be derived from the commutation of the prison sentences conceded some days ago to Croce and Canevese". Of this sum, 100 scudi were destined to the Inquisition in Pavia, to which a communication was immediately dispatched informing them they would receive some money "in part from the accord reached with Croce and Canavese, whose case originated in this court". "As for commuting brother Marc'Antonio Zerbi's exile in monetary punishment", the writer noted, moving on to treat the case of a friar prosecuted by the Pavia court, "we are not persuaded, as it does not seem appropriate to oblige Regular [clergy] to pay money".[34] In March, 1630, with the plague at a focal point, the Milan judge was given permission to transform corporal punishment ("*poenas corporales reorum*") into monetary fines ("*multas pecuniarias*") "despite whatever other contrary decree".[35]

Nor did Roman discretion invest only the possibility of fining culprits; it included, as well, determination of the amount of the fine inflicted as well as the possibility of modifying its entity. The Inquisitor of Pavia, who had tried to reduce the fine inflicted on a culprit from 100 to 50 scudi – probably because his accounts were for the moment in fairly good shape – found himself blocked by the fact that the money had already been assigned to another court "The necessities of the Inquisition in Reggio – to which the 100 scudi of the fine have already been assigned – are too urgent", decreed the Congregation, imposing upon the condemned man to "pay that which had been adjudged without further comment".[36]

It was, then, within a system of exceptions and *ad hoc* concessions already largely stable by the early 1600s that the Roman Inquisition administered the precious reserve of liquid assets constituted by monetary punishment during the entire early modern period. Forms of mediation between the official norms regulating sentencing and day-to-day practice were devised case by case, often to remedy problems deriving from the pervasive incentives which spurred inquisitors to impose fines on the convict with reckless ease. "Father Inquisitors are not less forbidden to impose monetary punishments than they are prohibited from turning other punishments into coinage", the cardinals in Rome reminded a seventeenth-century inquisitor in Bergamo:

> So your reverence without our consent should not have commuted the prison sentence of the medical doctor from Curlago into [a fine of] 100 scudi, as you did. However, informed of the nature of the offence and [that of] the person, these, my Most Illustrious Lords, for the moment approve and they close this matter, and let the 100 scudi be applied by you to extinguishing your credit with the Inquisition in Crema [to the sum of] 50 scudi and the other 50 [go] to provide the prison and its chambers with necessary equipment and to repair the attached House of the Clergy which is ready to tumble down.[37]

We cannot easily establish whether, and to what extent, the pressing need for funds might determine local inquisitors' decisions to prosecute possible culprits or condition the outcome of their trials. We can, however, note that, in cases brought against Jews, some trials and sentences appear to be blatantly determined by the urgent monetary needs of the office which sponsored them. In seventeenth-century Modena, after "serious penury" had allowed the judge of faith to impose monetary punishment, procedures – the specious nature of which the defending lawyers immediately denounced – were instigated against Jewish bankers.[38] Reading other sentences, it is difficult to avoid the impression that the judge of faith tended to consider first and foremost the wealth of the accused and his social status in fixing the entity of his fine. This is the case of the penalty inflicted upon Giovanni Siro, Prince of Correggio in 1618. Siro was found guilty of killing the Inquisitor of Reggio who, without the permission of the secular lord, had had two heretics removed from the lord's prisons and brought before him. After a number of partial payments and a number of extensions, in 1628 Siro still owed the Holy Office almost 2,000 Roman scudi:[39] a sum which could cover the budget of a first rank court of faith for several years.

The trial of Agostino Moneglia, a Ligurian heretic, carried out in Rome in 1582, was of much the same nature. Though, according to the sentence, he had talked and listened to the sermons of "Calvinist heretics"; behaved disrespectfully in church during the elevation of the Host; kept by him "a heretic wife and in the same way a heretic family"; ate meat on days of abstention; denied the existence of Purgatory and the sacrament of

Communion, as well as the efficacy of prayers and ceremonies of intercession for the souls of the dead – and, though tortured, had not denounced any accomplices – Moneglia was condemned to only a single year of house arrest. He was, however also condemned to pay 1,000 gold scudi to be distributed among the religious establishments in the city of Genoa.[40]

We have a still more evident example of the monetizing of punishment in the case of major sin-crime where individuals of notable economic or social standing were involved in the case of the trial of Carlo Gonzaga, son of Ferrante II, Duke of Guastalla (1563–1630). Gonzaga, who presented himself before the Inquisitor of Reggio Emilia during Holy Week in 1628, confessed to having engaged in magic rituals to discover the location of treasure supposed to be buried in Campobasso; to which territory he went in person, operating, therefore, within the jurisdiction of the Neapolitan Inquisition. After a number of attempts to evoke demons using formulae drawn from forbidden books which he had caused to be expressly copied for him (including the *Clavicula Salomonis*) – and having been deceived by a vague "Master of the Art", Carlo Gonzaga committed two murders.[41] The first was that of one of his accomplices in the episodes of magic, whom he suspected of intending to denounce him to the Holy Office. The sentence declared:

> Since he had asked you to allow him to come to Rome, so that he could not denounce you to this Holy Office you attempted to convince him to remain [...] but, [when he declared] he wished to depart to give notice of what had been done to his superiors, you struck him on the head, once lightly and then heavily [...] he fell wounded at the feet of your horse, which trampled him to death.

The second homicide perpetrated by Gonzaga was to have an acquaintance – who had refused to give him "a book in which he sustained that the seven spirits of the days of the week were "bound" – strangled.

The transferal of the trial of Carlo Gonzaga to the Congregation of the Holy Office was quite laborious: it was only in the final months of 1628 that the episcopal Vicar of Naples, Bishop of Molfetta, managed to send some objects to Rome, where they were essential to the trial. Faced with the customs difficulties created by the "trunk" sent on from Naples, the cardinal inquisitors did not hesitate to suggest an interesting stratagem to their representative in Naples:

> Once summoned these customs officials and having convinced them with the things packed on top that there is nothing which must pay taxes, they would not raise any problems at all: which your excellency can immediately do, showing them that they are old books and things which pay no duty [...] without needing to show the nature of the books – which they must not seek out, nor You display; and urge them graciously, for the resolution of this trial is urgent.[42]

The trunk, in fact, contained the "books, and other instruments of magic and the garments" acquired by the vicar of the Holy Office in Naples during the investigation.[43] The stratagem worked and a little over a month later the trial ended with an exceptionally clement verdict: reclusion in a place chosen by the cardinals "for a period at the will of the inquisitors", some salutary penances and the payment of 8,000 scudi "to be converted and spent on that which the Lord Cardinals shall command". The monetary punishment inflicted on the nobleman came to more than the entire annual expenses of the Congregation at the time. Last – but not insignificantly – the son of the Duke of Guastalla abjured privately (a prerogative of the aristocracy) in Castel Sant'Angelo witnessed only by the General Commissioner of the Holy Office: the noble preacher Father Ippolito Maria Lanci d'Acquanegra.[44]

The inquisitor and the convent

The Inquisition, then, began to function as a unified normative and procedural structure from about 1555, in large part due to the tireless effort of popes and the ministry to supervise, coordinate and take over trials, as well as setting up the policies and general criteria governing the behaviour of the local inquisitors. This policy expressed itself through a dense network of correspondence directed from Rome to the local outlying seats and from them to Rome. The Congregation intervened emanating what were, to all intents and purposes, decrees – though they often took the disarming form of simple letters, they carried normative weight and were binding for the whole of the Holy Office system.

So, almost insensibly for those not directly involved in its direction, the Inquisition broke out of the "nomadic work model" typical of the Middle Ages – a model not always based on unified rules and procedures – operating the radical constitutive innovation of introducing a constant, ineludible, flow of communication binding together centralized direction and local autonomies.[45] Correspondence between the centre and the periphery of the inquisitorial system gave rise to an autonomous body of law integrating, re-elaborating and clarifying the content of the papal letters which, from the Middle Ages, had presided over the formation, continuation and juridical definition of the Roman courts of faith. The decrees of the Roman Ministry were occasionally collected in codex, of which a few precious examples remain in the archives (especially those of the Vatican).[46] For a long time, the Supreme Congregation forbade inquisitors to print papers, letters or thematic summaries of their correspondence with Rome;[47] that is why reconstructing the overall sense of the process shaping the life and work of the Inquisition in early modern Italy – careful and capillary (though invisible to most of society) – is particularly difficult today.

From the story we have followed, it seems clear that creating a general stable, uniform, normative situation in all areas, including the economic plane (while also ensuring its adaptability to local conditions) was one of the chief traits of the history of the Roman Inquisition in the late sixteenth and early seventeenth centuries. This is well illustrated by an interesting document entitled *Notes for the Administration of the Holy Inquisition of Rome* ("*Ricordi per servitio della santa Inquisitione di Roma*"), compiled at the beginning of the seventeenth century for Pope Paul V (1605–21), it makes clear that the managerial and financial preoccupations had become of primary importance for the highest echelons of the Holy Office.

> Let the Lord Treasurer draw up a biannual résumé of expenses and income with the depositary and the unresolved debtors. Further, let a special account be kept for each debtor in a separate book.
>
> Let the Officials' commissions, prison expenses and extraordinary [expenses] be sent out each month, with a sole warrant for all.
>
> Let the warrants for extraordinary expenses be written by the chief notary with a note made of the date of the Decree and the Lord Cardinal's seal be affixed on each and every warrant (who then countersigns it: of which the secretary is to keep a confirmation).
>
> Regarding documents sent by the inquisitors *de partibus*, let the Lord Treasurer draw up a résumé of entry [*sic*] – which each Inquisition has – and it would be well to limit and clarify the ordinary expenses of each Inquisition.
>
> Every six months, the Lord Treasurer reports on the cases to prosecute in Rome and on whether they are going forward or are delayed; and the diligence be guaranteed.
>
> Every six months, let a report be made of letters regarding important negotiations to which the Ordinaries and the inquisitors have not provided answers.
>
> Every six months, let the assessor give report of the *de partibus* trials and prosecutions in course in Rome and the state in which they find themselves.
>
> Every six months, let the bishops and the inquisitors send résumé of the cases pending, in what situation they may be and so report also on the accusations presented to their courts and whether these are prosecuted or not.
>
> Every six months, let Ordinaries and inquisitors send their sentences and abjurations.
>
> No Grace on the part of the Holy Office may be considered for penitents if half the time of punishment imposed [upon them] has not passed; if not by order of Our Lord [the Pope] and the question must then be discussed before His Holiness [to decide] whether Grace is to be granted or not.
>
> Grace is not to be conceded but on three occasions each year: to wit, Christmas, Easter, and the feast of St Peter.
>
> Let the Holy Office notary forward the enabling licenses granted to various [people] within two months.

Let the censoring of books, proposals and other like matter to be carried out by Decree of the Holy Congregation, be made known *quid gestum sit* [what happened] within not more than six months.

Let whoever has the obligation of persecuting the nominative Index in trials make an annual report, [declaring] whether he has done so in past years, including as well as those just passed.

The Decrees of the Holy Congregation for the many years when the deceased Flaminio Adriano [was] Notary, displaying numerous cancellations and over-writings, so that they are indecent to see; besides making it difficult to read what they say – must of necessity be recopied and made neat.

Let the notary, the Treasurer, the assessor, and the other officials do for themselves that which their office imposes on them and not delegate it to others, *cum sit electa fides, et industria personarum*.

Let those who have the obligation to view trials, fail not to be present at them.

Let the Illustrious Lord Cardinals, General Inquisitors, deign to admonish [the members of] their households to refrain from meddling in negotiations with any of the imprisoned or penitents of the Holy Inquisition without an order from their most Illustrious Lords.[48]

This normative synopsis reflects the priorities and problems of the Roman inquisitorial system at the turn of the seventeenth century very well. Some points would be worth specific research: troublesome signs of "shady dealings" with prisoners by members of the cardinals' entourages; a tendency to be lax in reconsidering local trials, and in formalizing those held in Rome with proper documentation; and a generalized habit of not dealing seriously with business and delegating specific responsibilities even among officials with very delicate positions of authority. It is, as well, significant that the evident bureaucratic preoccupations in the memorandum – destined for a Borghese Pope – were occasioned by the financial management of inquisitorial organization.

After the crucial decades of anti-protestant repression, the 1550s and 1560s had slipped by in a state of substantial "deregulation", the Inquisition had been reorganized with a series of norms aimed at making the circulation and the use of money controllable and transparent both at the local level and within the Roman Ministry. The notes for the Administration of the Holy Inquisition set out the general policy pursued by the Congregation of the Holy Office on the basis of which – to use the document's words – "it would be well to limit" and "clarify" the ordinary expenses of each court. Here we have another confirmation that the popes and their Curia consciously desired the local Inquisitions to contain their budgets – and that the local seats found themselves in part obliged to make this choice as well, due to the scanty granting of sources of income.

It was chiefly under Gregory XIII that, between 1574 and 1578, the Holy Office emanated the first provisions aimed at establishing stable procedures for the economic administration of peripheral courts. These prescribed first of all the local appointment – in agreement with the bishops – of trustees: officials of proven honesty ("Who be trustees – and they must be persons of idoneous faith and substance – chosen by the bishop with the local inquisitors") who were to receive and register the income of the inquisitorial office, keeping regular accounts and transmitting them to Rome.

The tensions of various elements present in the relations between Ordinaries and the judges of faith are evident in the retreat of the Congregation from this involvement of the bishops in the nomination of the trustees only one year later when, in 1575, without further mention of the bishops, it deliberated definitively that such appointments were to be the exclusive preserve of the inquisitors.[49] This decision was taken while, on the one hand, the cardinals had begun to assign ordinary fixed incomes to the local courts and, on the other, to regulate the forms and the occasions of monetary punishments, setting controls and limits to their use and disciplining the impetuous surge of construction in the various Italian localities. It was in these same decades that the Holy Office established consistent exemptions in favour of local courts, forbidding the taxation of their real property and exempting from any tax all communications directed to them by the Congregation.[50]

These were both important aids for the local courts, though for different reasons: in the course of the most intense period of the war waged throughout Catholic Europe against heretics during the sixteenth century, the local Italian courts of faith had been accumulating a notable patrimony in property, especially through the confiscation of that of the condemned; on the other hand, postal expenses were to be a constant major item in court budgets for the entire early modern age. It was not by chance that the privilege of exemption from postal tax – which in a number of Italian states infringed the prerogatives of the Prince's treasury – became one of the main grounds of the secular, "civic", battle against the Inquisition which eventually led to the first eighteenth-century suppressions.[51]

Though it was still hesitant and contradictory, at the end of the sixteenth century an administrative principle whose symbolic importance was not less than its practical value had been established: inquisitors must keep orderly financial accounts, separate from their correspondence files and, especially, from the transcripts of trials and these accounts must be submitted to central control. In this manner, the economic dimension of the Office of Faith acquired a separate and specific documentary identity. In the cases we are able to reconstruct with some precision today, the location of the patrimonial and financial papers of the local Inquisitions which enable us to see clearly that, in the long run, this principle was generally respected.

This is the case, for example, in Milan, where the inquisitors kept the folders containing documents regarding their property in real estate, pensions and bequests in a "cupboard" built into the wall of the sacristy to the penitential chapel of the convent of Santa Maria delle Grazie. The "Holy Office Archive" was, instead separate; it was discovered when the Inquisition was suppressed, "divided into one hundred wooden containers of middling size [...] of which 94 numbered on the outside by temporal period, beginning with the year 1314 and ending with 1764". And, in Ancona, the inquisitor declared as early as 1609 that he noted all items of income and all expenditures of his office "in a special little book".[52] From the papacy of Paul V, the Congregation began keeping the accounts of each peripheral court separate and gave its fiscal officer the task of reviewing their expenses.[53]

Although the Ministry in Rome, as it now emerges from the organization of the Holy Office Archives, did not keep a specifically numbered documentary category just for the accounts of its peripheral courts, it did file carefully these periodic reports in the folders devoted to their general management. The rule imposing the regular transmission of annual accounts to Rome – though not always rigorously observed[54] – introduced a habit of management in the Inquisition which undoubtedly limited the decisional power which local judges had exercised in the accumulation and management of money, obliging them, at the same time, to cope with bookkeeping problems for which they were usually ill-prepared. It is, then, not surprising to see one of the editions of Matthias Kramer's manual, *The Bank Secretary* ("*Il Segretario di Banco*") and the anonymous *Letters Regarding the Study of Commerce* ("*Lettere sopra lo studio del commercio*"), shelved next to Eymerich's *Directorium inquisitorum* and Prospero Farinacci's *Praxis et theorica criminalis* in the libraries of inquisitors.[55]

A key operational component of the Inquisition was, of course, the active, engaged, participation of the Franciscan and Dominican "families". Since the Middle Ages these two mendicant organizations held the privilege of serving the cause of religious orthodoxy due to their centralized organizational structure, their capillary presence in the urban centres most permeable to the circulation of heterodox ideas and books, their consistent fidelity to papal policies and the high cultural profile of many of their most visible exponents who were, over the centuries, renowned theologians, teaching scholars and preachers. From the early years of the sixteenth century, it had been the Superior Generals of the two Orders who chose the inquisitors and the extraordinary commissioners destined to defend the orthodoxy of the Catholic faith. This task had subsequently been taken over by the Congregation of the Holy Office, within whose organization – both at the Roman centre and at the level of local seats – the preaching fathers always remained dominant. Less present at the various decisionary levels were the Minor Conventuals, the only part of the Franciscan "family" engaged with continuity over time in the justice of faith. The number of courts assigned to them was small compared to the number managed by Dominicans; their number, importance and continuity of representation were also scarce within the ranks of the Ministry in Rome. The prestigious post of Secretary of the Congregation of the Index was always covered by one of the Dominicans. Even for the task of guaranteeing continuity in the procurement of qualified personnel for the Inquisition's managerial necessities, the popes were quick to establish the criteria that friars who had posts in Holy Office courts should benefit from this situation for advancement in their career within their Order. Finally, an obligatory, fixed, minimum of years of service in the post of local inquisitor dissuaded those who thought to take on this position only as a stepping stone in a rapid ascent to the post of Provincial.[56]

We have seen, as well, that the close links between the Holy Office and the Mendicant Orders were of decisive importance in the efficient economic management of the structure of repression. The convents were the material hosts of the inquisitors in the forms we have seen, acting as the lungs inhaling and exhaling monetary air – from which they, too, drew significant economic advantages. When a fellow friar who was an inquisitor died, his convent competed with the Holy Office in the disposal of his patrimony: a procedure, as we have seen, of great sensitivity, fraught with potential controversy; so much so that, in Turin, the popes definitively assigned the patrimonies of all friars who died outside convent walls (*"extra claustra"*) within the territories of the Duke of Savoy to the Inquisition.[57] Indeed, it seems that convent superiors did not always look favourably on the conferral upon their friars of inquisitorial responsibilities – even as vicariates – because of the negative effects which might sometimes ensue for the gathering of alms and, more generally, for the image of the monastic structure itself. On a number of occasions the Congregation found itself obliged to fight the attempts of the Orders to transfer inquisitors from one convent to another for reasons which were not always transparent.[58]

The persistence of this discordant counterpoint of internal requirements and partisan interests soon prompted the popes to attempt regulation of the relations between the Inquisition and the convents. From 1550, it had been decreed that all those who preached must expressly criticize Lutheran doctrines in their sermons and that whoever should abstain from so doing would be tried on suspicion of heresy: the following year the Congregation decided that the costs of the trials and the prison expenses of accused friars were to be covered by their respective Orders, in the attempt – not necessarily successful, as we shall soon see – to destroy the solidarity between culprits and their brethren.[59]

But it was Gregory XIII who resolved the important question of the position due to inquisitors within the hierarchic structure of the convent, establishing – as Father Giacomo Angarano da Vicenza would tersely put it in the normative synthesis he penned in the mid-seventeenth century – that, with the sole exception of the host convent's prior, "the inquisitor must receive immediate precedence in every situation".[60] Sixtus V, who was himself an expert inquisitor and a Minor Conventual, only a few weeks into his pontificate formulated a general directive aimed at disciplining the relations between inquisitors and convents which, from its very first paragraph took on the question of money:

> The money of the Holy Office is to be in the hands of a faithful and secure depositary, and when [the inquisitors] need money for the service

of the Holy Office, they are to emit a warrant in which the manner in which [the funds] are to be spent is stated: this [document] is to remain in the hands of the depositary.[61]

The punctilious document also fixed the basic structure of the local inquisitorial offices, with particular reference to the organizational and operative situations involving the convents. It was thus established that the inquisitors could not have their own "family [i.e. household] separate from [their] fellow brothers", except for a cleric and a lay brother (that is a secular servant who acted also as prison guard); for other positions – including that of notary – the judges of faith were to use personnel drawn from the friars in the convent in which they resided.

Any appointment of vicars for peripheral inquisitors must be approved by the Suprema, Sixtus continued, ordering the judges of faith to "pattern themselves in conformity to other friars" in observing the Rule of their Order "in way of life as in clothing and shunning any singularity", since they continued to be subject to the rule of obedience to their superiors, who were at liberty to command them as they might any other brother. Inquisitors were further ordered: not to keep a horse for riding "in the ordinary way, for this will keep them more stably at home and they shall be free of the expense"; to spend no useless money on construction or on furniture for (existing) chambers, conserving with care, instead, whatever was inventoried at the moment of entry into service. Gifts in money, whether to lay persons or to members of the clergy, were forbidden as was the acceptation of any viaticum when leaving a post to assume another elsewhere. It was equally forbidden to keep supplies of food and wine in Inquisition Chambers; "if they house prisoners there [with them]", the rules declared, referring to the judges of faith:

> they can provide them on a day-to-day basis with some soup or victuals of the convent such as the brothers normally eat, paying the just price; and in the event that they should have a goodly number of prisoners, they may order from the convent cook whatever may be required for [them] to eat, without setting up a separate kitchen.

Convent structures were openly solicited to support the Holy Office in one of its most costly and complicated incumbencies – the provision of meals for prisoners and the storage of the supplies of food required. Sixtus' regulations forbid inquisitors to feed or house witnesses participating in the trials and imposed upon them to "avoid energetically too much familiarity" with lay persons, and clergy both regular and cloistered; where possible, they were to gather the information necessary for a trial through the use of deputized "vicars". A further sign of the "immobilization" of the peripheral inquisitor into a uniform "terminal" of central power may be seen in the rule Sixtus included in his operational manual prohibiting judges and their vicars from leaving the city in which they operated "in the course of prosecution, if not obliged", preferring always the convocation of those to be examined at the convent. From that moment, the payment of the expenses of convocation of witnesses – postal as well as for detention – and other expenses linked to the trials were regulated, and the requirement that judges of faith forward to Rome "the names of prisoners and the number of days held, and, analogously, that the tortures and punishment and other extraordinary expenses for which the poor are unable to pay" be made explicit. Finally, the courts of faith were forbidden to impose payment of the cost of trials or the copy of the transcripts and sentences, reiterating the obligation to submit the accounts of the local courts to the Congregation and to await their approval before undertaking extraordinary payments.

Sixtus' detailed procedural code overhauled and rearticulated the structure of the Curia, reforming the system of the Congregations, this was to be the managerial template of the Roman Inquisition courts until the very moment of their suppression nearly 300 years later. The code manual was sent out periodically to the cardinal protectors and the heads of the Orders as a sort of silent "rap on the knuckles". Indeed, the note accompanying the document opened with a brisk: "Most reverend father, Your Reverence will make known to all inquisitors of your Order that the money of the Holy Office must be placed in the hands of a trusted and secure Depositary".[62]

Yet such decisions could not alone confront and resolve so complex a problem. The serious difficulties still unresolved in the relations between the Inquisition and the convents emerged sharply from a long letter Sixtus V – as Supreme Inquisitor – had his clerk send to the preachers' General in December of 1588:

> Our Lord having been informed that the inquisitors of religion of San Domenico, with the Holy Office's warrant, allege themselves to be entirely immune to [the obligation of] obedience to their superiors; do not want to obey like the other [brothers], nor serve the Rule, going forth from the monasteries [at will], with no one knowing where they go, and causing their companions – vicars, notaries, and other ministers – to fail in like manner, a great lassitude in obedience to the Rule ensues, with disservice to God and scandal among those who are close by; and that, on the other hand, the inquisitors complain that they cannot carry out the tasks of their Office because of the odd quirks of their regular Superiors, and the uncertainty they might displease princes and gentlemen and [bring] general hate upon the convent – but, instead, are often hindered and numerous difficulties are created by their very Superiors; [when] because his Office obliges him, [the inquisitor] must institute investigation of some brothers of his Order, under the pretext of customs and the observance of the Rule, [the inquisitor/s] are persecuted so that they may not live in peace, save by abandoning procedures against their brethren: which is what it has greatly displeased His Holiness to learn has occurred.[63]

The intricate web of problems which was the result of centuries of interrelations between the Inquisition and Mendicant Orders, had, in the decades in which the Holy Office had not hesitated to prosecute – alongside the bishops – authoritative figures at all levels of the regular hierarchies, become so intricate as to allow little further play. The judges of faith – whose economic relations with the convents were decisive for the efficiency of their courts – challenged the discipline of obedience and monastic life under the Rule, enraging the superiors. Yet the difficult problem of the spread of heresy within the Orders (as well as that of the protection which, inside their jurisdiction, could shield heretically inclined brothers) led to the fear that inquisitors, operating in such contiguity and communion of interests with the convents, might find themselves entangled by superiors in endless pretexts. The Congregation addressed a strongly worded "request" to the Dominican General asking him to inform the Provincials and the Priors of his Order that they were to make every effort to support the work of the Inquisition, assuring him that, in exchange, its own local personnel would submit to convent discipline. At the same time, the Congregation explicitly affirmed that inquisitors who failed to prosecute their own brethren were to be punished.[64]

The institution of organic logistic, economic and organizational links between the Inquisition and the monastic Orders produced, then, the formulation of regulations and an increasingly detailed control over convent life in the latter half of the sixteenth century. This process multiplied the practical traffic between the sphere of the justice of faith and that of life under the Rule: the continual overlapping of functions at Santa Maria delle Grazie in Milan – where on land belonging to the convent, in 1608 new prisons were built and new apothecaries, chambers for the prior and door keeper, a hay loft, stalls and a room with a printing press, all of which indifferently occupied and used by the convent or by the Inquisition – offers an excellent example.[65]

We find further proof in documents like the deliberation signed by Urban VIII on February 10, 1633, three days before the illustrious Pisan scientist Galileo Galilei arrived in Rome to be tried by the Holy Office; with this decision the Pope bestowed land which had been bequeathed to the Minor Observant Friars of Livorno to the Inquisition in Pisa.[66] We have, as well, new dispositions emanated by the pontiffs (specifically in their capacity as Head of the Holy Office) which expressed the day-to-day reality of the Orders under the supreme authority of the Inquisition in terms that became increasingly explicit. This trend is clearly evident in the provisions to guarantee the moral profile of those accepted by the Orders and the behaviour of friars within their convents. Among these is a decree emitted by Sixtus V as head of the Congregation in September, 1578: "to the end that they [i.e. the friars] may not perform *comoedias* under any pretext; and so that there may not be received among the brothers thieves, assassins, killers, homicides, falsifiers and other like persons".[67] Taking over a long-term process aimed at eroding monastic and conventual prerogatives (which the Church of Rome had already begun to pursue at the height of the medieval period), the Inquisition in the full Counter Reformation could not tolerate even marginal discretion in the local seats of its capillary repressive apparatus.

Among the reasons which might create conflict between the Inquisition and the Mendicant Orders was the ambiguity of the financial relations in which both were involved; an ambiguity which, as we have seen, was, in turn, an integral element in the administrative model on whose foundations the Holy Office stood. "It has always been the custom that the convents where inquisitors dwell bear the expenses usual to the Inquisition itself without any special recognition", the Congregation could baldly declare to its justice of faith in Faenza in 1594.[68] Still, not everywhere did the money move from the latter to the former between inquisitors and convents, as was the case in which when their credit was passive or extraordinary expenses loomed, judges of faith turned to the treasury of their Orders. The inquisitors might, in turn, give money to convents in difficulty without always informing Rome that they had done so.

This type of transfer – displacing Inquisition funds in favour of the convents – was very often motivated by logics and events deriving from the development of specific, local relationships among friars; unfortunately, surviving documentation offers us little aid in reconstructing such situations. Still we do have, again, the dense material, as well as an ephemeral network of exchange connecting the structures of the Holy Office and of the Orders; making them, willy-nilly, interdependent. It was, for example, only after the death of an inquisitor that the Holy See discovered, as it did in the 1630s for Brescia, that he had lent 300 scudi to his convent; this moved Rome to command his successor to recover the money and redistribute it to needy local Inquisition courts. Contextually, a vicar was appointed to investigate the expenses of the deceased Brescian inquisitor: a notable expense of 250 scudi thus came to light, of which 60 had been spent on a walnut cupboard for the local Dominican convent (which now claimed it as its own): "it seems best to leave it to them", opined the Congregation in a conciliatory tone, "since the expense of 60 scudi for such use seems excessive".[69] Again, the money which, in the same years, the deceased inquisitor in Padua had paid into "the treasury of this convent" – and which, therefore, to all intents and purposes, belonged to the Dominican order, was assigned by Rome to the payment of still outstanding arrears in salaries and debts incurred by the deceased inquisitor "to serve [his] Office".[70] This is a further example of the flexible distinction between the Inquisition's treasury and the treasury of the convent in which it was housed – besides demonstrating the unwavering decisional supremacy exercised by Rome in the resolution of situations which might give rise to serious conflicts.

The pressure exercised upon the convent by local inquisitors to secure margins of operative independence, their tendency to distinguish themselves and to isolate themselves from the fraternal community, the appropriation by the Inquisition of collaborators and bureaucrats who, according to the precepts of the Canon, were to be chosen among the brothers. All these were, in turn, organizational aspects of the justice of faith viewed askance by the Priors and Guardians, who were guarantees of the respect and tranquillity of regular life. A frequent cause of discord was constituted by the inquisitor's need to call upon the brothers who participated unwaveringly in their work – serving as notaries, vicars, clerks, simply aides or theological consultants – without regard for the concomitant violation of the prescribed timetable of convent life. Superiors might react with forms of opposition or retaliation; they might refuse to contribute to the inquisitor's keep and to eventual supplements to the honorarium paid to convent friars working for the local Inquisition.

To block such controversies, the Congregation had already deliberated in the early years of the seventeenth century that convents in which an inquisitor operated were to provide for his maintenance and for that of his collaborators, guaranteeing them the same material conditions as those enjoyed by fellow brethren. The convents were also charged with paying any extraordinary fees which might arise for the notary and the lay brother who served the inquisitor. However another disposition, accepted by the General Chapters of the Orders in 1611, provided that friars assisting the inquisitors, when not wholly occupied in that capacity, were to be considered wholly at the disposition of the convent and that the judges of faith could not, therefore make a habit of calling upon collaborators in hours dedicated to religious duties. None of these general agreements between the Holy Office and the Orders ever limited in any way the decisional prerogatives of the Congregation concerning the local use and the transferal of inquisitors – even when they were assigned to posts not directly within the area of faith Offices. To give a single illustrative example: the concession of a permit allowed the Inquisitor of Belluno to reside "outside the ecclesiastical convent ['*extra ecclesia conventus*'] to serve as Director of the Office for the Poor".[71]

In the seventeenth century, the Roman Inquisition had, then, established a juridical tradition and an operative stance in its interaction with the Orders and their leadership at various levels that were conciliatory and circumspect. Small exchanges of goods and services between inquisitors and convents began to be carefully monitored and recorded by Rome, where the Congregation of the Holy Office ended up dedicating considerably more attention to this area than it conceded to most of the trials prosecuted by local judges whose transcripts were to be referred on to the Holy See only in especially complex cases ("*in arduis causis*").[72] In practice this meant, for example, that the Dominican convent in Crema had to apply for a special authorization from Rome to provide its resident inquisitor with medicines and his lay brother; or that the Franciscan Guardian in Adria relinquish his "habitual incumbency" in favour of the Holy Office's local vicar, along with the wood, the oil and the candles the convent habitually lent the inquisitor and his vicar in the course of their activities.[73]

Ad hoc negotiations established the division of expenses for the maintenance of prisoners who were members of an Order: in their context, the Roman cardinals decided not to weigh upon the convent treasury, but, rather, to seek out forms of partial refunding and of payment in instalments over time. Therefore, in the 1600s the Inquisition in Pavia was ordered to avoid billing the Franciscan Order for the expenses involved in the prosecution and trial of the Minor Observant Friar Bartolomeo da Castiglione, since "their convent has no property at all"; "in all like situations", the Office, however, dryly advised its local inquisitor, in the future "your reverence may so dispose that the convent shall provide, day-to-day the necessary meals, such as the other friars [in the convent] eat".[74]

In its first century of existence, the Holy Office's recognition of the situation of nearly absolute power and independence which the inquisitors enjoyed was accompanied by the imposition of severe controls aimed at protecting the power, independence, efficiency and secrecy of the enterprise which was the justice of faith. This was accomplished while the leadership of the Orders were invited by the highest authorities of Catholicism – in accents which made no room for reply – to recognize the priority of the war against heresy and to accept as a consequence the inquisitor's right to pre-eminence in exchange for a more or less blanket recognition of the legitimacy of prevailing hierarchies within convents. Rome required its judges, as it harshly informed the Inquisitor of Venice in 1578, to "dedicate [yourself] to your Office of the Inquisition with that diligence which is necessary and abstain from becoming entangled in convent affairs and in its government: knowing that you will have done just as you should, as you will have satisfied (as you must) the duties of the Office which are sufficient to keep you busy, without getting mixed up in other things".[75]

Yet the will to calm or immediately dispel possible conflicts between inquisitors and convents did not imply that the various protagonists might forget the existence of a hierarchy of powers which had become a "given": "This holy Congregation considers it crucial that, for the proper service of God and the court, there subsist between the father inquisitors and the priors of the convents where they reside that friendly exchange and peace which is natural to the religious". Rome could write to the Venetian inquisitor some 50 years later in the context of a policy of "soft" relations which did not, however, mean to become acquiescence "when, in some particular instance the contrary should occur, we should be advised [of it], so that proper remedies may be applied".[76]

The construction of an ethos

We have now considered in some detail key aspects of the normative structures which the leadership of the Catholic Church in Rome set up to consolidate and strengthen the network of courts gathered under the direction of the Congregation of the Holy Office in the mid-1500s to resolve a series of problems deriving from the administration of the inquisitorial "enterprise". The structure and managerial procedures of the Roman Inquisition in the early modern period were not, however, established only by a normative structure that was stable and valid over time; it was, instead, in continual evolution through a process of capillary memos, reminders, critiques, appeals to tradition and recommendations, both moral and practical. Over centuries, a myriad of informal ties sprang up around the local decisions of the peripheral inquisitors acting day after day, backed by the attentive management of the Sacred College – allowing it to extend the activity and the real presence of officially promulgated norms (and making them more flexible and responsive to particular situations and needs).

This constant prescriptive groundswell, of which we shall now attempt to give some examples within the economic field, laboriously shaped the material and moral procedures of the inquisitors and their offices during the whole of the Counter Reformation era. Within the single units of the Inquisition's territorial network, a common ethos slowly filtered down, layer upon layer, as well as behavioural codes accepted by the friars and their immediate interlocutors without whose respect the Holy Office could hardly have continued to maintain at such length in its strong social roots and the substantial participation of an ample part of the population of the *Ancien régime*.

In the very delicate area of the gathering and investment of money, the Congregation of the Holy Office went far beyond promulgating general rules valid for all its courts. During the entire period we are considering, the process of ethical consolidation of the inquisitorial structure had, indeed, one of its most significant manifestations in the organization of interventions of "moral suasion" on the part of the leading figures of the Roman hierarchy, aimed at producing "good habits" of economic management in the local organs of the justice of faith. Although, as we have already seen, questionable links might exist between the way in which a trial turned out and the potential economic advantage it in fact produced, and however much (or because?) the inquisitor might be conditioned by a managerial model rife with incentives to prefer certain types of penal action over others, on a number of occasions the Congregation made it a point to intervene to block sentences it found dubious due to their pecuniary advantages for local inquisitors. In 1626, disavowing the intentions of the inquisitor in Piacenza, Rome succeeded in blocking the release of Matteo Gatti and Battistino di Carpinato, two condemned heretics from whom a conspicuous fine might have been forthcoming, "and the means of providing your reverence with the 100 scudi you wish to have to complete [your] construction, are not easily discovered"; still, the writer concluded, "thought shall, however, be given to how some aid may be offered you".[77] A fundamental element in assuring the financial correctness and the transparency of relations between inquisitors and the population was the prohibition to engage in monetary transactions – to "do business" – with anyone who had been involved in cases considered by the courts;[78] a practice which, however – as we have seen – was not always respected by the cardinals themselves in the inquisitorial activities they themselves prosecuted.

The orders from Rome which obliged the local judges of faith to make good personally any misappropriations or embezzlements on the part of their collaborators were part of this policy of responsabilization of local courts. In the seventeenth century, for example, the Bishop of Civita Castellana was urged to intervene directly to repay one Dedalo Fortunato "monies wrongfully extorted by your vicar on behalf of the Holy Office [...] and should he not comply within said term, lay it upon him as a duty under serious penalties, as well as others at the will of the Congregation itself [...] as we desire to proceed at all costs to indemnify the speaker".[79] Besides the embarrassing task of obliging a dishonest subordinate to give back money improperly acquired, it was the local inquisitor who was usually delegated to remove from office vicars who had embezzled funds.[80] The Suprema acted directly only in cases where the sum required to cover the dishonesty of local inquisitors was too large for peripheral finances in 1583, for example, it was obliged to refund David Lunello, a Jew residing in Cuneo, 100 gold scudi "for damages sustained to books and objects of his" confiscated by the Pavia inquisitor in forms that were, evidently, illicit.[81]

The unease Rome felt concerning the use of money by the inquisitors and the relative persuasive measures taken to make economic activity as transparent as possible, was not limited to the judicial context. On various occasions Rome reminded its inquisitors that friars who, as inquisitors, received donations or post-mortem bequests had the obligation to cover the expenses of their positions and all their duties, however minute, including frequently, the celebration of regular masses, or of masses in suffrage, keeping chapels and altars clean and in good repair, giving alms or guaranteeing the feeding or the necessities of life for the poor, the ill and the orphaned.[82] Moreover, in situations in which conflicts sprang up between the inquisitors and the local population concerning the management of land and buildings belonging to the Holy Office (which might range from boundary squabbles to the management of irrigation canals or agricultural leases), the Suprema invariably invited inquisitors to maintain "that care which justice requires". As the directive addressed to the Inquisitor of Milan put it in the course of a case posed by the refusal of a certain Cesare Luini to pay part of the expense of keeping a canal carrying common water running between his terrain and the Milan court's property in good repair. Showing a decisiveness which in itself, testifies to the importance of such problems within the economic and symbolic world of the time, and so to their potential negative repercussions on the court's reputation and that of its exponents, Luini did not hesitate to defy the Milanese inquisitor addressing a memorandum to the cardinals of the Suprema in which he complained that he had been forced to pay expenses for which he had no legal obligation. And the cardinals immediately gave instructions to the inquisitor as to how he should resolve what was only apparently a banal squabble, without prejudice for the public image of the institution.[83]

Within this same spectrum of "image preoccupations" were Roman policies aimed at enhancing the Office's respectability through the attentive protection of its financial reputation and its fame of solubility. "The Holy Congregation is pleased by the urgency with which your reverence has extinguished this debt", the Inquisitor of Tortona is commended[84] in reference to the payment in bills of exchange received by Rome. In this same logic, risky financial operations were discouraged by decrees instructing inquisitors on how to invest in eventual budgetary surpluses. Whenever an inquisitor found himself with strong liquidity, perhaps as the result of the recovery of a credit from some debtors, Rome granted him "permission to liquidate the deed and recover the money so that it may be deposited with the amounts previously identified when you do not find a way to use them in property equally solid, and having good security".[85]

In brief, the Roman Inquisition "firm" developed over time an ever stronger consciousness of the positive connection between good economic management, correct relations with the subjects whose interests were close to – or even the same as – its own, a reputation for financial solvency and the fostering of public consensus within the various social ranks and institutional subjects of the *Ancien régime* communities. Cultivating diplomacy and discernment, administering carefully and transparently the patrimony with which he was entrusted, the local inquisitor – territorial representative of the good name and the prestige of the Roman Congregation as an entity – embodied the mission of the Office of Faith as much as he did when directly engaged in carrying out the justice of faith in his court.

It is with this broader optic, and not merely as mere patrimonial solicitude, that we must view the frequent reminders urging local inquisitors to be precise and diligent in administering properties acquired over the years and stimulating them to "proceed in the negotiations left hanging [in your jurisdiction]" – as the Office prompted the Inquisitor of Como in the 1600s – "succeeding in getting in hand the monies owed as soon as possible, and once you have exacted it, look to it to invest it as you ought, according to the instructions laid out in the apostolic memorandum we have already sent you". "And when you should find yourself unable to lay hold upon the money", concluded the Congregation, "at least do not fail to recover the lands [which have been] sold, so that this Holy Office risk not finding itself without the real estate and without its price in coin".[86]

Even commercial relations between the Inquisition and religious entities were to be founded upon an affability which did not forego claiming forcefully what was due after having in vain "used all the most urbane of tones" with the Procurator of the Jesuit *Collegio di Brera* to convince him to contribute to the expenses of modifying the banks of the canal irrigating the Office's property, the inquisitor in Milan was then urged to "insist upon his rights" by appealing to the competent courts.[87] Yet, at the same time, Rome might advise the Inquisitor of Perugia that, to the Suprema, it had "not seemed well done to cause the money usually distributed each year by the [Apostolic] Chamber to various persons of this city as Castellans of certain towers [to be] assigned to the Inquisition",[88] recalling the exigency that the war for the orthodoxy of the faith should be waged, even within the borders of the Church's state, in the context of stable and correct economic and institutional relations.

Roman, Spanish and Portuguese inquisitions: compared economies

Let us now attempt a synthetic comparison between what we have seen of the economic behaviour of the Holy Office in Italy and what we know today in the same area in so far as regards to the Spanish and Portuguese Inquisitions. The other European countries never experienced institutions directly comparable to the Inquisitions in Catholic, Mediterranean, areas although, before the French Revolution, ecclesiastical authorities and the secular governments, as well, almost everywhere in the West set up institutional controls of doctrinal orthodoxy and religious practice which could inflict punishment and even bloodshed.[89]

From the monumental and indispensable work of Henry Charles Lee, the Spanish Inquisition – in virtue, too, of its superior preservation of the documentary sources – has been the object of detailed research. The administrative models of the Spanish Inquisition, instead, despite (or, perhaps, due to) the overwhelming quantity of surviving documents, are still largely to be research.[90] Its creation in 1542 makes the Congregation of the Holy Office the last of the three Mediterranean Inquisitions to be instituted: it is more than 60 years younger than Spain's (1478), though only a few years younger than Portugal's (1536). The sequence of this chronology is not irrelevant when it came to deciding how their Inquisition should be organized and administered, the mid-sixteenth century popes and the Roman Curia could take into account the advantages – but also the problems and the limits – which, at least for the Spanish Inquisition, were by then evident. The organizational structures of the Holy Office and its Portuguese counterpart, instead, developed more or less in parallel, though with important differences.

First among these differences were, of course, their juridical and statutory structures. The Roman Holy Office drew its canonical and jurisdictional – as well as its theoretic and spiritual – legitimacy directly from the Pope and from him alone (and, in a subordinate measure, from the Cardinals of the Congregation, of which he was the Head) and it answered only to them. The Spanish and Portuguese Inquisitions, instead, were born – and remained for as long as they existed – as instruments of the secular policy of kings, politically and institutionally subject to the two Crowns, which obtained their institution, respectively, from Pope Sixtus IV (1478) and Paul III (1536). This did not, however, mean that they were fully State courts: the authority and the jurisdiction of their inquisitors derived from Rome as well as from their kings, for without the chrism of canonical legitimation they could neither have been created nor could operate.

Once they had secured the Pope's permission to create a Hispanic Holy Office under their control – chiefly to the end of acting, using the pretext of prosecutions in defence of the faith, against converted Jews – the Catholic Monarchs of the first, terrible, years of activity, based their administrative structure upon the medieval model of itinerant ecclesiastical inquisitors. A few years later, in 1484, a new central directorate was created: the Council for the Supreme and General Inquisition [*"Consejo de la Suprema y General Inquisición"*] was on the same level as the other administrative councils serving the Spanish Crown. It was presided by an Inquisitor General – Tomás de Torquemada, still famous today, the first to hold the post – who drew his legitimacy and authority from the pope, from whom he received his powers after he had been chosen by both monarchs.

Therefore, the early modern Spanish court of faith was born as the result of an institutional link between ecclesiastical jurisdiction and State power; indeed, it was precisely its nature as an ecclesiastical court controlled by the State which made it a highly supple and powerful repressive tool, able to break out of the canons of medieval norms to operate with striking harshness and great liberty of action. As a consequence, Henry Kamen, an authoritative contemporary historian of the Spanish Inquisition, has construed its operative structure as fruit of a "plural headship" at once secular and religious, deriving from differentiated centres of power. As the Hispanic Suprema's fiscal officer recalled in a memorandum to its members as late as 1817, at its heart was the pact of union constituted by "the Royal and Apostolic jurisdiction".[91] All the officers of the Spanish Inquisition were considered ministers of the monarch and, as such, their salaries were paid by the sovereign. With the creation of the Council, the monarchs delegated to it the temporal jurisdiction and the economic direction of the Inquisition "business", appointing an Accountant General who brought together the various accounts of the local offices which collaborated with the inquisitors in their prosecutions, above all, as we shall soon see, when the confiscation of property was involved.

The popes continued to have and to exercise a notable power of intervention on the Spanish Inquisition: the bull with which, in 1520, Leo X imposed the resignation en masse of all officers and dismissed all of the clerks and other personnel – with the sole exception of the Inquisitor General, Adriano di Utrecht – is a striking example. In attempting to put control into the hands of the Ordinaries and the diocesan Chapters (as well as, taking into account the complaints of the *conversos* (converted Jews), to limit the recourse to confiscation, to moralize the use of money and to reply to the accusations of Cisneros, Regent of Castile, who declared that Leo X meant "to sell the Catholic faith"), the Pope aimed at regulating the selection of Spanish inquisitorial personnel stringently, destroying conflicts of interest even when professional, and punishing corruption and extortion with severity. It is not without significance that in some surviving Vatican codex, Leo X's bull *Pro Sancto Officio Inquisitionis Hispaniarum* was included already in the sixteenth-century compendia of Decrees by Congregation popes dealing with the organization of the Roman *Officium fidei* – testifying to the contemporary perception of a continuity between the organizational interventions of the Medici Pope and the later efforts to predispose the Italian Inquisiton's management.[92]

Creating the Congregation of the Holy Office and, in the following decades, consolidating and regulating its activity and local and central financing, the apostolic See must, then, have taken the Spanish experience into account in some measure. This antecedent had, of course, already given rise to significant repercussions on the organizational and financial model of the Portuguese Inquisition, whose administrative structure was modelled on Spain's, with, however, significant adjustments in the areas of finance and confiscation.

What, then, were the fundamental characteristics of the economic model of the Spanish Inquisition between the end of the 1400s and the early 1500s? We know that the sovereigns, Isabella and Ferdinand, in instituting their Inquisition – as a component of the material and symbolic edification of the monarchy as a guide of the reconquered Spanish nation – did not expect the court to be financially autonomous, but that it should bring the State new funds, deriving them chiefly from confiscation of the patrimonies of the converted Jews. To this end, the sovereigns openly and decisively excluded any requests for assignment to Rome of a portion of confiscated wealth or funds deriving from monetary punishments. When the first Spanish inquisitors were invited to Seville in 1480, they were not assigned any guaranteed income, they were however, assigned royally appointed officers who would accompany them to their posts and remain with them as receivers of confiscated property. It was certainly due to the strong and constant pressures of the royal treasury that, in Spain, inquisitorial usage for many decades included routine confiscation of property even in cases of abjuration and subsequent reconciliation of the culprits. And this was the case even though the official sentences often failed to record it: whether because confiscation was taken for granted, or when – as would occur later in some Italian states like Milan – a local public magistrate (the "*alcalde*") had simply pocketed it.

Only in the case of spontaneous presentation within the so-called "period of grace", having abjured and denounced their accomplices, the culprits might enjoy reconciliation, saving themselves not merely from imprisonment, but from confiscation. For the Spanish Inquisition, outside the period of grace, for many years there was no possibility for the culprits to save themselves from confiscation. In this, as we shall see in the chapters which follow, the Roman Inquisition was to differ notably. The greater fiscal harshness of the Spanish Holy Office played a fundamental role in the popular demonstrations which broke out in Milan and Naples in the late 1500s at the prospect of an extension of its jurisdiction into Italy where, as we have seen, the Roman "mode" prevailed.[93]

The detailed studies of Henry Charles Lea have shown how, at the moment of arrest, the Spanish Inquisition at once discovered and inventoried the lands belonging to the culprit. This phase should not be confused with that of the actual confiscation which – at least in the Italian context – was, necessarily, subsequent to the sentence of the court of faith. Among Roman inquisitorial practices, however, we find no indications of that successive phase which the Spanish system called "Household Hearing" ("*audiencia de hacienda*"), during which the culprit was closely questioned under oath as to the entity of his properties, his debts and credits, what his matrimonial accords entailed; endowments received or granted; donations received or given; and eventual transferals of property in favour of offspring. The Spaniard who found himself under investigation was also obliged to declare formally that he had not hidden any asset in view of the arrest and any refusal to answer questions posed in this preliminary phase of the trial of faith fully and sincerely was viewed as false testimony. In Spain there were even cases in which the confessors of those condemned to death spent the final night before execution exhorting them to reveal any remaining bits of property which might not have been discovered in previous investigations. In the early decades of the persecution of the *conversos*, the Spanish Inquisition went so far as to offer substantial commissions to those who should furnish information of the property of condemned individuals which had escaped the fiscal officers' investigations, creating as well actual professional "detectives" capable of ferreting out new clues to hidden assets.[94]

An integral part of the original economic physiognomy of the Spanish Inquisition was formed by the income derived from monetary punishments, specifically, the fines – whose entity was largely left to the local inquisitor's fancy and whose payment had to be immediate – and the rarer "penances" ("*penitencia*"), monetary punishments (usually larger) inflicted solemnly on public occasions and auto-da-fé. The Spanish Holy Office, too, could concede "dispensations" or commutations of corporal into monetary punishment; consequently these forms were over decades a source of income less important than confiscations, but far from negligible.

Only after Isabella's death in 1504 did the Spanish Inquisition begin to experience a tendency to see its income from confiscation decline: in 1509 it took in about a tenth of what it had received in 1498. The sporadic nature of local sources makes it impossible to formulate estimates on the financial performance of the Spanish courts from 1480 to 1559, a period in which the existence of the various local offices was still based on income each must autonomously seek out. As Torquemada had laid out in his 1498 *Instructions*, each local court was made up of two inquisitors (a jurist and a theologian, or two jurists), flanked by the usual notaries, medical aides and servants – clerical and operative – whose maintenance required ever greater patrimonies. In Spain, too, the administrative apparatus would grow rapidly, by the end of the 1500s, the most important courts in Spain had three inquisitors each, surrounded by an ample "household". The blatant stripping of Jews and *conversos*, as a direct consequence of the obligation of self-financing and the syphoning of funds into the Crown Treasury imposed upon Spanish inquisitors between the end of the 1400s and the early 1500s, led historians of the Spanish Inquisition to believe that it was the dearth of funds which chiefly spurred its creation and its operation over its early decades.[95]

This troubling scene, together with the bold attempts at reform imposed by Leo X, obliged the sixteenth-century papacy and secular monarchs to reconsider the basic financial structure underpinning the Spanish courts of faith. After an unsuccessful attempt at reform on the part of Clement VII, Paul

III, with a 1536 decree, sanctioned the creation of a Portuguese Inquisition. Among the provisions was a ten-year exemption from confiscations for "New Christians" (*"cristãos novos"*, i.e. converted Jews) condemned to death, whose estates were to be inherited by Catholic relatives in the first degree. In addition, the reigning sovereigns – even when, in the middle decades of the 1500s it became possible for Portuguese inquisitors to execute confiscations of the patrimonies of heretics and new Catholics – unlike the Spanish monarchs did not permit the judges of faith to hold the property which they confiscated, it remained, instead, patrimony of the Crown of which the Inquisitor General was in each separate instance named administrator.

All of these elements obliged the organizational and territorial development of the Portuguese Holy Office to remain within existing local ecclesiastical structures, with the explicit goal of keeping their operating expenses minimal. As in Spain, in Portugal a General Council of the Crown directed the local courts, set up in three large district seats: Lisbon, Évora and Coimbra, to which, later, Goa was added for the Indies. The extension and the operations of the Portuguese Inquisition were very small until 1548, when Paul III, made aware of the material and organizational difficulties of that *Officium fidei*, endowed it with new, more ample, powers.

Creating and aiding the rise of an organizational structure and a territorial network for the Congregation of the Holy Office after winning a sharply waged battle between intransigent and conciliatory factions, which had been raging since the 1530s, Paul III and his immediate successors had, then, two intersecting historic patterns before them. One was the slow, steady dilation of the pontifical feudal structure which had begun to take shape between the eleventh and the thirteenth centuries until, in the late Middle Ages, the Holy See found itself permanently situated as a centre of temporal government and the redistribution of financial resources within the ecclesiastical structures of Christianity.

The process had been consolidated by feudal grants and pontifical benefices, initially pursuant to the construction of the Church State and they were conspicuously methodic and uncoordinated, constituting a sort of weak material and juridical Roman presence scattered across the territory, in whose context "the papacy seems never to have made full use of the tools of feudal law to increase its income and its powers".[96] This general structure would manage the assignment – as we have seen also largely casual and contingent, of ordinary, fixed, income to the Holy Office in the form of benefices. In the 1550s, the experience of central control of the justice of faith in Spain and Portugal offered a second, more recent, point of reference. There the abandonment of the medieval itinerant model of the Inquisition was complete, and could not fail to throw into relief organizational and financial ties – and opportunities – which the Curia, too, would have to consider attentively.

The Spanish sovereigns and their government, spurred by the end of the 1400s to guarantee ethnic purity to the new-born unified Spanish nation –

a problem which, albeit with different motivation, would engage some 50 years later the Roman Church, under siege by the Lutheran Reformers – had not based their Inquisition model on any long-term plan. The very fact that the confiscated wealth of the *conversos* flowed abundantly and constantly into Council coffers did not place the Spanish monarch under any obligation to make plans for an inquisitorial institution which could be guaranteed to function over the long period.

At first, the same, contingent, approach prevailed in Italy as well, as Kamen put it in viewing Spain, we too might say "the most surprising aspect of the administration of the [...] Holy Office is its – often inadequate – financing".[97] If, in 1501, Alexander VI had already tried to guarantee an affixed income deriving from benefices and pensions to all existing Spanish courts of faith, it was only after 1559 that this goal would, gradually, be reached. This was accomplished by Paul IV with a decree – aimed chiefly at freeing the Spanish Inquisition from the direct influence of the Crown – which provided that each court should be assigned annual incomes, to be obtained by the institution of a canonicate financed by all the cathedrals or colleges within the borders of the realm. The stable financial structure of the Spanish Inquisition, and, after the extension of Paul IV's bull, of the Portuguese Inquisition as well, dates from that moment, though the decree had no immediate repercussions in Italy. To achieve analogous provisions stabilizing finances – even if in a disorganized manner – most of the Italian courts had to wait several decades, and some never managed to gain any regular source of income at all.

Within the financial arc of the Spanish and Portuguese Holy Offices – as we have already seen in the Roman Holy Office between the late sixteenth and the early seventeenth centuries – we can discern a progressive accretion of ordinary, fixed, items of annual income, which appear alongside the slow bureaucratization and the physical settling of the Inquisition into the territory. In Spain, this evolution was accompanied by a decline in resorting to confiscation; the court in Llerena, for example, was awarded two canonicates in 1572, yielding 680,000 maravedis per year – a third of the total income of that court in that year; the remainder derived from confiscation.

In Portugal, instead, the effort to institute a new system of mixed financing for the Inquisition, combining confiscation with canonicates, diocesan pensions and royal grants was hindered by legal difficulties arising from the reluctant acquiescence to diocesan pensions. Therefore confiscation continued to be an important category in the annual accounts of the Portuguese Holy Office which, nonetheless, continued to suffer from shortfall compared to the expenses linked to rising salaries and fixed expenses. In the period of dynastic unity (1580–1640), the Portuguese Inquisition found itself, in a constant deficit which the income deriving from Crown Grants was never able to cover. In Spain, too, during the period of the union of the two Crowns, the progressive bureaucratization of the courts of faith saw the complaints of local inquisitors swell progressively at the increasing costs of administering the local offices, prosecuting the trials and keeping the prisoners and carrying out the auto-da-fé. In Granada, where in 1671 the expenses of the court of faith exceeded its income by 3 per cent, by 1705 they topped it by 27 per cent. In Córdoba, the court's indebtedness was chronic: in 1578 expenses were already 14.6 per cent more than income: in 1661 they had reached 33.8 per cent, and, by 1726, they had only been contained to 11.2 per cent.

The local accounts of the Spanish Inquisition were in perennial difficulty precisely because the bureaucracy had, from the second half of the sixteenth century, absorbed a growing portion of income. In Córdoba, whose court of faith counted 26 officials in 1578, salaries absorbed 75.6 per cent of annual income. These were large sums, especially as each court must obligatorily send part of its income to the Suprema to cover its increasingly conspicuous expenses. Indeed, in 1578, the Inquisition in Córdoba had to send the Council about a fifth of its income – for, at the time, this organ was spending about 5,800,000 maravedis in wages each year (including 1,500,000 for the Inquisitor General alone); local inquisitors received, instead, an annual income of about 7,000 maravedis. In Córdoba, an auto-da-fé cost about 2,000,000 maravedis in 1655, a period in which the annual income of that court was about 500,000.[98]

The large number of laws promulgated by the Council in regard to the inquisitorial *hacienda* from the latter half of the sixteenth to the early years of the seventeenth centuries show the difficulty with which, even in Spain, centralization of the economic management of the courts of faith was accomplished. The post of General Accountant ("*contador general*") of the Council was instituted in 1632, with jurisdiction over all the courts in Castile and Aragon. The birth of this position marks a fundamental organizational watershed, because it defined the accounting structure of the Spanish Inquisition throughout the rest of its history until 1820. The Accountant was delegated the centralization and the direction of the inquisitorial "firm", while the Council, from that point onwards, limited itself to promulgating detailed regulations tending to unify the form of presentation of the accounts and fixing in every detail, the role of the officials engaged in the managerial process.[99]

From the scarce information at our disposition today, the financial situations of the components of the Spanish and Portuguese Inquisitions do not appear to have significantly improved after Portugal became, once more, independent and a general debate developed around inquisitorial procedures. In this regard, the polemics regarding confiscation touched off by the Jesuit, Father António Vieira, who exhorted King John IV to use these sums to support the royal treasury, are worth mentioning. In 1655, the King ordered that control over confiscated property should pass into the hands of the Crown Economic Council, stripping the Holy Office of regular income (despite Innocent X's formal annulment of the royal decree with a counter papal decree, largely without practical effect). In 1674, Clement X went so far as to suspend the Portuguese inquisitors from their functions and to take upon himself the cases pending; the Portuguese court of faith resumed its activities only in 1681, continuing to survive, however, only thanks to confiscations and fines. So, at the beginning of the eighteenth century another offensive was launched against the New Christians: although we do not have detailed documentation of its economic results, there is no doubt that it brought significant patrimonial profit to the Portuguese treasury.

That was certainly what happened during the last, great persecution of the *conversos* which, in the decade between 1715 and 1725, terminated the financial crisis in which the Inquisition courts had stagnated. In the mid-eighteenth century, the ebbing of this new wave of persecution would have negative financial repercussions on inquisitorial finances – especially in Portugal, where there were no supporting canonicates and pensions like those on which the contemporary Spanish structure was based. The Marquis of Pombal's Reform, reassumed in the General Regulations of 1774, a year before the annulment of any distinction between old and new Catholic Christians, does not appear to have introduced significant changes in the Portuguese Inquisition's economy in a period which probably brought a new increase of the economic weight of the Crown in its activities until the Inquisition was definitively abolished in 1821.[100]

Between money and social penetration

In Part I of this book we have examined an aspect crucial to the understanding of the Roman Inquisition and its political, social and cultural consequences in the early modern period: the economic regulation of the overall mechanism of the justice of faith and the relations existing within its context between the Holy See and local courts. From this documentation – and the elements its examination have brought to the fore – I think we may now legitimately formulate some interpretations valid over the long period we are considering.

First of all, it seems clear that the birth of the Congregation of the Holy Office and the acute phase of repression of Evangelical and Reformed religious heterodoxy in the central decades of the sixteenth century, occurred without any system of financing and regular control of the administration of economic resources on the part of the peripheral seats: these are traits which would be institutionalized only at a later date – with unquestionable benefit for the efficiency and the transparency of judicial procedures of faith. That means that the debut of the modern Roman Inquisition and the period of radicalization of what may well be termed the mortal challenge of the doctrines of Lutheran derivation, developed without any general system furnishing peripheral courts with a regular monetary income independent of the outcome of prosecutions and trials (an income that would, of its nature, have served, too, as a guarantee of procedural probity for the accused); nor were there clear and respected rules providing controls over income and expenses. The income of the Congregation of the Holy Office itself took on quantitative and qualitative regularity in the final decade of the 1500s with the beginning of efficient management of the Conca estate and the assignment of its income to the Roman Ministry (which marked the emancipation of inquisitorial income from the opaque system of monetary punishment). The painful moments of the sixteenth-century Roman religious war – crucial for Italian history for many subsequent centuries – were characterized by an operational inquisitorial structure distinctly medieval in style, within which the judges of faith acted with ample managerial discretion within the limits of the human and economic resources at their disposition and they maintained indispensable financial and administrative relations with the convents and the Orders to which they belonged.

Throughout the sixteenth century, the inquisitors in many local seats remained without regular, certain, incomes and were thus not only without the highly valuable symbolic and political possibility of reassuring the local population of the independence of their judgements from any pecuniary consideration, but, also, the capacity to program any action in line with the grandiose nature of the mission assigned to them by the highest authorities of Catholicism, the protection of the purity of Catholic, that is to say "universal" doctrine. Only in the 1600s, though with the exceptions we have just noted, did popes and Cardinals Inquisitor apply systematic procedures limiting and controlling the imposing of monetary punishments which – like fines – most easily lent themselves to abuse by local judges. In the first years of the seventeenth century, an Inquisition in many ways strategic like that of Ancona was managed on an income of 60–70 scudi a year, "according to the price of the grain and wine" that could be produced by the benefice of the chapel *della Concezione* in the city's cathedral.[101]

The forms of ascertainment set up in the 1500s and 1600s were made more necessary still by the peculiar nature the early modern inquisitor's office had assumed. For the judge of faith, this structure implied the assumption of significant patrimonial, financial, risks – besides the risks to his good repute – as well as incentives to resort to monetary punishment to reduce these risks and to improve his overall performance within the period of his appointment. Even when, in the late 1500s and early 1600s – and well into the seventeenth century – the Holy See gave its courts of faith a somewhat organic system of finance, the limited amount of capital deriving from the benefices made the inquisitors continue to regard their stable financial bases as insufficient: and to spend virtually the entire sum assigned. The income at the disposal of the individual inquisitors – over the entire 1600, and the early 1700s – remained, then, lower (sometimes much lower) than that of the older and prestigious monastic entities scattered over the territory of the peninsula or that of the families of the aristocratic landowners from which a number of the popes and cardinal inquisitors of the Counter Reformation came.

It seems, therefore, difficult to deny that the resources placed at the disposition of the inquisitorial apparatus by the Holy See in the early modern era, were inadequate for the reach of a repressive project which was expanding in the increasing diversification of the profile pursued. The slowing down, during the 1500s and 1600s, of anti-heretic persecution – and, perhaps, of the seeking out of witchcraft – was counter-weighed by the reoriented (or renewed) prosecution of blasphemers, sodomites, bigamists, Jewish sympathizers, astrologists, "bearers" and "propagators" of popular superstitions, base confessors, scientists, quietists and Jansenists. The very limited consistency of regular, fixed, income at the disposition of the inquisitors may, perhaps, contribute – along with other, juridical or sociocultural factors – to explaining the tendency of the courts to pursue broad categories of crime within the various historic periods. A "sequencing" of the objectives of repression was, perhaps, also due to the need to focalize available resources and, therefore, to concentrate judicial prosecution on groups which were felt to be emergent. Piecemeal attention was abandoned or granted as a direct consequence, to those with which the inquisitorial mechanism felt it had already more or less fully and adequately dealt with in the past.

Why did the popes and the Roman Curia not worry about improving the relationship between inquisitorial intervention and economic resources, finding further, more efficacious, mechanisms to activate money and smooth out the financial imbalances produced by the local offices? Why was the mid-1500s triumph of the intransigent faction of the Roman Curia – and the subsequent development of the extremely harsh extirpation of the Evangelical-Reformed doctrines which altered the religious and cultural face of Italy for centuries – carried out without organizing and financing the inquisitors within a stable and secure framework?

At the moment, these are still open questions, to which we might attempt to furnish a few provisory answers. Given the relative modesty – and, consequently, the ease with which the sums in play might be reformulated, as well as the plurality of potential sources in the hands of the Roman Curia and the Holy Office itself with which Inquisition income might be increased – it seems impossible to invoke a scarcity of resources at the disposition of the Holy See. Still we ought not to forget that the conferral of benefices was, within the historic and cultural coordinates of the time, the most practical way to give a stable living to organisms which – like the Holy Office – were considered permanent entities within the Roman ecclesiastical constellation. The very nature of the assigned benefice, however, exposed it to contestations and impediments of all sorts (both secular and ecclesiastical), of which conflicts with the bishops were only the most evident and dense with consequences.

Choosing to resort to ordinary financing by assigned benefices implied, at the State level, setting the whole inquisitorial system on a course fully institutionalized and legitimated by government courts, at the price, however, of strong uncertainty as to the tempo and the modes of completion of the overall managerial model. A determining factor in slowing down the process of connecting ecclesiastical benefices to inquisitorial courts can be immediately identified in the resistance – in some cases insurmountable – opposed to it by some bishops and by those diocesan organs suffering the pain of these transferrals. In the mid-1500s, the attention to possible cases of heresy among diocesan pastors was strongly characterized by the will to defend their own authority even when protecting the interests and the internal equilibriums of local society, shielding the honour of families involved in the inquiries and the related privileges of the locality.[102] In the long run, this ended up favouring the persistence of heretical ideas within the ecclesiastical districts, so that a sedimentary layer of inquisitorial vindications formed, influencing – in the latter half of the century – the redistribution of resources carried out by the "inquisitor popes" in favour of the Holy Office, this, in turn, inevitably strengthened the resistance of the Ordinaries.

Giovanni Romeo has pointed out another element explaining the apparent paradox of a Roman Inquisition whose channels of resource distribution were fragmentary and disarticulated, though the initiative was meant to be capillary and "universal". Romeo observes that it is altogether possible that the paradox arises in a distrust of the religious Orders, of which the inquisitors were exponents, among the post-Tridentine popes. Such clamorous episodes as the flight of Bernardino Ochino, Vicar General of the Capuchins, to Geneva in 1542; the arrest – and the escape – of the Augustinian Giulio da Milano in the same year; the burning at the stake of the Minor Conventual Giovanni Buzio da Montalcino, in the first execution for heresy carried out in Rome by the Congregation of the Holy Office – not to mention the almost 30 trials of Dominicans celebrated in Rome between 1548 and 1558[103] may all have combined to induce the popes and the cardinal inquisitors to decide not to strengthen local powers of political negotiation and judiciary decision ("*arbitrium*"), and, therefore, the financial independence of the individual courts.

So, in the decades of the anti-heretical emergency, the apostolic See, in this view, cultivated a preference for direct diversion of the more important trials of faith, making use of Extraordinary Commissioners and nuncios, or bringing diplomatic pressures to bear upon the secular authorities to induce them to cooperate with their structures – considered more trustworthy and manageable than the upper levels and the important exponents of the Mendicant Orders.[104] Local inquisitors were tied to the Orders at many levels – including that of their financing, and this, as our brief analysis of Sixtus V's regulatory decrees makes clear, did not guarantee local judges the liberty of action and the autonomy to try and to sentence freely, without pressures and impositions, considered fundamental to any justice of faith.

The interpretation Romeo proposes finds corroboration in the analysis of the entity of the grants from time to time bestowed on the inquisitors in the latter half of the 1500s: relatively limited, both as compared to the total expenditures of the Congregation and to the sums granted to many diverse subjects who did not, themselves, exercise inquisitorial functions, but were evidently participants in the strategies which the Supreme Court handled directly. Further, since the relations between the inquisitors and the convents were the source of internal conflict in the economic no less than in other areas, the financial reinforcement of local courts on the part of Rome would have favoured the already accentuated centrifugal tensions the inquisitors produced within convent life, provoking the inevitable escalation of the contrasts between the Roman leadership of the

Inquisition and the leaderships of the Orders. This was a result which the Pope and the ministry – inclined in general to smooth out disagreements with the convents so long as they recognized the special prerogatives of the judges of faith – were far from eager to foster.

Another element which can explain the fragmentary nature of the policies of finance of the peripheral courts of the Roman Inquisition is constituted by fact that this very fragmentary nature contributed to maintaining the direction and the control of peripheral Holy Office courts securely in the hands of the Roman directors of the Holy Office. For the Suprema, there were indubitable advantages in terms of the exercise of power to be secured in making their own intervention indispensable to obtain benefices or occasional grants as well as to coordinate the forms of "state" solidarity among local inquisitors. First of all, this system allowed the popes and the cardinals to select the inquisitors and bind them to Rome, choosing and rewarding those among them who displayed the greatest haste in applying policies – and, in the future, might be able to assume positions of greater responsibility within the Curia or within the inquisitorial system. Second, a financial structure which permitted the Holy See to choose which local seat it would favour with benefices and/or grants gave Rome the possibility of continually renewing the terms of its centrality within the flow of information and resources that "standardized" the components of the justice of faith network.

In significant measure, the popes were able to maintain their position at the centre of the inquisitorial constellation for centuries thanks to the fact that they, and the central ministry, held the local courts under the double reins of an attentive surveillance and a parsimonious munificence. In this manner the highest levels of Catholicism guaranteed themselves what we might call a "boundary role" absolutely unchallengeable by other contemporary ecclesiastical entities, acting upon their borders and putting them into contact one with the other, not only from the patrimonial point of view. This role is well illustrated by the correspondence of Carlo Maria Vizzani, Assessor of the Holy Office in the mid-1600s, when the beneficiary framework supporting the inquisitorial enterprise had already taken form and become consolidated for some decades. "Our Lord [Pope Alexander VII] has informed me that your most illustrious worship, in conformity with what I communicated [to you] [...] has ready the establishment of an income of 50 scudi for the Inquisition in Fermo, and a larger one for Perugia", Monsignor Vizzani wrote to the Ordinary of the Archdiocese of Fermo in 1658:

> And I am commanded to send you notice of the Inquisitions which are in poverty, that you may consider if, with some leftover little convent, they might be set to rights. In this connection, I advise you that the inquisitor of Gubbio has no income at all; Modena, Reggio, Crema and Belluno have little. Siena is very poor indeed; has many cities under it and, however, heavy expenses for the maintenance of prisoners [...] [you might] cede them a little convent of the Minor Conventuals of Pienza.[105]

The assessor might, in another communication, point out the opportunity that "to the Inquisition in Siena be added a little, suppressed, convent [of the Franciscans situated] in Pienza, since in reality no seminary has been included – as is obligatory – in the one built [for them]", indicating once more with what difficulty the post-Tridentine dioceses fulfilled the obligation to form the clergy which the Council had laid upon them. "I informed Our Lord day before yesterday, who ordered me to communicate it to your most illustrious Lord – so that with that or with the income of the other convent [...] that Inquisition may be made comfortable."[106] Reminding his many interlocutors of the Pope's intention of "assigning some income to those inquisitors who have very little or none at all", or monitoring the incomes of convents which were on the verge of suppression – or might prove suppressible to the benefit of the Inquisition ("small convent of the Augustinian fathers of Monte Juliano, annual income 80 scudi; small convent of the Carmelite fathers in the same place, 70 scudi a year: small convent of the Augustinians in Montefortino, annual income 70 scudi"),[107] the Holy Office consolidated its centrality in relations between dioceses, Ordinaries, and the Roman Curia and bound inquisitors to an institutional-financial dependence it obviously felt to be indispensable for an adequate exercise of their mission.

A final interpretative element emerges forcefully from the documentation and it will oblige us, in the second part of this study, to broaden our observation, moving from the analysis of central decisions and the relations between the centre and periphery to the economic management of the Inquisition locally. Certainly, one of the most legally binding limitations on the incomes of local Holy Office courts (together with the basing of their ordinary income on benefices and the affirmation of the "entrepreneurial" and monastic model in their administration), was the stable inclusion of the courts in the local economy and local political and social life. It was only by accumulating a patrimony whose income was able to cover the costs of the court's activities – and only by ensuring its competent, careful, administration – that local inquisitors could assure their offices a dignified tenor of life and a continuity of initiative over time.

The period from the middle decades to the end of the 1500s, when the fervour of the war on heresy had been accompanied by a virtual financial deregulation (a sign, perhaps, too, that the serious results of the fourteenth-century trials for embezzlement among Northern inquisitors had been forgotten), saw the formation of a "patrimony of the Inquisition" due to the relative liberty to impose monetary punishments: fines and, above all, confiscation. At the end of the sixteenth century, when the popes began to restrain deregulation and to assign benefices to inquisitors, the properties and the capital accumulated by the peripheral courts had become a solid foundation of support whose "divestment" could be accomplished only through a policy of massive central financing which was never adopted. The very nature of the conferral of benefices, consisting chiefly in income deriving from the management of real estate, promoted a fusion with the managerial procedures developed over the years for the wealth accumulated by the courts in preceding decades, constituting, de facto, a unified patrimonial "package" under the direction of the individual inquisitors.

The image of the Inquisition we have explored so far – that of the flow of money and the managerial practices regulated by Rome and periodically redirected by Rome according to pontifical policies – has as its "retro" another, far more mobile and indistinct, image. It is the image of the local courts and their multiple needs of contact and interaction with the powers and the subjects who move on the shifting stage-sets of the regional states. Obliged to put down roots in small centres or in important cities, the feared judges of faith had to learn to engage in a dialogue with community representatives and their institutions, with the lessees and the agricultural workers who farmed their lands, with the artisan corporations occupying their shops, with the bankers who administered their savings and with the shop-keepers who benefited from their loans.

In short, the Holy Office system had to become embedded:[108] a step which imposed the integration of canonical "pure and harsh" practice with a more malleable – and, from various points of view, a more fruitful – relational "tone" aimed at the women and the men moving every level of the pre-industrial world's social pyramid.

This important and lasting economic dynamic of maintenance and perpetuation caused the Roman Inquisition to develop – alongside its relations with the Roman, central, authorities – a social presence which broke free of convent barriers as well as those of the Court Chambers, becoming a part of daily life. I believe, indeed, we may say that, in the 1500s, the firm intent of pursuing a capillary political, economic and social rooting of the courts in the territory was one of the strongest impulses spurring the popes and the Suprema to set up a sort of two-phase managerial strategy: establishing at first a policy of liberalization of inquisitorial financing – functional to the strengthening of prosecution in the mid-century and the accumulation of patrimony at the local level through monetary penalties – and, subsequently, turning to benefices and financial parsimony. It was a strategy which, as the 1600s opened, had given rise to an organizational and cultural model which placed the early modern Inquisition within the living body of the *Ancien régime*, making it an economic and social institution actively and pervasively operative on all levels of the material as well as the spiritual reality of early modern Italy.

Notes

1. Paolini (1999), pp. 442–3.
2. Ibid., p. 453.
3. The Venetian "*Liber contractuum*" and "*Liber possessionum*" have been published in Bonato (2002); see also Del Col (2006), pp. 141ff.
4. Benedetti (2008), p. 175.
5. Chialvo (1908), p. 65.
6. BAV, Barb. Lat. 6335, p. 55r, Rome, March 13, 1627. Monsignor Herrera and the Pope's nephew, Cardinal Francesco Barberini, engaged in a rich correspondence

(now in BAV, Barb. Lat. 6678) from 1627–1630, when Barberini was one of the supreme inquisitors of the Congregation.

7 De Frede (1999), p. 369.
8 Tavuzzi (2007), pp. 31–4.
9 Biondi (2008), p. 171. A long series of monetarizations of inquisitorial punishments inflicted on Jews in Modena between 1600 and 1604 is published in Biondi (1994), pp. 277–8. On the correction of Jewish books of the Reggio Inquisition between 1602 and 1604 and the items listed see Perani (1994).
10 BAV, Vat. Lat. 10945, p. 74v. The following year, Rome also ordered the inquisitor in Vicenza not to begin "to build anything with Inquisition money without first informing us and awaiting our reply" (October 29, 1580; ibid.).
11 BAV, Barb. Lat. 6335, p. 289v; Rome, November 27, 1627. At the same time a letter was dispatched to the Bishop of Tortona "so that with his piety and zeal he undertakes repayment, as we hope" (ibid.).
12 BAV, Barb. Lat. 6336, p. 60v, Rome, March 4, 1628.
13 TCD, Mrm, Ms. 1224, p. 84v, sentence emitted in Rome, October 22, 1560. On Bolano degli Accolti, an important printer, originally from Brescia, operating in Rome, information may be found in Barberi (1942), pp. 75 and 93; Tramezzino has been the object of more research; a first approach may be made with Masetti Zannini (1980). Other interesting cases of monetary penalties consisting of contributions to pious entities: TCD, Mrm, Ms. 1224, January 11 and 18, 1567, following an abjuration *de vehementi* on the part of two exponents of the Calabrian Baracca family: Mario, abbot of Santa Maria di Altilia and Alfonso, first baron of Lattarico. The family was just beginning its socio-economic rise in those years: see Palmieri (1999), pp. 276–7.
14 TCD, Mrm, Ms 1224, pp. 163r–164v and 165r–166v, Rome, September 20 and 21, 1567.
15 ACDF, So, St.st., LL5e, *Inquisizione di Milano*. On Semino see Bruzzese (2009).
16 ACDF, Oec 15 e 18, *passim*.
17 See, for example BAV, Vat. Lat. 10945, p. 74v, Rome, June 4, 1580, in which the Inquisitor of Vicenza is instructed to request permission before building. On the involvement of Ordinaries see, among others BAV, Barb. Lat. 1370, p. 29r, letters sent on October 10, 1588, and May 23, 1592, to the Patriarch of Aquilea – of which the second, delivered by the nuncio in Venice, threatened "to sequestrate your income to this effect to the end that this construction be completed within the month".
18 See, for example, BAV, Borg. Lat. 558, p. 51r, authorization granted the inquisitor in Milan, October 2, 1603.
19 Scaramella (2002), p. 265.
20 BAV, Borg. Lat. 558, pp. 22r, 28r and 29r.
21 ACDF, So, St.st., LL5e, *Inquisizione di Cremona*. 20 scudi constituted a significant sum for the annual income of about 300 scudi which the Cremona Inquisition had at the end of the 1500s, made up of a pension of 100 scudi per year deriving from a tax laid upon the income of the provostship of San Giacomo, and about 190 scudi in income, land and fees from property accumulated in preceding decades. It should also be kept in mind that the Cremonese Inquisition of the time had jurisdiction over the areas subject to the Duke of Mantua *in temporalibus* (BAV, Borg. Lat. 558, c. 70v).
22 ACDF, So, St.st., LL5e, *Inquisizione di Perugia*.
23 BAV, Borg. Lat. 558, p. 95r, Rome, January 21, 1610; April 22, 1610; May 22, 1610.
24 BAV, Barb. Lat. 6335, p. 277r, Rome, October 3, 1627.
25 See, for example, BAV, Borg. Lat. 558, p. 95r, where, on April 4, 1603, to an explicit query from the Inquisitor of Turin whether "in accusing, in cases carrying

monetary punishment, the sum applicable must be declared", the answer was "simply declare 'under monetary punishment'".
26 Lavenia (2000), p. 85.
27 BAV, Borg. Lat. 558, p. 451r, Rome, September 5, 1597.
28 BAV, Barb. Lat. 1503, p. 46, Rome, July 25, 1590. A case in which the Roman Ministry prescribed in detail the destination to various pious Neapolitan entities of a confiscation amounting to 400 scudi may be found in Scaramella (2002), p. 177.
29 See, for example, the recommendation to the Inquisitor of Vicenza "that, together with the bishop, the monetary fine be distributed to the pious places of said City without the intervention of the Rectors" (BAV, Borg. Lat. 558, March 31, 1604).
30 BAV, Vat. Lat. 10945, p. 49r: "We understand that some of them [inquisitors] impose and extort pecuniary fines [...] Yet, however, His Holiness and these my most illustrious masters, have ordered me to lay strictly upon your reverence the observation of the Decree, with which it has ever been forbidden to impose and extort monetary punishment without first informing this Holy Congregation. Content yourself, further, to give notice as well, as soon as possible, to all the inquisitors of this State"; with specific reference to missives sent to Venice on December 20, 1618; May 21, 1625 and August 28, 1632. We are not however, without examples of inquisitors who respected the rules: "I have received the renewal of the old decrees forbidding the laying of monetary punishments – which, without exception, I shall cause to be observed in this court, as I have always done in the past, too" wrote the Inquisitor of Bergamo to the Congregation on June 4, 1625 (ACDF, So, St.st., GG3c, p. 107r).
31 On Lateranense V see Various authors (1972), pp. 621–2. As for the Jews, in 1745 the Suprema still condemned two Jews living in the Modena ghetto to a penalty of 15 gold scudi and two months of imprisonment – later reduced to 25 silver scudi – for having conversed with – and attended parties where there were – Christian women. In Piacenza, the inquisitor decreed a fine of 15 gold scudi to be laid upon Jews related to Christians in various ways: see Caffiero (2012), pp. 235–6.
32 For example, in 1620 the Milan Inquisition commuted a soldier's three-year jail sentence into a 25 scudi fine, so that he might participate in the Thirty Years War, four years earlier, at the request of the Prefect of the Milan castle, a Captain Visconti had been released to the service of the sovereign on payment of a bond of 200 scudi, with the obligation of remittal to the inquisitor on request: see Fumi (1910), p. 31. In 1601 the death sentence of a Mutio Bove, imprisoned in Naples, was commuted to 45 scudi "due to the difficulties he suffers from asthma": Scaramella (2002), pp. 320 and 322.
33 BAV, Barb. Lat. 6334, p. 236r, Rome, August 22, 1626.
34 BAV, Barb. Lat. 6334, p. 249r, Rome, two letters to Milan and Pavia, September 5, 1626.
35 BAV, Vat. Lat. 10945, p. 27r, Rome, March 21, 1630.
36 BAV, Barb. Lat. 6335, p. 176v, Rome, July 24, 1627.
37 BAV, Barb. Lat. 6334, p. 223r, Rome, August 1, 1626.
38 Lavenia (2003), p. 347.
39 BAV, Barb. Lat. 6336, pp. 357v–358r, Rome December 30, 1628. The Prince of Correggio, raised to this rank in 1616 by the Emperor after the title of the da Correggio had, for centuries been that of 'Count', was imprisoned in Milan, where he was prosecuted in a trial which, at the end of the 1700s, was still closed in the inquisitorial archives: see Fumi (1910), p. 15. Siro was freed on the supplications of his mother, addressed to Paul V, evidently with the payment of a conspicuous monetary penalty, see Ascari (1969).

40 TCD, Mrm, Ms. 1227, pp. 279r–281r, sentence pronounced in Rome, December 3, 1582. The diversion of the Moneglia case by Rome had provoked protests from the Doge and the governors of the republic, who, however, "ended up once again giving up, in according to [their] usual procedure" – which moved from opposition to extradition, developed papal resistance and ended in the acquiescence to the request. See Canosa (1988), pp. 145–7.

41 TCD, Mrm, Ms. 1231, sentence pronounced in Rome, December 11, 1628, pp. 199r–208r, from which the citation is drawn. The books used by Carlo Gonzaga included "in particular [...] Cornelio Agrippa, Solomon's *Altitudine* [probably the *Ars Almadel*], Pietro d'Abano's *Lucidario*, and the *Latrùm* in which how to command the familiar spirits of Lucifer is explained, and the *Clavicola* falsely termed Solomon's" (ibid., *passim*).

42 BAV, Barb. Lat. 6336, p. 316r, Rome, November 18, 1628.

43 We learn this from TCD, Mrm, Ms. 1231, sentence emitted in Rome, December 11, 1628, p. 199v.

44 See ibid. the text of the December 11, 1628 abjuration, signed by Carlo Gonzaga. The episode is briefly noted in Hoffmann (1878), who, though not citing the source, obviously drew the material from one of the oldest historiographical explorations of TCD, Mrm, together with other cases dealt with.

45 This definition is formulated by Scaramella (2002), p. XV.

46 Many of these sources have been used in this study; they are cited in the appropriate notes. For a more general discussion of sources see, for example Jobe (1986).

47 See, for example, BAV, Barb. Lat. 1503 (a more easily read copy of Barb. Lat. 1502, though with slight variations), where we learn that on August 3, 1594, the Cardinals of the Holy Office "sent word to the scribes of the Lombard Inquisition, that they make no print copies, nor allow summaries, nor information regarding Holy Office affairs" (p. 56).

48 ASV, *Fondo Borghese*, series I, box 340–344, pp. 176r–177r, "*Ricordi per servitio della Santa Inquisitione di Roma [...] Alla Santità di Nostro Signore*".

49 See the decrees of January 7, 1574 and March 10, 1575, published by von Pastor (1912), pp. 32–3.

50 See again von Pastor (1912), pp. 37 and 42, on the prohibition to raise communal taxes on the goods and on the lease holders of the Inquisition in Faenza.

51 The eighteenth-century conflicts with secular power on the theme of exemption for postal expenses are abundantly documented in the reports sent to Rome by the inquisitors in 1749, collected in ACDF, So, St.st., LL5e and LL5f.

52 For Milan, see ASM, *Atti di governo. Culto, parte antica*, box 2106, folder "March 20, 1779", visit of the Chamber Notary, Antonio Silvola, March 13, 1779, convent of Santa Maria delle Grazie, pp. 2r–v and 3r, with a detailed list of the patrimonial documents found in the cupboard. On Ancona see ACDF, St.st., So, DD2b, p. 242r, letter from Friar Arcangelo, Inquisitor of Ancona, Ancona, September 24, 1609.

53 Davidson (1988), in particular p. 30, describes the reception and the application of these norms in the context of a local office.

54 See for example in ACDF, So, St.st., GG3c, unnumbered pages, the limited number of the biannual accounts for Bergamo in the first two decades of the 1600s, whose irregularity is remarked by a 1625 Roman letter of complaint, ibid.

55 ASM, *Atti di governo, Culto parte antica*, box 2106, folder "20 marzo 1779", "*Nota de' libri del soppresso ufficio dell'Inquisizione*" ("*List of the Books of the Suppressed Inquisition Office*"), pp. 1r and 3v.

56 As an initial approach to these themes see Paolin (2000).

57 This happened on January 20, 1579, with a bull by Gregory XIII (ACDF, So, St.st., LL5f, *Inquisizione di Torino*). This practice in favour of the Turin Inquisition, though generating conflict over the whole of the seventeenth century, continued to be habitual in Turin until the eighteenth century, generating sums by no means irrelevant: in 1617, the property of Brother Girolamo Cigotto, Curate of the parish of San Verano in Pinerolo, brought the inquisitor there 1,800 florins. The previous year, on the death of Father Costantino Favetta, who had become curate after having been a Canonical regular as well as a Cistercian monk, the Commendatory of Rivalta Abbey demanded his property; the Suprema, however, decided that "the patrimony of Costantino Favetta must go to the Turin Holy Office according to Gregory XIII's decree" (see ibid., also for other examples of such passage of patrimonies and the conflicts which they produced with the abbeys).
58 Romeo (2009).
59 Del Col (2006), p. 314.
60 On January 12, 1583, "at the presence of" Gregory XIII, the Congregation "declares the reverend inquisitors everywhere appointed to an Apostolic Seat must, in that office, receive immediate precedence in private and on public occasions; it is permissible for Dominican inquisitors to come after a prior of the same Order, the same applying to those of the Franciscan Order" (BAV, Vat. Lat. 10945, c. 104r). The quote is from "Soul of the Holy Office, emitted by the Supreme Court of the Holy Congregation, gathered by F. Giacomo Angarano da Vicenza, Preaching father, in the Year of Our Lord MDCXLIV"; manuscript.
61 See the long letter sent to the General of the Dominicans on September 30, 1585 in BAV, Borg. Lat. 470, pp. 597rff., citation from 597r, from which we draw the information that follows. Sixtus V became Pope on April 24 of that year.
62 A copy was, for example, sent, on July 14, 1597, to the cardinal protectors of the Dominicans, Alessandrino, and of the Minor Conventuals, Cusano, with the title: "Orders Deliberated by the Holy Congregation, to be Observed by Inquisitors". See BAV, Barb. Lat. 1370, pp. 124ff.
63 BAV, Barb. Lat. 1370, pp. 125rff., Rome, December 4, 1588.
64 Ibid., p. 127r.
65 Fumi (1910), pp. 10–1.
66 ACDF, So, St.st., LL5f, *Inquisizione di Pisa*.
67 See von Pastor (1912), p. 43, decree of September 3, 1587.
68 BAV, Barb. Lat. 1370, pp. 138v–139r, Rome, May 28, 1594.
69 BAV, Barb. Lat. 6334, p. 64r, Rome, March 14, 1626.
70 BAV, Barb. Lat. 6336, p. 36v, Rome, February 12, 1628.
71 BAV, Vat. Lat. 10945, pp. 126v–127r, letters July 4, 1626 and February 14, 1637; BAV, Borg. Lat. 558, p. 418r, authorization April 17, 1614.
72 See von Pastor (1912), p. 37, decree September 18, 1581.
73 BAV, Borg. Lat. 558, p. 418v, authorization on the years 1632 and 1641.
74 BAV, Barb. Lat. 6334, p. 56r, March 7, 1626.
75 BAV, Vat. Lat. 10945, p. 105r, Rome, June 7, 1578.
76 BAV, Vat. Lat. 10945, p. 105r, Rome, September 5, 1629.
77 BAV, Barb. Lat. 6334, p. 165r, Rome, June 20, 1626.
78 "The lord cardinals have ordered me to admonish your reverence that in the future you are in no manner to receive money from those who have been investigated by the Holy Office, even after their case has been concluded", Rome explicitly reproved the Inquisition in Vicenza at the beginning of the 1600s. See BAV, Vat. Lat. 10945, p. 27r, Rome, March 30, 1603.
79 BAV, Barb. Lat. 6336, p. 58r, February 26, 1628, which opens declaring: "Since the Holy Congregation has not yet seen any result whatsoever from the orders given your reverence".

132 *The economy of the Holy Office*

80 See, for example, the letter to the Inquisitor of Mondovì dated August 5, 1628: "These, my illustrious [Lords], have decided that your reverence is to remove brother Benedetto Maria Moglione from his office as vicar, that you are to oblige him to give back the sums of money he is accused – and confessed – of having taken to expedite the case of Bernardino Fasoletto and Caterina Grandi" (ibid., p. 211*v*).
81 ACDF, Oec 17, November 24, 1583.
82 See for example the letter sent to the Inquisitor of Cremona in BAV, Barb. Lat. 6334, p. 44*r*, Rome, February 21, 1626.
83 BAV, Barb. Lat. 6334, p. 43*r*, Rome, February 21, 1626.
84 BAV, Barb. Lat. 6334, p. 34*r*–*v*, Rome, February 14, 1626.
85 BAV, Barb. Lat. 6334, p. 34*r*, Rome, February 14, 1626.
86 BAV, Barb. Lat. 6334, p. 173*r*, Rome, June 27, 1626.
87 BAV, Barb. Lat. 6335, p. 31*r*, Rome, February 6, 1627.
88 BAV, Barb. Lat. 6334, p. 23*r*, Rome, January 24, 1626.
89 For a comparison which shows the profound differences between the Mediterranean Inquisitions and the other European courts of faith, see Brambilla (2006), pp. 169ff.
90 On the Spanish Inquisition see Lea (1906), vol. 2, pp. 315–88; Martínez Millán (1984); Martínez Millán (1993); Martínez Millán (2010); Kamen (1998), pp. 137ff. (p. 138); on Portugal see Marcocci (2009); Veiga Torres (1993); Cruz (2007); López-Salazar Codes and Marcocci (2010).
91 Martínez Millán (1993), pp. 885ff.
92 Cf. for example BAV, Barb. Lat. 1502, "Decreta generalia Sancti Officii et non nullae [*sic*] litterae apostolicae non impressae" and its copy, with some differences, in BAV, Barb. Lat. 1503, "Decreta et litterae apostolicae pro Sancto Officio". For the important historic significance of this bull, despite its substantial non-application, see Pastore (2003), pp. 125ff.
93 Lea (1906), pp. 315–20. On the theological foundations and the normative structure of the confiscations, see Lavenia (2004).
94 Lea (1906), pp. 320–5.
95 Kamen (1998), pp. 151–2.
96 Carocci (2000), p. 1035.
97 Kamen (1998), p. 148.
98 Ibid., pp. 151–5.
99 Martínez Millán (1993), pp. 902ff.
100 See López-Salazar Codes and Marcocci (2010).
101 ACDF, St.st., So, DD2b, p. 242*r*, letter written by Brother Arcangelo, Inquisitor of Ancona, Ancona, September 24, 1609. "The expenses are many", the writer added, "for usually you have to ride out to take care of the cases in these towns within the jurisdiction, and the money that comes in is not enough".
102 See for example Ragagli (2011).
103 Del Col (2006), p. 314.
104 Romeo (2009), pp. 11–12.
105 ASV, Armadio VIII, 92, *Miscellanea*, p. 272*r*, Rome, March 5, 1658.
106 Ibid., p. 275*r*, without date.
107 Ibid., pp. 246*r* e 277*r*–*v*, Rome, February–March 1658.
108 See the classic Granovetter (1985).

Bibliography

Ascari, T. (1969) 'Ottavio Bolognesi', *Dizionario biografico degli italiani*, volume 11, Rome: Istituto dell'enciclopedia italiana.

Barberi, F. (1942) *Paolo Manuzio e la stamperia del popolo romano (1561–1570). Con documenti inediti*, Rome: Cuggiani.
Benedetti, M. (2008) *Inquisitori lombardi del Duecento*, Rome: Edizioni di storia e letteratura.
Biondi, A. (1994) 'Gli Ebrei e l'Inquisizione negli Stati estensi', in M. Luzzati (ed.) *L'Inquisizione e gli Ebrei in Italia*, Rome and Bari: Laterza, 265–85.
Biondi, A. (2008) *Umanisti, eretici, streghe. Saggi di storia moderna*, ed. M. Donattini, Modena: Comune di Modena. Assessorato alla Cultura.
Bonato, E. (2002) (ed). 'Il "Liber contractuum" dei frati Minori di Padova e di Vicenza (1263–1302)', with the collaboration of E. Bacciga, Rome: Viella.
Brambilla, E. (2006) *La giustizia intollerante. Inquisizione e tribunali confessionali in Europa (secoli IV–XVIII)*, Rome: Carocci.
Bruzzese, S. (2009) '"Dor gran penciò dra vallada de Bregn": sulle tracce di Ottavio Semino pittore genovese, naturalizzato milanese', *Nuovi studi. Rivista di arte antica e moderna'* (15): 165–78.
Caffiero, M. (2012) *Legami pericolosi. Ebrei e cristiani tra eresia, libri proibiti e stregoneria*, Turin: Einaudi.
Canosa, R. (1988) *Storia dell'Inquisizione in Italia. Dalla metà del Cinquecento alla fine del Settecento*, volume 3, *Torino e Genova*, Rome: Sapere 2000.
Carocci, S. (2000) 'Feudo, vassallaggi e potere papale nello Stato della Chiesa (metà XI sec. – inizio XIII sec.)', *Rivista storica italiana* (112): 999–1035.
Chialvo, G. (1908) 'Una sentenza per eresia, apostasia e magia', *Bollettino storico bibliografico subalpino* (13): 63–70.
Cruz, M. L. (2007) 'Relações entre poder real e Inquisição (séculos XVI–XVII). Fontes de renda, realidade social e política financeira', in L. F. Barreto, J. A. Mourão, P. de Assunção, A. C. da Costa Gomes and J. E. Franco (eds) *Inquisição portuguesa. Tempo, razão e circunstância*, Lisbon and São Paulo: Prefácio, 107–26.
Davidson, N. S. (1988) 'Rome and the Venitian Inquisition', *Journal of Ecclesiastical History* (39): 16–36.
De Frede, C. (1999) *Religiosità e cultura nel Cinquecento italiano*, Bologna: Il Mulino.
Del Col, A. (2006) *L'Inquisizione in Italia dal XII al XXI secolo*, Milan: Mondadori.
Fumi, L. (1910) 'L'Inquisizione romana e lo Stato di Milano. Saggio di ricerche nell'Archivio di Stato', *Archivio storico lombardo* (35, 36, 37): 5–124, 145–220, 285–414.
Granovetter, M. (1985) 'Economic Action and Social Structure: The Problem of Embeddedness', *American Journal of Sociology* (78): 1360–80.
Hoffmann, F. (1878) *Geschichte der Inquisition. Einrichtung und Thätigkeit derselben in Spanien, Portugal, Italien, den Niederlander, Frankreich, Deutschland, Süd-America, Indien, und China*, Bonn: Reuffer.
Jobe, P. H. (1986) *Inquisitorial Manuscripts in the Biblioteca Apostolica Vaticana: a Preliminary Handlist*, in G. Henningsen and J. Tedeschi (eds) *The Inquisition in Early Modern Europe: Studies in Sources and Methods*, De Kalb, IL: Northern Illinois University Press, 33–53.
Kamen, H. (1998) *The Spanish Inquisition: A Historical Revision*, New Haven, CT and London: Yale University Press.
Lavenia, V. (2000) 'I beni dell'eretico, i conti dell'inquisitore. Confische, Stati italiani, economia del sacro tribunale' in *L'inquisizione e gli storici: un cantiere aperto. Tavola rotonda nell'ambito della Conferenza annuale della ricerca (Roma, 24–25 giugno 1999)*, Rome: Accademia Nazionale dei Lincei, 47–94.

Lavenia, V. (2003) 'Gli ebrei e il fisco dell'Inquisizione. Tributi, espropri e multe tra "500" e "600"', in *Le inquisizioni cristiane e gli ebrei. Tavola rotonda nell'ambito della Conferenza annuale della ricerca. Roma, 20–21 dicembre 2001*, Rome: Accademia nazionale dei Lincei, 325–56.

Lea, H. C. (1906) *A History of the Inquisition of Spain*, New York: Macmillan & Co, vol. 2.

López-Salazar Codes, A. I. and Marcocci, G. (2010) 'Struttura economica: Inquisizione portoghese', in A. Prosperi (ed.) *Dizionario storico dell'Inquisizione*, with the collaboration of V. Lavenia and J. Tedeschi, Pisa: Edizioni della Normale, vol. 3.

Marcocci, G. (2009) 'Trent'anni di storiografia sull'Inquisizione portoghese. Quesiti aperti, reticenze, prospettive di ricerca (1978–2008)', *Cromohs*, (14): 1–9, available online at: http://www.cromohs.unifi.it/14_2009/marcocci_storioport.html#fnB35.

Martínez Millán, J. (1984) *La hacienda de la Inquisición (1478–1700)*, Madrid: Istituto Enrique Flórez.

Martínez Millán, J. (1993) *Estructura de la hacienda de la Inquisición*, in J. P. Villanueva and B. Escandell Bonet (eds) *Historia de la Inquisición en España y Amèrica*, vol. 2, *Las estructuras del Santo Officio*, Madrid: Biblioteca de autores cristianos – Centro de estudios inquisitoriales, 883–1076.

Martínez Millán, J. (2010) 'Struttura economica: Inquisizione spagnola', in A. Prosperi (ed.) *Dizionario storico dell'Inquisizione*, with the collaboration of V. Lavenia and J. Tedeschi, Pisa: Edizioni della Normale, vol. 3.

Masetti Zannini, G. L. (1980) *Stampatori e librai a Roma nella seconda metà del Cinquecento: documenti inediti*, Rome: Fratelli Palombi.

Palmieri, L. (1999) *Cosenza e le sue famiglie attraverso testi atti e manoscritti*, Cosenza: Pellegrini.

Paolin, G. (2000) 'Gli ordini religiosi e l'Inquisizione: analisi di un rapporto', in A. Del Col and G. Paolin (eds) *L'inquisizione romana: metodologia delle fonti e storia istituzionale. Atti del seminario internazionale, Montereale Valcellina, 23 e 24 settembre 1999*, Trieste and Montereale Valcellina: Università di Trieste-Circolo culturale Menocchio, 51–72.

Paolini, L. (1999) 'Le finanze dell'Inquisizione in Italia (secoli XIII–XIV)', in *Gli spazi economici della Chiesa nell'Occidente mediterraneo (secoli XII–metà XIV)*, Pistoia: Centro italiano di studi di storia e d'arte, 441–81.

Pastore, S. (2003) *Il Vangelo e la spada. L'Inquisizione di Castiglia e i suoi critici (1460–1598)*, Rome: Edizioni di Storia e letteratura.

Perani, M. (1994) 'Confisca e censura di libri ebraici a Modena fra Cinque e Seicento', in M. Luzzati (ed.) *L'Inquisizione e gli Ebrei in Italia*, Roma and Bari: Laterza, 287–320.

Ragagli, S. (2011) 'Inquisitori e vescovi contro l'eresia nella Savona del Cinquecento', in G. Dall'Olio, A. Malena and P. Scaramella (eds) *La fede degli italiani. Per Adriano Prosperi*, vol. 1, Pisa: Edizioni della Normale, 153–68.

Romeo, G. (2009) *L'Inquisizione nell'Italia moderna*, Rome and Bari: Laterza.

Scaramella, P. (2002) *Le lettere della Congregazione del Sant'Ufficio ai tribunali di fede di Napoli 1563–1625*, Trieste and Naples: Edizioni Università di Trieste-Istituto italiano per gli studi filosofici.

Tavuzzi, M. (2007) *Renaissance Inquisitors. Dominican Inquisitors and Inquisitorial Districts in Northern Italy 1474–1527*: Leiden and Boston: Brill.

Veiga Torres, J. (1993) 'A vida financeira do Conselho Geral do Santo Ofício da Inquisição (séculos XVI–XVIII)', *Notas Económicas* (2): 24–39.
von Pastor, L. (1912) (ed.) *Allgemeine Dekrete der Römischen Inquisition aus den Jahren 1555–1597. Nach dem Notariatsprotokoll des S. Uffizio sum erstenmale veröffentlicht*, Freiburgim-Breisgau: Herdersche Verlagshandlung.
Various authors. (1972) J. Alberigo, J. A. Dossetti, P. -P. Joannou, C. Leonardi and P. Prodi (eds) *Conciliorum Oecomenicorum decreta*, Bologna: Istituto per le scienze religiose.
Various authors. (2000) *L'inquisizione e gli storici: un cantiere aperto. Tavola rotonda nell'ambito della Conferenza annuale della ricerca (Roma, 24–25 giugno 1999)*, Rome: Accademia Nazionale dei Lincei.
Various authors. (2003) *Le inquisizioni cristiane e gli ebrei. Tavola rotonda nell'ambito della Conferenza annuale della ricerca. (Roma, 20–21 dicembre 2001)*, Rome: Accademia nazionale dei Lincei.

Part II
The Inquisition and economic life

4 "The citizen dies, the man remains"
Confiscation

The confiscation of the patrimonies of individuals condemned by the courts of the Roman Inquisition has become very important in studies of the history of the Holy Office and, more broadly, of Italian economy and society in the early modern period. Still, our knowledge of these areas remains piecemeal and fragmentary. Vincenzo Lavenia has recently investigated the theological-juridical premises of the confiscation of goods ["*publicatio bonorum*"] as it developed in the Middle Ages and subsequently (with the determining contribution of the Salamanca school), as well as the complex relations which developed during the 1500s between the Holy Office and the governing authorities of various Italian peninsula states which, in various situations, contested the rights (and the fruits) of penal confiscation with the ecclesiastical courts.[1]

These important studies have confirmed that – at least during the sixteenth century – confiscations provided one of the most important sources of Inquisition income, as well as a crucial element of political and institutional negotiation between it and secular governments. It is not yet possible, however, to formulate secure hypotheses regarding the relative weight of confiscations within the overall income of local courts and of the Congregation of the Holy Office itself, whether for specific moments or over the medium-long period. We do not even have a specific outline of confiscation procedures, different in various statutory situations due to the varied compromises struck between inquisitors and sovereign organs. Somewhat murky, but in my opinion crucially important, is, as well, the relationship which developed in each location within inquisitorial procedures: between the penal trial itself and the phase of property confiscation, traditionally seen as merely an appendix dictated by the will to take possession of the condemned individual's property.

The historiography regarding the Spanish Inquisition, which has long studied the economic aspects, has, instead, made it clear that confiscation played a central role in financing the institution and, indeed, according to a number of scholars, the original characteristics of the repression of heterodoxy and of the ethnic-religious minorities in the peninsula. Discussing the first and crudest phase of the history of the Spanish Inquisition, William Monter has, indeed, affirmed that:

> The final scope of the terror that his [Torquemada's] organization unleashed across Spain had more to do with the need to maximize confiscation, and thus profits, in a period in which the long war against Granada had imposed unusual expenses upon the Crown, than with the will to eliminate heresy among the *conversos*.[2]

In regards to Portugal, too, recent studies – though referred only to the court in Lisbon – have suggested that confiscation, in the long run, acted as an instrument of social control besides being a source of accumulation of wealth. In the peculiar structure of the Spanish Inquisition, which, as we have seen, bound it legally to the Crown, the kings themselves benefited from a consistent portion of the property confiscated for crimes of faith. That money became a flexible source of income for the sovereigns and one which could be mobilized in periods of extraordinary expense or in financial situations which were critical for the state. We should note that in the Portuguese case too – as well as in in some Italian situations – it was not the ecclesiastical court which acted directly, but the secular officials who carried out the practical process of confiscation. As the historians who have recently studied these forms have commented, "the phenomenon of confiscation by the Portuguese Inquisition, far from being the creation of the Church, or serving to support it financially, must be analysed as a mechanism in the centralization of the state of the early modern period".[3]

In the following pages, after a brief look at the norms inherited from the Middle Ages, we shall look at some general examples of confiscations executed by the Roman Inquisition during the early modern era and the principal consequences for the functioning of the Holy Office and the relations between it and the Italian states. In the next chapter, we shall specifically analyse some cases of confiscation procedures to investigate the construction of social consensus towards the activities of the courts of faith and the contribution furnished it by the specific forms in which the confiscations were carried out, in which the ecclesiastical courts routinely worked with State institutions.

Confiscation as a cancellation of the past

In the essay *On Crimes and Punishments* (1764), a founding document of modern penal science, Cesare Beccaria wrote:

> Confiscations set a price on the heads of the weak, cause innocents to suffer the pain of the guilty individual and place the innocents themselves in the desperate necessity of committing crimes [...] All will be lost when the ostracism intimated by the law is such that it cancels all relations between society and a delinquent citizen; then the citizen dies and the man remains, and as regards the body politic, this must produce the same effect as physical death.[4]

Today there are few who recall that the legal institution of confiscation of the property of condemned individuals – which regarded above all those condemned to death – practised from the Roman era and throughout the Middle Ages and the early modern period was at the centre of a heated debate during the Enlightenment, chiefly due to its intrinsic moral and philosophical implications. In this passage, Beccaria summarized them cogently. First of all, confiscation of property legitimately accumulated by an individual meant extending punishment to relatives and descendants, though these were legally innocent; besides being morally unjust, this favoured the possibility that, being reduced to poverty, they too would commit crimes. Further, confiscating the property of a culprit even in cases which were not capital, would represent a de facto death sentence, with the end of any tie between him and civil society and the cancellation not only of his present and future, but of his past as well. Indeed, we see that confiscation – even and above all when decreed by the Inquisition – was retroactive; it involved the cancellation of economic transactions and legal and fiduciary pacts signed and sealed even decades prior to the condemnation.

Confiscation – we can add to Beccaria's list – also irreparably disturbed the social and fiduciary framework which induced active citizens to stipulate contracts – to buy and sell, to loan, to rent or lease, to bequeath and so on – counting upon the continuity of the guarantees of property rights and informal ties. Guarantees which were, instead, set at naught where confiscation was a frequent practice – or even only seriously threatened. With this subsequent extension, a dangerous veil of uncertainty and diffuse reciprocal mistrust was drawn over the whole network of daily transactions of the *Ancien régime*.

The Roman Inquisition confiscated the condemned individual's property acquired *a die commissi criminis*, that is, from the moment in which, on the basis of evidence produced during a trial, the culprit had first committed the sin-crime of heresy. All transactions carried out by the culprit from the moment in which he or she had fallen into sin-crime were, as we shall see in some examples, automatically annulled. This brought with it consignment to the confiscating authority – often the Holy Office, in collaboration with the Chambers of the secular princes – of properties which had, in the past, been the object of sale, donation or bequest, as well as the cancellation of nuptial agreements, concessions of credit, rentals, mortgages and everything else which had changed the consistency of the culprit's patrimony since the moment of committing the sin-crime.

We can easily imagine how the mere possibility that these lacerating economic and social factors might explode produced negative repercussions on the regular functioning of the financial and mercantile world, in whose context the respect of property rights and the daily exercise of trust were fundamental prerequisites. Also economic milieus, stimulated in Italy by merchants from predominantly Reformed European areas, or by peninsula colleagues who periodically visited – or had lived at length – in those areas as long as this was allowed (that is, as we shall see, until the end of the

1500s), saw in this situation the greatest of risks that their protagonists might remain entrapped in the nets of the Roman Inquisition. Whether co-nationals or foreign, the business associates of Italian Catholic merchants with strong international interests – or of German, Dutch, English or Swiss merchants operating in Italy – were then, in turn, subjects who might be seriously damaged by the repercussions of an eventual trial for heresy which involved them, with the consequent confiscation of their patrimonies and the annulment of their past economic transactions. And so, fears linked to the exercise of trade in an Italy subjected to the action of the courts of faith might lead foreign commercial firms to limit their activities in the Italian peninsula.

Alternatively, the foreign commercial firms based in heretic countries ("*in partibus haereticorum*") were obliged to procure Catholic agents who, at their risk and peril, acted as go-betweens on peninsula markets. As Pandolfo Bruchman, Protestant agent of the Nuremburg bankers Gewandschneider, told the inquisitors who arrested him in Ferrara in 1606 the night before his departure for the Bolzano fairs, his principles ("*maggiori*") aimed at "having a Catholic agent for their affairs in Italy"; an element which led him, after only a few days of imprisonment, to declare, almost with relief, that he was willing to convert to Catholicism – "for when he was in Italy, he always went about in great fear". Conversely, in the second half of the 1500s, Italian merchants who worked on foreign markets in areas prevalently Protestant, acquired the expensive habit of providing themselves with certificates – sometimes indeed notarized – attesting their secure Catholic faith.[5]

The great historian of the Spanish Inquisition, Henry Kamen, had already observed in pioneering studies of the 1960s that the confiscations operated by the Spanish court could not represent a direct cause for the economic decline of Spain between the sixteenth and seventeenth centuries. He did, however, offer a precious methodological indication, suggesting that "the real problem is the indirect contribution of the Inquisition; its impact on the activity of those who suffered the confiscations".[6] At present, available research does not allow us to establish whether, and in what measure, the Roman institution of confiscation for crimes of faith contributed to creating a climate of generalized uncertainty in Italian markets, such as to influence an undeniable reduction and provincialization of Italian international commerce and banking activities in the seventeenth and early eighteenth centuries.[7] Further research in the archives and the correspondence of the great European mercantile houses of the period is necessary to discover eventual races of precise strategies of isolation or commercial "declassing" of Catholic partners, or to ascertain whether the closing of Italian offices sometimes occurred after an explicit evaluation of risk in terms of the uncertainty of property rights due to the fear of trials of faith which such forms of exposition were thought to carry.

There is, however, no doubt but what in Italy, too, within the situation of inadequate financing of local inquisitorial courts and the vigorous conflicts for resources between the Holy Office and diocesan Ordinaries, the funds deriving from confiscation assumed, already in the 1500s, a role of conspicuous importance in the birth and the consolidation of the Inquisition network. The Siena office, for example, was sustained for decades almost exclusively by the confiscation of the property of the famous religious Reformer, Fausto Sozzini, who moved to Poland in 1579, dying there in 1604. Carried out in 1590, before Sozzini was burnt in effigy in the Church of San Francesco in the following year, the confiscation brought the Sienese Inquisition 600 scudi. Of these, 200 were immediately destined to restore the archive, and 400 invested in a property earning 7; in 1633, 200 scudi were drawn from it to build prisons.

Thanks to the income from this conspicuous patrimony, the seventeenth-century Sienese judges of faith could look with relative serenity at the fact that the Bishop of Chiusi refused to pay them the annual benefice of 14 scudi due to them. A sum which – "not withstanding the Holy Congregation [had] many times written to the existing Bishop of Chiusi pro tempore", as a seventeenth-century memorandum of the inquisitor, Giovanni Pellei da Radicofani, testifies – was never paid, nor was there ever "any reply whatsoever".[8] We should note that, already during the trial for heresy carried out against Sozzini in default in 1588, the questions posed by the inquisitors insisted on aspects which it is difficult to refer to the pure ascertainment of the orthodoxy of faith. After having learnt that Fausto's brother-in-law, Cornelio Marsili, lessee of his properties, had received letters from Kraków in which Sozzini spoke of "his business, of his Income, that you were to send him", he was asked explicitly: "of what are you to send income?" A second question regards "income" and "rents" belonging to "Fausto's properties", to which the inquisitor receives a reply which is a precise patrimonial overview: "He has five farms, one called the Popero, the other Casa Nova, the other the Chiusa, the other the Catenaio, and Monte Santo".[9] This patrimony in real estate had accumulated by the preceding generations of the Sozzini family, which had a number of prestigious scholars of canon law. Among these, Mariano Sozzini (1397–1467) who, ironically enough, had discussed the merit of the destination of confiscation in cases of heresy. He did not note the iniquity as regards to the descendants of the culprit, citing, indeed, a series of normative texts, secular and canonical, which justified punishing the sons for the sins of the fathers in some serious cases.[10] In any case, the confiscation of Fausto Sozzini's property shows the growth of the Holy Office's power of intervention in the dialogue between the institutions governing Italy in the early decades of the Counter Reformation.

Though condemned for heresy in default by the Bologna and Siena Inquisitions in about 1559, Fausto's paternal uncle, Camillo, had seen his property in Tuscany benefit from the protection of Cosimo I, who had blocked the entry in possession by the ecclesiastical court. Fausto tried to obtain the same intercession, writing from Kraków in 1588 to Cosimo's son, the Grand Duke Ferdinand I (at the time still a cardinal), without, however, favourable results, given the altered political and religious scenario:

The Inquisitor of Siena – not for any accusation brought for any crime of mine committed in that state, but because he says he has learnt that I have caused books to be printed, and preach and hold lessons public and private against the Holy Roman Church (things all false and in great part ridiculous) – not only has called me to appear personally before him under most atrocious menace of punishment, but has immediately seized what little property I have in the world, ordering the honourable Cornelius Marsili of Siena, my leasee and procurator, to pay me nothing, and disposing the governing of my properties as if they were transferred to the Inquisition: arriving, in brief, at acts of execution upon things that are mine, before he or anyone else has pronounced any sentence against me [...] The most serene, great, Cosimo, of glorious memory, Your Highness' father – my uncle Camillo Sozzini having been publicly condemned and excommunicated in default in Bologna and Siena of formal accusations and testimonies of crimes committed in the same locations, the Inquisition desiring at last to proceed to execute upon his property (or at least upon the income deriving from it) – did not allow them to do so in any manner. So how much less should Your Highness allow [them] to proceed upon my property, since I have only been called – or even should I be condemned in default – since such [a sentence] would necessarily be based on simple, false, suspicions and vain accusations of crimes committed in foreign places.[11]

Far from replying positively to Sozzini's petition, the Grand Duke of Tuscany did not hesitate to claim his right to the confiscated patrimony, sustaining before the Holy Office that it belonged to the secular fiscal system by both natural and divine right, as a part of regal attributes; and that the ecclesiastical sentence did not concern temporal, only spiritual, punishments. This act provoked an intense controversy with the Holy See on the question of Gran Ducal rights on Inquisition confiscations which, subsequently, was taken as a model by other contemporary states. During its course, the Pope was reminded that the trial of Pietro Carneseccchi, Apostolic Protonotary beheaded in 1567, had ended with conspicuous profit for Cosimo I's treasury.[12]

As we shall see more specifically, an operation like the confiscation of patrimony due to heresy was almost inevitably destined to stimulate appetites and give rise to controversies between secular and ecclesiastical authorities. Within the various Italian states, the whole second half of the sixteenth century saw the attempt to reach agreements and establish a more or less definitive adjustment between the Holy See and secular governments as to the assignment or division of wealth deriving from confiscation for sin-crime (*"fidei causa"*). Unpleasant incidents might arise even where such equilibriums seemed to have been established – as was the case for the State of Milan, governed by the Spanish Crown, where a compromise prescribed a tripartite division of confiscated heretic property whose parties were the Holy Office, the episcopal Mensa and the State treasury. In 1572, for example, after some members of the Appiani family had been condemned for heresy in Milan, the Bishop of Novara's Vicar went to Pallanza, accompanied by notaries, tax officials and other members of the diocesan court, to collect the 12,000 lire owed to the Appiani family by a local producer of wine. At the refusal of the debtor, whose property had already been sequestered by the secular Milanese courts which habitually carried out such activity, the Novarese Ordinary's representatives – as we learn from an indignant letter of protest – "took the wine and the equipment, threatening execution upon many others, because these goods have not respected His Majesty's jurisdiction".[13]

This episode is a good example of two of the aspects which we will consider with some attention in this and the following chapter. First of all, the ambiguous link between the inquisitorial process, considered as an examination of the orthodoxy of an individual's faith and "execution" upon that individual's property. This link which, as we shall see, was not limited to the attention precociously displayed by inquisitors for the entity of the accused's patrimony – a trait which appeared in *Ancien régime* usage, common even in secular courts: to start confiscation procedures well before a sentence had been pronounced. That link, in fact, included the possibility that confiscation might, in turn, be an instrument in the gathering of information and testimony to use as the basis of new inquisitorial trials. Second, Sozzini's story reminds us that patrimonial expropriation of a condemned individual's patrimony by the Inquisition – especially in cases in which it took on the character of "basic" confiscation that is of patrimony whose possession gave solidity and socio-economic roots to the local inquisition – enhanced the symbolic and communicative value of the Holy Office in the local ecclesiastical court's memory and in the eyes of society as a whole.

The manuscript *Book of Entry and of Expense of the Holy Office* ("*Libro dell'Entrata e dell'Uscita del Santo Ufficio*"), which Giovanni Pellei da Radicofani began in 1656 on his arrival in Siena from Treviso, was destined to hold the accounts of that locality until the 1710s: it opened with an account of Sozzini's case, on which it conferred the role of virtual "myth of the origins" from which all the successive history of the local courts appeared to derive.[14] In a like manner, a plaque over the entry to a house situated on an extensive property outside Porta Nuova in Milan – purchased with the funds from an Inquisition confiscation of 1570 – declared: "May 13, 1570 Father Zampa da Cremona, Inquisitor of the Preaching Order, from many and good heretic confiscations, took this property, cultivated the uncultivated and built a house to sustain the Holy Office of the Inquisition. God be Blessed." The inscription, still clearly legible two centuries later,[15] perpetuated and publicized a fearsome image of the Inquisition's power throughout the early modern period, a result which would be difficult to secure with the mere public execution of an ordinary sentence.

Today, the gaps regarding the practice of confiscation that we find in the history of the Roman Inquisition derive chiefly from the fact that the documents produced by the peripheral seats of the Holy Office have, with few exceptions, been destroyed. This makes it particularly complicated to study a phenomenon in large measure handled by the peripheral offices of the Inquisition, which there took on, as well, its greatest economic and symbolic importance. The Congregation of the Holy Office might, naturally, intervene to directly control confiscations whose execution might have troublesome political and diplomatic aspects. This occurred, for example, in the case of the "publication" of the property belonging to the Jew, Emanuele Mocata, which, in the early 1600s, found the Inquisitor of Reggio Emilia and the Marquis of Scandiano in disagreement. The small d'Este estate, only a short time before being acquired by the Bentivoglio, had a tradition of tolerance towards the Jews, who were allowed liberty of cult and ritual butchery, exemption from the obligation to wear the badge prescribed by Lateran Council IV and the possibility for some local Jewish families – and, in particular the Almansi family of Scandiano – to acquire land. Both the Inquisitor of Reggio and the Ministry in Rome had, from time to time, tried unsuccessfully to limit this policy of protection and concession in favour of the Jewish population.

In this tense situation, a controversy between the inquisitor and the feudal Lord as to the confiscation of Emanuele Moscata's patrimony was terminated by the Suprema, which limited itself to having the Marquis of Scandiano deposit 100 scudi directly in the Roman treasury. A sum that is "very slight, if one considers what the positions of the Holy Office are", admitted Rome to the Reggio inquisitor, who had tried to obtain much more and been blocked by Marquis Bentivoglio. Still, he admonished the local judge of faith, "This case – for the many particularities it brings together – must not, in the future, be brought into play as an example by others".[16]

The bull *Licet ab initio* (1542), with which Paul III created the Congregation of the Holy Office, indicated its scope as action "against all, and every single individual, deviating from the way of the Lord and the Catholic faith", through "inquisitions and investigations whether instigated by others or ex officio", even of "suspects previously indicated, released from prison". Once pronounced sentence, the decretal stated: "the goods of the condemned, according to law, will be confiscated".[17] From its origins, then, the early modern Inquisition considered the confiscation of property to be one of its pre-eminent functions. Its execution was explicitly included in a series of operations which linked it securely to the preceding procedural phases: inquiry; incarceration; sentence; and condemnation to punishment. At the same time, confiscation, in turn, pointed to the need to carry out all these phases in a juridical form coherent with prevailing canonical structures. By 1542, the institution of confiscation for crimes of faith already rested upon a millenary history which we must now review in its most salient moments.

The Justianian *Codex* already punished heresy with exile, classifying it as an offence against the King's Majesty ("*lesa maestà*"), while the death penalty was pronounced only for the most serious cases of doctrinal deviation carrying social peril. The Roman sentence of exile, conceived in the

Republican period when trials were held by the Centurian Meeting, was not an automatic sentence, but, rather, a sort of procedural alternative, avoiding a condemnation to death. When, in later centuries, exile became a sentence in its own right in Roman law, it still remained, however, within the concept of capital punishment, whose consequences were always and necessarily the loss of citizenship and the confiscation of goods ("*publicatio bonorum*"): not, then, a penalty in itself, but a necessary consequence of the penalty of exile. In any case, the Justinian and Theodosian Codes contemplated various forms of exile which, given their diverse characteristics, might be accompanied by confiscation, corporal punishment and/or fines.[18]

In the High Middle Ages, the *Lex Wisigothorum Recesvindiana*, emanated in 654 by King Recesvind, valid both for Romans and Goths, dedicated Title II of Book XII to heretics and Jews ("*De ominium hereticorun adque Iudeorum conctis erroribus amputatis*"), deriving the punishment of exile and confiscation from Roman-Christian law. Another important legal source of the time – the *Lex Romana canonice compta* – a ninth-century collection of Roman legal texts adapted to the life of the ecclesiastical structure (considered by jurists as a sort of intermediate step between the sources of secular law dealing with religion and those of canon law), envisioned the civil and military incapacity of heretics (defined "those who do not participate in the church"), disposing that women that found heretic should lose the dowry privilege if married, unless they converted to orthodoxy. This constitutes a repetition of Roman-Christian legal norms regarding heretics, without its harshness and its extreme consequences. Other compendiums of the canons and others prior to Gratian give various definitions and procedures regarding the heretic in which no explicit reference to economic punishment is made.

The Roman tradition as to confiscation was rediscovered and elaborated in the central years of the Middle Ages by the Bologna commentators. This local detail takes on great historic importance since the theme of monetary punishment of heretics, precisely due to the attention dedicated to it by this group, came to pervade the pontifical decretals emitted at the end of the twelfth century and, subsequently, the laws of Frederick II – that is to say those texts which set the definitive model within which the Holy Office acted throughout the early modern era. Secular commentators held a more subtle position on the *publicatio bonorum* applied to heretics. Irnerius and Azone gave a limitative reading, insisting on the incapacity of those guilty of heresy to transfer their property to living persons in whatever manner or under whatever title, but defending the possibility that such property might be transmitted as inheritance to orthodox descendants. Piacentini, however, took less indulgent positions introducing – though as a hypothesis – the possibility of confiscation including Catholic descendants, in virtue of the implicit crime of *lèse-majesté*.

In the field of canon law, from the time of the Gregorian Reform with Anselm of Lucca, and, later, Gratian and his commentators up until Huguccio of Pisa, confiscation was discussed in purely theoretical terms – though with careful references to the Roman constitutions. The situation continued, indeed, until the papacy and the Emperor found legal and repressive instruments which might bring the *publicatio* into the realm of the feasible. In 1163, the Council of Tours established the need to confiscate the property of heretics and isolate them socially: this translated into the prohibition for orthodox Catholics to engage in relations with them involving buying and selling. At the Council of Arras, in 1182, there was a first, practical, example of a division of confiscated, heretic, property, with a condemnation emitted by the Archbishop and the Count and the subsequent division of the property between them. In 1194, at the Council of Lerida, the confiscation of the property of sustainers of heretics was decided: an important innovation which was the consequence of the definitive identification of heretics as guilty of the crime of *lesa maestà*. Finally – at the 1197 Council of Gerona – the total confiscation of the property of local heretics in favour of the King of Aragona was decided; a third being reserved for the person who had denounced them.[19]

In Italy, the first cases of confiscation regarding heterodox-Catholics date from the early twelfth century. With the decretal *Vergentis in senium*, Innocent III had, in 1199, put heresy in the category of the Roman "*crimen lesae (maiestatis)*" ("*divine lèse-majesté*"), thus definitively establishing the public nature of the crimes of faith. Included in the *Compilatio tertia* and in Gregory IX's compendium, part of the third canon of Lateran Council IV (1215), the document assimilated the sovereignty of the Vicar of Christ and the body of the Church to divine sovereignty and the body of Jesus. However, as Othmar Hageneder's studies have authoritatively clarified, *Vergentis* was partially included in the *Liber extra* emanated by Gregory IX in 1234, and, thus in the *Corpus iuris canonici*. Only the last part of the text was included in the *Decretali* – the whole programmatic introduction was omitted and the note declaring that the law is directed against the proponents, the defenders and the adherents of the heresy, as well as the enumeration of the single types of infamy into which they had fallen.

Therefore, only the affirmations regarding the confiscation of property – though these too came with some significant variations – had become a part of the Canon Law ("*Corpus iuris canonici*"). The *Vergentis* became, instead, part of secular jurisprudence with Frederick II's 1220 laws; in particular, the law known as *Gazaros*, included in the Civil Law ("*Corpus iuris civilis*").[20] In 1207, Innocent III set up in Viterbo a procedure which divided the property derived from heretic confiscation into three parts: one-third to the authorities who had arrested the heretic; one-third to the court which had emanated the sentence; and the final third to build city walls in the location in which the culprit had been arrested. The dwelling in which the heretic had been housed was to be destroyed to the foundations, "and let no one have the presumption to rebuild it, but let it – which has served as the hiding place of the perfidious – become the receptacle of vile refuse".[21]

From that moment, the tripartite formula dividing confiscated heretic property among various secular and ecclesiastical authorities remained a constant among the norms and customs regulating this matter in the Medieval

Italian peninsula and into the early modern era. It was restated in Rome by senator Annibaldo in 1231 – on the eve, that is, of the definitive affirmation of the delegated papal Inquisition with its directive that the whole confiscated property of heretics: liquid assets and real property alike must be in hand within eight days after the ecclesiastical sentence had been pronounced, and be assigned for one-third to those who had discovered and arrested the heretics, for one-third to the Roman Senate and, for the final third, used for the restoration of the city walls and demolition of the house in which the culprit had found refuge. Frederick II's laws of the 1220s and 1230s brought no changes, if not to add greater detail and wider interpretations.

After the organizational phase of the Inquisition as papal "delegate" had been brought to its conclusion by Innocent IV's decretals *Ad extirpanda* (1252) and *Cum super inquisitione* (1254), subsequent canonical changes concentrated chiefly on the financial aspects linked to punishment, in a direction clearly intended to strengthen their potentials. In *Quod super nonnulis* (1258), Alexander IV established that the orthodox offspring of parents found guilty of heresy after their deaths – whose condemnation would deprive their descendants of their inheritance *ex post* – might defend their possession of it "producing witnesses who are trustworthy and, above all, zealous in their faith" to demonstrate that their parents had embraced heresy only on their death beds. If this proved impossible, post-mortem confiscation must be executed.

In the 1295 constitution *Cum secundum leges*, Boniface VIII set the fundamental principle which would regulate heretic confiscation in the following centuries: according to this principle; confiscation could not legitimately be carried out by civil authorities if not after an ecclesiastical sentence of condemnation, issued by the inquisitor or the bishop. The Pope himself specified that the dowries which orthodox wives had brought to their marriage should not be confiscated if, at the wedding, they had been unaware of the heretical state of the husband. The Dominican Pope, Benedict XI, intending to favour the inquisitors with respect to the bishops, in 1304 declared that the latter could claim no part of the funds deriving from the sale of property taken from heretics, while Clement V made excommunication the penalty for inquisitors who should extort money using their inquisitorial office as a pretext.

With this normative framework, the early centuries of the early modern period saw a rich juridical-theological production regarding monetary punishments: production which certainly influenced the decisions of the ecclesiastical courts and the accumulating local procedures and customs within the Inquisition itself. This accruing process turned upon the exploration of the link between the sin-crime of heresy – which imposed, together with the sentence, excommunication (and therefore derived directly from God) – and the subsequent confiscation of property, deriving from an ecclesiastical structure and thus of human origin. The *Cum secundum leges* provided that "the goods of heretics being *ipso iures* confiscated"; it was, at the same time, forbidden to "expropriate its occupant with temporal authorities before the legitimate ecclesiastical judges have pronounced themselves regarding the crime of heresy".[22]

The document gave rise to a prolonged juridical and theological debate on the nature of confiscation. In the opinion of many interpreters, its threat weighed upon the culprit, since it obliged the accused to consign his property spontaneously to the fiscal authorities, even when no trial had been held. Declaring confiscation an *ipso iure* (by operation of law) penalty meant, as well, the admission that it applied from the moment in which the crime was committed: this allowed the authorities to seize goods acquired or sold by the culprit during the period between the crime and the sentence. Boniface VIII's rules, therefore, annulled the validity of debts, commercial transactions and wills entered upon (with good or bad faith) by the accused after his sin-crime – with the further effect of stripping the unaware buyers, inheritors and debt holders in possession of the now illicit goods. Further, on the basis of the same principles, confiscation of the property of descendants (whether orthodox or not), of a heretic who had died without having sustained a public trial, was legitimated. Still, a partial contradiction persisted, since the constitution's dispositions regarding the act of confiscation itself – which excluded secular courts even from the final act of trials for heresy and made the sentence of an ecclesiastical court obligatory – remained operative and were applied.

In the mid-1500s there was also discussion – especially in Spain – as to the correctness of applying the mechanisms of excommunication *ipso facto* even in the course of the trial, so as to make the repression of hidden crimes more efficient and recover confiscated property – which might also have important repercussions in terms of the debated legality of appropriating the property of the unbelievers of the New World. Alfonso de Castro (1495–1558), Minor Friar and Spanish Bishop faithful to Emperor Charles V – considered one of the fathers of modern criminal law – sustained that the norms of faith (even when, as was the case with confiscation, they did not concern personal guilt) bound conscience to the point that the person of faith was legally obliged to give his property back to the ecclesiastical authority, denouncing himself in the event of heresy committed by himself or a family member who had died without trial. Consequently, Castro accused the more indulgent theologians and scholars of canon law of cheapening the Christian's duty to obey the norms of the Church in their conscience, and exhorted confessors to aid the ecclesiastical and secular courts in their efforts to reduce religious dissent and the moral violation of tributary norms.

In *De potestate legis poenalis* ("Concerning the Authority of Penal Laws") (1550) the Franciscan theologian sustained the theory that the criminal trial and the hearing of oral confession could be considered substantially the same, not merely because both were judicial in character, but, also, because of the mechanisms of self-accusation and "satisfaction" which human coercion might share with the laws of pardon present in the sacrament of confession. A crime like heresy and the consequent confiscation of property

– the result of the excommunication *latae sententiae* – could not avoid this punishment through the intervention of any human judge. Noting that casting doubt upon the obligation of confiscation weakened the coercive and fiscal structures of the state, he proposed a spiritual guarantee of obedience to secular laws by attempting to model the latter on ecclesiastical law and by strengthening fiscal norms as well.

Still, during the sixteenth century, jurists and theologians took up the question of conscience posed by the canon laws in general, usually refusing Castro's thesis and sustaining, instead, the conventional nature of human law which obliged the subject to respect civil norms without the burden of self-accusation. The Dominican scholar, Francisco de Vitoria, in his *Relectio de Indis,* pronounced in 1539 – and circulated in manuscript until the Lyons edition of 1557 – certainly recalled that heretics "incur confiscation from the day they committed their crime" which made "any contract" invalid.[23] Still, he replied to Castro declaring that the appropriation of the heretic's patrimony by the ecclesiastical and secular authorities should come about only after a sentence and that any punishment *a die commissi criminis* should be seen as an "obligation": not because his ownership was illegitimate, but rather because this would have placed him in the situation of committing the sin of fraud. Should the heretic be tried, the buyer would risk losing (during his lifetime or after his death) what he had acquired in a sale made in bad faith. All this, Vitoria affirmed, was a mere consequence of the laws on confiscation, which were not based on divine law and might, therefore, even be revoked. The Dominican theologian thus suggested that the obligation of awaiting a sentence before materially acquiring the property confiscated *ipso iure* be recognized and the heretic be allowed legitimate use of his patrimony before condemnation, this would free many innocents from unjust sanctions – which also threatened the paralysis of trade.[24]

The Council of Trent came to an end without taking any explicit position on the doctrinal problem of the relation between laws and individual conscience, while, in the latter half of the century, the debate on the application of confiscation became a largely formal exercise given the reorientation of the economic structure of the courts of faith and the creation of the Congregation of the Holy Office. In any event, with the end of the Lutheran emergency, the courts tended to recur more frequently to the procedures of self-denunciation and spontaneous presentation which, even in the most serious cases, usually guaranteed the preservation of patrimony. Still, the threat of confiscation continued to seem real and terrible to people: in both the anti-inquisitorial riots in Naples in 1547 and the Milanese and Neapolitan disorders of 1563–4 (as had been the case in Naples in 1510 and would occur not much later in the anti-Spanish revolt in the Flanders), the people's fear of plunder and confiscations played an important role. Nor did juridical studies on these themes peter out, as the many pamphlets and essays cited in the course of this text (including judicial "opinions" addressed to popes and to the Roman ministries well into the 1600s) demonstrate.

In addition to an authoritative late sixteenth-century comment on Nicholás Eymerich's famous medieval inquisitorial handbook, *Directorium inquisitorum*, the Spanish jurist, Francisco Peña, was the author of a vast canonistic production – both in print and in manuscript – within which the question of confiscation had an important place. It was he who – with the Fiscal Procurator of the Congregation of the Holy Office – signed a consultation in 1610 on the case we have already cited of the defaulting "judaizer" Emanuele Mocata, condemned to confiscation by the Inquisitor of Reggio, whose property the Marquis of Scandiano claimed as his due. On this occasion, Peña sustained that the secular authorities could claim no right to the property confiscated by the ecclesiastical courts since the confiscation was an "accessory [...] to the sentence of condemnation" and fully part of the inquisitorial trial. A trial which, of course, recognized no *mixto foro* (that is, a joint competence of the secular and the ecclesiastical powers, allowed for other crimes like blasphemy, sodomy or – at least into the early modern period – witchcraft). Peña further sustained that the Pope had absolute dominion over the world and, therefore, also over the temporal sphere, since he acknowledged no limit to his direct jurisdiction ("*potestas directa*").[25] Unlike the situation in Spain, where the devolution of confiscated property to secular tax authorities occurred only where the dependants of the Inquisition court were maintained by the state, in Italy during the seventeenth century conflicts on the nature of taxation and the fiscal jurisdiction of the Holy Office increased, obliging the Holy See to engage in constant mediations with the various authorities of peninsular government.

"From the day of your committed error"

With the almost total disappearance of local Inquisition archives, and the only partial survival of the central Holy Office archives, singling out the basic directions which governed confiscation policy in the middle centuries of the early modern era is arduous. We can observe that sixteenth-century legal studies continued to place *publicatio bonorum* at the heart of the procedure and to insist upon the highly dangerous right of ecclesiastical courts to confiscate – or have the secular judiciary confiscate – the property of individuals condemned for heresy *a die commissi criminis*, from the moment in which the individual had committed the crime of heresy, regardless of the date in which the trial had been completed and the sentence pronounced. Nor did the retroactivity of the confiscations ordered by the *Officium fidei* regard only the property possessed by laymen, it invested the whole system of the concession of ecclesiastical benefices. Even the previously cited 1556 decree annulling the benefices of religious figures suspected of heresy, had, in fact, declared that "the benefices of heretics, from the day of commission are invalidated". The principle of confiscation *from the day of commission of the crime* was also constantly cited in the weighty pre-Tridentine *Summae confessorum* – among which, the influential *Summa tabiena* – as well as being cited in all the reference works present in the libraries of the Italian inquisitors.

The Dominican friar and Commissar General of the Holy Office, Umberto Locati, spent a good deal of time on it in his renowned *Praxis judiciaria inquisitorum*, in which the section on confiscation was reproduced almost exactly in the *Opus quod Iudiciale inquisitorum dicitur* of 1568. Zanchino Ugolini repeated it with the authority of the medieval tradition in *De haereticis*.[26] In its first book, the monumental and quickly deemed classic even in Italy, *De origine et progressu Officii sanctae Inquisitionis* (1598) – work of the Spanish Inquisitor Ludovico da Páramo, active in Sicily at the end of the 1500s – situated the roots of the Holy Office in the act with which God, in *Genesis*, drove Adam and Eve from Paradise, confiscating their property de facto ("Overthrowing all goods, he cast them out of the comforts of Paradise; thus the Inquisitor proscribes the property of heretics"). Páramus then inexorably recalled: "The property of heretics has not to be confiscated if not from the time the crime is committed".[27]

Even the broader mercantile jurisprudence of the early modern period, in so far as regarding the general traits of confiscation, was quick to indicate the dangers of holding property acquired from heretics, recalling that they might be confiscated only if the heretic had owned or sold them from the moment in which he had committed the crime and that in which he had been sentenced. So property acquired by heretics after the sentence had been pronounced were to be considered safe.[28] As a reminder of how inextricably secular and canon law were still intertwined in the early modern era, we should note that even secular jurists dedicated ample space in their treatises to the crime of heresy and the economic problems which might derive from it, damaging even the affairs of orthodox Catholics.

Sebastiano Guazzini's 1611 *Tractatus de confiscatione bonorum*, for example, specifically warned its readers that neither the prince nor secular judges could impede the confiscation of the property of a person condemned by the episcopal or inquisitorial court, and the inquisitor himself had no faculty to grace a heretic out of the so-called "period of grace", during which even the confiscation was prohibited. Guazzini further informed his reader that, in so far as goods alienated *post delictum* were concerned, ecclesiastical courts might request a "declaration" regarding the manner of acquisition of the property by third parties.[29] Confiscation *a die commissi criminis* was in any case considered permissible even by secular jurisprudence and secular juridical practice in cases where it had been imposed for the crime of human *lèse-majesté* and this represented a determining affinity in the consolidation of the principle of retroactive confiscation of heretic property since, as we have seen, heretics were considered guilty of the crime of divine *lèse-majesté*.[30]

The concept of divine majesty ("*maiestas divina*") was a crucial element in the power system on which the *Ancien régime* was founded. As Mario

Sbriccoli has illustrated so well, the crime of divine *lèse-majesté* was "built up – in method, in the rationale on which it rested, and in the elements employed in its fashioning – with the same framework as that which concerned human majesty (*"maiestas humana"*), which it reproduced down to the least detail, constituting a nearly specular image of it".[31] Emblematically, in the early 1600s, Paolo Sarpi advanced a sharp jurisdictional critique of the parallelism between the crime of human *lèse-majesté* and that of divine *lèse-majesté*, judging them to be disparate and drawing the consequential conclusions as to confiscation. On this point, too, the Cardinal Assessor of the Holy Office, Francesco Albizzi, centred his polemical reply:

> Fra' Paolo [...], convinced not merely as a liar, but as a hypocrite (as he remains also a convinced ignoramus), while he pretends to persuade [us] that confiscation is not an obligatory punishment for heresy, declaring – so he says – that the reason for the crime of human *lèse-majesté* is not the same as that for divine *lèse-majesté*, since in that former occurs for malice, whilst the latter, very often for ignorance; so that this deserves compassion – and that, never.[32]

The retroactivity of confiscation of heretics' property with regard to the moment of condemnation was set in canon law and therefore unavoidable: not always, however, was this retroactivity explicitly mentioned in the sentence. We can, however, cite as an example among others, the 1551 sentence of the "relapsed Lutheran heretic", Galeazzo da Trezzo from Sant'Angelo Lodigiano, recalling his sentencing that "the good of the heretics [had] to be inflicted with confiscation from the day of the commission of the crime as punishment for such iniquities",[33] as well as that inflicted in 1570 upon the Vicentine Giulio da Thiene, "for many and many years a well-known heretic", which provided "that all thy property, both liquid and real, be confiscated from the day of thine committed error", with the contextual detraction of 100 scudi for the expenses and immediate needs of the Holy Office. The material execution of the confiscation in Thiene occurred in 1580 and faithfully cited that the sentence provided that "all of his property, mobile and real, be confiscated, from the day the crime of heresy was committed, and leased and incorporated by the Office of the Holy Inquisition".[34]

The same retroactive rigour was explicitly part of the sentences pronounced upon heretics emanated by the episcopal courts, as in the case of Aurelio and Giovanni Battista Mosconi of Adria, condemned in default in 1581 by Bishop Giulio Canano to be consigned to the secular arm with the confiscation "of all goods [...] from the day of the commission of the crime".[35] That "his memory be damned, annulled and cancelled from the memory of the faithful and when his bones and body can be discerned from the bones of the faithful, [the court] determines that they must be disinterred as fetid and unworthy of a holy place and that they be [...] thrown away in some profane location; besides this, we declared that all his belongings pertaining to his person be confiscated, both mobile and real, assets and shares in whatsoever location they may be, as at this present we confiscate them from the day in which he committed the crime", provided, as well, the fulminating post-mortem sentence pronounced by the Cremona Inquisition on December 22, 1581 upon the mysterious Neapolitan priest, Andrea Luzio. Luzio, preaching in the parish church of Saint George and "having, with many simple and many qualified persons, made the effort to dogmatize various highly pernicious, reprobate and heretic, opinions", had, the court averred, made himself "Master of the Darkness and Leader of the Blind".[36]

In the mid-1500s, the influential *Responsa* of Pietro Belo, Chief Advisor and Fiscal Procurator of the Holy Office in the 1550s and 1560s under Paul IV, Pius IV and Pius V, defended authoritatively the retroactivity of heretic confiscation.[37] To the query as to whether the orthodox children of heretics, whose property had been confiscated, had the right to a living allowance from the treasury, or if they might subtract the sum necessary for their support from confiscated properties, Belo responded negatively: "it is human to maintain oneself", he admitted, but the sin of heresy, inasmuch as it was a crime of divine *lèse-majesté*, must be considered so serious that "it may furnish no living, nor funds".[38]

During the seventeenth century, too, the Holy Office continued to emanate rulings, and stated that the citations to canon laws which provided confiscation of heretic property should occur from the moment in which the sin-crime had been committed. The various seventeenth-century examples we might cite can be reassumed in those found in the pages of the *Confiscatione* described in the manuscript *Most Accurate Index Compiled upon the Final Section of the Arsenal of the Holy Office* ("Indice accuratissimo compilato sopra l'ultima parte dell'Arsenale del Sant'Officio"), an updated synthesis of the famous inquisitorial manual by Eliseo Masini, *Sacred Arsenal* ("*Sacro arsenale*"), written down in 1673 by the Dominican Father Domenico Francesco Pellegrini da Como:

> *Confiscation.* All the property of the relapsed heretic be confiscated *a die predicti delicti haeresis*. The goods acquired by the penitent heretic after the sentence are not confiscated. So the goods of others which are with his, when he is sentenced, go to their owners; indeed, the tax office is to satisfy creditors, who were acquired before the heretic fell into error. Children of relapsed heretics and of founders of heresies, though they may receive the sacraments, remain deprived of inheritance. Goods are not to be confiscated in punishment for default, but only for adjudged heresy, indeed, so great is benevolence that, if the heretic returns to the bosom of the holy Church, if not relapsed, his confiscated property is condoned. Heretic confiscation, even though imposed *ipso iure*, does not take effect, if not after the pronouncing of the sentence.[39]

The norms outlined by Inquisitor Pellegrini indicate, in their very brevity, the level of seventeenth-century familiarity with confiscation as a practice that had become routine. The instances accumulated over the preceding decades had found certain and categorical answers which suggest at least two important implications. First of all is the fact that, between the sentence and confiscation, the precedence of the former must be rigid: a disposition guaranteeing the accused which, however, was not always efficient since, as we shall see, a substantial part of the confiscation – the so-called *Seizure* (*"apprehensio"*) – occurred prior to the pronouncement of the sentence by the inquisitor and, therefore, might in some measure influence it. Second, we should note the effort required of the court of faith to honour the obligations of third parties weighing upon the confiscated patrimonies, should these claim rights be greater than those of the Holy Office. This was a procedure which, permitting third parties to present recourse, complicated the liquidation of confiscation considerably, exposing the court (and this, too, would be the object of successive bargaining) to a notable administrative effort. This was probably the reason prompting the popes and the Congregation to accept the usage, present for centuries in some territorial states, of dividing the results of confiscation with the secular authorities and/or the episcopal courts, obtaining, with other results, the possibility of using their offices in the management of the bureaucratic aspects of requisitioning and, if necessary, selling – usually by auction – the expropriated goods.

The division of patrimonies between secular and ecclesiastical powers

The agreements between ecclesiastical courts and secular governments in the early modern period, in so far as regards to the division of patrimonies confiscated for crimes of faith, were set up in the central decades of the 1500s, while the battle against the spread of Reformed doctrines proceeded throughout the Italian peninsula. Relations between the Holy Office and secular governments in so far as regarded pecuniary punishments – particularly for the important theme of confiscation – were never simple, especially within the states territorially larger and politically more influential. Here public authorities were less controllable as compared to the dynasties of minor principalities and they were better able to conquer more or less ample margins of intervention. The relations between the ecclesiastical courts and secular authority were especially difficult within the borders of the republics, where the jurisdictional autonomy of the inquisitorial courts was a long-standing tradition and greater space was allowed for the intervention of the civil magistracy, both during the trial and on the terrain of eventual extradition and confiscations. In Venice and Genoa secular judges regularly took part in the plenary hearings of the Inquisition court and in the reading of its sentences, as a means of control.[40]

The Republic of Lucca was the only peninsula State to block the stable penetration of the Holy Office courts, though – or precisely because – the merchants and leaders were found to be amply "infected" with Reformed ideas. Here, in 1545, a secular court of faith was created – the Office on Religion – which projected, among other ends, incentives to denounce, promising a monetary recompense through the Office of Heretic Properties. The laws of Lucca, in fact, provided that the heterodox individuals incriminated for the first time, even for having read forbidden books or exchanged correspondence with heretics for commercial purposes, must pay the secular tax office a fine of 50 gold ducats and, in the event of a second infraction, suffer total confiscation of property, accompanied, should there be a third trial, with the death penalty.

Lucca, too, would experience a wave of confiscations in 1580 at the height of the anti-heretic repression conducted by the Tuscan republic. Even in the Republic of Genoa, where there was only one Holy Office court – in the capital city (so its jurisdiction was wide) – there were tensions between secular and ecclesiastical authorities concerning the confiscation of heretics' property. In 1593, for example, the treasury of the *Dominante* seized the goods confiscated from Augustino Mortara without consulting the Congregation of the Holy Office, enraging the cardinals who only with difficulty managed to oblige the secular tax authorities to hand over the funds to the pious institutions of the Inquisition. In the mid-sixteenth century, Venice even managed to impose the prohibition of confiscation of the property of condemned heretics upon the Holy Office. In the event that confiscation had already occurred, the *Serenissima*, instead, reserved the right to repossess the patrimonies to restore them to the orthodox descendants, chiefly to avoid negative repercussions on trade. These norms provided for an exception with regard to those who were "judaizers", that is, converted Jews who were accused of cultivating their ancestral faith in secret, and whose property was appropriated by the Venetian authorities.[41]

Within the pontifical dominions, where inquisitorial procedures were facilitated by the fusion of the secular and the ecclesiastical dimensions at the various levels of government, judiciary and public bureaucracy, it was natural for the Holy Congregation to hold the monopoly of collection and possession of confiscated property. Confiscation, together with fines imposed on individuals and on the Jewish universities, represented a decisive source of income for the Roman Ministry, especially in the central and latter decades of the 1500s. This remained true at least until the income deriving from the various economic activities connected to the management of the Conca estate and the regulation of monetary punishments became more stringent; events which made the phase "forgiving you the confiscation of your property" become more frequent at the end of the sentences pronounced by the Roman court of faith.[42]

Tens of thousands of scudi were obtained in 1556 from the sequestration of property belonging to Portuguese subjects living in Ancona, after more than 50 trials for charges of "judaizing" undertaken by the Neapolitan jurist, Giovanni Vincenzo Falangonio, Commissioner Extraordinary sent by Paul IV. Falangonio himself benefited illicitly from his position, fleeing Ancona after having aided a group of people under Inquisition to escape – and having taken possession himself of their property. An uncertain number of people – between 24 and 27 individuals – who refused reconciliation, after having been condemned as "influenced by Jews", were sent to the stake and burnt between the spring and summer of 1556, while the credits of all the expropriated subjects were transferred to the Apostolic Chamber. The cultural and emotional impact of this dramatic episode on the world of Judaism was enormous, giving rise to an internal tradition of elegies, chronicles and comments which continued down the centuries. Other confiscations, to the value of about 40,000 scudi, executed upon Jews, were launched between 1567 and 1568 after various trials in Bologna, providing funds for the local Mount of Piety and the new House of the Catechumens.[43]

In the same period, the confiscations imposed on the leading figures of important wealthy families, condemned for heresy, afforded conspicuous sums. Between the 1570s and the 1580s, the Holy Office took in, for example, 3,000 scudi from the agreement reached with the heirs of the Hermit of St Augustine friar, Giulio da Milano (Giulio della Rovere), whose property had been confiscated after his escape from prison in Venice in 1543 and during his residence in various Three Leagues localities, where he served as a Calvinist minister. In 1578, the first instalment of a total sum of 1,000 scudi was registered with a note "which Giulio della Rovere must pay", while, after his death in Tirano in 1581, his brothers reached an agreement to pay another 2,000 gold scudi to the Supreme Court.[44]

In the event of confiscations imposed upon wealthy Roman families, too, the patrimony involved might equal, and even exceed, the funds available to the various local merchant groups engaged in commerce and finance, unleashing many appetites. This was the case when, during the pontificate of Clement VIII, a notorious confiscation was executed upon the Cenci family. Though its result did not directly involve the Holy Office, it did give rise to historiographical scenarios which ought to be more closely examined from the point of view of confiscation for crimes of faith. As a tenacious posthumous memory informs us, in September, 1599, Beatrice Cenci, her brother, Giacomo and her step-mother, Lucrezia, were executed for patricide in the course of a dramatic, public, ceremony in front of Castel Sant'Angelo. Their property was promptly confiscated and destined (as was the practice in such cases) to be sold at auction. In May, 1600, however, with a *motu proprio*, the Pope authorized the governor of Rome to sell the rural Cenci holding called Torrenova to his nephew, Gianfranco Aldobrandini (who already owned a confining property), for 91,000 scudi: a sum probably inferior to one-quarter of the holding's market value. This episode began a long controversy between the Cencis and the Aldobrandinis which lasted almost 30 years, ending with a few compensations during the pontificate of Urban VIII.[45]

From the institutional point of view, the only Roman organization able to contest the Holy Office's power to appropriate the property of those condemned for crimes of faith was the Apostolic Chamber; its periodic attempts to claim prerogatives, however, were never completely recognized. The Pontifical Chamber ("*Camera thesauraria*") had been established in the eleventh century to administer the finances of the Curia and the temporal goods of the Holy See. Between the thirteenth and the sixteenth centuries – along with the traditional functions regarding the verification of income, the custody of the treasury and payments – it had acquired judicial competence in fiscal, civil and penal matters.

In particular, in 1379, Urban VI had extended the Chamber's jurisdiction to all cases concerning – even indirectly – its rights and interests. From the fifteenth century, the titular *camerarius* was always a cardinal with a permanent substitute – the Vice-Chamberlain ("*vice camerarius*") – a post later fused with that of governor of Rome. Pius IV reorganized the Apostolic Chamber between 1561 and 1564, not only with the intent of destroying the influence of the Carafa family (which had affirmed itself during the pontificate of Paul IV – and the nepotistic creation of the post of Regent of the Chamber) but, as well, to confer efficiency and prestige upon an institution which remained crucial for the government of the Catholic Church and the pontifical State in the centuries of the early modern era.[46]

The Apostolic Chamber's attempts to supplant the Holy Office in receiving confiscations or fines for crimes of faith were usually made on the occasion of particularly important sums. In 1713, for example, when the time came to exact a large sum from another Apostolic Protonotary (after the clamorous sixteenth-century case of Pietro Carnesecchi). The target was the Marquis Pietro Gabrielli, a noted collector of art, who had been a personal attendant to Pope Innocent XI.[47] Arrested in 1690 with two of his secretaries, Filippo Alfonsi and Giuseppe Pignata, Monsignor Gabrielli spent a year in prison in Castel Sant'Angelo, and abjured *de vehementi* before the cardinals of the Congregation, who condemned him to perpetual incarceration. The following year he was transferred to the convent of the Minor Observants of Saint Bernardino (1704), just outside the walls of Urbino.

Here Gabrielli was held under a bond of 40,000 scudi which, in the event of flight – as the dispositions of his transferal declared – was to be "paid to the court or Treasury of the Holy Office". A brief incursion of the prisoner into a field adjacent to the convent was deemed – perhaps speciously – an attempt at evasion, and here a long legal controversy arose with the Gabrielli family (especially Pietro's brother, Angelo) on the payment of the bond. In 1711, under the papacy of Clement XI, when the Congregation finally obliged the Gabrielli family to deposit 25,000 scudi, divided in a series of payments, in the Banco di Santo Spirito, "in a separate account in credit to the Court and Treasury of the Holy Office", an unpleasant conflict developed with the Apostolic Chamber on the destination of the funds; a conflict which very quickly broadened to regard, more generally, the jurisdiction over the property confiscated from heretics.[48]

The Chamber Procurator – listing all the legal arguments concerning heretic confiscation from the Roman period to the medieval bulls and Frederick II's constitutions – appealed to the centuries long custom of dividing expropriated property among ecclesiastical entities (or between these and the secular governments) as precedents demonstrating the non-exclusive canonical pertinence of the Holy Court regarding confiscated property, though its right of ultimate judgement in trials of heresy was unquestionable. The Chamber also denied that the various examples of past consignment of confiscations to the Holy Office constituted a precedent to which the Congregation might appeal, since what really counted was the letter of canon law which, in the opinion of these jurists, did not explicitly envision the sole competence of the *Officium fidei* for monetary punishments of heresy. The same beneficiary provisions set out by the popes in the 1500s and the 1600s in favour of the local courts were expressly cited to deduce the adequate capacity to sustain – and thus the moral and financial sustainability – of the requests advanced by the pontifical treasury.[49]

On its part, the Holy Office replied to these pressures with a memorandum interpreting medieval canon law in terms favourable to its own position and restoring full dignity of juridical precedences to the numerous confiscations it had received into its coffers over the centuries. The only case of attribution to the Apostolic Chamber of the fruits of a confiscation by the Holy Office, they sustained, had been that connected with the property of Giacinto Centini, a maternal nephew of Cardinal d'Ascoli, accused with two friars of having attempted to assassinate Urban VIII with sortileges invoking demons, burnt in Rome in April, 1635. On that occasion, the Congregation recalled, Centini's confiscated patrimony had been given to the Chamber:

> because that was the will of the majesté of Urban VIII, who considered that Centini's principal crime was *lèse-majesté* due to planning the death of his holiness by charm (the instrument of his crime), so that the death and the confiscation did not proceed from these acts, but from the other crime, as the Pope himself expressly declared in the decree.[50]

Since, then, the Pope himself had decided that the condemnation had been pronounced for attempted assassination – and so for human *lèse-majesté* (for divine *lèse-majesté*, as we have seen, would, instead, have given the Inquisition full competence and thus, with it, confiscation), the fruits of punishment were, on that occasion, assigned directly to the pontifical treasury. In the moment in which they found themselves defending their economic prerogatives, the directors of the Holy Office also openly cited the existence of a financial link between the crucial question of the conversion of the Jews and the income deriving from confiscation. They did this by recalling that the Congregation directly financed pious initiatives "like the

Houses of the catechumens in Ferrara and in Bologna" which, the essayist averred, they could not do if the fruits of confiscation were to go to the Apostolic Chamber. The recourse to this argument, even within a patrimonial controversy, indicates once again how crucial conversion was within the early modern history of the Roman Inquisition.[51]

Finally, during the controversy over the disposition of the Gabrielli bond, the Roman Ministry produced a documented memorandum, entitled "A Note on Some of the Many Examples Which May Be Furnished of Punishments and Confiscations Regarding the Holy Office" ("*Nota di alcuni fra li molti esempii, che addurre si possono delle pene, e confiscationi applicate al Sant' Officio*"), presenting an ample series of confiscations carried out in the course of the seventeenth century and, with all probability, destined to the attention of the Pope.[52] Among the cases cited, was the 1624 condemnation of Antonio Camerata to ten years in the galleys, with a 4,000 scudi fine; that of Francesco Burri, in 1672, which, after negotiations with his brother Cesare, was transformed into 150 scudi, to be paid to the Milan Holy Office; and that of the counts Aloisio and Geronimo de Malvasia, whose properties were confiscated by the Inquisitor of Bologna in 1675. It is interesting to note that, along with the income represented by sums deriving from crimes of faith in the strict sense, the Holy Office broadened its recourse to confiscation to defend its operative continuity, using it to punish crimes of blood against its own exponents. This it did by applying an extensive interpretation to the concept of divine *lèse-majesté*, as it did on May 23, 1657, in the case of condemnation in default of Carlo Mezzanotte, found guilty of having killed a Carlo Riccio, operating in Gubbio as agent of the Holy Office. Mezzanotte was tried by the Inquisition and accused of divine *lèse-majesté*, which led to a life sentence to the galleys and the confiscation of his goods.[53]

These examples allow us, perhaps, to assign a more political – and not merely juridical and theological – connotation to the already cited decision of Urban VIII to entrust the fruits of the Centini confiscation to the Apostolic Chamber on the basis of the argument that, in the event of an attempt upon the life of the Pope through enchantment, the accusation of homicide was to be considered dominant – and thus the crime of human *lèse-majesté*, rather than that of heresy and apostasy attached to the casting of spells. Clearly, the application of the category of divine *lèse-majesté* to the agents of the Holy Office should have regarded even more closely the presumed attempt of Centini to assassinate the Pope, Head of the Congregation. Faced with an accusation by the Holy Office which explicitly brought divine *lèse-majesté* into play, with attendant confiscation in favour of the Holy Office, Urban VIII none the less decided (probably to favour the Chamber financially) that "the confiscation [is a result] of the crime of human *lèse-majesté*, from an attempt upon his sanctified person". So this episode constitutes a useful example of the not always linear policy of papal intervention in the management of the Supreme inquisitorial court in all fields, including the economic.[54]

Princes and inquisitors between "large" and "small" states

In the early years of the modern period, secular princes had wielded broad decisional power in the question of appropriation of property belonging to heretics. In 1545, Hercules II d'Este, with a printed edict, established a sort of secular "period of grace" after which those who had been condemned as heretics – or as in possession of heretical documents – and had not denounced themselves would, for a first offence, be liable to a fine of 100 gold scudi; and in the event of a second offence, to that of 2,000 gold scudi and banishment. The still obstinate heretic would suffer the death penalty and the confiscation of all his or her property, to be assigned to pious organisms listed in the document. In 1563, Giudobaldo II della Rovere, Duke of Urbino, autonomously declared the nullification of testamentary provisions aimed at countering the confiscation of heretic properties which, as we shall soon see, had rapidly become widespread among the Italian landed gentry.[55]

In the regional states which originated in and centred upon a small city, the tradition of the supremacy of princely houses and the continuance of an often daily relationship between the dukes and the exponents of the ecclesiastical courts favoured a habit of direct negotiation of the terms of confiscation due to crimes of faith (in whose context the Church met fewer obstacles compared with what occurred in larger states). An example is what happened in Mantua in May 1568, following Carlo Borromeo's sentence of heresy pronounced against a group of important citizens, among whom was the duke's tax commissioner and the architects Cesare Pedemonte and Giovan Battista Bertani – prefect of ducal buildings and principal local pupil of Giulio Romano.[56] A few days before the ceremony of public abjuration, which would involve some of his closest aids, Duke Guglielmo Gonzaga visited Borromeo and "with great modesty and humility" successfully begged him to condone imprisonment of Pedemonte and Bertani and their arraying in the ignominious "shift" contemplated by the sentence. He went on, then to "speak of the confiscations", declaring that it would have been sufficient for the inquisitor to exhibit:

> some declaration of the Pope contrary to that which he claims as his and that, in his words, it also be clear that he would be equally placated, as there is no Bull regarding the matter, should his holiness wish to write [with a letter that might be] display[ed], that only half of the confiscation is to go to him, showing he has no stake in this matter that is so important to him.[57]

Another eloquent example is that of Piacenza – since 1545 passed on by Paul III Farnese to his natural son Pier Luigi, who made the city capital of a new duchy and principal seat of the Inquisition. The judges of faith in Piacenza had established vicariates in Parma (1585) and Crema (1614). Until suppression in the eighteenth century, the Piacenza Inquisition was one of the few never to have been awarded a fixed ordinary income based on benefices. Its income – in the mid-sixteenth century already worth about 35 scudi a year (while it also gave the Parma office 35 scudi annually) and, a century later, nearly double that figure – derived entirely from the confiscated properties of the condemned.[58] The highest amount of income was reached in 1560, when the already cited author of *Praxis judiciaria inquisitorum*, the preacher Umberto Locati – who would subsequently rise to the position of Commissar General of the Roman Ministry – was appointed Inquisitor of Piacenza. In his principal work, Locati himself gives us a testimony of his activity in Piacenza in these years, recalling 14 cases of trials, some of which ended with confiscation: among these, the trial of the notary Alessio Ruinagia. Head of a wealthy local family which, in the fifteenth century, along with customs duties and taxes linked to trade, as well as collecting horse and salt taxes, in 1564, Ruinagia was found guilty of practising Calvinism since 1552: that is, in the period in which – after the assassination of Pier Luigi Farnese, power had been wielded by Ferrante Gonzaga, as Imperial substitute, through the Governor don García Manrique. The governor's wife, Isabella Brisegna or Brisena, sympathized with the local exponents of Reformed ideas, having frequented in Naples the circle of the *Spirituali*. Then, expatriate in Chiavenna and Zurich, Isabella was aided by Giulia Gonzaga, through the good offices of Pietro Carnesecchi.[59]

What took on all the traits of a "pay back" began when the stabilization of the Piacenza political scene in the hands of Ottavio Farnese – bitter foe of don Ferrante – made it possible for the Piacenza Inquisition to turn an investigative eye upon what had been going on in the city in the years of indulgence towards heterodoxy. With the duke's acquiescence, Alessio Ruinagia was captured in Genoa in 1563 and his extensive estate confiscated directly by the inquisitor. The sentence of confiscation began from the year in which Ruinagia fell into sin: the various land holdings were confiscated even if their management had already passed into the hands of third parties and he had retained only legal possession, receiving payment of rent.[60]

The possibilities of strategic alliances and reciprocal support between princes and inquisitors were not the only elements which – until the 1631 devolution to the pontifical State – gave the "little states" of the Farnese, the Este and the Gonzaga a greater liberty of action with the Holy Office even in the area of patrimonial expropriation. Though this group had far from homogenous experiences in civic and religious areas during the sixteenth and seventeenth centuries – the Ferrara of Renée of France, wife of Duke Hercules II who received Calvin personally as a guest in 1536 is certainly not the seventeenth-century Parma of the diabolic spells feared by Ranuccio I Farnese although they do present some common institutional and political traits. As the minor territorial entities lost political centrality throughout the Italian peninsula as well as internationally, their reigning dynasties and their governmental structures felt a growing need to negotiate with more important courts, desiring to receive and concede protection and signs of good faith, a network of agreements regarding reciprocal financial or military aid, the aspiration to titles, positions and other forms of honorific recognition.

A dense agenda of relationships bound all the "minor states" in an effort to set up alliances and create consensus which, as Daniela Frigo has observed, "seems, finally, to have as its fundamental object to point out the existence of their lords – of the minimal level of territorial sovereignty that could still claim [...] its own role and its own autonomous function".[61] Proceeding, in so far as possible, together with local inquisitors; repressing the forms of religious dissent and the heterodoxy of usage together – and permitting the representatives of the Holy Office to play a prominent role within local society even from the point of view of the accumulation and the administration of patrimony both real and financial – became, then, an almost obligatory phase for the dynasties feeling their way across the changing Italian board of the Counter Reformation.

On the other hand, during the seventeenth and much of the eighteenth centuries, the role of the spiritual and cultural climate determined by the spread of panic concerning possession, conjuration and witchcraft and baroque devotional enthusiasm, should not be under-valued in the creation of alliances of intent (or at least of reciprocal non-interference) between dukes and inquisitors. There was, too, a notable presence within the Po valley duchies, of Jewish minorities and their sometimes real – sometimes only feared – "closeness" to the sphere of magic and occultism. Minorities for centuries, object of ferocious economic depredations, as we shall see more clearly, were among the most frequent victims of confiscations decided by the ecclesiastical courts.[62] The period and the figures of the Duchess of Modena, Virginia de' Medici, wife of Cesare d'Este, "cured" in 1607 by exorcisms from a Dominican friar – whose illness led to the imprisonment of several women suspected of casting evil spells – as well as the already cited Ranuccio Farnese, Duke of Parma and Piacenza from 1592–1622 (he, too, obsessed with fears of possession and diabolic spells), represent well the atmosphere of the time.

In the 1610s, Farnese personally carried out a vast inquiry into witchcraft, from which he drew important patrimonial advantages, spreading artfully the voices of an inexistent community of intent with the Inquisition (which did not, however, provoke opposition from the judges of faith). The inquiry was broadened to include at least ten women, two "wizard" priests and various nobles whom the Farnese did not care for: these were later, tortured, confessed to an extraordinary magic plot aimed at some Italian princes, 18 cardinals and the pope. At the end of the trials, in May, 1612, Parma's main square saw the execution by decapitation or hanging of ten individuals in the course of a theatrical public ceremony lasting three hours. In August, the two prelates accused of witchcraft were hanged. Ranuccio Farnese took the castles and held in feud by the condemned and, in particular, the very desirable Colorno feud, belonging to Gian Francesco Sanvitale and his mother, Barbara, married to Orazio Simonetta, all of whom were executed. Girolamo's son was imprisoned in Borgo Val di Taro, where he died of the plague. Other castles were taken from Bartolomeo Riva, the Farnese's ambitious General Treasurer – a member of a local family of the middle classes – who had conceived the idea of having a secular court put on a trial for witchcraft without reaction from the inquisitor. The judge of faith of Parma, in fact, never turned up during the entire trial until 1613, when he claimed jurisdiction over a few witches who had not yet been judged by the ducal court.[63]

Another eloquent case in which inquisitorial jurisdiction, political considerations and economic interests overlapped with the opposite results, occurred in the 1630s in the city of Turin, centre of the large Duchy of Savoy with its international aspirations. Here, Margherita Roera, an impoverished noblewoman, exorcized by a Dominican friar with the approval of the judge of faith, Friar Girolamo Robiolo, accused the ducal president and plenipotentiary, Lelio Cauda, of having ensorcelled Duke Vittorio Amedeo I, the general of ducal finances and two other aristocrats. On that occasion, the inquisitor, in conjunction with the exorcist, staged a false possession complete with a ringing prophecy in the roaring tones of a diabolic voice, to the sole end of ruining Cauda, a wealthy landowner whose brilliant career had displaced leading bureaucrats and nobles of the Savoyard entourage, inciting their envy. Once the truth had come to light, two investigations were instituted: one by the Holy Office; the other by the archbishop. Vittorio Amedeo himself, who had for some time been attempting to curb the powers of the Inquisition in the duchy, opened an investigation, carried out by the royal treasurer with a procedure that led to the arrest of the inquisitor by the Dominican Provincial. After a controversy which went on for years, in 1638, the Congregation of the Holy Office condemned the exorcist to life imprisonment, Roero to a public whipping and the two aristocrats involved in the plot to confiscation of their property, while the inquisitor was stripped of his office.[64]

These examples of the intertwining of politics and the Inquisition in early seventeenth-century Parma and Turin, though displaying all the variations of a history which often eludes any general scheme, do offer two clear tendencies which may prove useful in understanding the contemporary policy of confiscation for crimes of faith. In the Po valley duchies of the early modern era, and in the surviving feudal enclaves which persisted even within the largest states, the practice of confiscation was necessarily liable to local negotiation between the inquisitors and the secular government. Here, though the duke or the feud holder might advance objections and vaunt privileges when confronted with the patrimonial appetites of the Holy Office. The entire negotiation was conditioned by the overall system which saw the princely dynasties attempting to fit themselves securely into the dance of military alliances, requests for protection and the assignment of episcopal, cardinal and pontifical posts which shook the Italian peninsula during the middle centuries of the early modern period. In that political context, it was much easier for the Congregation and local judges to establish momentary and partial accords with the duchies, or to claim a margin of operative liberty subsequently, in compensation for some past concession.

The situation was very different for regimes like that of the Duchy of Savoy: a State whose territorial and dynastic aspirations had always looked beyond the Alps: and which, in the 1600s and 1700s, could still maintain an active political and military strategy at European level – and, during the sixteenth century, had had to come to terms with considerable heterodox religious minorities within its own territory. Here the properties confiscated in the context of the religious wars had often been conferred on functionaries or military figures, or directly absorbed by the state, chronically in debt and therefore very reluctant to allow the fruits of confiscation slip into ecclesiastical hands. After 1572, for example, Emanuele Filiberto expropriated the property of those who had escaped the Saint Bartholomew's Day massacre taking refuge in Savoy, by devolving it to the ducal treasury.[65] Despite negotiations conducted by Rome through the nuncio during the entire 1580s, contrasts persisted throughout the Piedmontese territories (when there were not actual abuses, perpetrated against the property of those being investigated, or condemned, in trials of faith).

In 1610, up to half of the fines imposed for the possession of forbidden books in Savoy territory was destined for the secular tax office, while the princes published edicts of their own providing for the confiscation of the property of heretics and "witches" to the benefit of the treasury. In this and other cases of harsh competition on the terrain of economic resources between government and ecclesiastical institutions, besides the administering of justice, the possibilities for the inquisitors to bring negotiations with the princes to a happy ending were liable to many, complicated, limitations. Frequent impatient letters sent from Rome to the judges of faith operating in Piedmont stigmatizing their weakness in dealing with governmental authorities during confiscation procedures show this clearly. A letter addressed in 1602 to the inquisitor in Turin accuses him of "moving ineptly" in a negotiation regarding property in emphyteusis held by the Benedictine abbey of San Giusto in Susa, taken over by the ducal treasury ("and in the future notify [us], if similar confiscation concerning goods in ecclesiastical emphyteusis is undertaken by the ducal tax office").[66]

The dynamics of political and institutional negotiation, then, considerably influenced the formation of a patrimonial base for the inquisitorial seats scattered throughout the various Italian states. We have already observed that the Piacenza Inquisition was able to subsist throughout the entire early modern age on local income from bequests, fines and confiscations, without any other beneficiary income. In the mid-1700s, the office drew a notable revenue from 36 rents deriving from properties and incomes which had accumulated over the sixteenth and seventeenth centuries. The very fragmentation is, in itself, an eloquent testimony to a patrimonial sedimentation, formed over decades.[67] The twin office in Piacenza drew the major part of its income – besides that deriving from the property of the

Church of San Michele degli Umiliati, assigned to it by Pius V – from the confiscated inheritance of the well-to-do sixteenth-century jurist, Giuseppe Caverzago: a man of impeccable orthodoxy, but brother of the heretic Alessandro, burnt at the stake in June, 1564. When Giuseppe Caverzago died in 1569 without descendants, his property was included in the *publicatio* concerning his brother. Ottavio Farnese – though he had intended to claim part of the patrimony in question, was obliged to take a conciliatory stance after a Holy Congregation decree of 1589 ordered the Inquisitor of Piacenza to take possession of the Caverzago properties and, from them, confer upon the struggling office in Parma a perpetual pension of 252 local lire. Caverzago's widow, Margherita Bassi, expropriated de facto of her inheritance, was persuaded to retire into the Piacentine monastery of Santa Chiara, where she was maintained by the inquisitor until her death.[68]

Punishments and investments though the centuries: the case of Ferrara

An interesting case of able management of inquisitorial confiscations over the long period in an urban territory is that of the Ferrara Inquisition, whose economic history we shall now observe in some detail, so as to draw some general considerations at the end of this chapter.

The Holy Office's d'Este patrimony was for the most part composed of property accumulated before 1598, when the duchy devolved upon the Church's state. Indeed, a sum of about 3 scudi, paid annually by the House of d'Este on a building with land which, from 1598, the Ducal Chamber of Modena continued to pay until the suppressions, dated from 1398. Further, in 1396 the Marquis Nicolò III d'Este had allowed a Gerardo della Fratta to build a chapel dedicated to Saint Augustine in Ferrara cathedral and to endow it with property which was bequeathed (together with the faculty of naming the chaplain) to the Inquisitor of Ferrara. In this case, too, the income – which, in 1514, was already 24 gold scudi per annum – continued to be drawn until the court was terminated. In September, 1405, a Pietro Confettori named the Estense Holy Office as his heir and testamentary executor, giving it direct dominion over various terrains in emphyteusis; the same thing occurred in 1448, when Pietro's sister, Margherita, left the *Officium fidei* "many lots of land", immediately leased out.

In the sixteenth century, the Holy Office in Ferrara was very enterprising from the patrimonial point of view as well. In 1516 it spent 100 lire on land which had previously been cultivated by others; three years later, a plot which had been purchased not long before was leased out directly by the inquisitor; in 1535 three houses were bought and immediately rented out with incomes that continued well into the 1600s. In 1564, a certain Ottaviano Gillioli was condemned "for heresy" to the monetary punishment of 300 gold scudi, part of which the inquisitor ceded to the duke of Este, probably to honour an agreement on division. Still "as neither Ottaviano nor his sons were able to pay this sum, due to the many debts they had (besides which, they had already paid the Ducal Chamber of Ferrara 150 scudi – which had been assigned to the Father Inquisitor – and another 50 scudi directly to the Father Inquisitor) they remained debtors of 100 scudi". In 1567, the Gillioli family were obliged to give the inquisitor another property, with immediate conveyance of the use of the land through emphyteusis. On the death of Ottaviano Gillioli, the Montisti family of Rome took possession of his property and assumed, as well, the payment of the annual fee to the Holy Office. The same thing occurred – again in 1564 – when a Ercole Calzone, condemned to a monetary punishment of 200 lire "due to heresy", discovered to be insolvent, covered his punishment by ceding a plot of land – which was then given in emphyteusis by the court of faith to the same Calzone at an annual rent of 10 lire (remaining a stable entry for the local office at least until the mid-eighteenth century).[69]

The economic life of the Estense Holy Office, then, proceeded with a substantial continuity of income and expenditure throughout the crucial decades of the sixteenth century. The edicts and the prohibitions regarding heresy emanated from 1550 by the dukes, in any case, attributed increasing financial concessions to the local inquisitors.[70] The fact that "the friars of San Domenico [claimed] that the inquisitor can confiscate the real property of citizens" was, on the other hand, well known within the Estense duchy, as the deposition of the Modenese Cataldo Bozzale, arrested and tried in 1566 attests.[71] The Ferrara Inquisition displayed an accentuated patrimonial vivacity even after the devolution of the duchy to the pontifical state, when, indeed, it may be presumed that the confiscation procedure became more simple and direct.

In 1602, with the money from a monetary penalty, buildings and estates were purchased, among which one guaranteed by land at Belriguardo where, since the fifteenth century, the Marquis Niccolò III had caused the celebrated residence *Delizia* to be built. Once that estate was freed by its debtors in 1610, with the 300 scudi the inquisitor immediately purchased another; this, in turn, was transformed into capital deposited with the local Mount of Piety, where it continued to produce income until the middle of the eighteenth century. And for the entire seventeenth century and the early eighteenth century, as a highly accurate retrospective compiled in 1749 on the vast archive unfortunately now lost to us testifies, the Ferrara Inquisition continued to purchase land and to renew scrupulously the fees, rents and leases on an increasingly extensive patrimony.[72]

Other deductions may be formulated following the story of a single investment managed by the Estense Holy Office from the seventeenth to the eighteenth century, starting with the confiscation of 3,000 Roman scudi from the "Jew" Vita – whose patronymic we do not, unfortunately, know.[73] With about half of this sum – equivalent to some 11,000 Ferrarese lire – in years in which the annual salary of an Estense mason was about 70–80 lire,[74] the inquisitor bought, in 1610, a vast estate which the duke had declared immune to any taxation since 1552. The remaining capital was deposited with the Mount of Piety at 5 per cent interest and remained there until 1646. When, in that year, the local Mount failed due to fraud,[75] the Ferrara Inquisitor was able to recover (and only with difficulty) half of the capital – that is, about 2,600 lire. After this negative experience with the institutional credit structures, the inquisitors judged it more profitable to engage in the ancient activity of small loans. A part of the capital which remained after the failure of the Mount was given to the Carmelite Fathers of Saint Paul, subject to annual tribute until 1656, when they freed themselves from the agreement. Immediately, in 1657, the sum repaid was lent out in like manner to a private individual, who redeemed it at the end of the same year. Perhaps to reduce the risk of loss of income over the medium-long period in a moment of market stagnation deriving from the effects of the plague of 1630 and the successive wave of 1656, in December, 1657, the Ferrara Inquisition divided the sum in two parts: one, 450 scudi, was lent out at 8 per cent; the other, 200 scudi, at about 6 per cent. These sums were renewed regularly throughout the first half of the 1700s.[76]

Such detailed operative résumés provide precious general information. The very length of the chronology within which the patrimonial base of the Estense Inquisition was built up shows how funds deriving from confiscation and the larger fines produced medium or long term economic effects. For the Holy Office courts, the acquisition of the properties of the condemned was a formidable instrument consenting hoarding and the re-enforcement of power, whose effects were felt throughout the entire early modern period. We should keep in mind, too, that fines and confiscations were distinct forms of monetary punishment, which might not only "over-lap" – as those condemned to heavy fines were often obliged to sell property to pay them (transforming the fines de facto into confiscation) – but also work together, since the eventual failure to pay a fine could produce a court order of confiscation, increasing both the coercive and the deterrent powers of this punishment. When, for example, a don Giovanni de Silva, sentenced in 1595 to a fine of 500 scudi, to be paid to the Hospital of the Incurabili in Naples had not, after four years, made payment "with diverse subterfuges", "making illusory the punishment imposed upon him", the Suprema ordered the Ministry of the Holy Office in Naples to summon the culprit and, in the event that he should continue to refuse payment, proceed to confiscate his property and recoup the missing sum.[77]

Precisely due to its benign effects on the Holy Tribunal's finances over the long period, confiscation not only significantly improved the patrimonial situations of the local offices: it also increased the desirability and the prestige of the offices which had shown themselves most active in the eyes of the inquisitors themselves. This is evident in the letters of complaint sent to Rome by inquisitors destined (sometimes on various, successive, occasions of transferal) to fill roles in seats considered "poor", and therefore without attraction. A "flourishing" court might attract more qualified and ambitious judges of faith, allowing them to break free of the economic support of the convents of the Orders and from the attendant equivocation in day-to-day material relations which we have seen prevailed within their walls. So the accumulative mechanism of confiscation was a means – and it was, indeed, probably considered *the* means by the inquisitors – to improve their own position and the importance of their office within the hierarchy of choice presented by the local seats of the Holy Office. So, when the inquisitor carried out a rich confiscation, he was not working only for himself – responding to incentives activated, as we have seen, by the double nature of his post – but, as well, for the reputation and, we might say, for the future importance of the local office in which he found himself within the whole system of the justice of faith.

Nor can we exclude the possibility that, on the terrain of confiscation and heavy fines, some specific mechanisms of path dependence through which, over time, the single courts consolidated virtuous forms of administration and patrimonial accumulation, grew up and came to fruition. This is the case, for example, with the Faenza court which – as we have seen – was still quite wealthy in the mid-1700s (due, among other reasons, to the strategic ability already displayed in the early phases of the sixteenth-century anti-heretical repressions). Here a particularly violent action against the citizen council led, in the mid-1500s, to almost 20 years of conflict, ending in extremely heavy sentences with rich patrimonial aspects. When, later, Faenza's city government attempted to avoid financial collapse by collecting at least the tax on "the many properties confiscated for the Apostolic Seats due to the crime of heresy, which many in this city have incurred", Pius V – always on the advice of Pietro Belo – had his secretaries respond in writing that all the properties seized at the pontiff's command were immune from taxation. This was, furthermore, a competitive advantage which all inquisitors' property enjoyed throughout the Italian peninsula, as it might be extended to those who worked in such property, or assumed its management. This was a further source (with the jurisdictional exemptions) making it easy for the Holy Office to find leases for its real estate, another question we will need to look into further on.

The case of Ferrara also affords a second order of considerations regarding the efficacy with which the judges of faith administered their money. The secure capacity to acquire land and buildings already producing income, or rapidly rentable or available for fixed fee management, the prompt and efficient structuring of loans (evident even in situations where the necessary capital had been precociously redeemed and therefore the rapid identification of trustworthy borrowers with towards whom one might open new credits, are all elements showing the inquisitors' command of the logics governing local relationships and local informative networks, as well as the attention and ability in evaluating the opportunity of investments.

The variety of financial instruments to which the highest levels of the courts of faith recurred – their very elasticity in reutilizing them in the face of a case of dramatic institutional failure like that of the Mounts of Piety, are of themselves indicative of an active presence within the social and economic fabric of pre-industrial communities. In periods in which the chronic lack of diffuse liquidity, the canonical prohibitions concerning the concession of loans at interest – often included by theologians under the broad heading of usury – as well as the fragility of the chief institutions of the time offering credit, spurred investors and, in our case, the inquisitors and their managerial collaborators, to take refuge in credit agreements we may generically term "tributary". The tribute ("*livello*") or state ("*censo*") of the early modern period was, in practice, a contract activating a mortgage on property – usually a plot of land or a house. The property was held by the secular or religious lender and the debtor reacquired possession by paying back the sum of money lent in the form of an annual "tribute" for a period of nine or ten years, with several possible renewals. In this way, the loan was masked as a sale, since the agreement usually afforded the possibility for the seller to end the obligation to pay the "tribute" fixed by giving the buyer a sum equal to that for which he had "sold it" (that is, the sum loaned). The operation carried no fiscal charges for the buyer, since the taxes to which the property was subject continued to be paid by the "seller". The obligation to pay the "tributes" did not, obviously, end with the death of the debtor, if the sum had neither been repaid nor "extended". It fell, instead, upon the real property which served as a guarantee and so upon the heirs.

The lending activity of the Inquisition in Ferrara, exercised directly with the concession of capital and, indirectly, with contracts of "tribute" and "state", put the Holy Office substantially in the same category with the various secular and religious entities holding capital or real estate – from the confraternities, to the monasteries and the convents – which, during the 1500s, began to operate increasingly as regular institutions of credit for local populations. The period in which the Congregation of the Holy Office was created – and in which it consolidated the economic management of its territorial network – was the same that saw, together with population growth, an increase in consumption and prices as well as infra- and inter-regional expansion of trade. Though these elements were not accompanied by an adaptation of bank credit, nonetheless a growing number of people and institutions became familiar with financial techniques of some sophistication, and began to concede money on loan. So a connective tissue of minute, diffuse, credit sprang up, functioning on the basis of social mechanisms of reciprocal trust and the circulation of information and guarantees of good repute between lenders and debtors. These were mechanisms within which the public fame of orthodoxy certainly played an important part. From the end of the sixteenth century and in the following periods – at least until massive industrialization – credit represented one of the most powerful public means of social communication and transmission of value judgements regarding community members, which "involved and linked together the whole social body in their networks".[78] In rural areas and in smaller centres, especially where the network of institutions offering credit – public banks, Mounts of piety, private bankers, brokers, and other subjects – were less widespread and stable, private lending on the part of religious institutions and the inquisitors themselves, contributed to financing regional economies and making them more dynamic.

Certainly the process involved the mobilization of the growing forced savings of religious holdings as well as those of sanctuaries, charitable organizations and the confraternities, and the continuing confiscations and fines deriving from trials of faith. But it found completion in the transformation of these funds into direct investments, chiefly to the advantage of agriculture and small commercial activities. The forms of patrimonial accumulation pursued by the local courts of the Holy Office (and the Roman Congregation) contributed, over several centuries, to the creation of something that was more than – and different from – the original organization: courts of justice, canonically empowered to conduct trials and pronounce sentences within the religious sphere. Therefore, in the next chapter, we will need to look at the final products of this evolution to understand whether, and how, it transformed the repressive activity of the Roman Inquisition and the efficacy of its procedures.

Notes

1 See Lavenia (2000, 2003, 2004, 2010).
2 Monter (2006), pp. 18–19; Kamen (1965).
3 Antunes and Ribeiro da Silva (2012), p. 410.
4 See the edition by Venturi (1958), p. 68. The reference to "natural death" is in opposition to the institution of "civic death" which, inherited from the *Ancien régime*, was still contemplated by the article 22 of the *Code civil* (1804). It provided that whosoever was civically dead, besides being without the capacity to accumulate and transfer property to heirs, was barred from holding posts and occupations open to full citizens; such an individual further saw his or her marriage annulled and the links to family relationships dissolved. Civic death was abrogated in France in 1854.
5 Mazzei (2001), p. 396. On the Milanese merchants, Gallarati and Capriano, who travelled to Geneva to collect their credits only after securing a written certificate attesting the solidity of their Catholic faith, see Savoja (1985), p. 53. On Vicenza see Demo (2014), which confirms that, among the merchants about to venture into "infected" lands, the practice of going to a notary with witnesses who could declare that one was "a good Christian" was common.
6 Translation of Kamen (1965), p. 524.
7 A discussion of this question may be found in Malanima (1998), pp. 112–21.
8 ACDF, Si, *Libro dell'entrata e dell'uscita del Sant'Offitio*, p. 1r. The letters of the Siena Inquisition are testimony of an interest in the destination of Sozzini's property which persisted for many years, despite repeated attempts of relatives to obtain redress. See Prosperi (2010), pp. 301–12.
9 ACDF, Si, vol. 16, folder 26, "Contro Fausto Sozzini detto Il frastagliato", interrogation of September 30, 1588 to Cornelio Marsilii, pp. 406r–407r. This quote does not appear in Szczucki (2001). "The jagged" was the name attributed to Sozzini within the Senese Accademia degli Intronati.
10 Di Renzo Villata (1999). The main reference is Mariano Sozzini's *Mirabilia commentaria in primam partem libri quinti decretalium*, printed in Venice (1593).
11 Fausto Sozzini to Ferdinand I Grand Duke of Tuscany, Kraków, December 14, 1588, in Fabronio (1792), pp. 118–20. On the broader hereditary question then

"The citizen dies, the man remains"   173

troubling the Sozzini family, which also involved Fausto's property, see Tedeschi (1964).
12 Lavenia (2000), pp. 58 and 75. In BAV, Borg. Lat. 558, pp. 30vff., we discover that, already in 1590, there had been correspondence between Rome and Florence concerning property confiscated by the Inquisition; between 1597 and 1603, in an intense exchange of letters, the grand duke is reminded that Pius V's donation *in toto* of the goods deriving from a confiscation (most probably that of Pietro Carnesecchi's property) to the Tuscan Ducal Chamber was to be considered exceptional, with Rome insisting many times that the local "inquisitor tell them what was done in other confiscations" or obliging him to "act as usual". In 1609, ducal ministers were still blocking the inquisitor in Siena from confiscating the property of a recalcitrant heretic who had already been executed, "alleging that it belongs of the duke's treasury".
13 ASM, Fc, b. 215, folder "Appiano Bernardo [...]", letter dated July 26, 1572 to the Governor of the State of Milan, pp. 1v–2r.
14 ACDF, Si, *Libro dell'entrata e dell'uscita del Sant'Offitio*, p. 2r. Before the confiscation, the ordinary fixed income of the Siena court was very modest, consisting of 30 scudi a year, provided by the Florence Inquisition, and 25 contributed by Pisa: see Lavenia (2000), p. 58. The dates in which Giovanni da Radicofani was in Treviso and became Inquisitor of Siena are in Ribetti (1710), pp. 561, 656 and 658.
15 As the inquisitor's manuscript shows: see Ermeneglido Todeschini's *Storia della fondazione, ed origine della santa Inquisizione di Milano ora esistente nel convento di santa Maria delle Grazie nel borgo di porta Vercellina de frati Predicatori della provincia di Lombardia* [...] in ACDF, So, St.st., LL–5e, *Inquisizione di Milano*, p. 11r.
16 BAV, Barb. Lat. 6334, p. 153v, Rome, June 10, 1626. See also Bergonzoni (1998), pp. 27ff.
17 *Bullarum editio* (1860), pp. 344–5.
18 Maceratini (1994), pp. 74ff., 122ff.
19 Paolini (1999), pp. 445ff.; Piergiovanni (1974), pp. 175–98.
20 Where in *Vergentis* we see, as in Innocent III's *Registri*, "In terris temporali nostre iuristitioni subiectis bona eorum statuimus publicari, et in aliis idem fieri precipimus per potestates et principes seculares", Gregory IX's *Decretali* instead of "eorum" have the word "hereticorum". Hegeneder believes this implies that, while in 1199 the papacy meant to strike down not only heretics, but those who protected them as well, with the most serious punishments established for these cases (that is the confiscation of property), Raimondo di Peñafort, compiler of *Liber extra*, believed that such action might be taken only against the former. It is difficult to establish whether the change in direction of the whole edict is simply the result of Raimondo's editorial interpretation, or reflects a change in papal policy on heresy and those who sympathized with it. Weighing in favour of the second hypothesis – that is, a renunciation on the part of the Church of Rome to persecute external support of heresy severely – is the fact that the third *constitution* of Lateran Council IV, held in 1215, repeated almost to the letter *Vergentis* on sympathizers, repeating the consequences for infamy already cited (like the destitution from office and benefices for members of the clergy guilty of heresy already present in *Ad abolendam*), but without any mention of confiscation of their property: see Hageneder (1963).
21 Paolini (1999), p. 450, from which the information which follows below is also drawn.
22 Lavenia (2004), p. 137.
23 Ibid., p. 157.
24 Ibid., pp. 35ff. and 156ff.

25 Lavenia (2000), pp. 56–7.
26 Cagnazzo (1517), p. 242v, par. 9 ("et [...] intelligant a die commissi criminis"); Locati (1583), p. 31; Ugolini (1579), p. 181; *Opus* (1570) – first edition 1568: see Errera (2000), p. 106. On the 1556 decree see Firpo and Marcatto (1998–2000), vol. 1, p. 16. See also the Index of BAV, Barb. Lat. 1370: "Beneficia haereticorum vacant a die commissi delicti et sunt reservata".
27 á Paramo (1598), p. 45, col. 1.
28 See for example Guazzino (1611), p. 249 ("bona acquisita per haereticum, a die commissi delicti citra usque ad sententiam non veniant in confiscationem bonorum, sed ea tantum quae tempore delicti possidebat").
29 Ibid.
30 "Hoc enim dicitur in crimine laesae maiestatis, ut [...] multo ergo fortius in hoc immanissimo crimine": Locati (1583), p. 116; "Confiscatio honorum in omni capite criminis laesae maiestatis [...] fiat ipso iure a die commissi criminis, requiritur tamen declaratio iudicis, aliter fiscus non potest apponere manum" (ibid., p. 63); "Alienata post delictum per haereticum ipso iure dicuntur applicata fisco": Guazzino (1611), p. 243.
31 Sbriccoli (1974), pp. 346–7.
32 Without author (1678), p. 278.
33 Fumi (1910), p. 212.
34 TCD, Mrm, Ms 1225, pp. 257r–259v.
35 TCD, Mrm, Ms 1226, pp. 412v–414r.
36 TCD, Mrm, Ms 1226, pp. 412v–414r. Mention of Luzio's case may be found in Peyronel Rambaldi (1995), p. 607.
37 BAV, Vat. Lat. 5468, pp. 303v–307v.
38 Ibid., pp. 507v–509r.
39 BAV, Borg. Lat. 660, pp. 16v–17r.
40 Del Col (2006), pp. 748ff.
41 On Lucca see Lavenia (2000), p. 63 and Ragagli (2001); on Genua BAV, Barb. Lat. 1370, p. 75r, Rome, August 20, 1593 and May 20, 1594; Lavenia (2000), p. 86; on Venice see Del Col (2006), pp. 466–8.
42 See for example the sentences located in TCD, Mrm, Ms 1224, 1225, 1226, 1227.
43 A reconsideration of the Ancona episode in the light of an ample, and previously unpublished, documentation, can be found in Ioly Zorattini (2001–2); on Bologna see Lavenia (2003), p. 338.
44 ACDF, Oec 15, year 1579, p. 5r; So, St.st., L3b, "Instrumenta diversa", pp. XVv–XVIIIr. Perhaps erroneously, this material mentions an accord between Giulio and Bartolomeo de Revere, brothers and heirs of "that Antonio de Revere", "heretic and deceased among heretics". For an up-to-date survey, see Rozzo (2011).
45 Fraschetti (1935), pp. 158ff.; Di Sivo (2002).
46 Cherubini (1988); Giannini (2003).
47 On this interesting figure of a "learned libertine", see Frascarelli and Testa (2004).
48 The pertinent documentation may be found in ACDF, So, St.st., I5a, unnumbered subfolder.
49 "Just as, with the supreme popes, Gregory XIII and Alexander VI, Italian inquisitors were granted many benefices and pensions, whose provision was at the expense of the court, and prisoners fed [...] there is no reason to hesitate, since the utility of all goods deriving from confiscation belong by right to the Apostolic Chamber": see the printed papers *Sacra Congregatione coram Sanctissimo Romana confiscationis in causis haeresis. Pro reverenda Camera apostolica contra promothorem Fiscalem Sanctii Officii*, Typis De Comitibus, Roma 1712, p. 4r, contained in ACDF, ibid.
50 Ibid., Memorandum destined to the pope, without date or signature, pp. 3v–4r.

51 Ibid., p. 3*v*. The historic situation in which this episode occurred is reconstructed in Visceglia (2011).
52 ACDF, ibid.
53 ACDF, ibid., p. 1*r*.
54 In the margin, the person writing the *Note* explains "the affair was resolved in this manner because confiscation could not be imposed for a heretical spell, but for human *lèse-majesté* [it could], not being [then] due the Holy Office" (Ibid., p.2*r*–*v*).
55 Lavenia (2000), p. 60.
56 Pagano (1991) and Carpeggiani (1999), p. 278. On Bertani see Rebecchini (2000). Borromeo, already Archbishop of Milan, was sent to Mantua in 1567 by the Congregation to support the local inquisitor, Camillo Campeggi.
57 As Carlo Borromeo himself wrote to Cardinal Scipione Rebiba, secretary of the Congregation of the Holy Office: see BAM, F 41 inf, Mantua, May 21, 1568, p. 183*r*.
58 On the situation in the mid-1600s, when Piacentine income was made up of income "produced by properties acquired through confiscation", see BAV, Borg. Lat. 558 (quote p. 47*r*); on the mid-1700s see Chapter 1. For a general view see Ceriotti and Dallasta (2008).
59 On relations between the two women, see Peyronel Rambaldi (2012), pp. 259ff. The sentence condemning Carnesecchi declared "you were well aware of an income of one hundred scudi a year that a very close friend of yours, under investigation and attainted of heresy, sent to donna Isabella Brisegna, heretic and fugitive in Zurich and later in Chiavenna among the heretics": Firpo and Marcatto (1998–2000), vol. 2, tome 3, p. 1367 (also for the attribution of the name of Giulia Gonzaga to the "very close friend").
60 Castignoli (2005). On Locati, see the entry by Ragagli in *Dizionario* (2005).
61 Frigo (2011), p. 50.
62 Brambilla (2010); Caffiero (2012).
63 Dall'Acqua and Mondelli (1995). Surviving ducal documentation does not, however, consent a full understanding of how the exchanges between secular authorities and the Holy office were conducted: see Del Col (2006), pp. 598–602. On the complex relations between the secular authorities and the Holy Office on the question of jurisdiction in cases concerning witchcraft, see Lavenia (2001) and Romeo (2008).
64 This episode has been brilliantly reconstructed by Lavenia (1996).
65 Lavenia (2003), p. 80.
66 BAV, Barb. Lat. 1370, p. 75*r*, Rome, April 15, 1602.
67 ACDF, So, St.st., LL5f, *Inquisizione di Piacenza*.
68 Ceriotti and Dallasta (2008), pp. 106–7; ACDF, So, St.st., LL5f, *Inquisizione di Parma*.
69 It should be remembered that the peripheral offices of the Inquisition within the pontifical State survived the 1700s and 1800s abolition of that institution, functioning in the Kingdom of Italy until at least 1880, from what we can deduce from the appointment of inquisitors: see Del Col (2006), p. 793.
70 For example, where they insisted that the confiscated property of heretics must be "partitioned and dispensed among pious locations or initiatives without the Chamber or the Treasury being allowed to keep any minimal part for itself": Prosperi (2003), p. 130.
71 Ibid., p. 125.
72 ACDF, So, St.st., LL5e, *Inquisizione di Ferrara*.
73 Del Col mentions this case as well, see (2006), p. 467.

74 Prosperi (2003), p. 131.
75 The failure of the Mount in Ferrara brought with it the loss of about 500,000 scudi. The episode is mentioned, among others, by Frizzi (1809), p. 111.
76 ACDF, So, St.st., LL5e, *Inquisizione di Ferrara*.
77 Scaramella (2002), p. 272.
78 BAV, Vat. Lat. 5468, p. 537*v*. For further information on the Faenza episode, see Tre Re (1957). For a re-evaluation of the usefulness of the concept of *path dependence* in historical and economic studies, see David (2007).

Bibliography

à Paramo, L. (1598) *De origine et progressu officii Sanctae Inquisitionis*, Madrid: ex Typographia regia.
Anonymous [Albizzi, F.] (1678) *Risposta all'Historia della Sacra Inquisitione composta già dal r.p. Paolo servita*, Rome, n.p.
Antunes, C. and Ribeiro da Silva, F. (2012) 'In Nomine Domini et In Nomine Rex Regis: Inquisition, Persecution and Royal Finances in Portugal, 1580–1715', in F. Ammannati (ed.) *Religione e istituzioni religiose nell'economia europea. 1000–1800 – Religion and Religious Institutions in the European Economy*, Atti della Quarantatreesima settimana di studi, 8–12 maggio 2011, Florence: Florence University Press, 377–410.
Bergonzoni, D. (1998) *Storia degli ebrei di Scandiano*, Florence: La Giuntina.
Bullarum editio (1860) *Bullarum diplomatum et privilegiorum sanctorum romanorum pontificum taurinensis editio*, tome 4, Turin: Franco ed Henrico Dalmazzo editoribus.
Brambilla, E. (2010) *Corpi invasi e viaggi dell'anima. Santità, possessione, esorcismo dalla teologia barocca alla medicina illuminista*, Rome: Viella.
Caffiero, M. (2012) *Legami pericolosi. Ebrei e cristiani tra eresia, libri proibiti e stregoneria*, Turin: Einaudi.
Cagnazzo, G. (1517) *Summa Summarum quae Tabiena dicitur*, Bologna: in edibus Benedicti Hectoris bibliopole Bononiensi.
Carpeggiani, P. (1999) "Sgabelli pieni di carte disegnate quasi per la maggior parte indarno", in M. Rossi and A. Rovetta (eds) *Studi di storia dell'arte in onore di Maria Luisa Gatti Perer*, Milan: Vita e pensiero, 277–84.
Castignoli, P. (2005) 'L'attività penale del Sant'Ufficio di Piacenza nella seconda metà del Cinquecento. II. Il notaio Alessio Ruinagia costretto all'abiura: un errore giudiziario?', *Bollettino storico piacentino* (100): 205–13.
Ceriotti, L. and Dallasta, F. (2008) *Il posto di Caifa. L'Inquisizione a Parma negli anni dei Farnese*, Milan: FrancoAngeli.
Cherubini, P. (1988) (ed.) *Mandati della reverenda Camera apostolica, 1418–1802*, Rome: Istituto poligrafico e Zecca dello Stato.
Dall'Acqua, M. and Mondelli, M. E. (1995) *La spia di corte. Da un carteggio inedito un intrigo nella Parma farnesiana*, Parma: Guanda.
David, P. A. (2007) 'Path Dependence: a Foundational Concept for Historical Social Science, *Cliometrica* (2): 91–114.
De Luca, G. (2008) *Il potere del credito. Reti e istituzioni nell'Italia centro-settentrionale fra età moderna e decenni preunitari*, in A. Cova, S. La Francesca, A. Moioli and C. Bermond (eds) *Storia d'Italia. Annali 23. La banca*, Turin: Einaudi, 212–55.
Del Col, A. (2006) *L'Inquisizione in Italia dal XII al XXI secolo*, Milan: Mondadori.

Demo, E. (2014) 'Mercanti ed eresia a Vicenza nel XVI secolo. Nuovi documenti e prospettive di ricerca', in G. Maifreda (ed.) *Mercanti, eresia e Inquisizione nell'Italia moderna*, special issue of *Storia economica* (1): 85–100.
Di Renzo Villata, M. G. (1999) 'La Constitutio in basilica beati Petri nella dottrina di diritto comune', in *Studi di storia del diritto*, volume 2, Milan: Giuffrè, 151–301.
Di Sivo, M. (2002) 'Vite nefandissime. Il delitto Cenci e altre storie', in Id. (ed.) *I Cenci. Nobiltà di sangue*, Rome: Fondazione Marco Besso-Colombo, 219–55.
Errera, A. (2000) Processus in causa fidei. *L'evoluzione dei manuali inquisitoriali nei secoli XVI–XVIII e il manuale inedito di un inquisitore perugino*, Bologna: Monduzzi.
Fabronio, A. (1792) *Historiae Academiae Pisanae*, volume 2, Pisa: Cajetanus Mugnainius in aedibus auctoris.
Firpo, M. and Marcatto, D. (1998–2000) *I processi inquisitoriali di Pietro Carnesecchi (1557–1567). Edizione critica*, 2 vols, Vatican City: Archivio segreto vaticano.
Frascarelli, D. and Testa, L. (2004) *La casa dell'eretico. Arte e cultura nella quadreria romana di Pietro Gabrielli (1660-1734) a Palazzo Taverna di Montegiordano*, Rome: Istituto Nazionale di Studi Romani.
Fraschetti, C. (1935) *I Cenci. Storia e documenti dalle origini al secolo XVIII*, Rome: Formiggini.
Frigo, D. (2011) *Politica e diplomazia. I sentieri della storiografia italiana*, in R. Sabbatini and P. Volpini (eds) *Sulla diplomazia in età moderna. Politica, economia, religione*, Milan: FrancoAngeli, 35–60.
Fumi, L. (1910) 'L'Inquisizione romana e lo Stato di Milano. Saggio di ricerche nell'Archivio di Stato', *Archivio storico lombardo* (35, 36, 37): 5–124, 145–220, 285–414.
Giannini, M. C. (2003) *Loro e la tiara. La costruzione dello spazio fiscale italiano della Santa Sede (1650-1620)*, Bologna: Il Mulino.
Guazzino, S. (1611) *Tractatus de confiscatione bonorum*, Venice: apud Antonium Pinellum.
Hageneder, O. (1963) 'Studien zur Dekretale "Vergentis" (X.V, 7, 10). Ein Beitrag zur Häretikergesetzgebung Innocenz'III', *Zeitschrift der Savigny – Stiftung für Rechtsgeschichte* (49): 138–73.
Ioly Zorattini, P. C. (2001-2) 'Ancora sui giudaizzanti portoghesi di Ancona (1556): condanna e riconciliazione', *Zakho*r (5): 39–52.
Kamen, H. (1965) 'Confiscations in the Economy of the Spanish Inquisition', *The Economic History Review* (3): 511–25.
Lavenia, V. (1996) '"Cauda tu seras pendu". Lotta politica ed esorcismo nel Piemonte di Vittorio Amedeo I (1634)', *Studi storici* (37): 541–91.
Lavenia, V. (2000) 'I beni dell'eretico, i conti dell'inquisitore. Confische, Stati italiani, economia del sacro tribunale' in *L'inquisizione e gli storici: un cantiere aperto. Tavola rotonda nell'ambito della Conferenza annuale della ricerca (Roma, 24-25 giugno 1999)*, Rome: Accademia Nazionale dei Lincei, 47–94.
Lavenia, V. (2001) '"Anticamente di misto foro". Inquisizione, Stati e delitti di stregoneria nella prima età moderna', in G. Paolin (ed.) *Inquisizioni. Percorsi di ricerca*, Trieste: Università di Trieste, 35–80.
Lavenia, V. (2003) 'Gli ebrei e il fisco dell'Inquisizione. Tributi, espropri e multe tra "500" e "600", in *Le inquisizioni cristiane e gli ebrei. Tavola rotonda nell'ambito della Conferenza annuale della ricerca. Roma, 20-21 dicembre 2001*, Rome: Accademia nazionale dei Lincei, 325–56.

Lavenia, V. (2004) *L'infamia e il perdono. Tributi, pene e confessione nella teologia morale della prima età moderna*, Bologna: Il Mulino.
Lavenia, V. (2010) 'Struttura economica: Inquisizione romana', in A. Prosperi (ed.) *Dizionario storico dell'Inquisizione*, with the collaboration of V. Lavenia and J. Tedeschi, Pisa: Edizioni della Normale, vol. 3.
Locati, U. (1583) *Praxis judiciaria Inquisitorum*, Venice: apud Damianum Zenarium.
Maceratini, R. (1994) *Ricerche sullo status giuridico dell'eretico nel diritto romano-cristiano e nel diritto canonico classico (da Graziano ad Uguccione)*, Padua: Cedam.
Malanima, P. (1998) *La fine del primato. Crisi e riconversione nell'Italia del Seicento*, Milan: Bruno Mondadori.
Mazzei, R. (2001) 'Convivenza religiosa e mercatura nell'Europa del Cinquecento. Il caso degli italiani a Norimberga', in H. Méchoulan, R. H. Popkin, G. Ricuperati and L. Simonutti (eds) *La formazione storica dell'alterità. Studi di storia della tolleranza nell'età moderna offerti a Antonio Rotondò*, tomo I, Secolo XVI, Florence: Olschki, 395–428.
Monter, W. (2006) 'The Mystery of Torquemada's Heirs', in A. B. Palacios (ed.), *Praedicatores, Inquisitores – II. Los Dominicos y la Inquisición en el mundo ibérico e hispanoamericano. Actas del 2° Seminario Internacional sobre los Dominicos y la Inquisición, Sevilla, 3–6 de Marzo de 2004*, Rome: Istituto storico domenicano, 13–25.
Opus (1570) *Opus quod Iudiciale inquisitorum dicitur*, Rome: apud Haeredes Antonii Bladii impressores camerales, Romae 1570 (1st edn 1568).
Pagano, S. (1991) *Il processo di Endimio Calandra e l'Inquisizione a Mantova nel 1567–1568*, Vatican City: Biblioteca apostolica vaticana.
Paolini, L. (1999) 'Le finanze dell'Inquisizione in Italia (secoli XIII–XIV)', in *Gli spazi economici della Chiesa nell'Occidente mediterraneo (secoli XII–metà XIV)*, Pistoia: Centro italiano di studi di storia e d'arte, 441–81.
Peyronel Rambaldi, S. (1995) 'Inquisizione e potere laico: il caso di Cremona', in P. Pissavino and P. Signorotto (eds) *Lombardia borromaica Lombardia spagnola 1554–1659*, Atti del Convegno di studi (Pavia 17–21 settembre 1991), Rome: Bulzoni, volume 2, 579–617.
Peyronel Rambaldi, S. (2012) *Una gentildonna inquieta. Giulia Gonzaga fra reti familiari e relazioni eterodosse*, Rome: Viella.
Piergiovanni, V. (1974) *La punibilità degli innocenti nel diritto canonico dell'età classica*, Milan: Giuffrè.
Prosperi, A. (2003) *L'inquisizione romana. Letture e ricerche*, Rome: Edizioni di storia e letteratura.
Prosperi, A. (2010) *Eresie e devozioni. La religione italiana in età moderna. II. Inquisitori, ebrei e streghe*, Rome: Edizioni di storia e letteratura.
Ragagli, S. (2001) *Il mercante come inquisitore nella libera Lucca del Cinquecento*, in G. Paolin (ed.) *Inquisizioni: percorsi di ricerca*, Trieste: Università di Trieste, 131–80.
Ragagli, S. (2005) 'Locati Umberto', *Dizionario biografico degli italiani*, volume 65, Rome: Istituto dell'enciclopedia italiana, 375–8.
Rebecchini, G. (2000) 'Giovan Battista Bertani. L'inventario dei beni di un architetto e imprenditore mantovano', *Annali di architettura* (12): 69–74.
Ribetti, P. A. (1710) *Giardino serafico istorico fecondo di fiori, e frutti di virtù, di zelo e di santità nelli tre Ordini istituiti dal Gran Patriarca de Poveri San Francesco*, tome I, Venice: per Domenico Lovisa.

R. Romeo (2008) 'Inquisizione, Chiesa e stregoneria nell'Italia della Controriforma: nuove ipotesi', in D. Corsi and M. Duni (eds) *"Non lasciar vivere la malefica". Le streghe nei trattati e nei processi (secoli XIV–XVII)*, Florence: Florence University Press, 53–64.

Rozzo, U. (2011) *Giulio (Della Rovere) da Milano*, in M. Biagioni, M. Duni and L. Felici (eds) *Fratelli d'Italia. Riformatori italiani nel Cinquecento*, Turin: Claudiana, 71–8.

Savoja, M. (1985) 'Aspetti del commercio nello Stato di Milano in epoca spagnola', in Archivio di Stato di Milano, *Aspetti della società lombarda in età spagnola*, Como: New Press, volume 2, 51–108.

Sbriccoli, M. (1974) Crimen laesae maiestatis. *Il problema del reato politico alle soglie della scienza penalistica moderna*, Milan: Giuffrè.

Scaramella, P. (2002) *Le lettere della Congregazione del Sant'Ufficio ai tribunali di fede di Napoli 1563–1625*, Trieste and Naples: Edizioni Università di Trieste-Istituto italiano per gli studi filosofici.

Szczucki, L. (2001) 'Il processo di Fausto Sozzini a Siena (1588–1591)', in H. Méchoulan, R. H. Popkin, G. Ricuperati and L. Simonutti (eds) *La formazione storica della alterità. Studi di storia della tolleranza nell'età moderna offerti a Antonio Rotondò*, tome 1, Secolo XVI, Florence: Olschki, 375–90.

Tedeschi, J. (1964) *A Question of Inheritance in an Italian Letter of Fausto Sozzini (1587)*, Bibliothèque d'Humanisme et Renaissance (26): 154–61.

Tre Re, M. G. (1957) 'Gli avvenimenti del sedicesimo secolo nella città di Faenza con particolare riguardo ai processi e alle condanne degli inquisiti per eresia', *Studi romagnoli* (8): 279–97.

Ugolini, Z. (1579) *De haereticis,* Rome: in Aedibus populi Romani, Romae 1579.

Various authors. (2000) *L'inquisizione e gli storici: un cantiere aperto. Tavola rotonda nell'ambito della Conferenza annuale della ricerca (Roma, 24–25 giugno 1999)*, Rome: Accademia Nazionale dei Lincei.

Various authors. (2003) *Le inquisizioni cristiane e gli ebrei. Tavola rotonda nell'ambito della Conferenza annuale della ricerca. (Roma, 20–21 dicembre 2001)*, Rome: Accademia nazionale dei Lincei.

Venturi, F. (1958) (ed.) *Illuministi italiani*, tome 3, *Riformatori lombardi piemontesi e toscani,* Milan and Naples: Ricciardi, 27–105.

Visceglia, M. A. (2011) 'Attentare al corpo del papa: sortilegi e complotti politici durante il pontificato di Urbano VIII', in V. Lavenia and G. Paolin (eds) *Riti di passaggio, storie di giustizia. Per Adriano Prosperi*, volume 3, Pisa: Edizioni della Normale, 243–57.

5   A pervasive Inquisition

A closer look at the dynamics and the results of the widespread enterprise of confiscation of the property of those condemned in trials of faith can help us better understand the plurality of cultural and operative levels brought into play. The physical localities of religious repression initiated by the Holy Office in early modern Italy will be identified far from the convent walls and the episcopal and papal palaces. The will to confiscate unavoidably shattered the secrecy of the courts' procedure and drew the Inquisition to the centre of society. Necessarily, the formal rules governing the procedure in cases of faith had to be adapted to accommodate specific agreements and "trade-offs" as well as tenacious and pervasive informal incumbencies or obligations, conventions, traditions and local usages in their more simple forms, as well as socially approved behavioural norms, ways of speaking/expressing, *ethos* and codes of conduct deriving from family, education, literacy, or from the professions, or an ideology.

All of the elements, which – from the initial phases of the Inquisition through to the condemnation – might be set aside or avoided with relative ease, suddenly appeared solidly before the inquisitors and the secular authorities collaborating with them as an intractable element of the still vital complex existential fabric in which the culprit-victims were enveloped and which – until that final moment – all of these authorities had assumed might be cut away with the mere pronouncing of sentence.

In confiscating, the Inquisition spread out through society, multiplying the dignitaries, the offices and the subjects who collaborated with it and, in the end, its own visibility and power. As we shall see in the pages that follow, the process of describing, apprehending, calculating the value, blocking attempts to withhold goods, selling the property which had belonged to individuals forever expelled from civic society meant that a large, varied, population both urban and rural, were subjected to the rituals and the will of ecclesiastical and civil magistrates. Men and women who would never have ventured into the by-ways of inquisitional procedure on their own, were mobilized by public and religious authorities who – by summoning them, questioning them, forcibly making them their representatives, directly or indirectly damaging their patrimonial rights – plunged them into the abyss of the repression of religious dissent. In this way, they were transformed into living testimonials to the superior power of the confessional courts to break up some of the fundamental moral bases of the social system – like the certitude of property rights, the perpetuity of familial inheritance procedure and the bond between patrimonial unity and family identity, which a serious sentence might destroy forever.

The evidence which emerges from our look into confiscation for reasons of faith indicates the arbitrary nature of a history which separates the phase of the inquisitorial process in its strict sense from that of the actual confiscation. The close analysis of some examples of appropriation of the property belonging to heretics will allow elements of affinity, of continuity – and of reciprocal interference – between the two phases to come into focus, offering arguments in support of the method which invites us to study these moments side by side and consider them linked together in a unified juridical and repressive strategy. Within the inquisitorial continuum which was the interweaving of investigation, trial, sentence and confiscation the phase of compilation of the various items composing the patrimony to be seized and estimating their value – sometimes carried out while the trial was still in court (and so well before any inquisitorial sentence was pronounced) – had a central role. The listing and the evaluation of a culprit's property might bring up new and relevant information, which might, in turn, determine new developments in the ongoing trial, or in other trials already or potentially in existence.

The collaboration among inquisitors, civil magistrates, central and local governing institutions, feudatories and simple citizens in the carrying out of confiscations represented one of the privileged areas of dialogue between the two parallel legal codes – canon and secular – rooted in ancient Roman law. The medieval formation of an ecclesiastical legal system, founded on the interweaving of canon law and Roman-Byzantine law, allowed the inquisitors and the bishops to interact with "civil common law" quite easily on the question of confiscation for the crime of heresy, for it too was based on the ancient Roman structure to which the secular state's institutions looked.[1]

If ecclesiastical courts and civic authorities collaborated relatively harmoniously in appropriating the property of those condemned by the Inquisition within various Italian territorial regimes, this was not due solely to the monetary thirst of parched State coffers, nor the desire of secular governments to please the papacy and guarantee social stability and order through control of domestic religious dissent. Collaboration was possible because the ecclesiastical and the secular legal worlds employed the same juridical and cultural categories. That is to say that, fundamentally, they spoke the same language.

The "ultimate effect of the condemnation"

An important seventeenth-century example of confiscation for reasons of faith fell upon various members of the wealthy and influential Vaaz family, converted Portuguese Jews, living on the borders of the pontifical territories and those of the State of Naples. The three Vaaz brothers, Bento, Eduardo and Miguel, had arrived in Naples in the 1580s, after the popular revolt of 1585 had led to the lynching of the People's Representative ("*Eletto dal Popolo*") Gian Vincenzo Starace, leading the Spanish government to alter the forms with which the city was supplied with food. The Vaaz quickly gained a pre-eminent role in Naples' affairs, joining the principal local bankers and merchants in the grain trade and consolidating significant political influence. The economic and financial reforms undertaken after 1610 by the Viceroy, the Count of Lemos (in virtue of which the family consolidated the centrality of its role within the realm's financial structure) was largely devised by Miguel Vaaz.[2]

Precisely because it was so closely bound to Lemos' government, the family's situation changed when Lemos was replaced with the Duke of Osuna; strongly hostile to his predecessor due to internal factions within Philip III's Court, he set in motion a violent purge of the Viceroy's closest collaborators. In 1616, Bento Vaaz and his wife, Beatriz, were accused by the Inquisition to be "judaizers" in a trial probably instigated by the Viceroy. The following year it was Miguel's turn: the Duke of Osuna attempted to imprison him accusing him of conspiracy and correspondence with unbelievers because of the secret contacts the Vaaz family maintained with fellow New Christians ("*cristãos novos*") and Jews exiled by the Spanish monarchy and residing in London, Amsterdam, Leghorn and Venice. The wealthy Miguel – who had been created Count of Mola by Philip III in 1613, having purchased ample landed properties in that extremely fertile area of the realm (including the city after which his title was derived) – avoided arrest by taking refuge in the convent of the Celestines, which he was on his way to visit when the attempt to arrest him was made.

The next generation of the Vaaz family also engaged in commerce, though its principal branch was well integrated into the aristocratic milieu and into that of the educated professions and the Neapolitan judiciary. Their past troubles and their strong Portuguese origins continued, however, to provoke diffidence in governmental circles. After the disorders of 1647–8, they were suspected of being in touch with the Neapolitan exiles who had taken refuge with the Pope, whose projected uprising under the leadership of agents of King John IV of Portugal was well known.

Further manifestations of hostility towards the family appear in 1657, when the new Viceroy, the Count de Castrillo, ordered the arrest of Eduardo with the accusation of having favoured the son of an important judge in his activity as president of the criminal section of the Vicaria court. Imprisoned in Castel Sant'Elmo, Eduardo was further accused of being a "judaizer", with the immediate confiscation of his property. The Inquisition seems to have played no direct part in the initial phase of this procedure, with the arrival in Naples of Monsignor Camillo Piazza, Commissioner of the Holy Office in 1659, the accusation of being "judaizers" was extended to include many other members of the family, all arrested: Eduardo's brother, Bento and his wife, Grazia; Eduardo's sisters, Grazia and Fiorenza; his aunt Beatriz and his son, Emanuele, Duke of San Donato; his cousin, Grazia, with her husband, Eduardo de Rivera and her son from a previous marriage, Eduardo Mendez; as well as another cousin, Beatrice Vaaz, with her husband, Enrique Suarez Colonel and his brother, Antonio. Further, Rome had already requested – and obtained – the extradition of all the accused from the *Consiglio Collaterale*, the supreme political and administrative organ of the Neapolitan Viceroyalty.

Tried by the Congregation of the Holy Office in 1660, all the accused abjured *de formali* the following year in the usual ceremony of repentance, held in the Church of Santa Maria sopra Minerva, during which the sentences were read aloud. Eduardo Vaaz was sentenced to prison together with material and spiritual penalties, as well as the payment of 2,000 Roman scudi. His brother Bento – condemned to ten years in prison – and Emanuele Vaaz, were obliged, instead, to pay, respectively, 500 and 2,000 scudi; sums distributed "at the will of the Holy Congregation".[3] Informed of the definitive condemnation, the *Collaterale* decreed the definitive transfer to the treasury of the property already preventively confiscated. This brought on the violent reaction of Monsignor Piazza, who affirmed the precedence of the Holy Office, as well as that of the Neapolitan aristocracy which, as we know, had always been hostile to the confiscatory appetite of the Inquisition.

The application of Julius III's bull – which, as we shall see, forbade the confiscation of heretics' property in the Kingdom of Naples – was invoked. After prolonged judicial controversies, the Vaaz family obtained the restitution of a part of the confiscated property that had not yet been relinquished by the state, succeeding in regaining possession of the county of Mola. The Duchy of Casamassima and an important number of other liquid and real assets already transferred by the royal treasury at the moment of rearrangement were, instead, definitively lost. Although in 1671 Eduardo Vaaz returned to Naples after ten years in prison, benefiting from an act of papal clemency invoked by the *Collaterale*, the family had definitively fallen on the margins of the Neapolitan political and social elites. The descendants would never again hold important positions in the governing institutions of the Spanish era.[4]

This story offers many themes and lines of inquiry. First of all, it reminds us how tightly entangled politics and personal interests were: they might give direct or indirect origin to an inquisitorial investigation. This was especially true in the slippery area of the sin-crime of crypto-Judaism. Second, it invites reflection on the possible consequences of the diffidence with which foreign commercial and banking dynasties were viewed – in particular, when these families had gone through religious conversion. It was a diffidence which combined traditional popular hostility for those whose profession was handling money with the suspicion – a characteristic of Catholic ecclesiastical courts in the age of the Counter Reformation – towards the mercantile dynasties which had business relationships with those operating in international markets, situated in areas in which Reformed Christianity prevailed. Finally, the story of the Vaaz trials bears once more witness to the uneasy interdependence between ecclesiastical and secular authorities in the process of confiscation. The scenario in which they were executed might, in each instance, oscillate between smooth collaboration and keen competition, as the Neapolitan case shows so well.

Here, on April 7, 1554, after renewed anti-Spanish and anti-inquisitorial riots, Pope Julius III's bull *Ex tuae circumspectionis literis*, declared the non-application of confiscation in trials of faith in Naples. The norm was promulgated – as a memorandum sent by the Neapolitan authorities to the Congregation of the Holy Office would still recall a century later – "on the appeal of the said city of Naples, and to do something pleasing to said Emperor [Charles V], and said cardinal" (the Spaniard, Pietro Pacecco, Lieutenant and Governor General of the Realm during that year).[5] As we have seen in the Vaaz case, Pope Julius' brief was destined to ignite harsh contestations besides giving the Pope and the Congregation an excellent reason to press the Neapolitan authorities to transfer as many cases as possible to Rome and – when monetary punishment was possible – to secure that the maximum be directed outside the borders of the realm. In any event, these papal norms did not impede the Royal Chamber from proceeding autonomously to the seizure and sale of property confiscated in investigations of faith – as was the case of the decisions of the Viceroy, the Duke of Alcalá, in 1569 against the Waldensians of Calabria, tried and massacred in 1561. The goods of six "judaizers" executed in Rome in 1572 were also confiscated, even if, in three instances, the procedure could not be carried out for fear of tumults.[6]

In 1564 there was another, serious, popular uprising in Naples, led by local nobles; once again, it arose from fear of a jurisdictional expansion on the part of the feared Spanish Inquisition and its more sweeping recourse to property confiscation. Giordano Bruno, who was a direct witness of these riots in his youth, includes an allegory inspired by them in *Spaccio della bestia trionfante* (1584). Through it he could deplore "the great avarice which operates under the pretext of upholding religion" in the Spaniards and their Inquisition and, in particular – as Cesare Beccaria would deplore it two centuries later – the institution of confiscation, in virtue of which "in the culprit's punishment, many innocents participate as well – and sometimes the just; and withal the prince grows fatter". Bruno's voice echoes what the Neapolitan baronage feared, threatened in its property and its liberties by the substantial lack of application of Julius III's bull, mostly to the fiscal advantage of the royal treasury. At the end of the revolt, in March 1565, Philip II declared in writing that he did not have any intention of establishing the Spanish Inquisition in Naples, assuring that he would entrust to the Council of Italy the study of confiscation for cases of faith (from which the Neapolitan aristocracy would have liked to see culprits' families and noble descendants exempted, destining the requisitioned property to charity, rather than the royal coffers).[7]

An interesting testimony as to the connections between secular government and the Holy Office in the matter of heretic trials and confiscation in the period following that of the sixteenth-century Lutheran emergency, may be seen in the memoirs of the Judge of the *Vicaria civile*, later President of the Royal Summary Chamber and Advocate of the Royal Patrimony, Fabio Capece Galeota (1572–1645). Among his opinions concerning jurisdictional privileges, public domain and grants – areas often disputed between civil and ecclesiastical power – this jurist published a dissertation in 1628 entitled *A Discourse addressed to His Excellency, the Lord Duke of Alva, Regarding the Most Ancient Custom and the Inviolable Observance that, in the Realm, it is not possible to incarcerate Any Person for Heresy or for [the will of] the Holy Office without First Notifying the Lords Viceroy*.[8] Citing precedents going back to the fourteenth century, Capece Galeota touched on the question of confiscation, reassuming that:

> If the heretic's temporal belongings are consigned to the royal treasury even if they should be bishops and other ecclesiasticals [...] necessarily, it follows that the king and his ministers, as interested [parties] in the confiscation, must have notice of what is going on, and this from beginning to end, so that they may cooperate in the proper punishment.[9]

Capece Galeota's permissive attitude towards inquisitorial confiscation – precisely because it was situated in a treatise which, on the contrary, openly aimed at curbing the Holy Office's operative range, obliging it to make arrests in cases of faith with warrants from the secular authorities – is a good expression of the necessarily conciliating attitude adopted by the Neapolitan government in taking possession of patrimonies forfeited for heresy. It was an area on which State authorities were well aware that they could not always proceed decisively and autonomously.

Less accommodating was, in fact, an anonymous comment (in manuscript and, as far as can be ascertained, never printed), entitled *Answer to the discourse of Fabio Capece Galeota, Royal Councilor, given to the press, against the ancient and immemorial capacity which the Holy Office of the Realm of Naples has always held and holds to freely incarcerate laymen of whatever condition they may be for causes of their pertinence without making [this] known to, or asking the permission of, the Viceroy of this same Realm*, addressed in the same year of 1628 "to the Holiness of Our Lord Pope Urban VIII and to the Most Illustrious lords cardinal inquisitors throughout the Christian republic against the heretical depravity".[10] The author openly labelled "false" the crucial precedent cited by Capece Galeota and drawn from the era of Charles III of Durazzo (that is, that this sovereign gave his courtier, Tomaso Mariconda of Salerno, the confiscated property of Francesco Marchesino, Bishop of Trivento):

> not being the right of the king to put his hands upon, nor emanate decrees in the confiscation of property in holy Inquisition cases, for both the penal crime and the punishment which follows its author – and the nature of this – must be imposed by the judge of the crime, who also must apply it to the proper person.

In any case, only the prince who had been accorded the privilege by the Holy See, "or by a custom approved by the same", might, according to the *Answer*, freely assign the property of a heretic secular individual, while the property of an individual in religious orders confiscated for heresy "as all know" goes to the ecclesiastical treasury. The Holy Office consultant further sustained that even admitting the precedent invoked by Naples, it would be impossible to derive from it:

> that necessarily the king and his ministers must – as parties interested in the confiscation of property – have notification of what is going on, and what is done from the beginning to the end by the inquisitors in their cases, and much more are they to make known to the Royal ministers of the capture the laymen in the properties in which the king has all of his interest.

And he continued:

> But what is worse, it is impossible to understand in what way the Author infers that, because of this, the inquisitors must give notice of delinquent culprits and request warrants to capture them because, Charles II [sic] having emanated that decree for no other reason than that of the final effect of the condemnation – which was that, after that same inquisition pronounced the sentence and given the secular Tax office its part, there is nothing left to do but that the same fiscal office dispose of the sum; therefore, to do the work of the Royal tax office, it is not necessary for [the Officer] to have prior information about the delinquent individuals (much less foreseeable by the inquisitors), asking permission to capture them since, as we have said, what is due the Royal Tax Office as privilege is an act which presupposes all the free exercise that is the inquisition's right has already been completed [...] While it is assumed that Charles II [sic] in virtue of apostolic privilege, granted the heretic confiscations already made by the inquisitors, he could not – nor could anyone else – interfere in any other act concerning judgement in a case of faith, if not in the measure conceded him by privilege [...] Evidently, it follows that he could not, and should not, have intervened in the process – just as today is the case – and as is seen in the holy Inquisition in the realms of Spain where the confiscation of heretic's property is carried out by the Inquisition, and is given to the royal fiscal office in virtue of the apostolic privilege of His Catholic Majesty, [who] does not interfere with anything else, except these specific confiscations.[11]

This view of the prerogatives and the jurisdiction of the Inquisition significantly transcends the terms of the dispute between the Apostolic Seat and the Kingdom of Naples, assuming a general ecclesiological and political value. Recalling that "the penal crime – like the punishment which seeks out the author (and its nature) – is determined by the judge of the crime, who must also attribute it to whosoever is responsible", the Holy Office not only claimed the right to reserve to itself all decisions as to patrimonial or monetary punishments, but reaffirmed the untouchable unity of the crime–trial–punishment–confiscation complex. For the Holy Court the admission that a theoretical-legal distinction existed between the phases of the process: ascertaining that a crime existed, trial, judgement and sentence (of which confiscation was an integral part), and the material execution of that confiscation could, at least in principle, open an extremely dangerous path leading secular authorities to claim a power of decision over a part of that process – that is confiscation.

This was evidently inadmissible from the point of view of an ecclesiastical court whose jurisdiction canon law gave as universal. Here we find a decisive methodological point: it derives from the historiographical necessity of considering the crime-trial-sentence-confiscation series as a single, consolidated, unit, identifying accurately – where surviving documentation allows us to do so – all the possible interferences among the various phases of the trials.

The arguments invoked here by the Roman Curia imply, beyond the juridical, the political obligation of secular governments to consider support of, or action in conjunction with, the activities of the Inquisition as a concession, which might be revoked at any moment. Confiscation, in as much as it was "the final effect of judgement", is wholly and exclusively prerogative of the inquisitor; the sole possessor of the right to "pronounce sentence" in cases of faith, and to "assign the punishment to the secular treasury". The "privilege" granted secular governments by the Church to take part in confiscation is then expressly defined: "presupposing that all the autonomous actions which are the inquisitor's prerogative have already been completed". Naturally, in this view, there was the possibility that a State might receive – in part or in full – the fruits of a confiscation derived from apostolic privilege. In this regard, the precedent of the relationship between the Inquisition and the Crown in Spain was invoked, but it would also have been possible to cite what was happening within an outlying Spanish territory looking towards the heart of heretic Europe, Milan, the "portal" of Catholic Italy.

A web of visibilities

In the State of Milan, Spanish sovereignty and the work of Carlo Borromeo in the decisive historical phase of the second half of the 1500s led to the establishment of a model of wide operative liberty for the Holy Office and close collaboration with secular authorities in the area of property confiscation. Following a custom established in the course of the sixteenth century, the property seized for crimes of faith were divided into three parts between the ducal Chamber the episcopal Mensa and the local Inquisition, while the practical execution was carried out by secular authorities through the offices of the Magistrate for Extraordinary Income or Extraordinary Magistrate ["*Magistrato Straordinario*"]. Besides respecting a usage sometimes employed already during the Middle Ages and benefiting secular entities, the tripartite division of the fruits of inquisitorial confiscation was also recommended by prestigious commentators like Zanchino Ugolini.

With the founding of the Holy Office and the anti-heretic repressions of the 1500s, this system of division of confiscated heretic property was questioned by inquisitors who, like the Ferrarese Camillo Campeggi, felt that the Italian judges of faith were too poor and weighed down by too many expenses to allow themselves such generosity.[12] Tripartite division became common in this same period within the State of Milan, deriving from the procedure followed by monetary penalties, as seen in the case of some measures regarding books forbidden in a 1554 decree of the General Apostolic Commissioner Bonaventura Castiglione and the Archbishop of Milan Giovan Angelo Arcimboldi. These measures blocked anyone from "putting about, selling – nor causing to be sold – nor in any manner giving, books in Latin or in the vulgar tongue, of any kind whatever, in which Holy Scripture is treated" without the permission of the ecclesiastical authority, "under penalty of excommunication *latae sententiae* and 100 scudi for each time and for each counterfeiter, a third part to be assigned to the Office of the Inquisition, another third to the imperial Chamber, and the final third part to the accuser, who shall be kept secret".

The same monetary penalty and the same division of the sum involved was applied to the booksellers and the bookbinders who, within two months, should have completed an inventory of all their books – whether in Latin or in the vulgar tongues – presenting the same to the archbishop and the inquisitor, as well as for any "Lutheran, or other sort of heretic" who, according to the usual logic of the "period of grace", should spontaneously present themselves in the court, and should accept penitence and denounce their accomplices. A clause in the decree explicitly declared that the informer would obtain a third of the monetary punishment to which the denounced was sentenced.[13]

The agreement on three part division of inquisitorial confiscations was generally observed in the Milanese territories even in the seventeenth century, when Rome already considered it only local custom ("*stylum loci*"): responding to doubts expressed by the inquisitor in Alessandria, in 1626 the Holy Office recommended that he divide the confiscated property of the heretic Giulio Mocagatti with the bishop and the royal treasury. The judge of faith in the area of Cremona was also advised in 1609 to proceed, in the confiscation of the patrimonies of some defaulting Soresina heretics, in close collaboration with the *Podestà* who administered civil and penal justice in that feud – a property of the Marquis Barbò by grant of the King of Spain. So the equilibrium established in the Spanish area of northern Italy entered into crisis only in the Austrian era, when, in 1720, the Milan Senate established an important precedent, blocking the Holy Tribunal's attempt to expropriate the property of the Milan nobleman, Nicolò Cauzzi. "The Inquisition no longer holds the privilege of confiscation, and of fines", the Milanese judge of faith, Ermenegildo Todeschini, observed sadly, "regarding which the most excellent Senate is extremely cautious".[14] Of that community of action and objectives between ecclesiastical and secular institutions – which lasted some 200 years – precious testimony is still available today in the Milanese archives, which allows us to reconstruct the activities of both parties and understand the tenor and manner of their collaboration.[15]

In two examples, we can try to understand how a confiscation in a case of faith was experienced. On April 13, 1571, the Milanese nobleman Paolo Camillo Balsamo was judged "an obstinate heretic" by the Milanese Inquisition and since he had not presented himself despite repeated citations, was excommunicated, sentenced to be burnt at the stake in effigy – a punishment of elevated symbolic value which substituted the physical execution when the culprit had fled and been convicted in default – and the confiscation of his property. Balsamo, declared the sentence signed by the General Inquisitor for the diocese of Milan, Friar Angelo da Cremona, and the Archbishop Carlo Borromeo, had been in Geneva for years "studying" and there he had "come into profound error and sin", as had been denounced to the court of the Holy Office of Milan "by legitimate witnesses". "Let him be punished as impenitent heretic according to the laws", sentenced the ecclesiastical judges, "as we now command and order that to that court [the arm ['*brazzo*'] and secular justice]" be given and consigned a statue so that of it – since he is not in our power – a demonstration may be made as the laws and justice command, confiscating all of his properties and goods as we confiscate him and we assign them to our Holy Office".[16]

After the promulgation of this sentence, its text was promptly sent to the officers of the Extraordinary Magistrate, who gave immediate course to the procedure of confiscation. In less than two months – on June 16, 1571 – notices were posted inviting all who those who believed they had "better and prior legal right" upon Balsamo's patrimony to advance written opposition within a date set a few weeks later. Orders of the Senate dating from the mid-1500s, provided that these opponents must be presented directly and exclusively to the Extraordinary Magistrate: even in this phase the ecclesiastical court had no role at all.[17] So the inquisitorial sentence (which was partially inexact where it implied that Balsamo's patrimony would be "assigned" to the Holy Office alone), had set in motion a complex procedure which would see bishop and inquisitor, once again united in the activity of repressing heresy, each receive only a third of the value of the property confiscated. In the name of the State, the Extraordinary Magistrate, future beneficiary of the remaining third, would deal with all of the practical steps leading to and resolving the liquidation of the whole patrimony.

In mid-July of the same year Paolo Camillo Balsamo's two brothers – Ottavio and Scipione – opposed the confiscation, appealing to the secular authorities.[18] They disclosed the dispositions of their father Giuliano's will, drawn up in 1562, which named the three brothers universal heirs on an equal footing, save for a compensation of 2,000 gold scudi that Paolo Camillo was to pay to Scipione and Ottavio. Giuliano Balsamo's will contained, further, a trust clause – signing it he forbid his sons to sell any estate holding whatsoever until they reached the age of 32, or the bequests would be annulled. Further, very shrewdly, the Balsamo brothers' father provided in his will that, if any of his sons should, before the age of 32, be condemned of any sort of crime which might involve a sentence involving some form of confiscation of patrimony ("any goods [...] in whatever manner be confiscate"], their capacity to inherit would be nullified.[19] Giuliano Balsamo's foresight makes us aware of how, already in the early 1560s, the possibility of confiscation by the Inquisition was a possibility keenly felt among members of the upper levels of society as they considered the protection of the family patrimony over time – especially in cases in which a member of the family operated in areas where Protestantism was dominant. By the end of 1571, the magistrate admitted the Balsamo brothers' claim, judging them possessed "of a better power and prior legal right than the aforesaid chamber has", and deliberated the relinquishment of Paolo Camillo's sequestered property. At the moment of condemnation, he had not yet reached his thirty-second year of age.[20]

In the years following the condemnation of Paolo Camillo Balsamo, one of his two brothers also had problems with the Inquisition. Unlike Paolo Camillo, who had moved to Geneva when still young, Scipione Balsamo must have lived uninterruptedly in Milan, becoming an exponent much in view among the city's aristocracy. We know that in 1565 he was called to Pisa by the High Prior of the Ordine di Santo Stefano to testify to the nobility of an Alessandro Verri, a close collaborator of Cosimo I de' Medici and a descendant of one of the oldest and most noble families of the city, so he might be knighted.[21] We do not know on what bases the condemnation which led to the confiscation of Scipione Balsamo's patrimony rested:[22] from the documents of the Extraordinary Magistrate, we do, however, learn that, in June of 1578, the description of his properties was ordered (including those which were still held in common with his brother, Ottavio), in execution of a notice emitted a few weeks earlier. But it was not the secular officials who ordered the notary Francesco Melzi to organize the Description of the Balsamos' holdings: it was the Inquisitor General in person, Giovan Battista Clavenna, future judge of faith of Venice.[23]

The intention was always that of setting in motion a procedure, carried out by the State magistrates, aimed at confiscating heretic's property to the benefit of the Royal Chamber, the archbishop's *Mensa*, and the Milanese Holy Office.[24] But this confiscation saw the active participation of the inquisitor from the beginning; he personally ordered the notary to draw up the document of the *Description* ("*Descriptio*") and, on June 20, 1578, when it was written down, he was represented by a vicar and a collateral.[25]

In the absence of a general land office comparable to those existing in contemporary societies, any confiscation procedure set in motion in the *Ancien régime* required the interrogation of relatives, acquaintances and collaborators of the culprit to identify his properties with any exactitude, as well as to compile a first evaluation of the their entity. During these investigations, set in motion by the Extraordinary, the consul of a locality in which there were properties belonging to Scipione Balsamo affirmed, for example:

I have looked diligently, in your presence, notary, and of other persons who were with you, and considered well all things [of] the said possession, and for the experience that I have of the possessions of this territory for having been born and raised in this place I say that I consider that on this possession, for the named things – that is about eighty *mogia* of grain, not more, as not being sown more than about 200 at rye, because not much is sown [...] as for rice and maize I can make no judgement now because it is not the time to be able to judge that kind of stuff [...] and on this property alone there are about four *pertiche* of land sown in maize, and all this, though, with the fortune of no bad weather coming up; in which stuff I mean further that the farmer's part must be included.[26]

It should be noted that the *Description* of the patrimony of a condemned culprit, which preceded its *Seizure* ("*Apprehensio*") by the proper authorities, was not simply a preparatory phase for the confiscation itself.[27] Its completion, in fact, included a delicate legal and material passage: the official consignment of the properties seized to one or more persons chosen as fiduciaries.[28] In the case we are considering, it was the local consul who received the obligation – as the notary's formula declares to care for the Balsamo property, cause the land to be cultivated and worked, have the crops gathered and keep the accounts with the usual formula – "drawn up in orderly manner". All of this with the obligation to render the property, products and accounts of the Balsamo patrimony only to officials appositely designated by the Ducal Chamber, the Office of the Inquisition, or the Archbishop of Milan "under penalty of paying himself", plus a fine of 200 gold scudi. The consul certified the accomplished passage of the property.[29]

In the days following, the notary and his entourage went to the other localities in the Milanese countryside in which – according to information they discovered as they went – land owned by the Balsamos was located. He then consigned the several properties to the care of local consuls, employees of the Balsamos or farmers who already rented them, writing separate mandates for each (always in the name of the three confiscating organizations).[30]

So the *Description* was an important phase not only in the confiscation of the property of those condemned for heresy, but, more broadly, in the relationship between the Inquisition and society. The men named custodians of the properties subjected to a *Description*, began to act, in their area of residence, as institutional representatives of the prince – and of the inquisitor and the archbishop as justices of faith. And, where the confiscation did not benefit the secular authorities, the custodians of the described properties became in all senses the custodians of the properties which were about to become property of the Holy Office and the episcopal *Mensa*, so contributing (more or less voluntarily and efficiently) to enlarging its presence, functions and prerogatives. The situation of the custodian during confiscation was not easy, since – as, for example, Charles V's 1541 *New Constitutions* ("*Nuove costituzioni*") and a chaotic mass of specific regulations ordained for the Milanese area – imposed the payment to the treasuries of the competent courts (and so to the Inquisition) of the rents and the annual income deriving from capitals, land or buildings belonging to the heretic, in addition to regular taxes.[31]

So it is not surprising that many attempted to avoid this difficult position. In 1560, after the property of Giuseppe Bondiolo, condemned for heresy in Cremona, was subjected to the *Description* and entrusted to some neighbours, they protested to the Extraordinary Magistrate, declaring that his local representative had:

> molested four poor men of the Covesino district [...] to make them store with them in deposit the broad beans and fruits that should be gathered in some plots of land in said district which used to belong to a Josepho Bandiolo, whose property they said was confiscated for heresy, which is odd to us and it seems to them cruel [...] it being, at most, their habit to busy themselves in their own business during the day to earn something for their keep and their families', the more so because the [Ducal] Chamber can protect itself in other ways, best of all for such a sequestration making [custodian] the farmer of said land [...] and these poor men will be free of this tangle and freed of the suspicion of some evil which could occur.[32]

The mechanism of the *Description*, with its consequent consignment of property, liquid and real, to provincial administrators obliged to operate in the name of the archbishop-inquisitor duo – risking the penalty of heavy monetary punishments – created an efficient network of subjects able to spread the power of the judges of faith within the urban and rural society of the *Ancien régime*. The symbolic power of that act might, further, be amplified by the fact that, in cases in which the real entity of a heretic's patrimony was in doubt, public officials did not hesitate to enlarge the *Description* and the subsequent *Seizure* coolly. This occurred, for example, in Cremona in 1558 when, in describing the property of the Cremonese priest, Antonio Baruffino, condemned by the Inquisition for heresy, the appraisers wrongly included among his properties "certain plots of land situated in Castelnovo del Zappa". In reality, these had been purchased by the priest in 1541 with an agreement of "sale and return" and entrusted at once to third parties in administration. The legitimate owner immediately lodged a complaint which led to the annulment of the procedure already executed by the Referendary, who was the local representative of the Extraordinary Magistrate. However, the cancellation of the inventories from the *Description* was carried out by the notary in that case, "only for the third part due to the Royal Ducal Chamber": thus leaving the episcopal and the inquisitorial courts free to reject the opposition of the complainants.[33]

The work of those who administered temporarily the property seized by the Inquisition might go on for years, or even decades, for the suits linked to the confiscations were not always resolved with the rapidity in the case regarding Paolo Camillo Balsamo. The Extraordinary's sentence on Ottavio Balsamo's opposition to the confiscation of Scipione's property – whose value was estimated at more than 86,000 lire – was pronounced in July, 1585, seven years after the *Description* had been completed.³⁴ After all those years, in the perception of the inhabitants of both the city and countryside – as well as of the experts who carried out the procedures of confiscation – the ownership of the properties administered by representatives of the three confiscating organizations might well be attributed exclusively to the most awe-inspiring of them, the Inquisition; which thereby gained the greatest advantage in terms of public image. A testimony in this sense is the letter sent to the president of the Extraordinary by an appraiser who, with the engineer Bernardino Lonato of the ducal Chamber, in January, 1584, drew up the definitive appraisal of Scipione Balsamo's property. From it we see that he believed he had operated "in execution of the commission given me by your most illustrious lordships, that is that I should go with an engineer of the Royal Chamber to the place where the properties which were Mr Scipione Balsamo's are situated, *by the Royal Chamber of the Holy Inquisition confiscated*; and we should diligently see [and] measure them and then, having gathered the necessary information, we should make an estimation of their value".³⁵

In the 1500s, the episcopal Mensas, following the pattern set by Carlo Borromeo, often relinquished the third due to them, devolving it to the Holy Office, whose courts did not yet enjoy the benefices which the popes would later confer upon them.³⁶ This was the case, for example, in 1562, when the property of nobleman Francesco Fogliata, a refugee from Geneva, condemned for heresy in default in 1558, was confiscated: Niccolò Sfondrati – then Bishop of Cremona and future Pope Gregory XIV – devolved to the Inquisition the third which was owed to the Ordinary.³⁷ This trend, too, probably contributed to blurring the attribution of ownership rights so that, in the eyes of the population at large, they might often seem to rest entirely with the Inquisition.

Finally, to remain on the historical territory of the widespread perception of the forms of repression of heresy: even where it was the secular magistrates who carried out the practical procedure of patrimonial confiscation regarding heretics, the populations and the eventual appellants most probably tended to view the whole procedure as basically in the hands of the Inquisition. When, for example, in 1584, the confiscation regarding Gerolamo Orsini – stable master to the Bishop of Pavia, condemned for heresy by the local Inquisition – was carried out, his brothers, Agostino and Giangiacomo (the second a priest), in their appeal to the Referendary showed that they believed Gerolamo's patrimony had been "sequestered by order of the most reverend father inquisitor because of the death sentence with confiscation". This, despite the fact that the procedure had, as usual, been initiated and executed by the Extraordinary Magistrate, in the optic of the usual three way division of the property.³⁸

The very complexity of the procedure which led to the appropriation of the heretic's property contributed – despite (or perhaps, indeed, due to) the plurality of the subjects involved – to bolster the appearance of power which the Inquisition projected through confiscation. The collaboration of secular

Confiscation as an investigative tool

As our two examples clarify, in the State of Milan confiscation of the property of those condemned for heresy was executed along relatively simple lines. The ecclesiastical court transmitted the sentence to the civil authorities, who, with the inquisitor's aid, proceeded to draw up a description of the items composing the patrimony and clarifying the existence of other rights to the culprit's holdings; finally, it emitted a sentence regarding them. Subsequently, the confiscating organs seized the properties, transferring ownership directly to themselves or, more often, auctioning them off: often the buyers were the heirs of the condemned heretic who, in this manner, were obliged to buy back property which, without the condemnation of their relative for heresy, would have been theirs by right of inheritance. In addition, the secular magistrates took whatever actual coinage there was, since it was the Ducal Chamber which distributed the patrimony, for the remaining two-thirds, to the episcopal *Mensa* and the treasury of the Holy Office.

We have also seen that the secular magistrate – or any other officer who might proceed to describe the heretic's property and look into the claims advanced by third parties – had at his disposition only one tool with which to carry out the task adequately: he must undertake an investigation, in part similar to the one conducted months earlier by the inquisitor, and question witnesses who were informed as to the facts. How else would it have been possible to establish the fact that Paolo Camillo Balsamo was not yet 32 years old at the time of his condemnation and sentencing? The obligation that parish priests must keep separate registers of dates for baptisms and weddings, as we know, from the twenty-fourth session of the Council of Trent – and it was partially observed only from 1563; in so far as registration of deaths was concerned, the Council's command was effectively imposed by the 1614 emanation of the *Rituale Romanum*.[39]

So, for many decades, public officials continued to insist upon eye-witness testimonies to certify legitimate birth, the celebration of baptisms and weddings and even burial ("his cadaver this witness saw placed in its sepulture" the notaries holding the interrogatories translated into Latin; or, "whose cadaver this witness did not see; but of this death [there was] public knowledge")[40] of the individuals whom they were investigating.

In the cultural context of the *Ancien régime*, centred on public fame and, for this reason, too, characterized by the generous publicity given to acts which only later western society began to consider "private", State officials acted within a bureaucratic praxis radically opposed to that we know today. It was, in fact, characterized by strong scepticism concerning written, registered, data: even when this was available, as was the case of the estimates (earlier versions of the present day land office data), it was considered not very reliable for it was objectively both muddled and updated dilatorily. In administrative offices and, more broadly, throughout society, there was, then, a tendency to consider oral testimony as proof of secure truth, as being the immediate expression of the objectivity of visual perception, over the fallibility of written – or at any rate, indirect – documentation. It was a tendency in which the Court of the Inquisition itself participated fully: as we see in the *Sacred Arsenal*. For the judges of faith, too, it was upon the quality and the believability of eye witnesses that "the honour, the life and the property of the culprits depend".[41]

In considering the opposition to the confiscation of his patrimony advanced by the brothers of the heretic Paolo Camillo Balsamo, the secular Milanese magistrates had, then, to deliberate as to the culprit's age at the moment in which the Holy Office pronounced its death sentence: an apparently banal question, dissociated from any religious motive, but essential to completion of the seizure of that patrimony. To this end, the Extraordinary Magistrate had to undertake an investigation of his own. As with any investigation initiated in the *Ancien régime* on such occasions by the authorities carrying out a confiscation, this procedure had an ambiguous nature, as it was aimed at a double end: reaching a sentence in the case of the Balsamos' appeal and, at the same time, identifying and estimating the value of Paolo Camillo's property. Lacking a reliable land office, an efficient real estate market, a transparent, general, system of agricultural prices – and therefore a broad view of income patterns on which to base specific estimates – without certificated registration of contracts, improvements and property titles, the magistrate could not evaluate the entity and the value of the properties to be confiscated, if not through a wearying preparatory phase, involving the interrogation of witnesses, notaries, officials and experts. A system so complex – multiplied by the sentences pronounced in a year – made it necessary to have an articulated and expensive structure: a characteristic fruit of the uncertainty of property rights and the consequent massive demand for certification which debilitated preindustrial economic relations.[42]

Could the autonomous investigation carried out by the Extraordinary Magistrate, a secular authority, influence the activity of the Inquisition? To answer this question, let us reconsider the temporal sequence we saw in the Balsamo confiscation. The notice of the confiscation of Paolo Camillo Balsamo's patrimony was posted publicly in Milan in mid-June, 1571; his two brothers appealed in mid-July. In August, the inquest of the Extraordinary Magistrate was already underway. At that moment, the condemnation of Paolo Camillo Balsamo to be burnt at the stake in effigy – decreed in mid-April by Father Angelo da Cremona and the archbishop, Carlo Borromeo – must have already been performed. It had been preceded by public posting of announcements which vainly ordered the presumed heretic to present himself before the Milanese Holy Office. In mid-August, none of those who knew Paolo Camillo were, presumably, unaware of his destiny.

At this point we have no difficulty in imagining the state of mind of the witnesses – often illiterate peasants from the countryside, lessees, nurses and servants – as they appeared before the officers of the Extraordinary Magistrate to be questioned on the life and the properties of a heretic burnt in effigy. The inquiry conducted by the secular authorities thus inevitably produced the effect of enlarging the results of the condemnation, reinforcing the perception of the life and death power of the Holy Office among those who were involved, the members of their families and their acquaintances.

The great power of the Inquisition was probably on the mind of that Pietro Corteni from Vareggio, of "about" 50 years of age, who appeared before the Fiscal Officer of the Extraordinary on the morning of September 5, 1571, declaring:

> I met said noble Giuliano Balsamo and the noble Isabella Anzaverta, married in the chapter, who were legitimate husband and wife, and as such practising. I, in the time said master Giuliano lived in his house – because I served with Giovan Battista Anzaverta who was said Giuliano's brother-in-law – many and many times heard them named among themselves, and equally by those who knew them as if they were so: that is, held to be, treated, and reputed, legitimate husband and wife: and this I say because I know it for the reasons I just gave [...] It is true that in the recent past year of 1540 – in I can't say what moment exactly, but it was in the summer – the noble Isabella, wife of the above named Giuliano, gave birth to noble Paolo Camillo Balsamo in the locality of Liscate, parish of Settala, Vicariate of Milan, and from then on – being about his house for the reasons mentioned above – I heard many and many times the above nobles, Giuliano, Isabella and Paolo Camillo, address each other, treat each other and – properly reporting – consider each other legitimate father, mother and son; and I say that said noble Paolo Camillo was born at that time because – being then with said noble Anzaverta – he (noble Anzaverta) sent me to Liscate to visit a young girl who was his relative-in-law, and noble Isabella, his sister, to see how they were; and having arrived at said noble Isabella's to see her, she told me that I should tell noble Anzaverta then my Master (who was, as I said, her brother), that she was going to give birth to an infant and that he should go to Liscate for Saint George's Day which was then coming, for she wanted to have him baptized and, having told him, my Master on the vigil of Saint George's Day, went to Liscate to his said sister – and I went with his worship and on the next day (which was Saint George's Day), I saw him carry the said infant to the Church of Saint George in that locality to be baptized. And I saw him baptized and he was given a name, as I heard, by the same priest: who baptized him Paolo Camillo; and I say that that boy who was baptized and named Paolo Camillo, as I said, is the same who is named in the Article and at present lives, as I know him very well, having frequented him almost continually from his birth onwards; and I say I know that the aforementioned things were of said year of 1540 and I

have kept memory [of them] because in the same year a daughter was born to me who thereafter died at about six years of age.⁴³

In this stereotyped language, with its bureaucratic rigidities, we see the legal imperative of every testimony registered by every *Ancien régime* court, secular or ecclesiastical, to "prove" veracity, the detailing of what the inquisitor Eliseo Masini would have defined in the *Arsenal* as "the fount of knowledge" ("*la causa della scienza*"), the reasons for which a fact is known.⁴⁴ In the eyes of a civil magistrate – as in those of the Holy Office – "a witness [who appears] without citing the fount of [his] knowledge is like a body without a soul".⁴⁵ Due to this imperative legal principle, even the farmer renting Balsamo land, Pietro De Purseo from Albiate, of "about fifty-five years of age", had to make a declaration:

> In the grape harvest of the year 1540 recently past, the above named noble Giuliano and the noble Isabella, his consort, and others of his household came to Buffalora to harvest the crops I worked on their [land] then, and with them they brought – that is they caused to be brought – an infant boy [...] who, while they stayed here to carry out the said harvest, many and many times I heard called by said noblefolk, Giuliano and Isabella, Paulo [sic] Camillo, and [named] his legitimate and natural son and as such they treated him and reputed him – and by all those who knew them as I testify, for such was he held and reputed.⁴⁶

The numerous acquaintances of Paolo Camillo Balsamo called by the authorities of the State of Milan to certify his age – an indispensable step to seize a part of his property and allow the Holy Office and Archbishop Borromeo to do likewise – inevitably declared details of their own past, recalling small incidents of the past and naming other witnesses to substantiate their version of the facts. Even Pietro Corteni, when asked by the Fiscal Officer "if the said youngster" (that is Paolo Camillo) might "have changed his facial aspect in growing up", answered: "if he had changed face, I would know to declare it; for after he was born until the death of my said master (who died it is now some eleven years past), almost every day I was in the house of said noble Balsamo and saw said youngster".⁴⁷ And he added, "When said babe was baptized, noble Giovan Steffano da Cavaiono was witness, with various others I did not know". The "about" seventy-five-year-old Giovan Battista De Canobio was more precise: after having verbally certified the matrimony of Giuliano and Isabella and the birth of Paolo Camillo in 1540, he, too, cited the godfather, Giovan Stefano Da Cavaiono and added an Antonio Brigante da Melzo. And he clarified – most probably because questioned explicitly – that he recalled the event because "that same year, my daughter Cornelia was born – who still lives".⁴⁸ The "sixtyish" Violanta De Bombini recalled the year 1540 very clearly, "because it was the first time that I went to live with others and also because it was a year of very great abundance".⁴⁹

198   *The Inquisition and economic life*

In a few short weeks, between August and September, 1571, the stories of men and women who had happened to know a heretic passed through the hands and before the eyes of a handful of administrative officials of the State of Milan: they were small glimpses of daily life; births and deaths; memories of abundant harvests, extended families, political alliances, networks of patronage;[50] rich patrimonial holdings; and the objects of everyday life, minutely itemized in the inventories. Pietro De Pureo further declared:

> Said noble Giuliano, while he lived, enjoyed the mill in the territory of Carrate, with certain holdings linked to said mill – which might have been about 25 *pertiche*, he also enjoyed – and always did so until his death – possession of a holding in the territory of Boffalora called Boffalora a' Meletta, which is about 200 *pertiche* in vines, fields and woods; renting out these properties and receiving the fruits and rents at his pleasure – as is the use of true owners of their own belongings; and this I say I know for having held and worked it for the above declared period myself on the named possession of Boffalora of the said noble Giuliano and [...] after, I left said properties to go and live in Albiate – distant a crossbow – shot from said holdings.[51]

Could the prosaic elements which usually emerged during the patrimonial investigations needed to expedite a confiscation be important for the grave mission of the court of faith? To answer this question, we have to take note, first of all, that, in the course of the procedure regarding Scipione Balsamo, the Extraordinary Magistrate recovered – and had integrally transcribed (making them, therefore, a formal part of the acts of the investigation) all of the interrogations carried out years earlier in the confiscation regarding the brother, Paolo Camillo.[52] So the entire legal process concerning the patrimony of a family of heretics was carried over into the documents of a secular court, from January 23, 1580, the old investigations were added onto the new.[53]

In the secular court folder which holds the data regarding the entity and the value of the undivided patrimony of the Balsamo brothers, the existence of Paolo Camillo, condemned to death for heresy and burnt in effigy ten years before, is wholly obliterated. Following the rigid logic of condemnation of memory ("*damnatio memoriae*") imposed by the court of faith, Paolo Camillo's name was no longer mentioned in any way – not even in the secular documents. The witnesses, in what remains of their voices in the cold transcriptions of the notaries, do not seem to recall him in any way. In 1580, even for the Extraordinary Magistrate of the State of Milan, Giuliano and Isabella Balsamo had always only had two male offspring: Scipione and Ottavio.

At a certain point in the Extraordinary's investigation pursuant to the confiscation of Scipione Balsamo's property, the noble Galeazzo Pozzobonelli, an intimate friend of the family, was questioned. The question interesting the officials was a minor one: they wanted to discover what had become of (and what might be the value of) a horse which – after the *Description* had been compiled – some witnesses were sustaining had been among Balsamo's possessions and which seemed to have disappeared. On that occasion, Pozzobonelli affirmed:

> This is what I know: that in the year 1577, during Lent, living in the locality of Liscate – where the declarant [Ottavio Balsamo] and the noble Scipione, his brother, were housed for fear of the plague, since I had a horse with a dark chestnut mantle that I had brought from Rome, the said noble Scipione asked me to sell him it and we agreed on sixty scudi and two *moggi* of oats and the declared Scipione promised to give me the money within a few days, and afterwards he told me his brother, noble Ottavio, would give them for him; and the aforesaid noble Scipione left for the Baths in Flanders and took with him the said horse. Said Ottavio came and found me in Milan a few days after the departure of the aforesaid noble Sipione [*sic*] in the house where I then resided near his [house] close to Santa Margherita, and he told me he would give the said sixty scudi for the price of said horse – and I answered that I had need of it [...] and after a few days I sent my brother, nobleman Giuliano, to Bofalora – the locality where the responsible compiler was, to obtain said sum; and had it from the aforesaid noble Ottavio, nor have I knowledge of other debts paid by the aforesaid noble Ottavio.[54]

So, in 1577 – a plague year in Milan – Scipione Balsamo bought Galeazzo Pozzobonelli's horse for 60 scudi, and on it disappeared into Flanders. The horse, along with Scipione's other outstanding debts, was paid for by his brother Ottavio, allowing us to suppose that, as had already been the case for his brother, Paolo Camillo, the Inquisition had already sentenced Scipione in default (if not for other causes, because he had gone without ecclesiastical permission into a land of such fearful heresy as Flanders and violated – as we shall see – various related papal dispositions). And all this occurred at the very moment in which the Pacification of Ghent was in crisis and Don John of Austria, the hero of the Battle of Lepanto and of Tunisia, had, with the Conquest of Namur (1577), renewed the war against the Calvinists in the northern provinces. Most probably, the noble Balsamo had chosen to side with the forces opposing the philo-Spanish and philo-Catholic stance adopted in the period by large areas of the Italian aristocracy – from the Gonzaga to the Farnese, the Malaspina, the Spinelli and the del Monte.[55]

Pozzobonelli's testimony had been given in a legal context which was extraneous to the trial of faith, in that it was aimed at ascertaining the patrimonial situation of a condemned culprit through investigation by a secular official. It did, however, take cognizance of the way in which Scipione had suddenly departed (very suspicious from the viewpoint of canon law) and alluded to the complicity of Ottavio: an element of primary importance for any judge of faith who should learn of it. "Noble Scipione left Milan almost immediately after he bought the horse from me", Galeazzo reaffirmed in another part of his testimony, "and went into Flanders, as I have said".[56] From the readiness with which Ottavio paid his brother's notable debts, the judge of faith might even have thought that he was in agreement with Scipione's intent of abandoning Catholic lands for the "baths in Flanders". The reference here is to the famous baths at the eponymous Spa, near Liège, whose iron-rich waters (already renowned in the Middle Ages) had begun to attract the elites of Europe during the sixteenth century. In the second half of the 1500s, they were still in an area where the Catholic faith dominated: their evocation here by Pozzobenelli might therefore have been an attempt to cast a veil over the real reason for Balsamo's departure from Lombardy.[57]

If the suspicion that Ottavio was consciously helping his brother to flee were to be confirmed (especially in a family context which had already suffered at least one previous sentence of heresy), that would have made him automatically guilty of the crime of supporting a heretic and so placing himself on the same legal terrain – with serious penal and patrimonial consequences. After having discussed the disappearance of the horse, the Extraordinary Magistrate's officials asked Galeazzo Pozzobonelli for information concerning another group of items which were absent from the inventories notary Melzi had compiled but which – as had been discovered during the investigation – were in Ottavio's possession and which he declared to be his own, personal, property: a collection of drawings and paintings whose exact composition has not survived in any known records. Neither the inventory regarding the mansion in Milan, nor that for the villa in Boffalora – where the two brothers had taken refuge during the plague – mention paintings or drawings, except for some painted chests, "a large painting with the twelve apostles and the Lord God" and "a portrait of the noble father of the aforesaid noble brothers, an arm and a half long with a frame in poplar wood". But the public officials had ascertained that there was much more art. From the testimony of Galeazzo Pozzobonelli they learned that "noble Ottavio is a professional painter, that is to say he loves [doing] it; nor did noble Scipione ever engage in any 'profession' at all – indeed, he was irritated that the said noble Ottavio should do so".

It was on this basis that Pozzobonelli believed the paintings in question had been in part painted by Ottavio Balsamo himself, "in part [...] before the departure of the aforesaid noble Sipione [sic] and in part he did them afterwards"; "and I myself", he added, "made three portraits for him , two of women and one of him".[58] Other details were discovered by questioning Galeazzo's brother, Giuliano Pozzobonelli (1550–1636), himself a well-known painter active in the circle of Giovan Battista Crespi, known as "the Cerano".[59] He confirmed the fact that Ottavio, on Good Friday, 1577, "about fifteen or twenty days" from Scipione's departure, paid the money due for the horse with which Scipione had left for Flanders. And he added:

> The same year as the plague, after the aforesaid master Sipione [sic] had been gone many days, noble Ottavio bought the bay horse described in

the Chamber's name [that is, in the *Description* we have discussed] and that he still has at the present, and by certain soldiers who came from Flanders: and my brother, noble Galeazzo, was the one who fixed the sale, as I understood from my brother.[60]

And he concluded:

> As for the framed canvases, drawings and paintings, I know that the noble declarant, Ottavio Balsamo, has always professed that he understood such things and has by his own hand made some, and said canvases, drawings and paintings described and itemized in the Chamber's name are in part the work of his hand and in part he had them painted by a Flemish fellow he kept in his house and in part he bought them and this was in part before the aforesaid Scipione left and, in part, after the departure, but I wouldn't know now how to say which were before the departure of the aforesaid noble Scipione and which were made after his departure. I am pretty sure the Flemish fellow was in the house at the time the said noble Scipione was at home.[61]

In this declaration, too, elements that would raise suspicion in a trial of faith emerged. While the painter Giuliano Pozzobonelli tried to defend the patrimonial views of Ottavio Balsamo, he also testified that the missing horse had been the object of a deal with soldiers from Flanders and that the missing art works were Ottavio's (or by the Flemish painter who had been his guest both before and after his brother had left for Flanders). Without noticing it, with these affirmations Pozzobonelli further compromised the Balsamos' position from the Church's point of view, making them still more open to the suspicion of aiding heterodoxy or of listening to heterodox doctrines. From this point of view, the testimony of the servant, Giuseppe Brioschi, who had worked for Ottavio both in his Milan dwelling and in Boffalora, was less compromising. He confirmed not only that the horse was sold to "noble Galeazzo, a painter",[62] but also that:

> the canvases, drawings and paintings fully described in said *Description* and of which mention is made in said list marked "D", are all made by noble Octavio [*sic*] or caused to be made by him, or bought, too; and having departed the said noble Scipione and from when I began to stay in his house, I [worked at] grinding the colours for said canvases, drawings and other paintings.[63]

A zealous inquisitor who should happen to learn of all this movement of nobles, painters, horses and soldiers between Milan and Flanders in the 1570s might have initiated some further information gathering – even to calling upon the secular authorities to give him support. The government of Spanish Milan, politically and religiously borderland, had, from the 1560s, tried to reduce the human, political and commercial traffic with the areas of Reformed religion to a minimum. In 1563, the Duke of Albuquerque had promulgated an order forbidding all relations with the area of the Grisons, putting the Alpine passes under strict guard; on this basis, in 1566 a minor merchant from the Valtellina, Vincenzo Pestalozzi, had been arrested and prosecuted by the inquisitor Angelo da Cremona, obliged to abjure after torture with strappado, and freed on bond of 50 scudi.[64] This was the period in which Cardinal Scipione Rebiba, secretary of the Congregation of the Holy Office, wrote to Carlo Borromeo:

> It has come to the notice of Our lord that in Nuremburg there are a number of Italian merchants – and especially from Lucca, Florence and Milan; and in that locality, due to the exile inflicted on priests, no masses are celebrated, and the merchants cannot either say it, nor even less confess themselves sacramentally, if not by walking a distance of at least thirty miles. So that – although they say they live as Catholics in their own homes, it is not however believable that within their souls such a fervour of devotion has developed as to make them in any week undertake that uncomfortable trip. Yet His Holiness, to provide for the health of so many souls, has let it be known, through the Authorities of Lucca, to the merchants of that city how to become more suspicious – that, in any case, they should abandon the locality: and should they nonetheless continue to traffic with Germany, that they move in part to where they live as Catholics, or, at least, where one can exercise with safety some sort of Christian behaviour.

The merchants from Lucca would reply positively to the Pope's appeal, with the proviso that "the same precept be observed by the other [merchants], who must not have a special privilege of exemption". For this reason, Rebiba had written to Borromeo, asking him to discover "with your usual caution and ability" how one might "agree with the Marquis of Ayamonte some manner in which the Milanese merchants may be brought to depart as well". He was convinced that then the same result could be obtained "with the Florentine nation, and the combined example of all of them will thus certainly be followed by the rest of the Italian merchants".[65]

In the final decades of the 1500s, these attempts at containment of the relations between the Catholic Italian peninsula and Protestant Europe, would be the object of progressive institutionalization, arriving, finally, at the formal prohibition Clement VIII imposed in 1596. This document provided that no Italian could go and reside in any place in which exercising the Catholic religion was not possible and that, in the event that an Italian who moved to a locality in which both Catholicism and Reformed churches existed, (he) might not marry a person of such a Church, participate in baptisms or funerals or consult medical doctors who were not Catholic. The temporary permanence of a Catholic in lands with the free practice of Christian religions, where the possibility of practising the Catholic faith was contemplated, must be notified to the Ordinaries and the Inquisitors and the obligation to send a yearly certificate to the bishop and the judge of faith within whose extended jurisdiction the expatriate resided, testifying that the subject had confessed and received communion at Easter in that foreign land. The failure to fulfil the requirements indicated, was cause for the Inquisition to proceed on suspicion of heresy.[66]

In the legal and religious context of the second half of the 1500s, the testimonies registered in the context of the procedure of confiscation regarding the Balsamo family might, then, be compromising from various points of view – that is, of course, if a judge of faith acquired them. But could an inquisitor, in practice, really look into the documents of evaluation and confiscation produced by the officers of the Extraordinary Magistrate of Milan? We know that there was, indeed, a continual exchange of information and documentation between the offices of the magistrate and those of the inquisitor.

In 1570, during the confiscation of the property of a Lyonese merchant arrested in Milan (whose name was Italianized as Giacomo Viberto) – who escaped from the Inquisition's prison and was then condemned in default for heresy – the Extraordinary's notary regularly transmitted the minutes of the trials contesting the Announcements of confiscation of his goods to Friar Angelo da Cremona.[67] The documents acquired by the judges of faith through the confiscation procedures were of various kinds, and might include account books. It was the case in the investigation pursuant to the seizure of the property of the Appiani family. By long established tradition, account books were devoted not merely to holding accounts (themselves precious means of reconstructing any merchant's network of relations and so his possible contacts with colleagues who might be heretics), but all sorts of information about the family life of the individual under investigation. The first page of the Appiani family's account book – dated November 29, 1541 – opened with the debt of an Antonio known as "Cilino" from Vignono and closed with "Note that it is a Sunday that was June 10, 1560, at the first hour before day, [that] Rafaele was born".[68]

So, in the second half of the sixteenth century, a constant bureaucratic-informative stream began to link directly the offices of the secular judiciary and the inquisitor's Chambers, where labour is increasingly more systematic and rationalized. Angelo da Cremona – who, in 1566, had imprisoned and tried Aonio Paleario, extraditing him subsequently to Rome, where he was condemned to death[69] – is described by Silvana Seidel Menchi as the Dominican "who had a more limited and bureaucratic conception of the inquisitorial office than that of the previous generation"; "when he opened a procedure, his ambition was to close it; the continued presence of open cases clashed with the bureaucratic conception he had of his own function".[70]

All the information gathered by the Extraordinary Magistrate's inquiries was potentially available to him; he could proceed against anyone for heresy *ex officio* (that is, without any explicit accusation), for a mere suspicion or, as Eliseo Masini put it in *Sacred Arsenal* ("*Sacro arsenale*") – a murmur "in the Inquisitor's ear, and most of all by grave and honoured persons". People like the personnel of the second magistrate for power and prestige, after the Senate of the State of Milan.[71]

Still, the inquisitor did not always need bureaucratic aid to know what the daily work of the secular offices uncovered. We have already noted that in the Italian peninsula there were contiguities between the secular and the ecclesiastical courts in various situations, starting with those of the republics, even in the way in which trials of faith were carried out. This was true also of the State of Milan.[72] In this regard, a particularly interesting case is that of the condemnation for heresy in default inflicted by the Cremona Inquisition in 1552, upon a group of local citizens – which represents the little known continuation of the unsuccessful 1552 attempt to try the supporters of the two Benedictines, Friar Valeriano and Friar Sereno, arrested in Solarolo in 1550.[73] On May 7, 1558, the Cremonese inquisitor, Tommaso Gaiettani (or Caiettani) and the bishop, Decio Alberio, jointly declared the excommunication in default of some of those accused in 1552 and other individuals who were their relatives or acquaintances. The patricians Francesco Fogliata and Pietro Maggi, Alessandro Roncadelli, Gerolamo Crotto and Giulio Cambiago had, instead, been summoned in vain, with public bills posted, to appear within six days, before the court at the convent of San Domenico. The Holy Office considered them in default and, as heresy suspects, excommunicated. At the sentence, emitted in the episcopal palace of Cremona, a Milanese senator, Danesio Figliodoni,[74] was present; the citations posted on April 20 had also been written with the participation and the collaboration (*"cum interventu et assistentia"*) of Figliodoni and another Milanese senator, Juan de Varahona.[75]

For our ends, it is useful to note that Figliodoni and Varahona were two important figures for the ties that bound them together – and would bind them to the Extraordinary Magistrate. The former, originally from the city of Piacenza, in 1569 became president of the Extraordinary and would be included by the Marquis of Ayamonte in the list of four candidates for the regency which had become vacant in the Madrid *Consejo de Italia* on the death of Giulio Claro (who had been, in turn, president of the Extraordinary from 1653 to 1566),[76] Juan de Varahona (or Tarahona, or Barahona) had, instead, been the only Spaniard elected in 1541 in the Milanese administration as Master of Payments received of the Magistrature of Incomes – an organism created with the unification of the Magistrates of Ordinary and Extraordinary Incomes imposed by Charles V in 1541 and repealed in 1563.[77] From this post, Varahona went on to the Senate and, as Regent in Madrid, in 1561, became a member of the Grand Chancellory.[78]

Therefore both of the governmental exponents who participated in the Cremonese trial of 1558 were important political figures and, due to the forms in which they had carried out their administrative careers until that moment, expressions of the specifically financial and fiscal branch of government. So it is not fanciful to suppose that their presence and their incentives were intrinsically bound to the need for procuring funds for the public Chamber. It certainly could not escape the two senators' attention, for example, that the complex *Description* of Pietro Maggi's property – prelude to a confiscation in benefit of the Extraordinary, the episcopal *Mensa* and the Holy Office court – had been executed between April 28 and May 4, 1558: before, then, the excommunication; and in a moment in which the canonical 12 days for the self-presentation of the accused (indicated in the posted citation of April 20), had not yet expired.[79] Nor, probably, were Figliodoni and Varahona without knowledge of an aspect which, only two years later – when the announcements of confiscation of the properties of five condemned heretics had been posted and the suits of opposition were already in course – which the Referendary of Cremona made present to the Extraordinary Magistrate. The Referendary wrote:

> I have inquired of the reverend episcopal vicars and the holy Inquisition of this city to learn the truth [of] when the nobleman Peter Maggio was accused of heresy, and, in effect, I have had nothing other from the above said vicars, if not that no accusation at all was made to them about said Maggio, if not a few days before the announcement given to said Maggio; which was on April 20, 1558.[80]

So a fundamental legal element in the condemnation of Pietro Maggi and the confiscation of his property was acquired by the ecclesiastical courts only on the eve of the public posting of the Notice intimating the obligation to appear before the judges – and ten days before the beginning of the *Description* of the property. Yet, despite this, it does not seem that the two members of the secular government raised any objections: in mid-1561, the ducal Chamber's fiscalist, noble Giovanni Battista Porto, could already emit the orders liquidating the sum realized from the sale of the "condemned *de haeresi*" Maggi's property – to the advantage of the episcopal *Mensa* and the Cremona Inquisition.[81] Everything essential had happened very quickly in those few April and May days of 1558, but no one seemed to have thought twice about it.

The public official becomes inquisitor

In the institutional polyphony characteristic of the government of the *Ancien régime*, the inquisitors worked with many governmental organisms even in areas like the confiscation and evaluation of property belonging to persons condemned for heresy. Even holders of local feudal power, as we have seen, might be involved in the decisions of the Holy Office which touched the patrimonies of persons and families under their jurisdiction: indeed, in the eyes of the judges of faith, they held precedence over the central organs of public administration.

A typical example is offered by the conflict which broke out in 1572 when the offices of the Extraordinary Magistrate received the anonymous information that a certain Giovan Andrea Ferrari, known as "the Reckless" ("*Sbardelato*") and residing in the hamlet of Musso – which was under the jurisdiction of the Marquis Giuseppe Malacrida – had been condemned by the Inquisition of Como "to be burnt for heresy and [to] the confiscation of his property, as he then was burnt in effigy". The land rent contracts stipulated by Ferrari with a Bernardo Malacrida of Como, and a Giovan Giacomo Lampartengo had, according to the unknown informer, been taken over by the inquisitor, who was, at that moment, enjoying their returns – 12 and 13 lire a year, respectively – in open conflict with "common sense": that is, the custom which required the involvement of the ducal Chamber in the procedures of property confiscation. The note cited, as well, another inhabitant of Musso "condemned for heresy" – Giovan Andrea Pellizzari – who, after being burnt in effigy by the same Inquisitor of Como, had been stripped of a like land rent contract, formerly paid by a Sigismondo Merli from Menaggio, and now due to the Inquisition.[82]

On receiving this information, the officials of the Extraordinary acted immediately, writing to the Como Referendary to order seizure of the property leased by Malacrida, Lampartengo and Merli and belonging to Ferrari and Pellizzari, reducing them to consignees ("who hold sequestered everything they have – which belonged to the said Ferrar[i]") of the patrimony seized by the State of Milan, the Inquisition and the episcopal *Mensa* of Como. The magistrate had no doubts that – as the usual procedure established – the properties in question could rapidly be "given proper liquidation so as to give portions to each, as to the Office of the Holy Inquisition and the episcopal Mensa". Finally, the Como inquisitor was ordered to transmit the text of the sentences of condemnation – indispensable for the publication announcing confiscation – to the Referendary.[83] But when the Referendary, local representative of the powers of the secular state, went to Musso with the local consul, one of his notaries and his most expert agronomist to execute a *Description* of the contested properties, he was surprised to learn that the inventory had already been compiled by the Inquisitor of Como with the approval of the feudal lord, the Marquis of Malacrida.[84]

On being questioned, the Como judge of faith, Gaspare Sacco, replied that Giovan Andrea Ferrari had been condemned as a heretic in default by his predecessor in April, 1567, and that his property had, indeed, been confiscated directly by the Holy Office, including the two land contracts mentioned "which", the inquisitor declared polemically, "are not enough to pay the expenses sustained". As for the case of Giovan Andrea Pellizzari, Father Sacco confirmed that he had suffered the same sentence in default on July 1, 1570, and that his property had likewise been confiscated by the Como Inquisition. This patrimony, once in the Holy Office's possession, had been sold, at about 320 lire and this had occurred with the explicit agreement of the feudal lord who, in turn, had received ten gold scudi. "I desire the agents of the Royal Chamber to not molest me nor disturb things past", the Como inquisitor concluded arrogantly, promising that, "in the future [he] would observe their orders, approved by the reverend father inquisitor of Milan": he would, that is, respect the style of the tripartite division generally applied in the territory more strictly "Milanese".[85]

When, leaving the principal urban centre of a State where the organs of government were situated, one went into the minor cities or the countryside (where as often was the case in longstanding states, jurisdictional and prerogative structure had accumulated and had become blurred in antique, or recently constituted, feuds), the relations between the Holy Office and State institutions was less predictable and less schematic. In these same years, the inquisitor in Novara advised Carlo Borromeo that he himself had sent the experts directly to Pallanza to compile the *Description* of the property of the wealthy Appiani family, whose members were on trial for heresy. Again in this case, the judge of faith showed himself confident in the possibility of handling the successive sale himself, reassuring the archbishop "nor shall their alienation be completed without your Illustrious Excellency remaining more its proprietor than I".[86]

The Como inquisitor's attitude became known to the Senate and to the governor, Luis de Zúñiga y Requesens, future governor of the Spanish Netherlands, who was, at the same time in receipt of a communication from the Holy Office signed by Cardinal Scipione Rebiba.[87] At the end of the year, the controversy was resolved with a deliberation by the Secret Council, which ordered the Extraordinary Magistrate not to molest "the office of the Holy Inquisition in Como as to the contents of its report, so that, in the future, it looks to what is customarily done in Milan".[88] The first useful occasion to test the Como inquisitor's acceptance of the Milanese "style" came in 1579, when the Como Referendary once again received an anonymous letter. It revealed that the new inquisitor had summarily confiscated the property of Gerolamo Castiglione, an orthodox Catholic residing in the city of Varese. Decades earlier, the property had belonged to a heretic from the Valcuvia, whose name, Guarnerio Castiglione, was almost the same.[89] Almost simultaneously, when the Milan Extraordinary Magistrate, too, had received the same anonymous information; summoning his Barrister Questor, Juan Hurtado de Mendoza, he had his representative in Como officially informed:

> It has come to our notice that before the ecclesiastical judges of the bishop or of the inquisition of that city, a trial is in course against a noble Hieronimo Castiglione of Varese to divest him of a property with the pretext that it was purchased by the father of said Castiglione from a Luther de Castiglione of the Val Cuvia, heretic, who was heretic at the time of sale and before, and that, therefore – as confiscated due to the prior crime of heresy before the sale – the [sale] could not have been [made] as damaging to the confiscation. Which, when it were true, would give rise to no small marvel, since this matter would be ours [...] Nor has it ever been seen that ecclesiastical judges or the Inquisition have interfered in the patrimony of heretics; it is their part to condemn or absolve heretics; it is our task to apprehend and liquidate their property. And having carried out the liquidation, of the wealth remaining – once the costs have been deducted – we divide [it] into three portions, one-third to the Royal Chamber, another third to the Holy

Office of the Inquisition, and one-third to the episcopal *Mensa* of the locality where the heretics and their property are; and this has served always, and serves still today, with the judges of the most illustrious and most excellent archbishop of Milan, and of the other cities. That father inquisitor knows very well what was ordered for the contracts of the heretic from Musso and you are to discover in what manner it is effective to proceed to act upon those judges who do not intend to change anything at all – but, indeed, want to leave the case to us who shall, for the sake of justice, bring it to a close, hearing first what said inquisitor, or ecclesiastical judges, want to declare.[90]

One of the most important learned officials of the second Milanese court, Mendoza – who would, in turn, become the first Spanish President of the Extraordinary Magistrate[91] – raised two problems. The first regarded the Como Inquisition's unflagging intention of proceeding on its own, which had already shown itself a few years earlier in the dispute over the seizure of the property of the Musso heretics. The second – less evident – regarded the legal legitimacy of the principle of *a die commissi criminis*, regarding which Mendoza added only a punctilious "when it were true", an uncertainty which would not reappear in any other officer of the Extraordinary Magistrate in the course of the confiscation of Guarnero Castiglione's property.

The secular authorities, then, once again easily accepted the canonical principle of the retroactivity of property confiscation; a principle usually invoked by the Extraordinary itself at the moment of considering any opposition. A 1557 writ of acquisition (*"instrumento acquisitionis"*) held by the buyer of a mill belonging to the already cited Cremonese priest, Giacomo Antonio Baruffini – condemned for heresy only in 1558 – could be considered legally null by the State courts, "in that it was concluded after the crime of heresy was committed [...] for it was committed from the year 1550 inclusively, as appears from his condemnation, which is exhibited".[92] This point is particularly important in understanding one of the bases of the overall efficiency of the Roman Inquisition: that is the close interweaving of canon law and ordinary secular law during the centuries of the early modern era.

The structure rested, first of all, on the fact that the confiscation procedure followed by the secular authorities – in this case the Extraordinary Magistrate of the State of Milan – was saturated with Roman-Canonical procedural elements which had taken form in the medieval ecclesiastical courts. As Paolo Prodi has observed, "the detailed procedure for each phase, the formalization of the legal documents to be compiled, the prospect of appeals and suits of invalidation, the obligation to motivate the sentence" – in short, all of the executive requirements on which confiscation by the secular judiciary turned[93] – had already been elaborated from at least the thirteenth century precisely by jurists of the Church. These requirements – first through the secular municipal courts of northern Italy and then, over several centuries, through the secular courts of the emerging monarchies and principalities – were transferred into secular justice, permeating it in depth. The secular world took them to itself in a long process of accretion which was culturally crucial for the history of the West, serving as the foundation of the general structure of cooperation between the justice of faith and secular justice "which remains still closely anchored to the *definition of crime as a sort of sin,* directly damaging to society as a whole".[94]

On the basis of these premises, the Milanese State judiciary did not hesitate to abandon the vague perplexities Mendoza expressed; rather, they wholeheartedly embraced the canonical position of retrospective confiscation advanced by the Como inquisitor. The question of the ascertainment of entity and value and the confiscation of the property belonging to Guarnero Castiglione (sometimes called "Luthero" or "Guarnerio Eluterio")[95] went forward with the meeting between the Como Referendary and the new inquisitor, Stefano da Cento. This new inquisitor averred that Castiglione's condemnation for heresy had been pronounced in 1575 by his predecessor – who had not, however, proceeded to "any seizure nor description" of property. "It is, however, true", the inquisitor declared, that Friar Sacco had:

> investigated and sought diligently to clarify when Guarnerio fell into heresy, so as to see if the alienation of two of his properties in the years 1549, 1550 and 1551 – among which is included that sold to said [Gerolamo] Castiglione – was made after he had become Lutheran (and consequently to be confiscated, and its alienation declared invalid); and it is for him to clear up this doubt and that he does not intend to show the trial documents that regard it without the express order of cardinal Savello.[96]

So the inquisitor confirmed the intention of proceeding with the confiscation of Castiglione's property *a die commissi criminis* of heresy; citing the Congregation directly, he also declared the exclusive competence of the Holy Office in establishing at what point of the investigation/trial process the faculty of secreting the documentation was to be exercised. The Como judge of faith did not, however, make objection to hypotheses of dividing the sum deriving from the confiscated property with the Milan ducal Chamber while – mentioning the quarrel over resources we have seen between the Holy Office and various diocesan authorities – he did declare himself contrary to any participation of Como's episcopal *Mensa* in that division.[97]

Faced with the Como inquisitor's arrogant declarations, Milan's Extraordinary Magistrate, too, became rigid:

> The task of seeking out and liquidating the property of heretics belongs to us, his majesty's ministers for the orders and the custom of this State, approved by his predecessors and, as well, by papal Bulls; and it shall never be found that, regarding the property of heretics, the inquisitors and other ecclesiastical judges have meddled [...] And the reason that says it is your

concern to see if the sales made by this heretic were made after he had already become heretic, or not: that is not reasonable, for this understanding is our prerogative, after the investigation [of the Description].[98]

In reality, the inquisitor Stefano da Cento had not meant to sustain that, from the procedural point of view, his was the right to decide which acts of buying and selling of Guarneri's property were to be considered legitimate and what contradictions might or might not be admissible. Rather, as his conciliatory rejoinder promptly made clear, the ecclesiastical judge had intended to sustain that fixing the date of commission of the heresy – which was the crucial chronological moment dividing legitimate and illegitimate sales of items of the heretic's property – depended solely on his authority.[99]

With this cleared up, the ecclesiastical and secular authorities quickly overcame the problem of notifying the negative inquisitorial decision regarding Guarnerio Castiglione and his wife, Bona: it arrived in Milan, after insistent pressures, at the end of December, 1579.[100] It immediately became clear that, in 1575, Father Sacco had judged the heretic couple noting that – fearing the court of faith – they promptly had sold their real estate at cut-rate prices and fled beyond the Alps.[101] It is interesting to note that the sale of the properties at well below market value (cheapening the price ["*viliori praetio venditis*"]), practised by Guarnerio and Bona shortly before their emigration, was explicitly cited by the inquisitor as revelatory of the intent to flee Catholic lands rapidly, and, therefore, of an already openly Protestant religious allegiance on the part of the accused culprits. Here the Holy Office cited a number of factors and clues – including some regarding estimates of value – to formulate a sentence which set the beginning of the crime (the "*dies commissi criminis*") as early as possible, increasing the economic potentiality of the confiscation.

If the contract of a property sale predating expatriation were to be held valid by an ecclesiastical court as proof of a manifest state of heresy, that would mean that the *dies commissi criminis* existed prior to the date in which the culprit had lived in a heretical land – and the departure itself became the mere epiphenomenon of a heretical religious choice already made. This was a decisive legal step, because it allowed the Inquisition to seize the patrimony sold by a culprit even when the moment of the "fall" into the sin-crime of heresy could not be established with any certainty, simply by making the sale itself proof ("*terminus ad quem*") of the state of heresy, on the basis of an evaluation of market value superior to the actual price of sale. In October, 1579, a sentence signed by both the inquisitor Stefano da Cento and the episcopal vicar Alessandro Lucino fixed the fatidic 1549 as the time when the Castigliones' sin originated.[102]

It was then, in December of 1579, that it was finally possible to post the bills of confiscation. The compilation of the *Description and Seizure* of the Castiglione patrimony "in the name of the Royal Chamber, the Office of the Holy Inquisition of Como and others to whom it is due", presented, nonetheless, a number of important difficulties. The "goods and rights which, from the year 1540 to the present time belonged to noble Guarnero Castiglione, as [herein] follows" were now – 40 years later, in the hands of a number of owners, many of whom had carried out notable improvements, completely altering the original characteristics of the fields, infrastructures and buildings, and, sometimes, leasing them on to others.[103] The experts tried to establish the original value of the buildings, whether these had been renovated with "effort and construction", reconstructing their state in earlier decades. The results were laborious, complicated, estimates: "probably not more than a calculable two *carra* of wine and a half *staro* of mixed grains a *pertica* yearly"; "probably they weren't able to get more than about 7 scudi a year in rent"; "realistically, they might have got as rent some 3 *stara* of mixed grains a year"; "[a]nd questioned, said consul – and also Battista del Pastore, living in the aforesaid locality of Accio, affirmed with their oath that from that plot of land you could probably get a yearly rent of about 2 *brenta* of wine and 2 *stara* of mixed rye and millet, half and half, nor could it be rented out for more".[104]

Obviously, this confiscation procedure produced a wave of opposition on the part of those who had, in the meantime, bought and developed the properties which had belonged to the Castiglione couple: at its heart was the same contention. The sale of properties made by the couple after 1549 were not to be considered legitimate, because the purchasers did not know at the time that the Castiglione were heretics. According to the appellants, the time elapsed had, as well, proscribed the rights of the Holy Office and the Ducal Chamber. To clarify this intricate situation – already in some measure foreshadowed by the President of the Extraordinary Magistrate, Camillo Porro, in his harsh letter of April, 1579 – the Como inquisitor, the secular authority and the ecclesiastical court had to establish an alliance of procedure and intent, developing a form of integrated inquisitorial practice. To understand how this worked out in daily reality, we can try to further deconstruct this paradigmatic case and draw from it more articulated considerations on the historic exercising of the justice of faith in its broadest and most articulated form.

The defensive position of those who, in 1579, were the owners of property which had belonged to the Castiglione family until 1549 was both lucid and legitimate. They maintained that it was improbable that, in the 1540s, they might have known that the Castigliones were heretics ("*haberent vel verisimiliter habere possent aliquam notitia*"). The improbability was, they declared, demonstrated by the fact that – if the Castigliones had been clearly heretic – the Inquisition would have prosecuted them.[105] The Extraordinary Magistrate, authority of the State of Milan, now had to assume the obligation of establishing whether, after the legally fixed date of the beginning of the state of heresy of the Castiglione couple, that condition was also publicly notorious. The union of practice and intent between the secular and the ecclesiastical spheres reached its peak here, in what we can call an exchange of roles. A shared economic objective could, then – with the aid of a common cultural and legal substratum – give rise to what is only an apparent paradox: the exchanging of roles, in virtue of which the secular courts began to carry out

212   *The Inquisition and economic life*

investigations into the orthodoxy of a prince's subject, while the ecclesiastical court waited confidently for the final completion of what was a traditionally secular act, the confiscation of the property of a condemned criminal.

Thus, had an indiscrete ear passed beneath the open window of Antonio Francesco Gorla, notary in the city of Varese, locally responsible for the investigation as *Podestà* of the Valcuvia, they might have believed they were hearing the interrogation of a dedicated inquisitor. They might have heard Tommaso Capia, known as Matteo, an inhabitant of Cuvio, declare, more or less:

> I knew as an inhabitant of the locality of Cuvio [the] in said section described noble Guarnerio Castiglione, equally named after he came from Clivio to live in said place of Cuvio until afterwards he dismantled his home there. Though I declare that, as his acquaintance and neighbour for all the said time the said noble Guarnerio was held, treated and reputed by me (witness) and any other acquaintance of his as a man of good repute and a faithful Christian, for he often used to go and hear mass not only on holy days, but on weekdays, too, as I often saw him do at our church in Cuvio, and he held himself devotedly and to any who went to him gave only good advice and I even remember having seen him many and many times in our presbystery to hear vespers sung on holidays while I too also was there, and as far as I heard tell at that time when children were born to him he had them baptized as is usual and orderly among Christians; however this baptizing I did not see, [though] it is certainly true that he held also some babies like, among others, one of my newborn children, at [their] baptism.[106]

Castiglione was a person of note: he was himself a notary and was for two years, *Podestà* of Lomagna and, for another two, Lieutenant of the *Podestà* of Laveno; he met with and daily received individuals of every social rank, conversing with them and giving them his opinions and advice. Bartolomeo Del Chiocca of Cuvio, who was for an entire decade "acquaintance and neighbour" confirmed that Guarnerio "was publicly held by everyone to be a good Christian and a good man and devoted to the Lord God because besides the holy days, he went to mass often on work days with the others of his household as I often saw" and that "when children of his were born, he notoriously and openly had them baptized", adding that "he had a great deal of work as notary and attorney".[107] Antonio Barberi, who knew Guarnerio Castiglione well, "turning to him often in those years for my needs, both in litigation and for the preparation of contracts and documents", confirmed that "for all of the indicated period, I never heard anything publicly said such that from any [of his] neighbours it might be surmised that he might be heretical, or that any blemish of heresy might mark him – indeed, to the contrary, he was reputed one of the best men who dwelt in the valley and a faithful Christian."[108]

As was always the case in investigations conducted by the Extraordinary, highly delicate evidence on the level of confessional justice emerged during

A pervasive Inquisition 213

the proceedings and they mingled with information and opinions whose scope was the evaluation of property. Antonio Gerini from Cuvio, for example, after having delineated various aspects of Castiglione's fame as a good Christian, slipped without difficulty into an estimation of the improvements he had made after 1550 to a plot of land now owned by Pietro Peroso:

> And in my opinion commonly and most probably said improvements are permanently useful and worth at least the sum of 250 gold scudi and I and any other person informed of said quality to be found in said 'chiosso' and [because] of said improvements paid him said sum extra for said improvements, [more] than what would have been paid without them; and this commonly.[109]

Francesco Martinoli, was, in turn, prompted by the inquiring officials to recall:

> I went into Tuscany when I was young and I remember that in the year 1550 I arrived in Cuvio where then I had relatives and friends and after I made my home there, but at the time I stayed there in Cuvio about six or seven months in which I remember having seen countless times the plot of land in 'chiosso' described in said Items [...] as it was close to the above named terrains of Cuvio near which I passed going and coming from the vicarage so that I remember what it was like [...] Said improvements are by common opinion – mine and of every other informed [person] – useful and necessary and of common value of at least 200 gold scudi and more, and anyone else who was informed as above to contemplate said improvements, having to buy said 'chiosso' will spend said 200 scudi and more than I would have done and would do without said improvements.[110]

Martinoli's testimony was also important because it furnished an important indication of the buyer Pietro Peroso's ignorance as to Castiglione's heretical status. In fact, Martinoli added:

> Before the said Pietro Peroso bought the above mentioned 'chiosso' of said noble Guarnerio, he had been about ten uninterrupted years – and even longer – in the city of Ascoli in the Marche, and I know it because I was there and in his company we worked for a loan, and in the month of May of the year 1551 he left said city where I was, coming to this area where he then bought the said 'chiosso'; but I couldn't really say how many days he was here before said purchase; I think they must have been very few.[111]

This statement might have favoured Peroso, had the inquisitor – who had free access to this documentation – begun to suspect that he had knowingly bought the Castigliones' property cheaply ("*viliori praetio*") with the intent of making their flight easier. Abetting a heretic might, in fact, given the closely knit situation of canon and secular law, carry serious patrimonial, as well as penal, consequences for the accomplice. Already in the thirteenth century – first with Frederick II's laws on heresy and then with Innocent IV's *Ad extirpanda* (1252, which transferred them into canon law) – the confiscation of the property of those who had helped a heretic to flee or had hampered his capture, was obligatory.[112] Both canon and secular law would, in the centuries which followed, follow this line, establishing punishments (including forms involving patrimony) for all kinds of aid or comfort to heretics, such elements were, as we have had occasion to notice, perhaps even more successfully discovered in the course of the far-ranging investigations of the Extraordinary Magistrate than in the inquisitor's own interrogations.

Finally, a point that has remained until now implicit in the analysis of the case of the Castiglione confiscation – though it is fundamental for the comprehension of the juridical roots of the alliance of intent between ecclesiastical and secular authorities in the ideological and patrimonial persecution of heresy and the heretic – needs to be at least briefly touched upon. The basic assumption on which the entire investigation conducted by the Extraordinary – which involved those who had purchased the property that had belonged to the Castiglione couple – rested, was that the demonstration of the impossibility of knowing the heretical condition of the sellers would annul the rights of the confiscating authorities: the Holy Office; Ducal Chamber; and, perhaps, the episcopal *Mensa*. The category of Good Faith was at stake: if proven, it would make the buyers guiltless and the confiscators' right would, with the process of seizure, cease to exist.

But Good Faith was a Roman juridical criterion; it had never been accepted by canon law. In Justinian's Code the abolition of the distinction between usucaption and prescription (the purchase or the addition of "dominion" to the material possession of property which had been enjoyed over a period fixed by law) attributed to the prescription of all of the effects of the ancient usucaption based on five requisites: good faith; just title; capacity of the thing which one wishes to enjoy; the period defined by law; and continued possession. In Roman usucaption and, subsequently, in prescription, Good Faith – that is the opinion of justice and the validity of the title with which possession of the good was secured – were not sought in the concept of the contract; Bad Faith, occurring before the end of the period fixed by law for prescription, did not interrupt the process leading to prescription. Canon law – with a crucial correction of the secular model – required, instead, an uninterrupted condition of Good Faith: that is, until completion of the fixed prescription period.[113] Throughout the whole investigation conducted by the secular authorities which we are considering, the Extraordinary's officers made no attempt to investigate whether the Good Faith of those buying Castiglione's property remained constant – and so, *even after the sale was completed,* they had not realized that those selling the property to them had been tainted with the crime of heresy.

Thus, the secular judiciary reaffirmed – and the Holy Office accepted – a concept which belonged distinctively to secular jurisprudence rather than to canon law. It was, however, a difference which, still again, did not impede the community of action and intent between State and Inquisition, in the continuing dialogue reciprocal principles and organizational structures constituting the basis of legal and cultural development during the early modern era. And it is worth noting that this occurred with regards to an element that was anything but secondary in the respective juridical identities of State and Church, since it carried for the latter damaging implications of incalculable cultural and material scope.

In the previous century, Lorenzo Valla had, indeed, used precisely the canonical argument of the necessity for perpetual Good Faith against the Church itself, affirming the impossibility of the Papal State to acquire the territories which were object of what were called *Constantine's Donation* by prescription. Once the pretended donation was demonstrated philologically to be a counterfeit, the Good Faith – which previous popes had been able to invoke through ignorance – came, necessarily to an end. This, Valla declared, would block the acquisitive prescription of State property on the plane of canon law, though it would not impede it in secular courts.[114]

Notes

1   See Prodi (2000): the definition of "civil common law" is on p. 122. Of course this does not assume there is no distinction between canon and secular law. As Prodi makes clear, "If we speak of common law as a structural entity [*'sistema iuris'*] which developed as a creation of the Roman attitude, in a synthesis between Roman law and canon law, I think [...] that this never occurred; and that has been one of the myths which have most damaged – and still continue to damage the legal history of our time. Certainly, a 'canonic common law' existed becoming, over time, increasingly papal law; certainly, a 'civil common law', Roman in structure – to which the emperors, the legislators and the local judges made reference [...] There is no sort of citation to an abstract Roman-canon common law, if not in the mediation of juridical theory [...] but this scholarly law, universally diffused, cannot be identified with any sort of universal 'system'" (ibid., pp. 122–3). Berman (1985) offers a "law applicable to heretics" as "a gross exception to the principle of the division between ecclesiastical and secular jurisdictions", adding however, "this was an 'anomaly' on which eventually – in the sixteenth century – the entire 'model' foundered" (p. 186).
2   The information comes from Sabatini (2010).
3   ACDF, So, St.st., I5a, unnumbered subfolder, "Nota di alcuni tra li molti esempii, che addurre si possono [...]", p. 1*v*.; ACDF, So, St.st., BB3b, folder 1.
4   Sabatini (2010), pp. 649–51.
5   BAV, Borg. Lat. 558, "Sommario delle cose più prencipali che si conservano nell'Archivio Regio di Napoli, spettanti al Sant'Officio" pp. 308ff., p. 315*r*. On the story see Amabile (1892), tome I, pp. 218–9.
6   On the Calabrian Waldensians see cfr. BAV, Borg. Lat. 558, pp. 371*v*ff.; on the "judaizers", see Del Col (2006), p. 466.
7   See, also for the quotation from Bruno, Ricci (2002), pp. 134–40.
8   *Discorso indirizzato all'Eccellenza del signor Duca d'Alva dell'antichissimo costume e dell'inviolabile osservanza di non potersi poner mano nel Regno a carcerare nessuna persona per causa d'eresia o del Sant'Ufficio senza prima darne*

notizia alli signori Viceré. For information on Capece Galeota, a first overview may be found in Russo (1975).
9 Cited from the copy in BAV, Barb. Lat. 558, pp. 197r–221r, p. 207r–v.
10 *Risposta al discorso di Fabio Capece Galeota Consigliero Regio, dato alle stampe contro l'antico e immemorabile possesso nel quale s'è sempre mantenuto et si mantiene il Santo Officio nel Regno di Napoli di carcerare liberamente laici di qualsivoglia conditione che siano per cause ad esso spettanti senza farne consapevole o chiedere licenza alli Vice Re dell'istesso Regno* (BAV, Barb. Lat. 558, pp. 222r–249r, p. 222r).
11 Ibid., pp. 227r–229r. Cantù (1865), vol. 1, p. 88, mentions the trial for heresy which involved the Bishop of Trivento.
12 Prosperi (2003), pp. 125–6.
13 Regular application of the tripartite division of the results of confiscation in the Duchy of Milan during the 1500s is discussed in Lavenia (2000), p. 72. The 1554 decree is in Cantù (1865), vol. 3, pp. 35–7. On the tradition concerning the "Period of Grace" see Brambilla (2000), pp. 381ff.
14 See BAV, Barb. Lat. 6334, Rome, January 10, 1626, p. 9r; BAV, Borg. Lat. 558, p. 56r, Rome, February 7, 1609; May 21, 1609; February 12, 1626 (definition of *stylus loci*). See also Lavenia (2000), p. 94; I quote from Ermeneglido Todeschini, *Storia della fondazione, ed origine della santa Inquisizione di Milano ora esistente nel convento di santa Maria delle Grazie nel borgo di porta Vercellina de frati Predicatori della provincia di Lombardia*, in ACDF, So, St.st., LL5e, *Inquisizione di Milano*, p. 19r.
15 The documentation is deposited in the State Archives in Milan and organized in titled folders in the collection *Finanze*, series *Confische*, in the old part of the *Atti di Governo* archive. The presence of some of these folders was mentioned and briefly commented by Rivoire (1936); so are as I know, they were not subsequently object of further study. To date, there is no full history of the Milanese inquisitorial court; see, however, di Filippo Bareggi and Signorotto (2009), and the bibliography it includes.
16 ASM, Fc, box 310, folder "Balsamo, diversi", subfolder "Balsamo Paolo Camillo", sentence of April 13, 1571, signed by Friar Angelo da Cremona and Archbishop Carlo Borromeo, pp. 1r–3r. Galiffe (1881), p. 127, sustains that Paolo Camillo Balsamo resided uninterruptedly in Geneva from 1557.
17 From the documentation concerning the confiscation of the property of the Cremonese priest, Giacomo Antonio Baruffino, we see that, faced with the doubts expressed by the local referendary "concerning the difficulty arising from having sent the oppositions to the notices regarding the property of Antonio Baruffino and others condemned for heresy [indifferently] into our hands – or into those of the reverend father inquisitor and the bishop's vicar in this city [...]: the most excellent Senate yesterday took charge of the problem, ordering that the declarations of said oppositions are the responsibility of our office" (ASM, Fc, box 343, folder "Baruffino Giac[om]o Ant[oni]o", letter to the Referendary of Cremona, April 3, 1559).
18 See ibid. The opposition filed by the Balsamo brothers is dated July 14, 1571 "To both the Dean and the *Questori* of the royal ducal Extraordinary Income of the State of Milan" (p. 1r).
19 Ibid., pp. 1v–2r.
20 The sentence is ibid., Milan, December 18, 1571.
21 Barsanti (2003), p. 152.
22 Aristide Sala (1857), p. 452, cites a letter from Cardinal Giacomo Savelli, Secretary of the Congregation of the Holy Office, to Carlo Borromeo, dated August 2, 1578, in which Savelli announces he has written to the Inquisitor of Milan concerning the case of Scipione Balsamo.

23 This substitution came about in the same year of 1578 and is documented in the 1749 manuscript of the Milan inquisitor of the time, Ermenegildo Todeschini, in ACDF, So, St.st., LL5e, *Inquisizione di Milano*, p. 4v. According to this source, Clavenna was Inquisitor of Milan from 1573, succeeding Father Paolo Constabili da Ferrara, inquisitor only for 1572, and the previously cited Angelo Zampi da Cremona, who held his post in Milan from 1563 to 1572 (ibid.).
24 See the document in ASM, Fc, box 310, folder "Balsamo Scipione", notary Francesco Melzi, June 20, 1578, p. 1r.
25 "*Ad praesentiam reverendi patris Mauri de Nigris ordinis predicatoris vicarii predicti Officii Sanctae Inquisitionis*" and of "*Paridis de Valle collateralis peaedicti Officiis Sanctae Inquisitionis*" (ibid.). For the transcript of the investigation regarding the houses in Milan, and Boffalora, see Maifreda (2012b).
26 Ibid., pp. 3v–4r. One Milanese *pertica* was equivalent to about 654 square metres; one Milanese *moggio* was about 146 litres.
27 On the *Description* as a prelude to confiscation, see Guazzino (1611), p. 4.
28 Ibid., p. 6.
29 The formula is in ASM, Fc, box 310, folder "Balsamo Scipione", notary Francesco Melzi, June 20, 1578, p. 4v; the acceptance is on a single sheet, originally fastened to the document with sealing wax.
30 "Consigned [...] representative of the Royal Treasury, offices Holy Inquisition and Mensa of Archbishop"; see ibid., Acts of June 23, 1578 (citied from p. 6r) and June 25, 1578, both drawn up by Francesco Melzi.
31 Maifreda (2006).
32 ASM, Fc, box 525, folder "Bondiolo Giuseppe".
33 ASM, Fc, box 343, folder "Baruffino Giac[om]o Ant[oni]o", *Descriptio* of April 26, 1558; quote from the letter June 8, 1558 and the second *descriptio* dated November 26, 1558.
34 ASM, Fc, box 310, folder "Balsamo Scipione", sentence July 17, 1585.
35 Ibid., letter without date or signature, accompanying the estimate dated January 13, 1584; the italics are mine.
36 On Carlo Borromeo's relinquishing the third of confiscation due the episcopal *Mensa*, see Lavenia (2000), pp. 72–3.
37 This episode was still mentioned, in the mid-eighteenth century, in a report sent by the Cremonese inquisitor to the Roman Congregation: cfr. ACDF, So, St.st., LL5e, unnumbered sheets, documentation gathered in 1749. Francesco Fogliata was part of the group of "gentlemen" incriminated because of their friendship with the two Benedictines who had fled Mantua – Friar Valeriano and Friar Sereno – discovered and captured in Solarolo in the home of Giuseppe Fossa, studied by F. Chabod (1938), pp. 145–8.
38 ASM, Fc, box 2125, folder "Orsino Gerolamo", memorandum without date.
39 Prosperi (2001), p. 114ff. The spread of baptismal registration in the preconciliar years has, however, been noted in Alfani (2009), pp. 30–1.
40 See for example ASM, Fc, box 343, folder "Baruffino Giac[om]o Ant[oni]o", subfolder "Testes examinati in favorem d. Anne de Pirolis", transcript of the interrogations opened March 16, 1558, pp. 4v and 2r.
41 I have investigated these themes using the documentation produced by the activities of the Extraordinary Magistrate; see Maifreda (2012a). Quote from Masini (1730), first edition 1621, p. 233.
42 This is shown in Ago (1998).
43 ASM, Fc, box 343, folder "Baruffino Giac[om]o Ant[oni]o", transcript of the interrogation entitled "*Processi expedit*" opened on August 12, 1571; interrogation of September 5, 1571, pp. 15r–18v.
44 Masini (1730), p. 98.

45 Ibid. Masini continues: "and monsignor Rossi detested this lack then when I served him in the Holy Office in Rome". The author then gives an example of a testimony with "the fount of knowledge": "I know very well Gilberta, daughter of Castor Malgradi and Arnulfa Cellari, and wife of Menelao Santori; and it was I who held her at baptism" (pp. 99–100). In the context of a long example of inquisitorial interrogation, Masini several times repeats this: "One can always see the importance that is given, and must be given, to the fount of knowledge" (p. 129). "Here we have a new occasion to recall the requirement of the fount of knowledge; and I shall not do so again" (p. 133).
46 ASM, Fc, box 343, folder "Baruffino Giac[om]o Ant[oni]o", transcript of the interrogation entitled *"Processi expedit"* opened on August 12, 1571; interrogation of September 5, 1571, pp. 15r–18v.
47 Ibid., pp. 19r–v.
48 Ibid., p. 24v.
49 Ibid., p. 29r.
50 The political implications are clearly indicated in Alfani (2009).
51 ASM, ibid. On units of measurement see Note 26.
52 ASM, Fc, box 310, folder "Balsamo Scipione", attachment C, pp. 1–42.
53 See ibid., the interrogations included in the transcript in the envelope "November 22, 1581", section beginning with January 23, 1580.
54 Ibid., pp. 98r–98v.
55 On the decisive contribution of the Italian aristocracy to the war in Flanders, see Spagnoletti (2009). On the preoccupations that the situation in Flanders and the possibility that it might cause unrest in the State of Milan which it occasioned in the Milanese governing and ecclesiastical authorities – and even in Philip II, see Giannini (2001), pp. 92–3.
56 ASM, ibid., pp. 98v–99r.
57 An interesting example of the specious use of the "visit to the Baths in Flanders", in connection with the war in the Flanders, occurs in the treatise Cardinal Guido Bentivoglio, who had been papal nuncio in Flanders, wrote (1635): "At the beginning of July [1577], Margherita de Valois, queen of Navarre, passed through the borders of Flanders on her way to France, taking the opportunity to visit the Baths at Spa, in the State of Liège. This was the official reason for her trip, but the real intention was to support personally, more closely, the campaign in favour of the Duke of Alansone, her brother" (tome 1, p. 527).
58 ASM, ibid., pp. 101v–102r.
59 Some of these may be seen in AA.VV. (1981).
60 ASM, ibid., pp. 104r–105v.
61 Ibid., pp. 106r–107r.
62 Ibid., p. 110r.
63 Ibid., pp. 110v–111v.
64 This episode is examined by Balmas (2004), pp. 117–37. When Pestalozzi, returning to the town of Piuro, had the local *Podestà* write to the Governor of Milan to recover the 50 scudi bond he had given Friar Angelo da Cremona, their reply was: "Your excellency is advised the most reverend father inquisitor has not in any way disturbed the agreement reached by his Catholic majesty, our lord and the Swiss lords, and if he had Vincenzo Pestaloci [*sic*] jailed, he did so according to reason and prior to the declared debt, so that it is clear that the said Pestaloci [*sic*] committed the offence in this State and as subject of his majesty [held] his false opinion. [...] This being so, the Swiss authorities have no reason to complain that anything new has been done, nor he, Pestalocio [*sic*] has any just cause whatsoever to complain about the Holy Office nor the reverend inquisitor" (pp. 134–5). On the Alburquerque *grida* of January 30, 1563, see Maselli (1970), pp. 334ff.

65 BAM, F 83 Inf, Scipione Rebiba to Carlo Borromeo, Rome, March 24, 1576, p. 554r–v. On April 17, Rebiba, known as Cardinal of Pisa, wrote once more to the Ordinary to express his satisfaction: "His Holiness our lord has been pleased to learn of the beginning which your most illustrious lordship has given to negotiations with the Milanese merchants who are in Nuremburg and hopes that the conclusion of the effort continues to afford satisfaction, entrusting the treaty to you, who will know how to bring it to conclusion with your usual goodness and prudence" (BAM, F 83 Inf., c. 559r).

66 See Simoncelli (1976). The papal prohibition was criticized by Paolo Sarpi: see Cozzi and Cozzi (1969), pp. 1220–3; Sarpi, after having sustained that the Republic of Venice had not accepted the decree, on p. 1120 testifies its rigorous application within the State of Milan.

67 "Trial records consigned to be viewed to the most reverend inquisitor by me, Giovan Ambrogio Biorago, notary of the Extraordinary Chamber on the order of the most illustrious Magistrate, so that his most reverend holiness may view them and, should it serve him, may act upon them for the treasury." The folders consigned to the inquisitor on that occasion were "a trial of a suit brought by *domino* Agosto de Rò against the property of Giacomo Viberti, condemned for heresy; a suit regarding the property of Domino Jacomo Filippo de Rò, contesting the previous suit; a contestation brought by *domini* Giovan Maria and Jeronimo father and sons of Augustoni, contrasting the above; another suit brought by Domino Giovan Battista da Monte against the above" (Cfr. ASM, Fc, box 3172, folder "Confisca di Giacomo Viberto", Milan, April 28, 1570).

68 ASM, Fc, box 215, fasc. "Appiano Bernardo", note of delivery of the registers, March 23, 1572.

69 Caponetto (1979).

70 Seidel Menchi (1987), p. 263.

71 The quote from *Sacro Arsenale* (*cit.*) is from p. 18. As Benaglio (1711), p. 1, testifies, "the Courts are two which, after the Senate, have been and today still are of equal importance in Milan: that of the Ordinary Magistrate and that of the Extraordinary Magistrate; the former administers the normal income of the ducal Chamber, the latter, the extraordinary [income]; the one and the other being equal in formality, prerogatives and honours. They hold it as their maxim to conserve the ducal patrimony, considering at once the interests of the rulers and the benefit to the subjects. And it is certain that if the zeal of these courts had always been seconded on the occasions of great need, the ducal coffers would not be in such difficulty".

72 To date, we have proof of the presence of four lay consultants at late sixteenth century inquisitorial trials; only in the mid-1600s has the presence of a senator and five lay consultants – always collegiate jurists – been documented: see Zardin (2003), pp. 50–1 and 56. Borromeo (1977–8), pp. 234–41 cites various examples of the intervention of secular Milanese authorities in questions of inquisitorial procedure; they refer, however, to the first half of the 1500s. It should also be noted that, in 1566, the above mentioned Vincenzo Pestalozzi confessed its guilt, as the governor of Milan wrote, "in the presence of the most reverend noble Ormaneto, vicar of the archbishop, of noble Giovan Battisti Raynoldi, senator, and other attorneys expert in Law and in Theology": see Balmas (2004), p. 134; on Ormaneto, Borromeo (1986), p. 245. In Cremona, too, some senators participated, as representatives of the state, in inquisitorial decisions, see Peyronel Rambaldi (1995).

73 This situation was brought to light by Chabod (1938), pp. 145–50; still, he only touches on the successive reopening of the trial in a brief note on p. 161.

74 The sentence is in ASM, Fc, box 1720, folder "Maggi Pietro", p. 1v. ("in episcopali palatio Cremonae et solum deum preoculis habentes et habita et partecipatione cum illustrissimo domino Danesio Filiodono [...] Senator Mediolani").

75 See ibid. the undated letter transmitting the sentence to the Extraordinary Magistrate which, among other information, declares specifically that the citation already contained the specific indication of the sentence of confiscation should the accused fail to present themselves: "confessed under duress and convicted of the crime of heresy, so to the confiscation of all property and all the punishments the law of its own will imposes".
76 Petronio (1972), vol. 1, p. 101, note 24. On Arese (1970), p. 76, he is erroneously indicated as president of the Ordinary Magistrate, including him, instead, correctly among the presidents of the Extraordinary Magistrate on p. 46.
77 Petronio (1972), vol. 1, p. 77, note 218, and p. 147, note 178. The Income Magistrate was a very old institution, going back to the Viscontis; considered "second only to the Senate in authority and prestige" (ibid., p. 148), it had exclusive control of ordinary State income and of the patrimonial incomes of the prince; in some cases, especially regarding feudal questions, it found a limit in the competing jurisdiction of the Senate. The president of the Income Magistrate participated in the meetings of the Secret Council: see Leverotti (1997).
78 Petronio (1972), p. 76, note 216; Arese (1970), p. 39. It is not irrelevant that later, in the 1550s, the proceedings of the Cremonese Inquisition were followed by the only Spanish senator, Baldassarre Molina, and precisely in 1558 (Petronio [1972], p. 109, note 51).
79 ASM, Fc, box 1720, folder "Maggi Pietro, April 28, 1558–May 4, 1558, notary Francesco Bonelli.
80 Ibid., Nicolò Silva to the president of the Extraordinary Magistrate, Cremona, July 31, 1560. The announcement of confiscation was posted in Cremona on June 28, 1559, examination of the contestation began on September 5 of the same year.
81 Ibid.. Order of payment, June 25, 1561, for about 766 lire in favour of this episcopal *Mensa*, and the offices of the Holy Inquisition of Cremona of said two parts owed due to the said confiscation".
82 ASM, Fc, box 887, folder "Castiglione Guarnerio", undated letter, p. 1r.
83 Ibid., Extraordinary Magistrate to the Referendary in Como Gianbattista Maggio, Milan, July 12, 1572, pp. 1r–v.
84 Ibid., Referendary in Como Gianbattista Maggio to Extraordinary Magistrate, Como, July 13, 1572.
85 Ibid., inquisitor in Como Gaspare Sacco to Referendary Gianbattista Maggio, Como, undated.
86 BAM, F 122 inf., c. 144r, Father Domenico Buelli to Carlo Borromeo, Novara, May 9, 1571.
87 As we see in ASM, Fc, box 887, folder "Castiglione Guarnerio", Extraordinary Magistrate to the Governor of the State of Milan: "We informed your Excellency that we had not done the abovementioned thing in execution of new orders, but according to habitual custom and the orders of the Senate which have always been observed, in Milan and in the cities of this State; nor do we know for what reason the Como inquisitor can pretend to more than those who have preceded him claimed – not existing any reasons for a difference" (p. 2r).
88 Ibid., certificated extract from the register of decrees of the Secret Council, December 13, 1572.
89 Ibid, Referendary in Como Cinzio Calvi to Extraordinary Magistrate, Como, April 7, 1579. A brief mention of "propaganda" of Reformed doctrine in the early 1540s, "stirred up precisely by the laymen" among whom Guarnerio Castiglione is included, is in Chabod (1938), p. 117.
90 Ibid., Extraordinary Magistrate to the Referendary in Como, Milan, April 9, 1579, p. 1r–v.
91 Arese (1970), p. 102.

A pervasive Inquisition   221

92 See the Proceedings of the "Processus Jo Petri del Ventura contra Regium Ducalem Fiscum, Mensam episcopalem et Officium sanctae Inquisitionis, pro bonis Jacobi Antonii Baruffini confischatis», parere dell'avvocato fiscale Sappa", pp. 6r–7v, in ASM, Fc, box 343, fasc. "Baruffino Giac[om]o Ant[oni]o".
93 As we can see very clearly in the lengthy and highly detailed procedure outlined in *Titolo del Magistrato straordinario composto nella maggior parte dal presidente Giulio Claro dopo l'anno 1563*: see Benaglio (1711), pp. 201–40. On Claro's juridical positions – saturated in canon law – which, regarding heresy, totally embrace the opinion of the Church ("in whose faith I live and mean to die") see Massetto (1994), quote from p. 53.
94 The quotations are from Prodi (2000), p. 133, the italics are mine. An important group of canonic studies has reconstructed the cultural turn which, in the Middle Ages, led canon law to orient itself progressively towards the assumption that the salvation of the soul from sin must become its chief objective, as Clarence Gallagher (1978), p. 185, has written "the large body of canonical legislation enacted in the twelfth and thirteenth centuries against heresy is the most striking example of canon law being used as a deterrent and an instrument of reform".
95 ASM, ibid., President of the Extraordinary Magistrate Camillo Porro to *pretore* in Valcuvia, Milan, April 15, 1579, p. 1v.
96 Ibid., Referendary in Como to Extraordinary Magistrate, Como, April 24, 1579, p. 1r.
97 "[The inquisitor] also says that when he should discover that said properties were confiscated, he would make no difficulties [if] the Chamber published the edict, and, having liquidated, kept the third part which belongs to the Chamber, giving to him, however, the other two-thirds, because he sustains that the episcopal *mensa* has no right to any part at all" (ibid.).
98 Ibid., President of the Extraordinary Magistrate to inquisitor in Como, Milan, April 30, 1579, pp. 1v–3r.
99 "Having noble Guarnerio sell his property 25 years before he was condemned by the Holy Office, and the property not being confiscated unless *a die commissi crimini*, I believe it is up to the Office of the Inquisitor to discover that day, being to that end a really wonderful – to not say unique – a look into the sales [or better, the depositions] taken by the Holy Office from dutiful witnesses against this culprit and his preaching or talking heretically, and these relations are made to the inquisitors in person, who must not publish the transcripts nor communicate the proceeding outside of the Office for respect even to the assistants nominated at the moment – and an inquisitor easily communicates to other inquisitors, for they are all ministers of the same Holy Office" (Ibid., Inquisitor in Como to President of the Extraordinary Magistrate, Como, May 6, 1579, p. 2r).
100 Ibid., Inquisitor in Como to Extraordinary Magistrate, Como, December 22, 1579.
101 "*Quos iure cognovimus haeresi laborantes, et timore iustitia trepidanter bonis suis immobilibus viliori praetio venditis, praeteritus annis confugisse ad partes Lutheranorum, et ibidem hactenus traxisse vitam labe heretica infertam ducentes*": Ibid., sentence signed by the inquisitor in Como Gaspare Sacco, Como, January 1575, p. 1r.
102 "*Sententiamus et declaramus dictos dominos Guarnerium, et Bonam jugales, alias haereticae declaratos: usque de annu 1549 fuisse haereticos, et (ut per testes, et alia contenta in processu per nos, et Sancti Officii ministros, postea agitato patet) eos fuisse illo anno 1549 de haeresi inditiatos, convictos, et ab inde citra semper fuisse tales, et pro talibus reputandos, et reputatos, et propterea ab eo tempore supranominato 1549 eorum bona, iura, credita, actiones, emolumenta, etc. fuisse et esse confiscata, et consequenter per eos non potuisse in praegiuditium Fisci sanctae Inquisitionis et aliorum, ad quos pertinet alienari, pignorari vel hippotecari subiicii quinimo a dicto anno 1549 citra*" (ibid., sentence signed "Stephanus da

Cento inquisitor Comi et Allexander Lacinus vicarius episcopi", Como, October 26, 1579, authenticated by frate Egidio da Como). On Alessandro Lucino see Rovelli (1803), p. 299; on Stefano da Cento, future inquisitor in Venice and Bologna, see Fragnito (1997), p. 236 and Perini (2002), pp. 235ff.
103 ASM, ibid., January 22, 1580, notary Anton Francesco Gorla.
104 Ibid., pp. 2r–v.
105 "*Quia aliqui si pubblicus fuisset [...] stantibus decretis et ordinibus notoriis contra omnes qui scirent aliquem hereticum et seu de heresi suspectum omnino fuisse eo tempore delatus et processatus de quibus tamen non apparet*": cfr. ibid., collective opposition document presented only to the president to the Extraordinary Magistrate, authors Gerolamo Castiglioni, Benpensando Porto, Gabrio Leone, Pietro Saccomanni named "Picci", March 23, 1580, p. 6r.
106 Ibid., folder "Procesus Magnifici Aequitis Domini Hieronimi Castillioni et consorti", interrogation April 19, 1580, p. 9r–v.
107 Ibid., pp. 11v–12r.
108 Ibid., pp. 21r–22v.
109 Ibid., pp. 12v–15v. "Chiotto" or "closso": the term referred to flat terrain which was organized in a pattern of alternating areas containing crops and areas left fallow, especially where streams might overflow.
110 Ibid., pp. 16r–17v.
111 Ibid., p. 17v.
112 Hageneder (1963); De Vergottini (1952).
113 The contrast already emerges with particular evidence in Rocchetti (1847), p. 138 and in Ruffini (1892), wholly based on the assumption that in canonic theory the Roman and civil law principle that *mala fides superveniens non nocet* ('if bad faith later occurs, it does not invalidate') is radically altered to *mala fides superveniens nocet* ('if bad faith occurs, it invalidates'). Francesco Ruffini, in particular, not only sustains that the Good Faith is a unifying core of canon law, but, as well, that canonic *bona fides* – in contrast with the Roman concept – consists essentially in a state of absence of sin. A more conciliatory interpretation of the difference between the Roman and the canonic theory as to Good Faith, is in Scavo Lombardo (1944). See also Locati (1583), pp. 117–8.
114 Antoniazzi (1985), p. 101.

Bibliography

Ago, R. (1998) *Economia barocca. Mercato e istituzioni nella Roma del Seicento*, Rome: Donzelli.

Alfani, G. (2009) *Fathers and Godfathers: Spiritual Kinship in Early Modern Italy*, Burlington VT/Farnham, UK: Ashgate.

Alfani, G. (2013) *Calamities and the Economy in Renaissance Italy: The Grand Tour of the Horsemen of the Apocalypse*, Chippenham: Palgrave Macmillan.

Amabile, L. (1892) *Il Santo Officio della Inquisizione di Napoli. Narrazione con molti documenti inediti*, Città di Castello: S. Lapi tipografo-editore.

Antonazzi, G. (1985) *Lorenzo Valla e la polemica sulla donazione di Costantino. Con testi inediti dei secoli XV–XVI*, Rome: Edizioni di storia e letteratura.

Arese, F. (1970) 'Le supreme cariche del Ducato di Milano da Francesco II Sforza a Filippo V', *Archivio storico lombardo* (9): 3–100.

Balmas, E. (2004) *Studi sul Cinquecento*, Florence: Olschki.

Barsanti, D. (2003) 'Un interessante spaccato sulla nobiltà lombarda: il cavalierato nell'Ordine di S. Stefano della famiglia Verri (1564–1775)', in D. Marrara (ed.)

Ceti dirigenti municipali in Italia e in Europa in età moderna e contemporanea, Pisa: Ets, 151–76.

Benaglio, G. (1711) *Relazione istorica del Magistrato delle ducali Entrate Straordinarie nello Stato di Milano*, Milan: per Marc'Antonio Pandolfo Malatesta.

Bentivoglio, G. (1635) *Della guerra di Fiandra*, Cologne [Leiden]: per Bonaventura e Abraham Elzevier.

Berman, H. J. (1985) *Law and Revolution: The Formation of the Western Legal Tradition*, Cambridge, MA and London: Harvard University Press.

Borromeo, A. (1977–8) 'Contributo allo studio dell'Inquisizione e dei suoi rapporti con il potere episcopale nell'Italia spagnola del Cinquecento', *Annuario dell'Istituto storico italiano per l'età moderna e contemporanea* (29–30): 219–76.

Borromeo, A. (1986) '*San Carlo Borromeo arcivescovo di Milano e la Curia Romana*', in *San Carlo e il suo tempo*, Atti del Convegno internazionale nel IV centenario della morte (Milano, 21–26 maggio 1984), Rome: Edizioni di storia e letteratura, volume 1, 237–301.

Brambilla, E. (2000) *Alle origini del Sant'Uffizio. Penitenza, confessione e giustizia spirituale dal Medioevo al XVI secolo*, Bologna: Il Mulino.

Cantù, C. (1865) *Eretici d'Italia. Discorsi storici*, 3 vols, Turin: Unione tipografico-editrice.

Caponetto, S. (1979) *Aonio Paleario (1503–1570) e la Riforma protestante in Toscana*, Turin: Claudiana.

Chabod, F. (1938) *Per la storia religiosa dello Stato di Milano durante il dominio di Carlo V. Note e documenti*, Bologna: Zanichelli.

Cozzi, G. and Cozzi, L. (1969) (eds) *Paolo Sarpi. Opera*, Milan-Naples: Ricciardi.

De Vergottini, G. (1952) *Studi sulla legislazione imperiale di Federico II in Italia: le leggi del 1220*, Milan: Giuffrè.

Del Col, A. (2006) *L'Inquisizione in Italia dal XII al XXI secolo*, Milan: Mondadori.

di Filippo Bareggi,C. and Signorotto, G. (2008) (eds) *L'Inquisizione in età moderna e il caso milanese. Atti delle Giornate di studio (27–29 novembre 2008)*, special issue of *Studia Borromaica* (23).

Fragnito, G. (1997) *La Bibbia al rogo. La censura ecclesiastica e i volgarizzamenti della Scrittura (1471–1605)*, Bologna: Il Mulino.

Galiffe, J.-B.-G. (1881) *Le refuge italien de Genève aux XVIme et XVIIme siècles*, Genève-Paris-Bâle-Lyon: H. Georg Libraire-éditeur.

Gallagher, C. (1978) *Canon Law and the Cristian Community: The Role of Law in the Church according to the* Summa aurea *of Cardinal Hostiensis*, Rome: Università Gregoriana editrice.

Giannini, M. C. (2001) 'Fra autonomia politica e ortodossia religiosa: il tentativo di introdurre l'Inquisizione "al modo di Spagna" nello Stato di Milano', *Società e storia* (91): 79–134.

Guazzino, S. (1611) *Tractatus de confiscatione bonorum*, Venice: apud Antonium Pinellum.

Hageneder, O. (1963) 'Studien zur Dekretale "Vergentis" (X.V, 7, 10). Ein Beitrag zur Häretikergesetzgebung Innocenz'III', *Zeitschrift der Savigny-Stiftung für Rechtsgeschichte* (49): 138–73.

Lavenia, V. (2000) 'I beni dell'eretico, i conti dell'inquisitore. Confische, Stati italiani, economia del sacro tribunale' in *L'inquisizione e gli storici: un cantiere aperto. Tavola rotonda nell'ambito della Conferenza annuale della ricerca (Roma, 24–25 giugno 1999)*, Rome: Accademia Nazionale dei Lincei, 47–94.

Leverotti, F. (1997) 'Gli officiali del Ducato sforzesco', *Annali della Scuola Normale Superiore di* Pisa, special issue Gli *officiali degli Stati italiani del Quattrocento* (1): 17–79.
Locati, U. (1583) *Praxis judiciaria Inquisitorum*, Venice: apud Damianum Zenarium.
Maifreda, G. (2006) 'Culture popolari e culture dello scambio in età preindustriale. Idee per una ricerca', *Studi storici Luigi Simeoni* (56): 295–332.
Maifreda, G. (2012a) *From* Oikonomia *to Political Economy: Constructing economic Knowledge from the Renaissance to the Scientific Revolution*, Burlington VT-Farnham UK: Ashgate.
Maifreda, G. (2012b) 'L'arte assente. Gli inventari di Scipione Balsamo (1578)', in E. Rossetti (ed.) *Squarci d'interni. Inventari per il Rinascimento milanese*, Milan: Scalpendi, 155–64.
Maselli, D. (1970) 'Per la storia religiosa dello Stato di Milano durante il dominio di Filippo II: l'eresia e la sua repressione dal 1555 al 1584', *Nuova rivista storica* (3–4): 317–73.
Masini, E. (1730) *Sacro arsenale, ovvero pratica dell'uffizio della santa Inquisizione; coll'inserzione di alcune regole fatte dal padre inquisitore Tommaso Meneghini domenicano* [...], Rome: nella stamperia di S. Michele a Ripa (1st edn 1621).
Massetto, G. P. (1994) *Saggi di storia del diritto penale lombardo (secc. XVI–XVIII)*, Milan: Led.
Perini, L. (2002) *La vita e i tempi di Pietro Perna*, Rome: Edizioni di storia e letteratura.
Petronio, U. (1972) *Il Senato di Milano. Istituzioni giuridiche ed esercizio del potere nel Ducato di Milano da Carlo V a Giuseppe II*, Milan: Giuffrè, 2 vols.
Peyronel Rambaldi, S. (1995) 'Inquisizione e potere laico: il caso di Cremona', in P. Pissavino, P. Signorotto (eds) *Lombardia borromaica Lombardia spagnola 1554–1659*, Atti del Convegno di studi (Pavia 17–21 settembre 1991), Rome: Bulzoni, volume 2, 579–617.
Prodi, P. (2000) *Una storia della giustizia. Dal pluralismo dei fori al moderno dualismo tra coscienza e diritto*, Bologna: Il Mulino.
Prosperi, A. (2003) *L'inquisizione romana. Letture e ricerche*, Rome: Edizioni di storia e letteratura.
Prosperi, A. (2011) *Il concilio di Trento. Una introduzione storica*, Turin: Einaudi.
Ricci, S. (2002) *Il sommo inquisitore. Giulio Antonio Santori tra autobiografia e storia (1532–1602)*, Rome: Salerno editrice.
Rivoire, P. (1936) 'Contributo alla storia della Riforma in Italia', *Bollettino della Società di studi valdesi* (66): 55–88.
Rocchetti, A. (1847) *Delle leggi romane abrogate, inusitate e corrette nello Stato pontificio e altre nazioni*, Fano: Tipografia di Giovanni Lana.
Rovelli, G. (1803) *Storia di Como*, Como: dalle stampe di Carlo Antonio Ostinelli.
Ruffini, F. (1892) *La buona fede in materia di prescrizione. Storia della teoria canonistica*, Turin: Bocca.
Russo, C. (1975) 'Fabio Capece Galeota', in *Dizionario biografico degli italiani*, volume 18, Rome: Istituto della Enciclopedia italiana.
Sabatini, G. (2010) 'The Vaaz: the rise and fall of a family of Portuguese bankers in Spanish Naples', *Journal of European Economic History* (3): 627–55.
Sala, A. (1857) *Documenti circa la vita e le gesta di san Carlo Borromeo*, 2 vols, Milan: con i tipi di Zaccaria Brasca.
Scavo Lombardo, L. (1944) *Il concetto di buona fede nel diritto canonico*, Rome: Tipografia Failli.

Seidel Menchi, S. (1987) *Erasmo in Italia 1520–1580*, Turin: Bollati Boringhieri.
Simoncelli, P. (1976) 'Clemente VIII e alcuni provvedimenti del Sant'Uffizio ("De Italis habitantibus in partibus haereticorum")', *Critica storica* (13): 129–72.
Spagnoletti, A. (2009) *Le dinastie italiane e la guerra delle Fiandre*, in *Società e storia* (125): 423–43.
Various authors. (1981) *La Ca' Granda. Cinque secoli di storia e d'arte dell'Ospedale Maggiore di Milano*, Milan: Electa.
Various authors. (2000) *L'inquisizione e gli storici: un cantiere aperto. Tavola rotonda nell'ambito della Conferenza annuale della ricerca (Roma, 24–25 giugno 1999)*, Rome: Accademia Nazionale dei Lincei.
Zardin, D. (2003) 'La curia arcivescovile al tempo del cardinal Federico', *Studia Borromaica* (17): 31–56.

6 The inquisitor between land and finance

The Roman inquisitors of the early modern period were not – as a historiography wholly concentrated on the trials leads us to imagine – obscure, cloistered, theologians who, from time to time, slipped briefly from the dim cells of their convents to punish crimes of faith cruelly, returning immediately to a life of erudition and contemplation as they waited for a further occasion to persecute a new victim. The judges of the Holy Office were, instead, constantly immersed in the vital stream of political and social relationships; managing economic activities requiring prosaic, detailed and continuing attention.

In this last chapter, we shall try to put into focus the shifting material tasks which were an integral part of the day-to-day life of the inquisitors. We shall see how the exercise of the justice of faith and management of the economic sphere were inseparable and, from some points of view, interdependent; aspects in whose management inquisitors were far from isolated, since they had to deal daily with agricultural labourers, farmers renting land, merchants, aristocrats and other figures of pre-industrial economic reality. All of these might influence the work of the inquisitor within multiple contexts and undertakings.

Still, the judges of the Inquisition did not act upon the land, the money and the service "market" in the same manner as their potential competitors or business "partners".[1] They were representatives of a judiciary power which, between the sixteenth and the seventeenth centuries, had progressively spread out, until it controlled not only the religious credo, but also the way business was done and the movement of persons professionally engaged in the production and exchange of goods and money. The interlocutors who cultivated and bought and sold the crops produced on the estates held by the Holy Office competed, together with the inquisitor, on the land – or the loan – "markets" with families and individuals; or they might decide to take on the management of farms, the rights to purchase or shops which were the property of the courts of faith. Yet, at the same time, they were subject to their jurisdiction, a fact which might determine the material choices and the organization of their activity.

Income, loans and investments

Once the most impetuous – and from the organizational point of view unbalanced – period in the history of the Holy Office ended, the Roman Inquisition of the early seventeenth century moved towards a progressive stabilization and homogenization of procedure, accompanied by a rationalization of finances and the strengthening of its bureaucracy, with the attendant construction of housing for its courts, both in key centres and locally. Throughout the 1600s, local controls of orthodoxy were strengthened through the establishment of vicariates: decentralized structures, uniformly distributed in the inquisitorial district, bringing the urban courts closer to a rural world which, until then, had been marginal to their activity. In this way a historic void was eliminated, placing "the Inquisition in the woods", as the Bishop of Volterra had polemically observed in 1579 considering the earliest such inquisitorial initiative of which we know, undertaken by the Florentine court of faith.[2] The activity of the vicariates, the insistence on the "penitential" dimensions and the spontaneous presentation; the strengthened bureaucratic tendencies of the inquisitorial offices marked the Holy Office taking a less lenient line in a procedural and organizational stance which increasingly made the inquisitors' activity repetitive and routine.

This does not, of course, mean that in the seventeenth and eighteenth centuries the death sentences and the execution of heretics, "witches", "judaizers" and the other (in some measure new) objects of the attention of the Holy Office – like quietism, the simulation of holiness or the request for sexual concourse during confession – ceased. Still it is important to notice that the capillary assignment of benefices and the regularizing of income flow – which we have seen were the distinctive traits of the economic history of the Inquisition between the 1500s and 1600s – is part of a slow process of material and administrative stabilization of its courts.

This evolution is visible, too, in another important novelty which emerged in the course of the 1600s within the institutional structure of the Italian Inquisition; the multiplication of the Holy Office's "family members". As we have seen, one of the most serious problems of the peripheral seats restructured in the late sixteenth century was the limited personnel at the disposition of the local inquisitors, and the continual conflicts with the convents in which they were guests as they engaged in a wearying squabble for economic and human resources to pursue the tasks of the *Officium fidei*. Minimal central investments and severe legal norms made it increasingly difficult to finance the office with the monetary punishments inflicted and swelled the number of cases falling into prescription, obliging the inquisitors to extend the range of the collaborators and helpers beyond the convent walls. Reaching out to noblemen and burghers who, for some centuries had already been united in local secular confraternities boasting the names of Saint Peter Martyr or *Crocesignati*, the inquisitors guaranteed themselves service of various sorts in exchange for honours and privileges which we shall discuss in some detail later on. The service so acquired included armed "policing" interventions which permitted the inquisitors to limit recourse to State guards, who must be paid, more often still, however, the familiars or licensed aides of the Holy Office limited themselves to carrying out occasional secondary tasks gratuitously, enjoying the privilege of a "title" which brought them important advantages; the spread of this usage is a convincing sign of the consensus which inquisitorial institutions enjoyed among the elite of the Italian peninsula during the period of the Counter Reformation.

In the context of the processes of organizational and bureaucratic stabilization briefly outlined, the central court and the peripheral seats of the Holy Office needed to count upon a flow of income both trustworthy and constant compared to what they depended upon during the 1500s. To this end, the inquisitors learnt step-by-step how to transform themselves into administrators of the patrimonies accumulated by their predecessors through confiscation, fines, buying and selling, loans, bequests and various other forms of investment. Their attentive development became increasingly indispensable over the 1600s in maintaining the functionality of institutions which were now solid and which – one should never forget – the Catholic Church considered to be permanent. In this long march of accumulation and patrimonial management, many of the Roman Inquisition's courts showed a vitality which, though within the limits and the vigilance established by Rome, made them very like private property holders and led them to enter into important areas of the commercial and credit circuits of the *Ancien régime*.

An unequivocal indication of the economic dynamism of various seats of the Holy Office is offered by the incessant movement of their acquisition of real estate. Even in periods where judicial activity appears to be generally lethargic, this area shows a consistent presence of such transactions and sometimes even a tendency for growth. That is the case of the Rimini Inquisition, where the second half of the seventeenth and the first half of the eighteenth centuries saw a new and increasingly intense series of property purchases. They were most probably financed with the income from monetary punishments, as the modest pension from the seat in Faenza was, since the year 1580, the only fixed ordinary income of the court of the Romagna region. In 1662, the inquisitor in Rimini bought three farms, whose respective value was about 70, 278 and 166 scudi; in 1675 and 1677 he purchased two holdings with buildings at 173 and 91 scudi respectively – the second with funds paid for "victuals provided for Giovanni Zaccarelli, imprisoned in this Holy Office" by his wife, Maria.

Between 1701 and 1706, after having received eight donations in real estate from as many benefactors – a clear sign of the consensus the Inquisition enjoyed locally – the Rimini court bought four more properties worth a little less than 200 scudi; five more properties, with an overall value of about 150 scudi were secured with notarial deeds stipulated between 1721 and 1734. All leased out to some 54 individuals, this notable patrimony of houses and farms yielded, in the mid-eighteenth century, about 180 scudi a year, in addition to veal, broad beans, chickpeas, linen and hemp: more than seven times the Faenza pension.³

In some localities – including a number in Piedmont – it was the inquisitors themselves who managed the lands belonging to their office, in whole or in part, "in economy": that is using hired hands. This was the case in Alessandria, where the Holy Office took in about 13,000 litres of wheat, 1,850 litres of "pure" wine and 460 litres of "inferior" wine in one mid-eighteenth century year; or in Asti and Casale, where, in the same period, the judges of faith scrupulously listed hundreds of Piedmontese lire from the sale of dozens of "kegs" of wine, measures of hemp and sacks of wheat, maize and beans among the entries in their accounts, as well as mulberry leaves, wood, rye and some calves.⁴ In some urban centres with a more pronounced mercantile vocation – notably Florence – the income of the inquisitional court consisted chiefly in rent from shops and commercial premises. With only three agricultural properties in emphyteusis leased out in 1541, 1689 and 1714, the inquisitors received rent from a perfumery, two shoemakers' shops, a book-seller, a greengrocer and a gilder. The Florentine Office drew other income from seven warehouses and nine habitations, in addition to the agricultural activity centred on the property assigned by Urban VIII in 1628 "perpetually" to the San Salvatore Chapel – designated as "at Scandicci", though it had been built within the cathedral of Volterra.⁵

Courts of faith might decide to invest – simply on the grounds of economic advantage – a liquidity they deemed excessive in commercial structures, renovating and renting them out to new tenants. That is what the Milan Inquisition did when, in 1680, it spent 900 lire in Cagnola, in the commune of Villapizzone, to buy "two shops with a small stall, olive press and other [material]", subsequently repairing the press which was "rickety" and opening a butchery. Improvement continued in the eighteenth century, with the construction of a "storage place for snow or ice" (the inquisitors sacrificed an ancient tower-clock to finance this which rose over Cagnola's manor, but was "of no use except to the country folk and to travellers"). They also added a new room for the benefit of the tenant, paid "for the most part by the charity of benefactors". Later, in 1746, the new inquisitor, Ermenegildo Todeschi, opened a third shop: an investment, as he himself affirmed "for the use of a smith, for its greater utility to the Holy Office". The whole complex, with its land and its buildings was not liable to any taxation, royal or civic; even the meat and the other goods produced for the Inquisition's shops were exempt from custom duties, enhancing the project's attractiveness and its profitability.⁶

Managing large patrimonies required time and resources: their administration also produced inevitable disagreements and controversy with farm workers, shopkeepers, those renting, and those whose property ran along boundaries. It was probably also for this reason that, in the course of the seventeenth century, many judges of faith, taking advantage of a less intransigent stance on the part of the Catholic Church as to loaning at interest, preferred to convert land and buildings into financial investments.

In Tortona, for example, the local Holy Office – which had seen the popes confer upon it the land of the canonicate of San Pietro di Volpedo in the early 1600s – found itself entangled in suits dragging on for decades with bordering property holders over rights of transit for wagons and cattle. "To free themselves from quarrels and obligations", noted an eighteenth-century commentator, and in the 1630s the Tortona inquisitors decided to sell a substantial part of the land and invest the money received in various loan agreements at interest. The land which the local Holy Office still held – plots located in various places, distant one from the other (probably because they had been obtained through confiscation or bequest) – was complicated to administer "we have a hard time finding farmers to work these lands, scattered as they are", an inquisitor was still informing his superiors in Rome in the 1700s:

> being very hard to reach and causing a lot of time to be lost in going from the farmhouse to them, going this way and that with the slow pace of bovines already weary before they start work; and what should be days become half-days – and we pay them as full [...] Besides which, they are surrounded by the land of other owners, so they are subject to theft of wood to make stakes, and of other fruits; to the grazing of alien animals; to the stealing of hay and other fodder; to cutting down new trees; and usurpation of land, for the neighbouring owners take over some to the damage of the Holy Office.[7]

Evidently, the threat of trial by an ecclesiastical court – which, by time-honoured prerogative was the destiny of those who damaged the personal security and the property of the Holy Office and its officials – does not seem to have eliminated the possibility of petty theft and annoying damages; perhaps, indeed, they were a form of retaliation. Even with their loans, the Tortona inquisitors were not always fortunate: the local judges spoke of all sorts of "excessively expensive" arguments with the city which, for 30 years refused to pay the 8 per cent interest due to the Inquisition on a loan of 200 scudi contracted in 1630 in the terrible context of the plague. Local nobles were brought to trial and sentences pronounced by Apostolic commissioners, as well as seizures of property or goods; they even acted against a Secondo Serra, canon of the Tortona cathedral, who "almost always paid with great difficulty and after being solicited; and now is totally disabled, being apoplectic and confined to lying upon a straw [mattress], poor unfortunate".[8]

Despite these difficulties, as the early modern era came into maturity, the income from loans or bank deposits granted to individuals, families, institutions or communities represented an ever more important part of the income of the Roman Inquisition. The judges of faith of Capodistria and of Cremona continued, throughout the 1600s and well into the first half of the 1700s, to loan money, barter property, stipulate contracts and receive rent on capital and on property. In 1750, the Holy Office in Capodistria had some ten properties run by private citizens, while the Cremona office counted upon 20, including some rented out. These highly financialized properties were rounded out in the case of Cremona, with a pension paid by the city and another – amounting to 100 gold scudi – awarded it by Pius V in 1569 and paid by the Barnabite Fathers of the local Collegio di San Giacomo e Vicenzo, heirs to the patrimony of the mother church of the suppressed Order of the Umiliati.

In other cases, it was the judges of faith themselves who bequeathed securities, debentures and other titles to the courts in which they had served: on his death in 1639, the Dominican, Agostino Galamini da Brisighella – an inquisitor named Cardinal of Aracoeli by Paul V – left various properties of a Roman *Monte* to the Inquisitions of Milan, Brescia, Piacenza and Genoa, where he had served.[9] Another location in which resources had been largely engaged in financial ventures was Como. During the entire seventeenth century, the justices of faith there, with the permission of the ministry in Rome, converted a major part of their patrimony in real estate into titles of credit. In the difficult economic situation following the plague of 1633–5, several plots of land which were owned by the priory of San Martino in Valcuvia (assigned to the Como Inquisition in 1603 by Clement VIII) were sold and the money invested in eight bonds with the Banco di Sant'Ambrogio yielding, in the devastated context of the moment, a modest annual 2 per cent.[10]

The judges of faith habitually lent money, bought and sold, and accepted gifts and bequests from wealthy, aristocratic families. In 1573, for example, Como Inquisitor Gaspare Sacco bought a large estate in Cadorago from the Clerici family: in the mid-eighteenth century it was still rented out and returned a respectable income. In 1617, the noble Milanese Renato Birago named the local inquisitor, Gianmaria Fiorini da Bologna – to whom he must have been very attached, for he referred to him in his will as "his most dear and very close friend, the very Observant and Greatly Meritorious" – his universal heir. Since Birago's patrimony was bound by entail, the Milanese Inquisition, after dealing with a series of difficulties and law suits, had to pay a monthly sum to Renato's brother until 1673. In 1631, the same Milan office accepted the Bagnavacca holding at Trezzo d'Adda, on the borders of the Republic of Venice, with vineyards and "a nobleman's house", from the noble Paolo Camillo Landriani, feudal lord of Vidigulfo. The bequest stipulated that the income from the property must be spent "for the extirpation of heresy and other works in service of the Holy Office". Again on this occasion, bitter litigation ensued around a supposed entail, bringing the Inquisition to an expensive compromise after several decades. The Mantua Holy Office, whose patrimony had, throughout the 1600s, been in large part invested in financial ventures, received an annual interest of 6 per cent on a tributary-fee property yielding 1,000 small, local, scudi a year, granted to the Milanese feud holders, the Marquises of Arrigoni, decades earlier.[11]

It is not difficult to imagine that the formation of patrimonial ties – and of sentiments of gratitude – the result of friendly, trusting relations between the judges of faith and individuals, families and members of secular and ecclesiastical institutions as well as the inevitable legal residues deriving from questions over the inheritance, might present conflicts of interest and other difficulties of various nature for the smooth function of judicial activity. The effects of such difficulties should be taken into account case by case, with specific studies of local situations and of the individual close relationships within them.

Not infrequently the peripheral courts of the Holy Office held rights of taxation over territory, communities, canals or productive structures, which also generally derived from confiscation or donation. For over two centuries, the Cremona Inquisition held part of the right to conduct a public house, open a butcher's shop and sell bread in the territory of Azzanello, deriving from the seizure in 1562 of the property of the already cited heretic, Francesco Fogliata; in 1750, these premises were still rented out by the Holy Office for a yearly income of 30 lire.[12] The stewards of the Mantua ghetto's Great Synagogue, instead, paid 10 gold doubloons to the local inquisitor in tributes connected to land in the locality of Villa del Tabelano; in Modena, too, from 1564 until suppression, the Holy Office enjoyed two tributes inflicted upon the Jewish university in a decision taken by Alfonso II d'Este.[13]

Alongside various rents from land and buildings, the Novara Inquisition enjoyed the right to draw water from the Naviglio canal, across the territory of the powerful Counts of Langosco, to its own land in Lomellina. The income from these sources created a capital of more than 1,000 lire between 1635 and 1734, lent out at interest to the town of Cameri (Novara) and, subsequently, to the *Contado* of Novara: a representative authority through which (as elsewhere in Lombardy and in the Veneto during the early modern period) rural towns and villages tried to deal with the weighty fiscal impositions of central government and the overweening power of the cities – with the result, at least in this case, of falling into debt with the Holy Office.[14] This interesting practice, on whose basis many communities and representative institutions, both urban and rural, placed themselves in conditions of financial dependence upon an Inquisition court, is also exemplified, with regard to eighteenth-century Novara, by the court of faith's 1718 loan of 1,000 lire at 5 per cent to a Stefano Rosina, residing in the town of Trecate; "a sum of money derived from the residues of sales [made] by this Holy Office". When the sum was paid back, it was reassigned as a loan (always at 5 per cent) to the town of Trecate which, in the mid-eighteenth century, was still paying interest to the Holy Office.[15]

Through their entire history, then, the major seats of the Italian Inquisition displayed a financial and patrimonial enterprise that had some surprising aspects. For the inquisitors who dedicated themselves so attentively to managing the patrimony of local courts, representing the Inquisition could constitute a significant advantage on the credit "market", as well as on those of real estate and agricultural contracts. All the properties and the products of the Holy Office were exempt from the principal forms of ecclesiastical and secular taxation at least until the eighteenth century shift in political and State paradigms which, in some states, led to an erosion of the jurisdictional and fiscal prerogatives of the Church. Further, above all for those who rented land, houses or shops – or sought rights to draw upon or collect funds – becoming an interlocutor of the court could bring with it a number of advantages.

An excellent example is offered by the Bologna Inquisition, which had the right to draw almost 1,500 litres of grain from the production of a certain mill in that city, thanks to a confiscation which, in 1548, fell upon Peregrino Righetti, a "relapsed heretic". This quota, fixed in a percentage of the total quantity of flour produced annually by the mill, was still enjoyed by the Bolognese inquisitors in the mid-1700s. Due to the changing conditions of the market in the nearly 200 years which had ensued, the quantity of flour had progressively declined to little more than 1,000 litres a year because as the eighteenth century inquisitor observed, "said flour has for a long time become of very low quality and not very different from pure and simple rubbish", and because "the city mills [were] seriously damaged by the mills in the countryside, so their incomes have fallen". Perhaps it was also because of this that, in the course of the 1600s, the Holy Office had rented out its right to withdraw the annual quota to private parties. Faced with the progressive decline in the quantity of flour available, it was increasingly difficult for the inquisitors to find individuals willing to pay the annual 20 scudi fee they had been imposing. But the judges of faith had a persuasive argument for their potential "partners".

A Bolognese inquisitor offers, in 1749, a testimony illustrating clearly the way in which his predecessor had managed to overcome the impasse of a "partner" who suddenly refused to pay the agreed sum, given the increasingly evident fall in the quantity of flour produced by the mill:

> The predecessor of the actual father inquisitor becoming, then, annoyed with having to recognize the situation, though it was justly as presented [that is to lower the fee for the concession to 20 scudi, given the diminished quantity of flour that might be obtained], he took advantage of a person who – anxious to have the title of 'tenant' of the Holy Office, declared himself willing to take over the 'rent' of the mill's [flour] by assuming the burden of his predecessor's credit with the Holy Office and to pay him what the Holy Office owed him.[16]

"Since, however, for other more pressing reasons, this new, present, "tenant" has notably reduced his interests (so much so that it is thought he is close to bankruptcy)", added Father Tomaso Maria de Augelli, Bologna judge of faith, when the tenant had failed to pay the rent for two years, "it will be necessary to take away the licence [he holds] for this rent and, if another [person] is not found who, desiring to enjoy the licence, wants to take it over in the same manner", he warned the Congregation that it would be necessary to "fix things up as best we can".[17]

In this example, the economic interlocutor of the Holy Office, despite the shaky financial situation which had led to the deterioration of his own "interests", declared himself willing to take over the burdens of a rental whose terms had been established two centuries earlier in a market situation far more favourable for becoming associated with the Inquisition. So aristocrats, professional men and merchants, sometimes belonging to confraternities of laymen known as *"della Croce"* ("of the Cross"), placed under the protection of Saint Peter Martyr, had for centuries been linked to the Sacred Court to carry out policing and military duties, but, also, for mansions whose value was chiefly symbolic, drawing from this condition prestige and material advantages. The lay confraternities of the Cross – and thus known as the *Crocesignati* ("Cross-Marked") – first appeared in the thirteenth century and, in the cities where they were found, represented a virtual armed militia whose members were usually of noble birth and who aided the inquisitors in the arrest, imprisonment and transferal of culprits, legitimating with their own reputations and prestige, the work of friars delegated to the administration of the justice of faith. In the 1500s, faced with the renewed necessity of enlarging the executive personnel of the courts, and the scarcity of financial resources which accompanied it, the judges of faith recruited, alongside the Crocesignati, a broader network of helpers for the personnel able to carry out functions of control, arrest and custody.

In this way, a whole world of "helpers" flourished – often swelling out of measure – all somehow "part" of the local courts, in various localities. Growing on its own over the sixteenth and seventeenth centuries, this group came to include at least a fiscal attorney, a prosecutor of culprits, a notary, an usher, a prison director, two or three guards, secretaries, printers, treasurers, custodians, medical doctors, barbers, prison personnel, revisers of accounts, customs officials, and consultants in theology, law and medicine.[18] As bureaucratization and the territorial expansion of vicarian seats proceeded – and the Roman Inquisition needed to count on human resources able to support its officials at low cost or, indeed, at next to nothing – the number of those forming such families swelled without pause. The seventeenth-century attempts by Urban VIII, Clement X and Innocent XI, to reduce the network of familiars met with obstacles that seemed intractable. Already in 1625, the Roman Ministry tried to oblige courts in papal territory – like Faenza, Ancona and Rimini – to confine their families, respectively, to 50, 40 and 30 members. In 1690, the official, "licensed", members of the family of the Inquisition in Florence were 37; those of the Siena court 30; and those of the office in Pisa 17. To the 84 laymen were to be added 225 people in religious communities, a total of more than 300 individuals. According to the overview provided by an inquiry ordered by Benedict XIV in 1743, in the Pontifical State alone there were 2,814 individuals licensed by the Inquisition, structured over nine peripheral courts. Of these, 1,819 were laymen; to these were to be added about 1,000 familiars of licence-holders, each of whom enjoyed almost all the privileges of the "licensed", beginning with the right to bear arms. In early eighteenth-century Modena, the staff of the inquisitorial court still had 204 members, while, in the 1730s, that of pontifical Ferrara numbered more than 60 people, many of whom belonged to the upper echelons of the Estense aristocracy.[19]

The familiars "serve", we read in a report of the period, "to receive and accompany prisoners or things from one inquisition to another [...] and they do this at their own expense; and therefore they chose for them knights and citizens who can spend". In the centuries of the early modern period, the socials origin of "family" members were still generally aristocratic or professional; the elevated socioeconomic condition of collaborators of the Inquisition was meant to guarantee the court from the risk of venality and corruption, since their position was unpaid.[20] In exchange for their service, the familiars of the Inquisition, however, received not only the prestige of belonging to a notable power structure, but also an official standing and some important privileges. Among these, the most desirable was certainly the right to bear arms, in *Ancien régime* societies forbidden to subjects without a special permit. The *Crocesignati* and the licensed also enjoyed the privilege of the ecclesiastical forum – that is the right to be judged only by ecclesiastical courts even in cases where jurisdiction would normally have belonged to the secular system. In 1628, the Congregation responding in a session at which Urban VIII was present, to an inquiry from the Inquisitor of Malta – had decreed that even the slaves of "family members" were to be considered exempt from secular justice "since the person and the property of the familiar of the Holy Office includes the slaves, who *count among the properties* [*"computantur inter bona"*], [they] have no different forum than that of their owners".[21] Finally, familiars could share the fiscal exemptions which they enjoyed in almost all the Italian peninsula states with all the property and the persons who were part of their household.

The formation of a vast network of *familiares* ("familiars") of the Roman Inquisition (which also occurred in Spain and Portugal) was thus a crucial element in the shaping and the management of social and political-institutional consensus concerning the mission of the courts of faith, both at the centre (where the Congregation itself counted many patent holders) and on the periphery. Besides attributing bureaucratic, military and policing services to the Officers of Faith, familiars brought financial resources and, as we have seen in the Bologna example, might be willing to take on the management of Inquisition properties even where these were not economically attractive. In addition, appointments might be sold: in eighteenth-century Modena they cost from 60 to 100 lire.[22] In addition, familiars and *Crocesignati* often loaned or donated money to the inquisitorial office. In Parma, the confraternity of the Cross benefited from numerous bequests between the sixteenth and the seventeenth centuries and, at the moment of dissolution in the second half of the 1700s, its patrimony was much larger than that of the local inquisition: about 25,000 Parma lire to the Holy Office's 15,000.

In Milan, too, the patrimony of the Crocesignati at the time of suppression was 17,850 Milan lire, wholly deposited in certificates of the Banco di Sant'Ambrogio, purchased in eight groups between 1627 and 1711.[23] In various Lombard cities, where the *Crocesignati* were traditionally structured in three Orders and paid their licenses in proportion, the money involved officially served the needs of the Holy Office. Those who were not noble, forming the third Order – for the most part professionals, merchants and tenants – were under the obligation of a yearly act of acknowledgement proportioned to the possibilities of each individual: shopkeepers in candles, chocolate, or sugar; agricultural tenants in chickens and other farm produce. It is no surprise, then, that the Cardinal of Santa Severina should write angrily to the inquisitor in Cremona in 1603, ordering "let the Inquisition receive nothing at all – neither large nor small – not even something said to be just nice to eat, for appointing Crocesignati".[24]

The management of the Inquisition as an open system

The patrimonial and managerial structure of Italian inquisitorial courts we have described – characterized, though with significant local exceptions, by a high level of integration between agricultural activity and real estate, financial investment and rights of payment – cannot be challenged by an analysis of the seventeenth-century ledgers of the Congregation of the Holy Office where these have survived. We have seen a series of financial entries on the income and expenses of the Roman Ministry in the seventeenth century, the period of stabilization of its activities in the routine "efficiency of normalcy" which ensued after the religious turbulence of the latter part of the 1500s was over.[25]

A general examination of those accounts indicates that the income from the Conca estate – in some periods rented out and in others managed directly, represented the major part of the income of the seventeenth-century Roman Holy Office and, as the documentation of the following century shows, the eighteenth as well.[26] This income, from the mid-1600s, was increasingly integrated by money lending and financial activities, probably in correspondence with a reduction in doctrinal intransigence (and in that of the cardinals of the Holy Office themselves), concerning the whole question of loaning.[27] In a year which we might consider "average" for the total income of the Roman Holy Office, 1676, of about 8,860 scudi in income, about 5,590 came from the sale of the grain and wool of Conca lands.

The remaining income – amounting to a little under 3,300 scudi – came almost entirely from bonds of the Roman Mount of Piety or from tributes. Almost 600 scudi were interest from a feud worth 10,000 scudi assigned in 1666 to the Prince of Palestrina, a title bestowed by Pius V in 1571 on the Colonna family, then purchased by Urban VIII for the Barberini. Until the 1680s, the title was held by Maffeo Barberini, son of Anna Colonna di Tagliacozzo and husband of Olimpia Giustiniani, as well as the brother-in-law of Francesco I d'Este, Duke of Modena. The financial relations of the

Roman Holy Office with Maffeo Barberini were conducted directly by his cousin – the cardinal and supreme inquisitor, Francesco. Given the Roman social context, further research and reflection on the family (and the credit) relations which grew up between the Congregation of the Holy Office, the cardinals who were a part of it and the major local and peninsular dynasties, would be fruitful; here again considering, case by case, the rise and impact of the inevitable conflicts of interest.[28]

From the debit side, too, the habitual managerial stance of the Congregation's Roman seat shows itself as fundamentally based on property as well as a growing bureaucratization. In another year whose expenditures we can consider representative for the century, 1637, the central Holy Office ministry paid out 1,701 scudi of a total 8,046 to the iron contractors on the island of Elba to purchase ore for the Conca foundries, 400 per grain and spent the rest to maintain the upkeep of the bureaucracy, listing the sum as destined to "officials" of the Congregation for the daily costs of ordinary administration.

These proportions do not change in the other sample year of 1676: the Holy Office books cite specifically the purchase of wine and wood, the salaries of the archivist, the surgeon and the coal carrier, along with the investments and the expenses of managing the Conca estate and its activities. We can see beyond any doubt that, in the 1600s too, extraordinary economic aid from Rome for local courts was entirely sporadic, confirming the substantial patrimonial and managerial autonomy of the peripheral inquisitions set as a principle in the previous century. Considering the entire documentable period running from 1633 through to 1678, we find a grant to Ancona for 136 scudi, and another to Malta for 100, in 1634; in 1639, another 100 scudi were sent to the inquisitor in Malta, and the same sum again in 1653. Finally, in 1662, 500 scudi were sent "for the building of the Inquisition in Perugia". These were small sums indeed, compared to the 5,100 ducats spent in 1636 "for the purchase that must be made [...] in the Conca ironworks and other places"; comparable more to the cost of two silver fruit plates purchased in 1660 from the Roman artisan, Rocco Tamboroni, for 50 scudi than to the 444 goats the supreme inquisitors bought that same year at the impressive price of 700 Roman scudi.[29]

Even in the annual budgets of the local Roman Inquisition courts, debit and credit items concerning the investigations and the trials for heresy as well as the imprisonment of culprits were usually grouped indifferently with all the other types of monetary flow. In the inquisitors' papers, the administration of income from land, proceeds and expenses from the sale and purchase of agricultural produce, improvement of land and buildings, rents and financial income are mixed with the travel expenses incurred by the judges of faith, the costs of investigation and of the imprisonment of culprits, the sums spent on torture and on the medical aid to prisoners, fines collected and reimbursement for the maintenance of prisoners. In Perugia, the honorarium of 60 scudi due to the Dominican judge of faith for his official obligation to "read Scripture in the Duomo, or explain it, or cause it to be explained" was listed among the items of income of the local Holy Office (and it was also integrated by 6 scudi of "a fine laid upon two Jews" and a tribute paid by the Agostinian friars of Todi, who had a long-standing debt of 250 scudi at 7 per cent "what origin this money springs from, I have not been able to ferret out", wrote an eighteenth-century inquisitor in setting down this item in his annual budget). Among his expenses, the more than 20 scudi spent for "the capture and transport of a supposed Knight of death" and a "Domenico Giustini, alias 'Pancakes' [*frittellata*']", for the "capture of Massimo for stealing in the Holy Office's kitchen garden", and for the "transport of Luigi Terzi, known as the Macerata gypsy", were mixed in among the expenses for food, barbers, clothing for the inquisitor and his vicars and three scudi spent "to block a small window and open another behind in a segregation cell to prevent a prisoner from talking to another".[30]

In the Turin Holy Office budgets, expenditure on olive oil was mixed with that "for soldiers of justice to capture Giacinto Ballone and torture same", with the former costing more than four times the latter. From Belluno's accounts, we can learn that an eighteenth-century inquisitor felt the need to buy "eight printed sheets representing various palaces and gardens of Rome" and spend 16 Venetian lire for "a painter to make an outline of said sheets in colours upon the wall so as to frame them, to paint the platform the colour of air and give the wall framing the fireplace the colour of stone". In Udine, the judge of faith drew from the same treasury the sum necessary for "a gig to take me to San Vito to examine the Salesian nuns named in the denunciation laid against don Andrea their confessor", and the cost of wood to heat his premises; the costs of the "trip made to Venice, called by Monsignor Nuncio [Martino] Caraccioli for the imprisonment made by the secular court of the three youths spontaneously presented [*'sponte comparenti'*]" and Christmas gratuities; the "gondola for 11 days, when I found it convenient to remain in Venice and presented myself three times before his excellency Ruzzini, chief of the Council of Ten, and another three before his excellency councillor Tiepolo, and for returning from diplomatic missions and going to the father inquisitor at the castle, and always took the gondola since the season was very hot", but also a "supper and two beds in Codrojpo".[31] The "reception given for the high court, and the low, of Monsignor Nuncio on the feast of San Domenico, when he came to rest in the Holy Office after celebrating the mass", was not, in the annual list of expenses of the Venice Inquisition, separate from the "food for a poor prisoner" and "expenses made – as documented – in the capture executed in Tremosine, in the jurisdiction of Salò".[32]

This integrated approach to the judicial and extra-judicial dimensions of the inquisitor's activity (unclear on the material as well as the cultural level) is a phenomenon to consider carefully. Year after year, the inquisitors and the convents of their orders had to deal with the local office's operative results and, when necessary, act to redress financial shortfall which could not be compensated in other ways. So if the expenses of the central and the local inquisition courts included the whole arc of their activities – and thus both the administration of patrimony and the holding of trials – our historiographical conception of the Holy Office's organization and of the relationship between the inquisitors' judicial choices and the resources at their disposition, must also take into consideration the variables which were not always closely related to past, present and potential trials.

A wealthy and well-managed Holy Office – potentially able, then, to engage in more trials or at least to open them without necessarily taking into account their possible economic effects, or without the incentives we saw earlier troubling the inquisitors' decisions – was a Holy Office whose economic and financial activities were well equilibrated. In his management – intuitive as well (or even more) than practical – of the court of which he is responsible, the eighteenth-century judge of faith in Vercelli put the costs of his vicars' trips into the territory "to prove there the substance of three sacrilegious and heretical thefts" with the investments in oxen, beef cattle, cows, calves, pigs, hay, plough, scythes, shovels, hoes and cordage necessary "to build up the better part of the equipment for the farm at Cavenago, now directly cultivated [by the Inquisition]", as well as money "lent graciously to the needy Holy Office farmers". "The ordinary annual expenses for the clothing, honorarium, letters, paper, oil, candles and food for three persons must be added", the priest commented in a note:

> Since the convent furnishes nothing, expenses amounting to the sum of 1,200 lire: according to the extraordinary costs of the captures, the medicines, the food, the household furnishings, the trips and the repair of six buildings so that incomes are more or less absorbed and, from time to time exceed what comes in, and this, in fact, is what happened last year and this year, in which the farmers found themselves cast upon this Holy Office due to the death of their animals, this Holy Office entered necessarily into extreme debt, not for any satisfaction, for 1,350 lire spent in fixing up the farm.[33]

All these dimensions came together in a single budget and a single mental and operative structure; and all of this combined to make the Holy Office an institutional entity more or less well off or in need of aid, under the pressure of incentives to invest or to save, potentially bound by financial, relational and social constraints. An institution, then, *open* to the flow of the economic life of the territory in which each single court was situated, as well as the local social and family dynamics, and those at regional, State and international level which might determine or influence the results of investments in pre-industrial societies.

Viewing the management of the inquisitorial courts as an *open system* can help us to elaborate some hypotheses on the relation between the financial performance of the inquisitorial courts and the intensity of their judicial activity. Let us take a closer look at a Holy Office seat for which, despite a few lacunae, we can document over a fairly ample period the simultaneous budgetary situation and the judicial activity: Siena. The careful study of the operation of the Siena Inquisition in the latter half of the 1600s and the early 1700s is particularly important, for in that period, this Tuscan court displayed an unusual judicial activism.

While in the few other courts for which we have complete series of the early modern flow of trials – like Venice, Aquileia-Concordia and Modena – the high point in the number of accused is registered between the second half of the 1500s and the beginning of the 1600s (that is, in the years that saw the apex of anti-Lutheran repression and the hunt for "witches"), in Siena we find, instead, an unusual peak in accusations for crimes of faith precisely between the second half of the 1600s and the first decades of the 1700s. According to the estimates of Andrea del Col, the Siena Inquisition – with an average of 35 accused per five-year period involved in trials between the mid-1500s and the end of the 1700s – in the five years from 1696–1700, reached a peak of 337 accused; followed in 1711–15 by 434 accused and then, in 1716–20, by the striking figure of 614 accused. In the two decades 1661–70 and 1671–80 the number of accused was similar to the preceding period average between the late 1500s and the first half of the 1600s. Finally, the decade 1681–90 registered a number of accused decidedly on the increase, though inferior to those of the decades immediately successive.[34]

What hypotheses can we offer for this sharp rise in judicial activity on the part of the Siena Inquisition in the decades between the seventeenth and the eighteenth centuries? Why, in any case, do we see a significant difference in the number of the accused involved in trials of faith? There were probably many reasons; among them, the intensification of an intense persecution of the quietist heresy in Siena in the second half of the 1680s, though this is not sufficient in itself to justify the rise in accusations of the following decade.[35] Let us take a look in Table 6.1 at the list of inquisitors holding the Siena office and their respective budgets for the 1657–1713 period.

The list of Siena inquisitors shows first of all that, during the period considered, six judges of faith held the position of head of the court. This is a banally evident fact, but one not always taken into due account when studying the evolution over the long period of the series of trials initiated by local courts. We can intuitively surmise that the different inquisitors may have had different ways of operating during investigation and within the trial itself. They may have been more, or less, zealous in their questioning and in moving the case along, more or less responsive to the indications of the Roman Ministry and more or less sensitive to certain types of crime of faith.

Some of the differences we see in the trial situation of the Siena Inquisition in the second half of the 1600s and the first years of the 1700s, can without doubt be attributed to these different "inquisitorial styles". The arrival of the new inquisitor Giovanni Pellei (or Pillei) da Radicofani, for example, determined the collapse of the number of accused of the Siena Holy Office in the ensuing five-year period by about two-thirds as compared to the period under the preceding inquisitor (until then the highest reached in Siena) of

Table 6.1 Income and expenditure of the Siena Inquisition (Roman scudi, rounded off to the unit)

Inquisitor	Year	Income	Expenses
A	1657	112	320
A	1658	126	428
A	1659	152	487
A	1660	126	523
A	1661	178	470
A	1662	223	641
A	1663	165	613
A	January–February 1664	n.p.	n.p.
B (1)	March 1664–December 1665	251	442
B	1666	104	263
B	1667	157	285
B	1668	178	246
B	1669	143	244
B	1670	160	298
B	1671	160	302
B	1672	161	305
B	1673	172	281
B	1674	147	267
B	1675	160	286
B	1676	142	239
B/C (2)	1677	n.p.	n.p.
C	1678	113	n.p.
C	1679	171	n.p.
C	1680	143	n.p.
C	1681	89	n.p.
C	1682	171	n.p.
C	1683	146	n.p.
C	1684	91	n.p.
C	1685	121	n.p.
C	1686	111	n.p.
C	1687	95	n.p.
C/D (3)	1688	n.p.	n.p.
D	1689	138	335
D	1690	232	287
D	1691	187	250
D	1692	177	n.p.
D	1693	197	n.p.
D	1694	184	n.p.
D	1695	206	n.p.
D	1696	180	n.p.

continued…

Table 6.1 continued...

Inquisitor	Year	Income	Expenses
D	1697	198	n.p.
D	1698	175	274
D	1699	154	242
D	1700	154	317
E–F (4–5)	1701	177	220
F	1702	174	n.p.
F	1703	n.p.	n.p.
F	1704	n.p.	n.p.
F	1705	185	n.p.
F–G	1706	n.p.	n.p.
G–H(7)	1707	n.p.	n.p.
H	June–December 1707	123	115
H	1708	205*	153
H	1709	228*	203
H	1710	203*	170
H	January–September 1711	127*	191
I(8)	September–December 1711	78*	59
I	1712	197*	246
I	1713	158	345

Source: ACDF, Si, Libro dell'entrata e dell'uscita del Santo Ufficio; the elaboration is mine. The dates in which the inquisitors assumed their positions has been integrated from Schwedt (2009), p. XXXII. The budgetary data is expressed by the Libro in Florentine lire through 1676; thereafter, in Roman scudi. The coefficient of conversion here applied is 6.66 Florentine lire per Roman scudo: the same employed by those keeping the accounts (see, for example, p. 12v). The data have been standardized for the period January 1–December 31 of each year, re-elaborating the figures registered, in some years, according to the "Sienese style" – that is, to begin the year *ab incarnatione* (from March 25). "Expenses" includes the effect of surplus or deficit accumulated in the previous year.

n.p.: Data not present in the ledger or not determinable due to damage to the page.

* The figure includes surplus from the previous year.

(1) New Inquisitor assumes the post in March, 1664. The ledger holding the accounts has several missing pages.

(2) New Inquisitor assumes the post in July, 1677.

(3) New Inquisitor assumes the post in July, 1688.

(4) New Inquisitor assumes the post in January 25, 1701.

(5) New Inquisitor assumes the post in September 14, 1701.

(6) New Inquisitor assumes the post in June, 1706.

(7) New Inquisitor assumes the post in May 24, 1707.

(8) New Inquisitor assumes the post in September 15, 1711.

Inquisitors: A – Giovanni Pellei o Pillei da Radicofani; B – Giuseppe Amati da Massafra; C – Modesto Paoletti da Vignanello; D – Serafino Gottarelli da Castelbolognese; E – Giacomo Serra da San Giovanni di Bologna; F – Cesare Pallavicini da Milano; G – Domenico Antonio Ranieri d'Acquapendente; H – Giuseppe Baldrati da Ravenna; I – Giovan Battista Magni da Verucchio.

Inquisitor Giovanni Antonio Angeli da Bologna (March 9 to April 6, 1707) de facto never assumed the post.

almost 300 accused in a five-year period. The apex – reached in the 1690s – was occasioned by the arrival of Serafino Gottarelli da Castelbolognese in July 1688; the arrival, in 1701, of Father Giacomo Serra, and then his successors up to Giuseppe Baldrati da Ravenna implied, in the 1710s, a relative slowing down of trials. The high point of the 1710s, which led to the trial of 600 individuals in the second half of the decade, came about under the Inquisitor Giovan Battista Magni. Unfortunately, for the inquisitors who followed we do not have a complete series of reports, as our documentation is interrupted in 1713.

So the "inquisitorial style" of the judges who assumed the guidance of the local Holy Office courts might determine variations of notable entity in their operative results. Even from the point of view of management and account keeping, as the series of budgets presented in Table 6.1, though fragmentary, show, the various inquisitors seem to have had different criteria. We go from inquisitors who set down analytic and rigorous financial documents to colleagues who did not even organize a general estimate or jotted down single slips which only later were included in a ledger. The entries of the Siena court, though fundamentally tied to fixed tributes or rents deriving, as we have seen from the Sozzini confiscation, plus a few benefices and pensions accumulated from the sixteenth and seventeenth centuries, might vary reasonably from year to year. Often these variations were due to the greater or lesser regularity in the payment of rent instalments by the tenants or the institutions owing them. The zeal and the promptness of the inquisitor and his subordinates in pursuing payment could significantly condition the flow of coinage entering the coffers of a court.

The variations in income we see in Table 6.1, then, derive in part from delays in payment and the energy with which the specific office pursues the collection of its credits. But significant variations in the income of inquisitors were also determined by the sum provided by monetary penalties, concerning which, once again, the different habits of the various inquisitors appear to clarify. Father Pellei made ample use of fines: on September 29, 1659, for example, he received 105 Florentine lire from a don Emilio Landucci "as an account upon the sentence pronounced on don Biagio Cherubini da Chianciano" no small part of the overall income of 1,015 lire for that year (and followed the next year with a second, equal, payment).[36] In June, 1662, 500 Florentine lire were paid as an instalment of a fine of almost 1,500 lire inflicted on a Lumucenio Gagliardi. These two items made this a peak year. Indeed, it was financially the most successful of Pellei's term as inquisitor.[37]

Still, the recourse of monetary penalties on the part of the first inquisitor of our series did not guarantee positive budgetary results. In the period from 1657–80, that is in five-year periods of the second half of the 1600s which we can consider substantially homogeneous for the number of accused appearing before the court, a number analogous to that of the previous century – the Siena Inquisition found itself with consistently negative balances. In the period, as notes like "and the father inquisitor remains in credit for this sum, and we carry it forward..."[38] scattered through the pages of the ledgers of the time confirm, the inquisitors covered – from their own pockets, or with the aid of their convent and Order – negative balances which might even be very large. In some years, as we see in Table 6.1, the expenses were double income. The five-year periods of activity substantially "within the norm" for the number of cases were, then, also those in which a part of the budgets of the inquisitors were most seriously passive and, at the same time, fines and monetary punishments were most vigorously employed.

This evidence seems to confirm the hypothesis, put forward in the preceding chapters, that, in the presence of heavy "inquisitor's credit", the system of incentives we have seen encouraged the judge of faith to seek income in monetary punishment and/or the Roman Ministry to authorize this type of punishment more often.

On the other hand, in the decades between the end of the 1600s and the early 1700s, where the numerical series, though fragmentary, allow us to see a more efficient financial management and annual budgets in some cases actually active, the recourse of monetary punishment was almost wholly absent. We might conclude that the inquisitors most disposed to inflict monetary penalties were not necessarily the most "severe" from the point of view of the number of accusations. On the contrary, a sort of inverse proportion seems to exist between pecuniary punishments and indictments, this would lead us to suppose that the inquisitors who managed their offices and their trials less efficiently, undertaking fewer cases or favouring fewer spontaneous presentations, were more frequently tempted to right their accounts imposing fines or confiscations.

The inquisitor holding the post in Siena in the 1680s never registered his expenditures: another indication of the variety of administrative and accounting styles applied by the individual judges. In any event, the 1677–87 period shows a constant fall in income, which reached the historical minimum of 89 Roman scudi in 1681. So it seems possible to deduce that the first effective managerial discontinuity in the period we are considering was constituted by the arrival of Father Stefano Gottarelli da Castelbolognese. This inquisitor, who had been Provincial in Bologna, a bare two months after his arrival received "one hundred Roman scudi sent [...] from the Holy Congregation by the hand of the reverend Bragaldi":[39] a sum which, for the moment, contributed notably to reducing the shortfall. Gottarelli, further, inaugurated a series of good managerial practices which favoured the growth of income: these, in some years – like 1691 – came close to tripling the minimum of 1681.

The year 1689 saw the Siena Inquisition receive a grant of 6 scudi in "charity" from the Camerlengo of the Officiali della scala di Siena, an income which would continue to remain constant in the following years.[40] Gottarelli succeeded, as well, in sending his predecessor – already transferred to another locality – 8 scudi (probably as a reimbursement);[41] he also began to exact rents, pensions and tributes more rapidly and systematically than had previously been the case. Finally, he engaged in an inflexible battle (which he won in 1698) against the city of Siena for having damaged with public works a holding of the Inquisition, whose tenant had therefore arbitrarily reduced his rent by a scudo.[42] Following Gottarelli's action, the city had to pay a scudo a year to the court of faith: a minimal but symbolic victory by an inquisitor whose temperament is reflected in a veritable explosion of accusations for crimes of faith.

The expenditures for investigations, imprisonments and punishments increased notably. Among them, Gottarelli listed more than 60 scudi spent in 1699 "for having had two prisoners transported to Siena – one from Pitigliano and the other from Piombino the one and the other places distant many miles from Siena: in days of the executors, expenses for food for the same prisoners, provisions for three months; and in trials from the above places, [with] Narni, Bagnorea, Pitigliano, and Montemerano, and Rome".[43] Father Serafino had already spent 10 scudi a few months after his arrival, in November 1688, for the "Design", the material and the construction of a platform for the abjuration of a "Quietist hermit", as well as a "theatre in church", payment of the police and tips for the grand duke's guards.[44] Other expenses were sustained by the Bolognese inquisitor to repair and expand the building holding his office.[45] So, in Gottarelli's case, the excess of expenses as compared to income (though this did increase) we can see in the years for which we have certain data was functional to a powerful growth in the court of faith's engagement in prosecution.

The financial behaviour of the Siena Holy Office in the period considered seems, therefore, to suggest the existence of a significant link between the overall managerial competence of Inquisition courts and their operative efficiency measured in the number of accused involved in the various forms of procedure that might be set in motion by the Office of Faith. Indeed, the link seems to find confirmation in the data relative to the early years of the eighteenth century: in fact, after Gottarelli was transferred to Rome to take up the position of Qualificator of the Holy Office – and, after the confused period of Father Serra's stewardship and those of his immediate successors (for all of which our data is sporadic) – the Siena Inquisition, first with Father Baldrati da Ravenna (who had been a judge in Treviso and then in Florence), and, subsequently, with Giovan Battista Magni, another experienced inquisitor, actually reached an active balance in its budget and maintained it for several consecutive years.

These were the same years which, thanks also, to virtuous administration, served as a harbinger of the most sensational series of accusations in the inquisitorial history of Siena: accusations whose number exceeded almost all the quinquennial aggregations concerning the early modern Italian peninsula Inquisitions for which we have certain data. The 636 accused in the second half of the 1710s are, at our present level of information, second only to the number prosecuted by the Modena Inquisition in the five-year period from 1621–5 and exceed all the five-year aggregates of an important court like that of Venice between the mid-1500s and the mid-1700s.[46]

The case of Siena suggests that the forms and the operative results of a Holy Office court could have more or less striking repercussions on local prosecution and penal action and so, too, for the Roman inquisitorial system as a whole. Considering the Inquisition courts as open managerial systems, however, means recognizing also that their economic-patrimonial conduct was, in turn, sensitive to variables both within the inquisitorial organization per se and wholly extraneous to it. Internal variables were made up of the managerial actions of individual inquisitors as well as the conduct of the Congregation of the Holy Office, which established norms and ethos binding for all. The actions might be reflected in a more – or less – careful balancing of expenditures and income; and in a greater, or lesser, rationality in the expenses sustained and the overall model of formal obligations and informal data: that is, in the sense of a coherence of managerial devices employed in securing the desired ends. The external variables, instead, included all the unforeseeable events – climactic, environmental, cultural, social – which might influence the economic activities every inquisitorial office found itself, year upon year, managing and which generated profit or loss that could influence the internal life of the court of faith at various levels.

This "open" reading of the operation of Inquisition courts does not propose a flattening of their operation to a simple economic dimension. That would be epistemologically incorrect. And, at the present stage of documentation and research, it would be rigorously indemonstrable as well. It may, however, allow us to open up the interpretation of the work of the courts of faith to a plurality of variables and a circularity of decision and function whose multiple presuppositions and consequences are to be evaluated case by case.

Free trade, "a most powerful basis of heresy"

An *open* view of the management of the inquisitorial courts requires us to devote attention to the effects of their activity on the contemporary world of business and trade. In fact, as the inquisitors began to gather benefices, they also began to engage in regular contacts with secular institutions and the secular government, inflicted monetary punishments and property confiscation, administered the patrimonies of their courts (or sought new ways of investment) and found themselves constantly immersed in the socioeconomic milieu in which bankers, merchants, shopkeepers of various national and religious origins operated.

On the one hand, such subjects were suspect in the eyes of the Holy Office, since they were religiously, mentally and geographically mobile and, therefore, vehicles of heresy to be feared. On the other hand, they were interlocutors in affairs which could influence the forms and outcomes of the economic activities in which the inquisitors themselves were engaged and so enter directly – if to a degree which for the moment it is still difficult to establish – in the managerial and operative cycle of the justice of faith. So the first step is to discover through what modes the Inquisition chose to deal with these protagonists of the pre-industrial marketplace in an overall project aiming at the uprooting of religious heterodoxy within the Italian society of *Ancien régime*.

From Delio Cantimori's magisterial intuitions in *Eretici italiani del Cinquecento* (2002 – 1st edn 1939), studies on the spread of heterodox religious doctrines and practices have, over the years, clarified progressively the role of businessmen, operating on the local as well as the national and international levels, in circulating and developing ideas of Evangelical-Reformed inspiration. The pages of the inquisitorial trials which have come down to us are filled with the testimonies of weavers, millers, jewellers, financers and shopkeepers obliged to admit that they had talked about religion and formed commercial or personal relations with heretics in the inns and taverns, in market squares, during fairs, in the warehouses and in the shops. New research insists upon the familiarity between important peninsula bankers and merchants and heretic business partners, and upon the intense exchange between them in markets situated in the most dangerous areas of the heretic geography on the far side of the Alps.

As we know, the Republic of Venice, already rife with intense pro-Lutheran sentiments in the late 1510s – and where the multi-ethnic mercantile milieu was, at once, a bridge and a hotbed of tensions and incentives to spiritual renewal – worried the popes and the inquisitors. With the creation of the Congregation of the Holy Office, the Nuremburg merchants living under the *Serenissima* immediately began to find their normal economic activities hampered, despite the counter-pressures brought to bear by local German authorities upon the doges to secure their mediation with ecclesiastical authorities. At the same time, we see the first examples of financial solidarity between the merchants of the German Warehouse, who helped those of their number who were imprisoned in cases of faith taking up collections of funds. The political opposition of the local German authorities and the alliance among business dynasties did not however obtain the desired results in pacification and, with the advance of the sixteenth century, it became increasingly difficult for merchants from prevalently Protestant areas of Europe to exercise their activities and practise their religion freely.

In the seventeenth century, the only religious, Christian, minority which was able to organize itself as a community was that of the Reformed Dutch, while the Germans who were not Catholic were obliged to finance their community – and a spiritual minister[47] – secretly. Still, the fluid Venetian reality continued to solicit preoccupation in the Catholic Church, as some passages in an "Instruction", the Congregation of the Holy Office sent in 1645 to Angelo Cesi, Bishop of Rimini, whom Innocent X had recently named nuncio in Venice, show:

> Your lordship will keep equally in mind that, in the city of Venice, as port of the Eastern world, and due to the great wealth of every sort of traffic, and merchandise, many schismatic [individuals], Turks, Jews,

Englishmen, Dutchmen, and other like nations, without the true faith or contaminated by error, come together; so it is necessary for you to be on guard so that in practice and through bad example, they do not infect the souls of those who, through cunning, or ignorance, or to enjoy greater liberty – a most potent basis of heresy – may let themselves be drawn into some pernicious error. And with this intent, you will show yourself diligent and zealous in a continuing assistance to the questions of the Holy Inquisition, drawing example from the supreme pontiffs who, save for serious illness, or other unavoidable occurrence, do not let a week go by without holding a meeting of the Congregation of the Holy Office in their presence, judging that, for the vicar of Christ, any other question may be, with less incongruence or damage, entrusted to the care of others, than that of the Holy Faith of which he must be the first and, as far as he is able, immediate, promoter.[48]

The Holy Office was also troubled by the hardworking Venetian Countryside where, in the second half of the sixteenth century, first rank mercantile firms carried on continent-wide trade and might, therefore, represent potential vehicles of infiltration for heterodox religious ideas and practices. To block such risks, the Inquisition tended to subject the circulation of individuals and merchandise to prohibitions and forms of severe scrutiny, consisting in licences to leave the territory subject to the approval of the inquisitors and the bishops, and in the obligation to certify the regular recourse to the sacraments in the case of prolonged stays abroad. "We hear that some [individuals] from your honour's diocese go out of Italy to localities where the [population] is heretic, taking the occasion to trade, where they prevaricate against the faith", Rome wrote in 1580 to the Ordinary in Venice, a city already full of religious ferment animated, among others, by silk workers and dyers, like the Pellizzari brothers, of a deeply humanistic culture and in close contact with Alessandro Trissino:

> To remedy this inconvenience, your Lordship should be content that, under your tutelage, those who set out in this manner demand permission of you, or of the father inquisitor – something which may be introduced ably, a little at a time – and, in the permit they must be enjoined to return home after a fixed number of years; and, meanwhile, they are to send – or to bring with them – testimony approved by the Nuncios, or by the Catholic Ordinaries, that they have confessed and have taken communion as Catholics once a year.[49]

The Pellizzari had arrived in Vicenza from Chiavenna in the first half of the sixteenth century and operated in their palace in Borgo Pusterla, a meeting point and exchange of heterodox ideas for the local upper class of the time. At the heart of a commercial network of primary importance, including operators from the Grisons, Florence, the Valtellina and Flanders, the Pellizzari periodically shipped the raw silk produced locally to firms managed by relatives and colleagues in Lyons, Chiavenna and Geneva. Their lucrative trade went bankrupt in 1587, when a terrifying shortfall of about 230,000 scudi became public knowledge. The Venice Holy Office investigated some of the protagonists of the company with great attention, as the collection of commercial letters exchanged between them in the years from 1558–63, today filed among the surviving inquisitorial folders, testifies. This investigation resulted in the accusation, among others, of Gian Antonio Pellizzari, who liaised between Geneva and the Veneto, for having moved "to live there freely with Lutherans and heretics". The judges of faith discovered as well – during a blockage of their merchandise executed by the Milan Holy Office in 1563 – that, in a box hidden among the bolts of cloth, Nicolò Pellizzari had carried compromising letters regarding religious matters. The Bonanomi, too – silk merchants operating between Milan, Naples, Antwerp, the Veneto and France, whose business moved thousands of ducats and who, in part, resided in Chiavenna, were investigated in 1569 by the Inquisitions of Venice and Piacenza, who sequestered a large consignment of goods on its way to Lyon: goods among which, once again, suspect religious writings were found to be hidden.[50]

These are episodes which show us how searching goods circulating in international trade – which, as we shall soon see more closely, was among the prerogatives of the inquisitors presiding over the principal commercial marketplaces of the peninsula – worked in practice. It might give origin to trials in which various Holy Office seats cooperated, in a sort of operative network, specializing in cutting the ties which might exist between the circulation of money and merchandise and the spread of the "heretic infection". As Marino Berengo observed in *Nobili e mercanti nella Lucca del Cinquecento* analysing, in this Italian classic, another republic which was dynamic and frightening for the custodians of orthodoxy, "the men of the age of Charles V and Philip II, who did not stray from Catholic orthodoxy, were almost always prone to explain the spread of the new religious ideas as a contagion".[51] It was the same theoretic conception of heresy as a contagious disease, propagated by international carriers from across the Alps which prompted the Catholic Church and the secular authorities of the sixteenth century to develop a new diffidence concerning free trade and the cosmopolitanism of its chief exponents. Already in 1533, the Bishop of Lucca, Giovanni Guidiccioni, the first to denounce the penetration of heterodox ideas in the small republic, had declared in his sermons that he was convinced this was the work of the principal merchants of the city.[52]

Another explicit indication of the spread of Reformed ideas among artisans, merchants and those engaged in finance was the massive emigration to Geneva, in the mid-1500s, involving hundreds of active individuals, chiefly working in textiles. The first consistent mercantile communities to move towards Calvin's city were from the area centred on Cremona and people from Lucca. Though their patrimonies had, in some cases, been heavily curtailed by confiscations decreed by the Inquisition and the secular courts in preceding years, they managed to bring consistent wealth with them to Geneva and continued to produce and trade with Italy as well, practicing a Reformed religion at the same time.[53] As the inquisitorial repression became more severe, it was increasingly evident that some of the most important protagonists of the Italian religious renewal of the sixteenth century – among whom, for example, the Florentine Francesco Pucci – had begun to cultivate heterodox ideas and frequent circles of Evangelical inspiration during a commercial apprenticeship abroad. The fear "in particular of those who here send their sons for reasons of commerce to heretical lands, where they learn heresy", as the Cardinals of the Congregation wrote to the inquisitor in Vicenza in 1609, inviting him, in the Pope's name to use "all possible diligence to have notice of such persons and, having sufficient indications, proceed against those you shall find guilty", became then – and remained for many decades – the basic motor of the repressive action of the Holy Office, though it was long neglected by historians.[54]

Among the first commercial marketplaces to cause panic among the inquisitors was Lyons, in the era of the Reform an extraordinary crossroads, drawing operators from all of Europe, from the King of Portugal's stewards to the agents of the most important banking houses of Augusta (Augsburg) and Nuremburg. The fairs held in the city of the two rivers (Lyons) were an essential part of the system of monetary transferal, while the cosmopolitan merchants dealt in spices and luxury goods, among which a good part of Italian silk was included. In Lyons the principal houses of southern Germany had offices, whose personnel was often Lutheran. Books from Geneva were sold next to products of the flourishing local presses and other, German, printers, while the merchants of Lyons, in turn, travelled regularly to the Frankfurt fairs, carrying written matter and goods of all sorts.

At the other end of the continental commercial area in which Reformed ideas spread was the city of Kraków which, in the latter half of the 1500s still constituted the chief market for Lucca's silk. The first person to obtain the privilege of Krakówian citizenship, in 1571, was, emblematically, the Lucchese merchant Pietro Santini, of secure Reformed faith, who moved to the city, launching a mercantile firm. Emanating, from the religious point of view too, was the beginning of a florid traffic established in the Polish coeval capital by two brothers from the prestigious Florentine dynasty of the Soderini. The elder, Bernardo, arriving from Lyon, rapidly increased the number of Italians in his household. After 1570, Kraków became a crossroads for Italian exiles in flight from Geneva and the Grisons; the Soderinis themselves had contacts with men who were certainly adherents of the Reform, like the Zborowski brothers, placing their banking services, as well, at the dispositions of the Sozzini family when it became necessary to furnish the exiled Fausto with funds from his family; the youngest Soderini brother, Carlo, had contacts in Poland with the Piedmontese anti-Trinitarian, Giovanni Alberto Alciati.[55]

The representatives of the most important commercial and financial Italian houses were not always continuously resident in a sole foreign locality. Sometimes parental influence permitted the creation of offices in a number of cities, with comfortable transfer from one to another promoting contact with varied ideas and cults. Operators like the Florentine Bartolomeo Panciatichi and the Genoese Agostino Centurione, investigated for heresy, developed heterodox religious sensibilities working regularly in Antwerp and Lyon and dealing, along with goods and money, with forbidden beliefs and texts. Inquisitors were obliged to take the growing indifference towards Catholic alimentary restrictions of merchants used to transnational life into account, in particular that forbidding meat on "lean" days of abstinence. In the depositions of the trial of Agostino Centurione – a representative of one of the most wealthy and influential families of Venice – held in Trent in 1563, we find, for example, the admission that, in Lyons, Lent "among merchants is not, generally, observed due to the opinion that the air is unhealthy".

Those travelling frequently beyond the Alps, moving often from Frankfurt, where the famous fairs were held, and Basel, an important crossroad of the commercial routes linking Italy and northern Europe – and Reformed cities – had learnt that, as Centurione added, "in many places in that part of the world, on "forbidden days" you have to eat what you can find and what the hosts of those places want to make". Panciatichi, too, had come into contact with heretical doctrines in Lyon where, in any case, he had also been born in 1507, since his father headed one of the chief houses trading in spices there. As an adult, he became an academic in Florence, where he openly supported pro-Reformation religious positions and benefited from the open protection of Cosimo de' Medici. There, in October, 1551, Panciatichi was mentioned to the Bologna inquisitor by don Piero Manelfi in the context of his famous denunciation of the Italian Anabaptist network. Whereupon the duke wrote to the Fiorentine Inquisition declaring his preoccupation that such an "accusation" might seriously damage Panciatichi's "negotiations" "in French places and elsewhere where he, as you know, engages in activities of trade which are quite important".

Bartolomeo's problems with the Inquisition coincided (though we do not know whether casually or purposely) with the onset of a crisis in the Lyon bank. Because of "letters of credit written by said Bartolomeo, which were not accepted, nor paid, and came back protested", the Lyon "Panciatichi and Company" went bankrupt in the months in which its principal figure was involved in a trial for heresy. Cosimo's intervention, in a year in which the protection of a powerful figure could still influence the outcome of an inquisitorial trial, was decisive both for the economic interests of the Panciatichi and on the plane of its problems with faith. The property of the Florentine merchant could not be alienated to satisfy creditors without the consent of the future Grand Duke of Tuscany, while the accusation of heresy was dropped.[56]

The social networks encouraged by merchants, who supported and financed the circulation of individuals, books and heterodox ideas across the Alps, emerge, too, from the inquisitorial trials of Vittore Soranzo. Among these merchants was Francesco of Bernardino della Costa, known as "Belinchetto", active in trade with Switzerland and the Realm of Naples, and linked to the leading exponents of the heretic movement in the area around Bergamo, as well as to Pier Paolo and Aurelio Vergerio. Arrested with his brother, Alessandro, in 1556, Belinchetto managed to escape from prison and find refuge across the Alps. The confiscation of their property by the Inquisition was declared illegal by the Venetian Council of Ten, while the brothers, from the Grisons, continued to carry out their economic activities and maintain relations with dissidents still in Italy. In 1568 they rented an iron mine in Bergün and, the year after, obtained citizenship in Chur. The names of Alessandro Bellinchetti, "a quiet man and most modest" and of his brother, Francesco, "a good man and honest", "good as his brother", appear in the correspondence of the Valtellinese Reformers with Heinrich Bullinger until the 1570s.[57]

Many more examples of practical and spiritual ties between the peninsula protagonists of international trade and the spread of Reformed religious sensibility in Italy might be offered, as might the revocation of the condemnations and the confiscations through which the Holy Office tried to cut them off. We have already seen the reasons why the patrimonial confiscations affecting bankers and merchants were potentially devastating not only for their personal activities, but for the commercial network of which they were a part, as well: the sequestration of property and the destruction of contracts had, in fact, retroactive value, suddenly cancelling rights of property held by third parties because of transactions concluded even decades before the inquisitorial sentence had been launched.

For those ruling the Counter Reformation of the Catholic world, however, the protection of religious homogeneity in the Italian peninsula was a goal to be pursued even at the cost of compromising the patrimonial situations and the commercial equilibrium of an economy – like that prevailing in Italy in the late 1500s and the 1600s – already weakened by the critical contemporary economic situation. From the point of view of the courts of faith, the two fundamental problems which the traditional international reach of the major peninsula markets provoked were, on the one hand, the presence in Italy of foreign operators, coming from areas which were mainly Protestant and, on the other, the periodic expatriation of Italian merchants into heretical territories ("*in partibus haereticorum*"). We shall deal with them now in that order.[58]

The first groups of questions linked to the Holy Office's intention of breaking the bonds between trade and the circulation of heterodox religious doctrines and practices centre on the increasingly rigid regulation to which, between the sixteenth and seventeenth centuries, the prolonged residence in Italy of foreign merchants was subjected. The inquisitors were first of all worried about the foreign presence in Italian ports outside the Papal State: chiefly, Venice, Genoa, Livorno and Naples. In Livorno, Medicean policy had, from the time of Cosimo I, been directed to transforming the modest port – which had sprung up in an area ravaged by malaria – into an organized city able to fulfil the ducal ambition for economic and demographic growth. From 1547, Cosimo granted exemptions and privileges to foreigners who set up residence in Pisa and Livorno, attracting, in particular, Jews and *marranos* from the Iberian peninsula. Among the various decrees of the following decades, the best known and incisive were those of the so-called *Livornine*, addressed to "All of you merchants of any nation whatsoever, Levantines, Westerners, Spanish, Portuguese, Greeks, Germans, [and] Italians, Jews, Turks, Moors, Armenians, Persians, and others". This was a hodge-podge of cultures and religions which could not fail to disturb the sleep of bishops and inquisitors who, in the course of the seventeenth century, obliged a number of the so-called "*sponte comparentes*" to abjure if they wanted to continue to trade freely (leaving the ecclesiastical authorities, none the less, in doubt as to the authenticity of their conversions).

In Florence, as well, the presence of a stable and numerous English community drew, from the early years of the seventeenth century, close scrutiny from the inquisitor, who described its behaviour in great detail in his letters to Rome.[59] In the Kingdom of Naples, the Congregation turned frequently to the apostolic nuncio for details on the presence and the habits of the sailors and merchants from predominantly Protestant areas of Europe. Nuncio Bernardino Ricci, for example, in 1666, reported:

> There are many heretics in Naples and the chief reason they are tolerated, observed through age-old custom, is that the city itself is maritime and receives through their commerce the benefits of the various goods they bring here. The English, in particular, live here with the king of Spain's permission, due to the above mentioned commerce with their Nation, and with the agreement that, superficially, they are to be treated as if they were Catholics; that, encountering the Holy Sacrament, they must kneel: in church, they must bare their heads and perform all the acts of reverence usual to the faithful. These same [individuals] eat meat every day in their own homes and are rigorously ordered, and prohibited from, conversing with and frequenting women.[60]

The Anglican presence in Naples was under surveillance by the inquisitor throughout the whole of the seventeenth century, in line with the policy of vigilance generally applied by the Holy Office in the Italian contexts that were most active economically and socially. It was a policy which posited a substantial tolerance towards those foreign commercial operators who did not manifest their heterodoxy openly, accompanied by an implacable severity should they offer an occasion of "public scandal" with declarations on religious questions or by engaging in explicitly heterodox practices. Thus, the permanence of the "English heretic", Enrico Gaudiniero might, by these criteria, in the opinion of the Cardinals of the Holy Office, "[be] tolerated, so long as he does not give rise to scandal, nor commit anything contrary to the holy Catholic faith", as Cardinal Giovanni Garzia Millini wrote to the Neapolitan archbishop, Decio Carafa, in 1616. This was a tolerance which did not, however, imply the recognition of the Anglican merchant's full legal parity with his local competitors and colleagues. Finding himself involved in commercial litigation, Gaudiniero had asked the archbishop to write a letter of advice to be sent to Catholic merchants, something which the Congregation openly disapproved, declaring:

> In no way can this benefit be due against a Catholic, in favour of heretics, who, the day they commit this crime, are stripped of all their actions and reasons and are excluded from all civil actions, and so much the more when they attempt to secure the aid and benefit of holy laws, with constriction […] against Catholics.[61]

So the margin of indulgence conferred by ecclesiastical authorities on merchants of Reformed religion residing in Italian peninsula territory definitely did not imply full parity with their Catholic competitors. The activities of those operators were, indeed, subject to surveillance and limited in its possibility for travel: elements of certain competitive curtailment which – with the serious risk of being denounced to the ecclesiastical courts by envious or vindictive competitors – could not fail to discourage foreign mercantile houses desiring to open commercial seats or send established agents to Italy.

In exercising controls over merchants of Reformed religion active in Italian locations, and limiting their activities, the ecclesiastical courts – as had been the case with confiscation – sometimes met with resistance from secular governments, generally little inclined to humour bishops and inquisitors when their decisions might damage the economy of the State and its treasury's finance. This occurred, for example, in 1622 when the inquisitor in Casale Monferrato, Giovan Battista Boselli (who had imprisoned the two Schöbingen brothers, merchants of the St Gallen textile mills operating in his area and in stable relations with colleagues living in Alessandria and Turin), tried to persuade the Duke of Mantua to expel them permanently and forbid their activity within the borders of his realm. "I wore myself out", wrote father Benelli to Rome, "trying to persuade him of the spiritual and temporal damage and I told him they had not been imprisoned simply because they were passing through, but because for ten years and more they live as they like in this state, selling merchandise". Still, the inquisitor, with all his insistence, secured his objective only in part, for, the following year, the two merchants:

> Already expelled from this jurisdiction, have appeared in this city and gone to my Lord Duke of Mantua, who is now here and will leave in a few days, and have – for what I have been able to discover – supplicated his Highness to leave Turin (where they are now) and come back here to live as they did before, or at least to have permission to come and stop [here] for a short time or as 'traffic', and they have lent him a great sum of money (for this, I understand).

The subsequent developments of the episode show that, although the duke did decide to satisfy the insistence of the inquisitor, ordering the merchants to transfer elsewhere their local warehouse, the Holy Office did not succeed in banishing the two men from St Gallen from the Gonzaga dominions altogether. The Schöbingens continued, in fact, to frequent local taverns "claiming they had to use up their credit" as the judge of faith complained in 1624. A new attempt by the Inquisition in 1635 saw the defensive action of the Catholic Cantons and the St Gallen abbot; in that situation, the Milan authorities were obliged to refer the question to Rome, though they declared their full willingness to intervene to see ecclesiastical will enforced.[62] Due to the serious disturbances provoked by the 1628–31 wars of succession, Urban VIII chose to defer the expulsion of the St Gallen merchants from the Gonzaga domains without, however, refraining from noting the canonical intolerability of their continuing presence, as Rome wrote the Bishop of Mantua a few years later:

> The Holiness of Our Lord took pity upon the miserable state in which the wars – then raging – had reduced the Monferrato, so that His Beatitude condescended to concede the noble Duke of Mantua a year's postponement in which to end all the traffic of the St Gallen merchants, so long as the business was carried out by Catholics and so long as the wars should last; now that the time has passed and, through God's grace arms have ceased, [he may] believe in the piety of our Lord that without further notice he has put an end to the dangerous traffic; when that should not be so, Our Lord desires his excellency, immediately, following the example on his own volition, remove this contagious presence, which habitually gives birth to bad issue.[63]

Despite the strenuous ecclesiastical opposition, however, we know that at the end of the century, there were still St Gallen merchants with warehouses in Casale, Alessandria and even "with the aid of Catholic merchants".[64]

Other indications of the contested application of ecclesiastical prescription at the end of the seventeenth century in so far as regards to the presence of foreign merchants of Reformed religion present on Italian soil, can be found in the Duchy of Savoy. There, as we have already seen, in the latter half of the 1500s, secular authorities had not been much inclined to embrace Roman norms on confiscation of heretic property, as they were, too, in the case of confiscation regarding the Jews (as we shall soon see). Thus, in the early decades of the seventeenth century, Rome contested the Savoys' support in Turin of the few German and Swiss firms whose owners belonged to Reformed churches. With some difficulty, the dukes managed to maintain their positions until at least 1624, objecting to the nuncio that the presence of heretic merchants was allowed in Bologna in the Papal State and insisting upon the fact that an eventual expulsion would bring with it "serious, immediate, detriment to trade". Still, already in 1613, the Saluzzo Inquisition had been solicited, again by the nuncio, to revoke the concession given to a number of heretic merchants to reside in the city, acting in this in agreement with the bishop; other decrees, attesting the imprisonment of some heretic merchants passing through Saluzzo, were emanated by the Supreme in 1632.[65]

In the first half of the seventeenth century, the Modena inquisitor lamented Duke Alfonso III's lack of collaboration in his efforts to contain the presence of merchants from northern Europe. Even in Bologna – as the Savoy magistrates had pointed out polemically – to revitalize an urban silk production in crisis, the pontifical government had followed a policy of tolerance with regards to foreign merchants. Still, the life of cosmopolitan merchants was certainly not simple in a city like Bologna: the Bruni brothers, Paolo and Errico, for example – though Catholic in religion – had to request a permit from the Congregation of the Holy Office to go abroad on business, depositing each time a 10,000 scudi deposit.[66] Indeed, in 1589, the Bologna Inquisition had already arrested some Swiss merchants and others from Nuremburg (among whom was Johann Praun, a member of the powerful German commercial dynasty which had, for several generations, had offices in Ferrara and Florence as well). The Prauns tried all possible means to liberate their brother, turning to Archduke Maximilian III – in the period a candidate for the Polish Crown and administrator of the Teutonic Order – as well as putting pressure upon the Swiss cantons which presented requests to the Pope and the inquisitors and threatened reciprocation on Italians living in their territories. In reply, the arrested Swiss merchants were freed, while Praun's imprisonment dragged on for years.[67]

As the overall economic situation grew worse in the opening decades of the 1600s, Cardinal Legate Roberto Ubaldini conveyed tacit qualms over the pressures of the Holy Office, dispatching a dense memorandum to Rome on the benefits of the presence and the commerce of Swiss merchants in the manufacture of silk. It was with concern, then, that the Bolognese inquisitor communicated in 1627 that he had "discovered that every day people from totally heretic localities beyond the Alps – like Saxony, Silesia and other similar places – turn up here, and that they stop in rooms staying for four or five months, sometimes more", asking the Congregation cardinals whether it was not the opportunity to intervene. The official Roman decision was, once again, intransigent and a priori intent upon containing the public visibility of heterodoxy: the judge of faith was invited to investigate whether the merchants were Catholic and, if they were not, order them to leave the city – provided they had caused no religious scandal. Should there be, instead, explicit transgression of canon law, the inquisitor was, instead, to proceed against them with regular trials.[68]

This mosaic of rigid official positions and flexible searches for compromise with local secular government seems to suggest that – even on the grounds we are considering – once the harshest phase of sixteenth-century anti-heretic repression was over, forms of accommodation between the letter of the law and the real forms of its application (not at all unusual for *Ancien régime* society) were established in the major Italian cities. Equilibriums which must have seemed all the more necessary as the marginality of Italian markets compared to the great European and extra-European commercial flow – accompanied by the spread of plague and war – became more marked in the first half of the seventeenth century. The Italian states could not afford to acquiesce passively to the harsh attitudes held by the Popes and the inquisitors on the presence of foreign merchants within their borders. In addition, secular governments and regional markets of the time were trying to deal with the negative results of the second important group of Holy Office interventions in relations between commerce and heresy: the presence of Catholic economic operatives in lands where Protestant religion was dominant; a question we must now look into somewhat more closely.

We have already mentioned the decree with which, in the summer of 1596, Clement VIII forbade those living stably outside Italy to reside where the Catholic cult was forbidden, disciplining control of compliance rigorously through certification of access to the sacraments by anyone who should reside in foreign places in which the exercise of Catholicism was guaranteed.[69] In practice, this document gave an overall organic organization of a multitude of local – and not only ecclesiastical – solutions which, in the preceding decades, had in varying degrees, fixed limits of circulation on persons and things from and for the Italian peninsula, especially in border areas. Leaving aside here the ample area of the printing and selling of forbidden books – on which notable bibliography already exists – we can mention, for a commercial marketplace as delicate as was Milan, the *Bannum civitatis Geneprie pro heresi* ("Civic Genevan Prohibition for Heresy") emanated by the Duke of Albuquerque in 1569 so that no subject "should dare to go to, nor treat personally, for his own particular [ends] or those of others, with Geneva". This was a norm that placed the principle of freedom of trade between the Milanese area and the Swiss Protestant areas – sanctioned by accords dating from the age of Charles V – in discussion, and it had been followed in subsequent years by other laws further restricting the area of application of the Caroline agreements.[70] Even in a dynamic urban commercial reality like Florence, at the end of the 1560s, the Cardinal of Pisa recommended the inquisitor to "keep your eyes open continuously, and above all on foreigners and people from across the mountains, of whom one can reasonably fear much worse than from those of the city".[71]

In the second half of the 1500s, the highest Roman authorities began to follow the evolving economic-diplomatic relations between the Italian peninsula and the countries beyond the Alps with growing apprehension, attempting to limit them with the authority of a parallel governing force. Sixtus V did not hesitate to threaten the interdiction of the Milan market to all Swiss merchants – evidently confident that he could exercise more than a spiritual authority in the moment in which Helvetic pressure on the borders of Catholicism should prove too invasive. Having learnt of a project on the part of "the leaders and gentlemen of the heretic Swiss cantons" to build a college in Teglio in the Valtellina, in 1588 the Pope ordered Carlo Borromeo's successor, the Archbishop Gaspare Visconti, to bring pressure to bear upon the governor to block this project in every possible way, and to negotiate directly "with those Swiss and their heads and agents so that they desist from such innovation, threatening to prohibit them from trading with this state if they vote to persevere in such a project".[72]

In another long letter couched in legal language, addressed to the Milanese inquisitor at the end of the 1500s, the Congregation cardinals reminded him that "the tolerance of practices under the heading of 'commerce'", emerging from certain agreements signed in 1581, "regard no other than Swiss, and the Grisons, for all the others were within the common laws", and so canon law as well. If "the commerce of letters" was to be allowed in the Grisons, that is "with those persons with whom the trade of merchandise and other things is tolerated", trade "with heretics of other nations is not to be tolerated in any manner". Merchandise coming from areas that were prevalently heretic and directed to Milan were to be rigorously searched by judges of faith, to seek out hidden forbidden books or compromising letters. Bales of merchandise coming from the same regions, but transiting the Milanese marketplace only to reach other peninsula markets, might instead, be allowed to pass without inspection, since their inspection was the duty of the inquisitor with jurisdiction over the place of arrival. As to the merchants who "usually reside in heretic localities or come home several times yearly", concluded the detailed memorandum, "we need not say more, if not that you are to make them observe the orders of this Holy Inquisition".[73]

By the dawn of the 1600s, European movement of Italian goods – like the remaining population, Catholic and not Catholic – of the peninsula, was thus rigidly under surveillance and minutely disciplined by the inquisitors and the Congregation of the Holy Office. Rome reached the point of decreeing, case by case, whether single individuals could go the localities that were prevalently Reformed, basing their decision on documents illustrating the reasons for the trip and certificates attesting the petitioner's orthodoxy elaborated by the local inquisitor. If a "citizen", as was the case in Venice in 1598, asked his local judge of faith's permission "to go to Geneva to recover many thousand scudi which came to him on the death of a Catholic relative of his, who traded with France" – motivation in which the effort to dispute the religious legitimacy of the operation seems quite clear – the cardinals, once they also had in hand the "report which you [the inquisitor] give of his great goodness and Religiosity", could approve the request. Not rarely – as is the case in this example – the Congregation did, however, insist that the local inquisitor himself request the consent of the local ordinary or, in the case of Venice, the patriarch.[74]

The early seventeenth century does not seem to have seen, then, any significant easing up of the ecclesiastical discipline as to surveillance of the flow of trade. In 1625, after having mentioned explicitly Gregory XV's recent renewal of part of Clement VIII's decree, Rome once more ordered the Milan Inquisition to allow "*Retis et Helvetiis*" to sojourn in the city for some day to do business while, for everyone else, the usual norms applied to heretics would still be valid. Three years later, on the occasion of a new request to the Milan inquisitor for a licence by "heretic not confederated merchants", Rome declared that permission must be conferred in agreement with Archbishop Federico Borromeo, after a careful examination of the names of the operators (which were to be transmitted to the Congregation). Concession of the relative permits was to be considered applicable only to merchants who had "long traded", that is had been active in Milan for some time; again, in this case too, "tolerance and not giving scandal are expected". "But the door is to be wholly shut to those who should desire to introduce new traffic", the cardinals decreed, "for, as it is more desirable, rather, that [traffic] shrink, than enlarging its practice". The inevitable negative effects on the volume of business which the rigidity of surveillance would cause did not seem to preoccupy ecclesiastical courts. It was, indeed, declared openly that "the mind of the Holy Congregation is to come to an accord only with such as have ongoing commerce and must complete it and not continue". Adding:

> It has indeed seemed strange and new to hear that not only has traffic with Germany been undertaken, but that there are negotiations with the English and the Dutch, enemies of this Crown; so that your reverence, with all vigilance, is to procure information to let us know more certainly, so as to put an end to such pernicious abuse, and remedy such a serious difficulty [...] We also wish to make clear that] under the category of Merchants [to be tolerated] are included no others but those who treat large affairs and mercantile traffic, and not those who come only to buy clothing or the like, as this is being too easy handed and fills this State with people infected, with danger of contaminating Italy – which must, however, be entirely excluded.[75]

The tolerance accorded the few heretic merchants operating in "the doorway to Italy" was, then, to be considered limited to "big deals"; even the sojourn of the "heretic coach-drivers" accompanying the merchants had strict time limits. In the 1700s, the local inquisitor still kept an up-to-date *Copybook-Register of the Names of Jews and Heretics Allowed to Stop in Milan with License of the Inquisitors,* an indication that vigilance in this regard persisted for a very long time.[76]

It is difficult to establish whether so stringent a norm – whose application was, moreover, so full of problems – was, indeed, really operative in the daily realities of Italy's contemporary commercial marketplaces. As for the first half of the 1600s, Giovanna Tonelli's detailed research in the Milanese notarial archives has, for example, shown that Lombardy's capital remained open even to foreign merchants of Protestant extraction. Letters of credit drafted beyond the Alps continued to arrive in Milan from localities like Lyon, Paris, Cambrai, Constance, St Gallen, Zurich, Ulm, Augsburg and

Nuremberg; from centres which were – or had been – seats of important fairs, like Frankfurt-am-Main and Besançon, as well as from the great northern European emporiums like Hamburg, Amsterdam, Antwerp and London. The most important foreign merchants operating in Milan – like the Italian merchants and firms present beyond the borders of the State – were, in the period, able to maintain solid links with their commercial firms of origin or with its foreign branches. Studies of Lucca have also shown that economic relations were maintained between local merchants and various foreign locations from Moscow to Lyon (among these the feared Nuremburg).[77]

On the other hand, we can get some sense of the fearfulness of inquisitorial norms, at least in the late 1500s, not only from the already cited cases of merchants incriminated by the Holy Office after the discovery of letters and forbidden books hidden in their goods, but as well, in the frequent notices of disputes among secular authorities, economic operators and inquisitors, due to the periodic obstacles the latter threw in the way of the free circulation of goods and people. A typical incident occurred at the end of the sixteenth century between the Pavia inquisitor and the Milanese government, when the former imposed an obligatory licence from the Holy Office upon the boatmen in the Milan basin of the regional canal system: its resolution was reached only through the mitigating intervention of the Pope. The contemporary angry protests of the customs officers dealing with Milanese merchandise due to restrictions imposed on traffic by the inquisitor on the occasion of the Frankfurt fair – which led the merchants to ask government authorities to intervene through the ambassador in Rome to promote the indispensability of free trade as a principle – are another indication suggesting that businessmen did not take the norms elaborated by the Holy Office lightly, reading them as prejudicial to their own rights.[78]

In any case, further research would be indispensable to establish whether – and how – ecclesiastical norms from the age of the Counter Reformation, aimed at disciplining Italian commercial life so as to maintain peninsula religious homogeneity, encountered wide application in the medium and long term; and whether or not they significantly influenced the restructurings of general economic equilibriums in contemporary Italy. While, until the mid-1500s, Italian merchants and bankers had been the most numerous and dynamic in all the commercial centres of Europe, there is no doubt that, after 1570, the overall number of Italians operating abroad diminished, while foreign merchants present in the peninsula grew.[79] Clement VIII's late sixteenth-century measures were certainly a sharp change in the way in which the Church of Rome dealt with the problem of the connection between commerce and heresy, as well as in the perception the economic operators themselves had of ecclesiastical intervention in the economic sphere.

Let us now take a closer look at the immediate circumstances of the application, and the limits of these set of rules, to catch some of the broader implications and illustrate some of the general questions in which historians have until now shown little interest.

As we have already noted, with the 1596 provisions no Italian could reside habitually where the cultural and sacramental practice of Catholicism was not guaranteed; further, whoever should go into regions in which Catholic practice lived alongside Reformed practices, could not marry anyone of any other Christian religion, participate in Reformed baptisms or funerals or resort to non-Catholic physicians. These ordinances were immediately damaging to Italian merchants residing in Nuremburg: a city which the nuncio in Prague, writing the previous year to the Cardinal di San Giorgio, Cinzio Aldobrandini, the Pope's nephew, had defined "most perfidly heretical". For years, the Congregation of the Holy Office had been putting secular governments on guard as to the fact that the presence among heretical customs ("*more hereticale*") of their merchants in Nuremburg could constitute a cause of "infection" for Italian cities. And, only a few weeks after the emanation of Clement's bull, various inquisitors' reports reached Rome forming a virtual census of the Italian merchants active in Nuremburg: it included the Florentine Torrigianis and Mancinis, the Vertemanis from Prato, the Genovese Crollalanzas, the Portas and the Odescalchis from Como, the Vicenza Morellis, the Moraris and Gaspare Gerardini from Verona, the Lucca firm of Butini and Borti and the Milanese Arconatis: all with households of up to eight members, counting family and collaborators.[80]

Among the most important of those interested in the Clementine dispositions were, then, the Torregiani, powerful Fiorentine merchants present since the late fifteenth century. The nuncio in Prague – that Cesare Speciano who only a few years earlier had worked to assure Francesco Pucci to the Holy Office – wrote of them:

> The Masters Torregiani are very close friends of mine, and I have found them most loving on every occasion, even in the service of Our Lord [Pope Clement VIII], and of this Holy See, for which I consider them to be good persons, Catholic and most honoured [...] but with all this I do not wish to abandon the humility I owe, and desire to bring to your most illustrious lordship's consideration that, despite the things they have proposed to Your Beatitude and written in the letters that treat this negotiation – that the whole time that they, Torregiani, and their elders, have lived in Nuremburg, they have gone, from time to time, to mass, and that every year all – or almost all – of their family takes communion in a Catholic church – it is, nonetheless, also very true that when some person of their family is ill, he has neither the consolation nor aid of any Catholic, for they die without the most holy sacraments, and are taken to the heretic's graveyards, and by the same heretics with their damned rites.[81]

Enjoying influential friendships and protections – having given service to and done favour for the Pope himself, the Torregiani leaned upon their connections and obtained an immediate extension of their stay in Nuremburg, provoking the resentment of their colleagues who had, instead, been obliged to move to Bamberg and Regensburg, or return to their cities of origin in Italy. In January, 1598, the Congregation of the Holy Office, in the presence of the Pope, decreed, however, that the Torregiani could have no further postponement and that the inquisition must proceed against them if they did not abandon Nuremburg (*"nisi discedant Norimberga"*).[82] In March, the apostolic nuncio was once more alerted:

> Of the Italian merchants resident in Nuremburg, I need not tell you more, if not that His Holiness is firm in his resolve that everyone must leave the place and a new order has been given the inquisitors to proceed against their most important members, who are in Italy, and it is believed certain they will obey; and the Florentine inquisitor advises [us] that Francesco Caponi, tutor of the Turegiani heirs, has already given orders to his correspondents to close shop in Nuremburg and transfer to Regensburg; for, if they do so, they will more easily free themselves from any delays and appeals from others. But I really doubt this, because their agent, Guicciardini, says that it cannot be so and that he will want to make use of the postponement conceded; just so they close shop; His Holiness seems inclined as the sum to be received is large, they say more than 200,000 scudi.[83]

In this already tense situation, the prior of Santa Maria sopra Minerva in Rome received an anonymous accusation which regarded two Torregiani administrators in Nuremburg, Carlo Albertinelli and Benedetto Giorgino, defined as "open heretics". Albertinelli whom the accusation also declared to be a "negromancer", had left Florence for Nuremburg in 1568, when he was only 16. He had been closely acquainted with Francesco Pucci from the time in which the latter worked in the Rinuccini bank in Lyons and he had moved between Antwerp and Cologne, frequenting other Italians in exile "due to religion", among whom was the unfrocked Antonio Volpe from Basilicata. The accusation ended with a sentence which reflects the turbid atmosphere that had developed due to the different treatment accorded to merchants who were equally residing "in heretic parts" – but not equally furnished with supporters in ecclesiastical circles "The rest of us Italians were supposed to go wandering off straggling like the Jews – and the heretics stay here with their business".[84] But, at the moment in which the inquisitor in Florence was about to excommunicate the Torregiani, the cardinal nephew stepped in once again, ordering, in the name of Clement VIII, that they "abstain from proceeding against them, even though you have precise orders from the lord cardinals of the Holy Office".[85]

Indeed, nothing untoward occurred until 1606, when a Pandolfo Bruchman – a Lutheran Nuremburger who usually went to Bolzano four times a year for the fairs, and travelled in the peninsula "to pursue [his] business affairs" – was arrested in Ferrara. The records of his trial indirectly opened old problems, reminding the Holy Office that only some of the merchants identified a few years earlier by the Holy See had actually left Nuremburg as ordered. Bruchman, in fact declared:

> In Nuremburg there are no churches of Catholics of the Church of Rome, nor not even priests; there are there a good lot of French and Italian merchants that they let live in their [own] way and they stay there for their business [...] There are the Torrigiani of Florence who have a house and say they are heirs of Lucca, and they are numerous, [...] and there are also from Luc[c]a the Buttini and Buti, Lucchese, nor do I know their names, but I know them only by sight, and there are others from Como, Odescalchi.[86]

Immediately – with a decree of the Congregation – the merchants still resident were ordered to depart. Still, the Torrigiani once again called upon Carlo Albertinelli, who was in Florence at the moment, and he immediately went to Rome to present "in his own voice and with humility" to Pope Paul V a memo lucidly defending with every possible argument (including those strictly economic) the positions of commerce as compared to those of religion. The memo was read to the Congregation, in the Pope's presence, on March 15, 1607. Among other considerations, it declared:

> The damage and the difficulties which would follow the abandonment of Nuremburg is inestimable, both to goods and to bills of notable sums as has been said, as well as to the trade and profit which the above mentioned nation – and many and most infinite Italian merchants – draw from it each day. And all this would fall under the power of the heretics [...] You must realize that, in Germany, there is not another city where like movement of exchange is custom, habit – or, to put it still better, where such a movement of commerce can exist – save Nuremburg, passing virtually all through the hands of the Italians; without whose utility so many, infinite, exchanges, tricks and [other things] useful for all Christianity cannot be brought to conclusion; which, being things of commerce I shall not bother to relate, but – touching indeed upon the spiritual in this matter of selling and exchanging – let me add that if the Italians were not there, the Germans would try to find a way to send out and cause things to arrive in Italy, from which writing and frequency follow. Nor are those lacking who, avid for wealth, will send there from Italy – and so among these bands – boys and young lads, not to reside there, but to buy and sell and make contacts, from which those who have little [religious] practice can easily slip into error.[87]

The experienced worldliness of the cosmopolitan businessman allowed Albertinelli to present the governing authorities of the Church a prospectus of the consequences which would ensue for the Italian economy, and for the continental system of exchange in general, given an abrupt disarticulation of the economies of scale, of the information networks and of the reproductive strategies of competences which had been consolidated in centuries of Italian presence in the major Western commercial markets.

For today's historians, these declarations should represent an important agenda for research, whose investigation and elaboration through adequate documentation would allow us to evaluate properly the effects of the normative interventions of the Holy Office on the economy of the Italian peninsula in a period in which it was already in a situation with serious elements of involution. The fact that the Torregiani and other Italian merchants continuously residing abroad (among whom the no less powerful Corsinis of London), were given further postponements – in 1622, Gregory XV renewed Clement VIII's letter and once again posed the problem of the presence of Italian merchants "in heretic localities" – does not mean necessarily that their work went forward smoothly. It is difficult to imagine that the continuity and the efficacy of commercial and financial performance remained undamaged by the continuous uncertainty which the shadow of the Inquisition cast upon them; and that their Protestant interlocutors did not feel in some lack of incentive to negotiate with counterparts constantly overshadowed by the threat of confiscation which, like the swipe of a sponge, could cancel the transactions and the contracts of years.

We also need to consider the situation of those "Italians" who – as the anonymous letter denouncing the Torrigiani to the Holy Office after the Clementine decrees put it – had had to "go wandering off straggling like the Jews", abandoning their habitual places of work and repositioning themselves in new and unfamiliar marketplaces. It was certainly a sizeable group, though, unfortunately, we do not know how large it was: nor its composition; the size and extension of its traffics; or the fate of its components. They were, as Federico Chabod observed (though referring to other contexts), "refugees in some safer land even before local authority and inquisitors saw them as heretic [...] so that their names are lost, obscure wanderers as they have become".[88] Probably they were small or medium agents who enjoyed no powerful protection, with modest family connections, whose meagre papers and accounts are today very hard to locate, when, indeed, they have not been lost.

In some cases, it is precisely in the Inquisition's trial documents that we can catch glimpses of this basic level: in the interrogation of an international merchant the judges were often interested in his collaborators and in the organization of his various foreign offices. When, for example, in 1573, the Holy Office called Giovan Battista Michelozzi, one of the most important Florentine bankers of the period, to appear before it in an investigation into the circulation of capital between him and his colleague, Prospero Piovana – in turn a client of the Kraków Lenzi, from whom he purchased bolts of damask and satin – the judge pressed him with insistent questions regarding his "business in Transylvania" and his negotiations with other merchants. And there is some indirect news of merchants who, in the second half of the 1500s, abandoned marketplaces for reasons of faith; information of which an attentive census and a systematic evaluation should be undertaken. The abandonment by commercial houses of areas which had become prevalently Protestant has even been documented for the Republic of Lucca, the only Italian State which had not allowed the Inquisition to extend its jurisdiction within its territory. It was from Lucca that a group of merchants who, in 1577, abandoned an Antwerp which had become Calvinist, came. Passing through Geneva on their way home, they met some fellow citizens who had expatriated and resided there: on their arrival in Lucca, they went immediately to the Gonfaloniere to denounce their colleagues who had taken refuge in Calvin's city. Indeed, the Office on Religion – Lucca's "Secular Inquisition" – kept a very vigilant eye upon the religious life of the colonies of local merchants living abroad, as the survival of "Easter certificates" dispatched from Lyon and of the annual warnings addressed to merchants resident in Cologne, Nuremburg, Augsburg and London – to which the businessmen responded reassuring the secular judges of the regularity of their recourse to the sacraments – show.[89]

There are, as well, significant traces of the pressure constantly brought to bear by the inquisitors on secular government to limit the presence of their merchants in Protestant countries (and, indeed, their trade itself), in the exhortations to enforce respect of papal decrees and other actions upon the management of politic-commercial relations between states. The relations in the seventeenth century between the Holy See and the Republic of Genoa (in whose context Genoa was the object of constant pressures to recall its merchants residing in prevalently Protestant areas, while the Ligurian Inquisitor was persistently reminded that he must proceed to incriminate should they fail to do so), show this very well.

Relations between Genoa and England created particular concern after Orazio Pallavicini became an Anglican. Named "Collector of the Apostolic Decime" in the reign of Mary Stuart (Queen of Scots), the patrician Pallavicini converted and was naturalized in 1586, becoming thereafter personal banker to Elizabeth I; and was sentenced to death in default.[90] In 1598, Clement VIII ordered the inquisitor in Genoa to proceed against Bartolomeo Riccio (perhaps a relative of his father-in-law's broker), "who has taken in wife the daughter [Lucrezia] of Horatio Palavicino, heretic" as well as against a certain Eliano Giuliano Calvo "who has bought a lot of property around London".[91] Concerning other Genoese residing uninterruptedly in England, Clement VIII considered it more prudent not to undertake direct judicial action at the time; he did, however, urge the local judge of faith to "procure information as to how they live and operate there as regards the practice of the Catholic Faith".[92] These were censures which had repercussions on diplomatic relations between the Republic of Genoa and England – as the fact that, in 1599, the Pope did not allow the inquisitor to authorize the governing authorities to communicate in writing with the Queen of England, tolerating only contacts regarding the recovery of three Genoese ships captured by the English, testifies. The Genoese authorities were also forbidden to address Elizabeth by the title of Holy Majesty, since, because of the Inquisition, only that of Most Serene was tolerable.[93]

Finally, it would certainly be worth attempting an overall historiographical evaluation of the various forms of normative, religious and cultural self-discipline adopted by the merchants themselves and their corporative organizations to align with the prescriptions of papal decrees – or forestall repressive acts on the part of ecclesiastical courts. Among these was, for example, the prohibition on marrying local women, imposed by contract on young men about to leave for cities where the Reform had definitively triumphed, already formulated in the central decades of the sixteenth century by the Florentine *Arte di Calimala*, the powerful guild of the cloth finishers and foreign cloth merchants. This corporative norm was more restrictive than the canonical norms of mixed marriages in force in the Roman Church, and its repercussions on business are, once again, difficult to assess: in terms of a lack of social linkage to the areas of emigration, of greater difficulty in intercepting dowries furnished by foreign families and in creating strategic parental ties in foreign marketplaces. We need to understand better whether, and in what degree, ecclesiastical authorities exercised direct or indirect pressure on corporations to oblige them to alter their statutes so as to conform them to new prescriptions – or whether it was the climate of control and reciprocal suspicion which developed in the second half of the 1500s through the intensification of the activity of the courts of faith which induced the arts to self-discipline.

It was, in any case, well known at the time that many of the places where international merchants gathered – including the taverns where they carried on their mercantile contracting – seethed with informers: like the merchant Philippe Dauxy who, as agent for Margaret of Parma, Governor of the Netherlands, kept an eye on the activities and the declarations of Calvinist colleagues in Antwerp in 1566, recording his findings in a carefully crafted report. The awareness of the risk of being spied upon and denounced to the ecclesiastical courts – even as retaliation by competitors – certainly made economic operators more cautious and reserved in transmitting information; the subsequent difficulty in gathering information due to the reliability and credit standing of businessmen provoked, at least in some periods and markets in which there were greater religious preoccupations, the spread of informative asymmetries and the rise of transaction costs.[94]

Evaluating the secondary effects of the creation of the Holy Office, and of the renewed harshness of the sixteenth-century Roman justice of faith on the functionality of the contemporary and successive Italian business world – and, more broadly, upon the development of those "opposite cycles" which, from the seventeenth century, saw Europe begin to travel along separate lines of economic development – is an arduous task and, with our present levels of knowledge, one that cannot lead to a unified response. In this, as in other aspects of the repression operated by the courts of faith on religious liberty, freedom of action and thought, censorship and the self-censorship of ideas and the limitation – and self-limitation – of operative individual and collective acts and choices, were inextricably connected.

This makes distinguishing between exogenous and endogenous factors especially difficult when the intent is to look into the results of what was certainly an articulated attempt to limit freedom of enterprise and commerce over the transformations the Italian economy suffered in the second half of the early modern period. It seems necessary, however, to open up this territory without preconceptions and therefore to start with what documentation has survived, broadening our research agenda, recovering the historiographical analysis of microeconomic elements which have, until now, been neglected by studies on the relations between trade and the Inquisition.

Notes

1 The metaphor "land market" is, of course, inadequate to represent an articulated and complex reality like that of the buying and selling of landed property in the pre-industrial era; we can, however, cite Polanyi's comment, according to which "the description of work, of land, and of money as merchandise is wholly fictitious [...] It is, none the less, with its contribution that labour, land and money markets are organized": see Polanyi (1980). On the limits of the approach which considers preindustrial commerce of land to be dominated by the automatic play of demand and offer/supply, see Levi (1987), Delille and Levi (1989).
2 Romeo (2009), pp. 68–70.
3 ACDF, So, St.st., LL5f, *Inquisizione di Rimini*.
4 ACDF, So, St.st., LL5e, *Inquisizione di Alessandria, Inquisizione di Asti, Inquisizione di Casale*.
5 ACDF, So, St.st., LL5e, *Inquisizione di Firenze*.
6 ACDF, So, St.st., LL5e, *Inquisizione di Milano*, paragraph "*Possessione della Cagnola*".
7 ACDF, So, St.st., LL5f, *Inquisizione di Tortona*.
8 Ibid.
9 ACDF, So, St.st., LL5e, *Inquisizione di Capo d'Istria, Inquisizione di Cremona* and, on the Cardinal d'Aracoeli, *Inquisizione di Milano*.
10 ACDF, So, St.st., LL5e, *Inquisizione di Como*.
11 ACDF, So, St.st., LL5e, *Inquisizione di Milano* and *Inquisizione di Mantova*.
12 ACDF, So, St.st., LL5e, *Inquisizione di Cremona*.
13 ACDF, So, St.st., LL5e, *Inquisizione di Mantova* and *Inquisizione di Modena*.
14 ACDF, So, St.st., LL5f, *Inquisizione di Novara*. On the structure of the "Contadi" or "Territori" see Maifreda (2002); on Langosco, Covini (2005).
15 ACDF, ibid.
16 ACDF, So, St.st., LL5e, *Inquisizione di Bologna*.
17 Ibid.
18 Prosperi (2009), p. 184. For an overview, see also Brambilla (2006), pp. 109ff. and Romeo (2009), pp. 71ff.
19 On Faenza, Ancona and Rimini see ACDF, So, *Decreta*, February 5, 1625, p. 26r; on Tuscany see ACDF, So, St.St., LL5e, *Inquisizione di Firenze*; on the 1743 total number and on Modena see Brambilla (2006), p. 114; Prosperi (2009), p. 184.
20 Recent studies on the case of Milan have, however, shown how, in the first half of the 1600s, admission to the confraternity of the *Crocesignati* might be requested by people who were compromised, or in the process of being judged (even for serious crimes); perhaps with the intention of re-establishing a good reputation, or creating social alliances which might mitigate their sentences: see Coppo (2011–12), pp. 110–11.
21 BAV, Vat. Lat. 6336, p. 123r, Rome, May 13, 1628.
22 Righi (1986), p. 54.

23 On Parma see Ceriotti and Dallasta (2008), p. 105; on Milan ASM, *Culto parte antica*, box 2016, un-numbered folder "Della veneranda Congregazione de quaranta Crocesegnati privilegiati di San Pietro Martire di questa città", p. 1*v*.
24 Fumi (1910), p. 23.
25 See the title of Visintin (2008); Table 1.2 in Chapter 1.
26 Ample documentation on the administration of the Conca estate over the long period may be found in ACDF, So, St.st., L3c and in the sources indicated by Marino (2009).
27 For the seventeenth-century evolution of the positions of the Church and the Holy Office on the question of loans see Vismara (2004) and Vismara (2010).
28 ACDF, register "Entrata e uscita banco S. Offitio", fuori Stanza storica, *ad annum*. November 10, 1666 saw, in fact, the expenditure of 10,000 scudi "paid with Order number 976 to the Most Excellent Prince of Palestrina" for an annual tribute [*censo*] of 400,000 scudi, imposed upon the holding of Campo Leone, sold in favour of the Holy Office (ibid. p. 51, which illustrates Francesco Barberini's role as intermediary). For information on the Principality of Palestrina see Tosi (1968), p. 147.
29 ACDF, register "Entrata e uscita banco S. Offitio", fuori Stanza storica, pp. 94, 98, 110, 134, 96, 127.
30 ACDF, So, St.st., LL5f, *Inquisizione di Perugia*.
31 ACDF, So, St.st., LL5e, *Inquisizione di Belluno* and LL5f, *Inquisizione di Torino* and *Inquisizione di Udine e Concordia*.
32 ACDF, So, St.st., LL5f, *Inquisizione di Venezia*.
33 ACDF, So, St.st., LL5f, *Inquisizione di Vercelli*.
34 Del Col (2006), pp. 778–9. The data includes denunciations and 'informations', formal trials, and summary procedures. In Modena, too, we find a significant increase in trials of the court of faith in the second half of the 1600s, analogous to what occurred on Malta – for which we have, however, no sixteenth and early seventeenth century data (ibid.).
35 Malena (2003), pp. 111ff.
36 ACDF, Si, register "Libro dell'entrata e dell'uscita del Sant'Offitio", pp. 4*v*–5*r*.
37 Ibid., p. 6*r*.
38 For example ibid., pp. 54*v*–55*r*.
39 Ibid., p. 18*v*.
40 Ibid., p. 19*r*.
41 Ibid.
42 Ibid., pp. 94*v*–95*r*.
43 Ibid., pp. 101*v*–102*r*.
44 Ibid., p. 85*v*.
45 Ibid., p. 97*r*: "For having had a vaulted ceiling built in the loggia – material in wood, ironwork, plaster, bricks and workmen, scudi 37; in doors, windows and window panes, most necessary to make the whole inquisition liveable, scudi 24; without which construction, one could not, with the terribly cold, live out the winter there, save in one single room".
46 See the figures cited by Del Col (2006), pp. 774–9. The financial aspects of Giovan Battista Magni's intense inquisitorial activities are abundantly documented in ACDF, Si, register "Libro dell'entrata e dell'uscita del Sant'Offitio", pp. 106rff.
47 On Venice see Firpo (2004), pp. 37ff. and his bibliography. On German merchants see Kellenbenz (1983), p. 117.
48 BAV, Vat. Lat. 10447, pp. 89rff., *"Istrutione a vostra signoria monsignor Cesi vescovo di Rimini destinato da Nostro Signore suo nunzio a Venezia"* ("Instructions to your Lordship monsignor Cesi, Bishop of Rimini appointed by Our Lord his Nuncio in Venice"), Rome, March 11, 1645, italics are mine.

49 BAV, Vat. Lat. 10945, p. 124r, Rome, January 16, 1580. On Pelizzari and the religious climate in Vicenza, see Olivieri (1992), pp. 379ff., and Demo (2014).
50 Demo (2003) and Vianello (2004), pp. 112–13. On the religious heterodoxy of the mercantile milieu in Chiavenna and Lyons see Scaramellini (2014), Faggion (2014).
51 Berengo (1999), pp. 399–400; Adorni-Braccesi (1994), pp. 319ff.
52 Berengo (1999), p. 401.
53 Mottu-Weber (1987); Perennoud (1990), pp. 56–7; Berengo (1999), pp. 419ff.; Monter (2006). On the very wide international range of commercial and financial traffic activated by Cremonese merchants in the seventeenth century see Demo (2006).
54 On the role of religion in Pucci's mercantile formation in Lyon, see Caravale (2011). The letter to the Vicenza inquisitor which explicitly declares "Our Lord orders you to use…" is in BAV, Vat. Lat. 10945, Rome, October 31, 1609.
55 Mazzei (2007), pp. 464–5.
56 Mazzei (2007), pp. 461–3. On Manelfi's accusations Ginzburg (1970) remains fundamental.
57 Firpo and Pagano (2004), tome 1, pp. 50–60, note 17.
58 In the last chapter of the Italian edition of this book I have also looked at the economic presence of the Jews in Italian society of the time and the many aspects of their relations with Christians – which were attentively scrutinized, in turn, by the Holy Office: see Maifreda (2014), pp. 289ff.
59 Toaff (1990), p. 419. On Leghorn and Florence see also Fosi (2011), p. 161.
60 Fosi (2011), p. 170.
61 Giovanni Garzia Millini to Decio Carafa, Rome, October 22, 1616: see Scaramella (2002), pp. 450–1.
62 Fosi (2011), pp. 160ff.; on Milan, 1635, see Savoja (1985), p. 53.
63 BAV, Borg. Lat. 470, p. 82r, Rome, undated.
64 Fosi (2011), p. 160.
65 BAV, Borg. Lat. 558, pp. 104r–107r; Rome, May 20, 1604; August 4, 1616; March 4, 1624; December 5, 1613; October 30, 1632.
66 BAV, Barb. Lat. 6334, p. 145r, Rome, May 30, 1626.
67 Kellenbenz (1983), pp. 119–21.
68 Fosi (2011), pp. 160–4.
69 The papal letter, renewed several times in the years that followed, was regularly sent to the inquisitors in the principal commercial Italian cities. For Venice, see, for example, BAV, Vat. Lat. 10945, p. 124r, Rome, December 13, 1598 and May 12, 1606: "His Holiness, Our Lord, has once more made it a perpetual norm that Italian merchants and businessmen cannot, outside of Italy, reside in cities, territories or localities in which the free and public exercise and the practice of the Catholic religion, of church, of priest, of mass and other divine offices, and the holy sacraments is forbidden and interdicted. I send you herewith a printed resumé".
70 On the book trade in the 1500s, an overview may be found in di Filippo Bareggi (1988) and Nuovo (2003), completed with an ample bibliography. On the links between the book trade and ecclesiastical censorship, an initial view is offered by Fragnito (2005); on regulations regarding the Milan area see La Rosa (1985), pp. 89 and 99; Savoja (1985), p. 53.
71 ACDF, So, St.st., LL5e, *Inquisizione di Firenze*, folder "*Transunto delle lettere della Suprema scritte dal signor Cardinale di Pisa al padre maestro fra' Francesco Giberti da Saponara Minore conventuale, inquisitore di Firenze nel pontificato di San Pio V*" ("Transcript of the Letters from the Suprema Written by the Lord Cardinal of Pisa to Father-Master brother Francesco Giberti da Saponara,

270 *The Inquisition and economic life*

    Conventual Minor, Inquisitor of Florence in the papacy of Saint Pius V"), p. 1r–v, Rome, January 22, 1569.
72 BAV, Barb. Lat. 1370, pp. 14v–15r, Rome, January 9, 1588.
73 BAV, Barb. Lat. 1370, pp. 9r–11r, Rome, July 3, 1593.
74 BAV, Vat. Lat. 10945, p. 124r, Rome, January 24, 1598.
75 BAV, Borg. Lat. 558, p. 59r, Rome, June 16, 1625; Barb. Lat. 6336, pp. 149r–150r, Rome, June 3, 1628. For an overview of the Milanese commercial market in the 1600s, see Tonelli (2012).
76 The preoccupation regarding the effects of "heretical coachmen" is documented in BAV, Barb. Lat. 6336, p. 150r
77 See Tonelli (2002); Tonelli (2014); Sabbatini (2012), p. 28.
78 On cases in the area of Pavia or in that of Milan see La Rosa (1985), pp. 99–100.
79 Malanima (1998), pp. 117ff.
80 On Aldobrandini see Mazzei (2001), p. 403, note 21; the Cardinal of Santa Severina's letter to the authorities of the Milanese government is cited by La Rosa (1985), p. 99. The "census" of the Italian merchants residing continuously in Nuremburg is, instead, in BAV, Barb. Lat. 1370, pp. 1r–v, Rome, July 26, 1596.
81 Mazzei (2001), p. 405, note 25.
82 See the letter of the Florentine inquisitor in BAV, Vat. Lat. 1370, p. 3r, Rome, January 19, 1598.
83 BAV, Barb. Lat. 1370, p. 3r–v, Rome, March 28, 1598. On April 29, 1598, a letter addressed to the inquisitor in Florence repeated the pontiff's desire that all the Italians leave Nuremburg (ibid., p. 3v).
84 Mazzei (2001), p. 406.
85 Ibid., p. 415, note 50. The Holy Office had already written to the nuncio on June 30, 1598, that Clement VIII had decided to allow some Torrigiani agents to remain in Nuremburg "to collect pending credits provided the bank remains closed; no buying, no selling, nor any new negotiations, but that the bank transfer to Regensburg as they have offered to do" (BAV, Vat. Lat. 1370, p. 5r).
86 Mazzei (2001), p. 416, note 51.
87 The complete transcription of the 1607 memorandum by Carlo Albertinelli in Mazzei (2001), pp. 425–8, quote from p. 426.
88 Chabod (1938), pp. 162–3.
89 On Lucca see Sabbatini (1998), pp. 135–6; on Michelozzi see Mazzei (1999), pp. 188–9.
90 De Frede (1999), p. 338.
91 The possibility that Bartolomeo Ricci was so related is the hypothesis of De Montaner (2011), p. 437.
92 The citation is from BAV, Barb. Lat. 1370, p. 7r, Rome, April 4, 1598; for other pressures brought to bear by the local inquisition, see p. 5r, Rome, July 5, 1598.
93 BAV, Barb. Lat. 1370, p. 7r, Rome, May 28, 1599. An analogous censure of the Genoa inquisitor for having permitted an exchange of letters between the Genoa Senate and the Queen of England is ibid., Rome, p. 6r, October 11, 1591; the judge of faith was, further, pressed to contact the Genoa "Duce" to make known to him "the grave error committed in this action in the manner of address, as also of treating with the most pestiferous heretics in the world at least without making this holy Congregation participate in it".
94 On the Florentine *Arte della Calimala* and Dauxy's secret report, see Mazzei (1999), pp. 181 and 184; on the repercussions, within economic transactions, of the rapidity and the efficacy of the circulation of information, see Maifreda (2011). For the Roman Church, the indispensable condition for a dispensation allowing a mixed marriage in pluri-confessional regions was that the Catholic spouse be protected in his or her faith and that the Catholic education of any offspring be assured: see Scaramella (2011), p. 407.

Bibliography

Adorni-Braccesi, S. (1994) 'Una città infetta'. La Repubblica di Lucca nella crisi religiosa del Cinquecento, Florence: Olschki.
Berengo, M. (1999) Nobili e mercanti nella Lucca del Cinquecento, Turin: Einaudi.
Brambilla, E. (2006) La giustizia intollerante. Inquisizione e tribunali confessionali in Europa (secoli IV–XVIII), Rome: Carocci.
Cantimori, D. (2002) Eretici italiani del Cinquecento e Prospettive di storia ereticale italiana del Cinquecento, ed. by A. Prosperi, Turin: Einaudi (1st edn 1939).
Caravale, G. (2011) Il profeta disarmato. L'eresia di Francesco Pucci nell'Europa del Cinquecento, Bologna: Il Mulino.
Ceriotti, L. and Dallasta, F. (2008) Il posto di Caifa. L'Inquisizione a Parma negli anni dei Farnese, Milan: FrancoAngeli.
Chabod, F. (1938) Per la storia religiosa dello Stato di Milano durante il dominio di Carlo V. Note e documenti, Bologna: Zanichelli.
Coppo, A. (2011–12) Al servizio dell'Inquisizione. La confraternita dei Quaranta crocesegnati di Milano, MPhil thesis examined at the Università degli Studi di Milano, a.a. 2011–12, tutor Professor S. Peyronel Rambaldi.
Covini, N. (2005) 'In Lomellina nel Quattrocento: il declino delle stirpi locali e i "feudi accomprati"', in F. Cengarle, G. Chittolini and G. M. Varanini (eds) Poteri signorili e feudali nelle campagne dell'Italia settentrionale fra Tre e Quattrocento: fondamenti di legittimità e forme di esercizio, Florence: Florence University Press, 127–74.
De Frede, C. (1999) Religiosità e cultura nel Cinquecento italiano, Bologna: Il Mulino.
de Montaner, P. (2011) 'La marranerie come injure d'origine espagnole utilisée hors la péninsule Ibérique, XVe–XVIIe siècle', in P. Bonte, E. Porqueres i Gené and J. Wilgaux (eds) L'argument de la filiation. Aux fondaments des sociétés européennes et méditerranéennes, Paris: Éditions de la Maison del sciences de l'homme.
Del Col, A. (2006) L'Inquisizione in Italia dal XII al XXI secolo, Milan: Mondadori.
Delille, G. and Levi, G. (1989) (eds) Il mercato della terra, special issue of Quaderni storici (65).
Demo, E. (2003) 'Sete e mercanti vicentini alle fiere di Lione nel XVI secolo', in P. Lanaro (ed.) La pratica dello scambio. Sistemi di fiere, mercanti e città in Europa (1400–1700), Venice: Marsilio, 177–99.
Demo, L. (2006) Dall'auge al declino. Manifattura, commercio locale e traffici internazionali a Cremona in età moderna, in G. Politi (ed.) Storia di Cremona. L'età degli Asburgo di Spagna (1535–1707), Bergamo-Cremona: Bolis-Banca cremonese-Credito Cooperativo, 262–87.
Demo, E. (2014) 'Mercanti ed eresia a Vicenza nel XVI secolo. Nuovi documenti e prospettive di ricerca', in G. Maifreda (ed.) Mercanti, eresia e Inquisizione nell'Italia moderna, special issue of Storia economica (1): 85–100.
di Filippo Bareggi, C. (1988) Il mestiere di scrivere. Lavoro intellettuale e mercato librario a Venezia nel Cinquecento, Rome: Bulzoni.
Faggion, L. (2014) 'Fuori dai confini: itinerari e reti di mercanti tra Vicenza, Lione e Ginevra nella seconda metà del secolo XVI', in G. Maifreda (ed.) Mercanti, eresia e Inquisizione nell'Italia moderna, special issue of Storia economica (1): 143–62.
Firpo, M. (2004) Artisti, gioiellieri, eretici. Il mondo di Lorenzo Lotto tra Riforma e Controriforma, Rome and Bari: Laterza.
Firpo, M. and Pagano, S. (2004) I processi inquisitoriali di Vittore Soranzo (1550–1558). Edizione critica, Vatican City: Archivio segreto vaticano.

Fosi, I. (2011) *Convertire lo straniero. Forestieri e Inquisizione a Roma in età moderna*, Rome: Viella.

Fragnito, G. (2005) *Proibito capire. La Chiesa e il volgare nella prima età moderna*, Bologna: Il Mulino.

Fumi, L. (1910) 'L'Inquisizione romana e lo Stato di Milano. Saggio di ricerche nell'Archivio di Stato', *Archivio storico lombardo* (35, 36, 37): 5–124, 145–220, 285–414.

Ginzburg, C. (1970) *I costituti di don Pietro Manelfi*, Florence-Chicago: Sansoni-Newberry Library.

Kellenbenz, H. (1983) 'I rapporti tedeschi con l'Italia nel XVI secolo e all'inizio del XVII secolo e la questione religiosa', in *Città italiane del '500 tra Riforma e Controriforma. Atti del Convegno internazionale di studi Lucca, 13–15 ottobre 1983*, Lucca: Maria Pacini Fazzi editore, 111–25.

La Rosa, M. (1985) *"Peste luterana". Intolleranza religiosa e focolai eretici nella Lombardia del Cinque e Seicento: documenti e annotazioni*, in Archivio di Stato di Milano, *Aspetti della società lombarda in età spagnola*, vol. 1, Como: New Press, 87–115.

Levi, G. (1987) 'Economia contadina e mercato della terra nel Piemonte di antico regime', in P. Bevilacqua (ed.) *Storia dell'agricoltura italiana in età contemporanea. II. Uomini e classi*, Venice: Marsilio, 535–53.

Maifreda, G. (2002) *Rappresentanze rurali e proprietà contadina. Il caso veronese tra Sei e Settecento*, Milan: FrancoAngeli.

Maifreda, G. (2011) 'Intermediari bancari e società civile (1861–1913)' in L. Conte (ed.) *Le banche e l'Italia. Crescita economica e società civile 1861–2011*, Rome: Bancaria editrice, 27–61.

Maifreda, G. (2014) *I denari dell'inquisitore. Affari e giustizia di fede nell'Italia moderna*, Turin: Einaudi.

Malanima, P. (1998) *La fine del primato. Crisi e riconversione nell'Italia del Seicento*, Milan: Bruno Mondadori.

Malena, A. (2003) *L'eresia dei perfetti. Inquisizione romana ed esperienze mistiche nel Seicento italiano*, Rome: Edizioni di Storia e letteratura.

Marino, M. (2009) 'L'attività economica: la tenuta di Conca', in A. Cifres and M. Pizzo (eds) *Rari e preziosi. Documenti dell'età moderna e contemporanea dall'archivio del Sant'Uffizio*, Rome: Gangemi, 48–63.

Mazzei, R. (1999) *Itinera mercatorum. Circolazione di uomini e beni nell'Europa centro-orientale 1550–1650*, Lucca: Maria Pacini Fazzi editore.

Mazzei, R. (2001) 'Convivenza religiosa e mercatura nell'Europa del Cinquecento. Il caso degli italiani a Norimberga' in H. Méchoulan, R. H. Popkin, G. Ricuperati and L. Simonutti (eds) *La formazione storica della alterità. Studi di storia della tolleranza nell'età moderna offerti a Antonio Rotondò*, vol. 1, Florence: Olschki, 395–428.

Mazzei, R. (2007) 'I mercanti e la circolazione delle idee religiose', in *Il Rinascimento italiano e l'Europa*, volume 4, F. Franceschi, R. A. Goldwhaite and R. C. Mueller (eds) *Commercio e cultura mercantile*, Treviso and Costabissara: Angelo Colla editore, 455–78.

Monter, W. (2006) 'La colonia protestante cremonese a Ginevra nel XVI secolo', in G. Politi (ed.) *Storia di Cremona. L'età degli Asburgo di Spagna (1535–1707)*, Bergamo-Cremona: Bolis-Banca cremonese-Credito Cooperativo, 334–49.

L. Mottu-Weber (1987) *Économie et refuge à Genève au siècle de la Réforme. La draperie et la soierie, 1540–1630*, Genève-Paris: Librairie Droz-Librairie Champion.

Nuovo, A. (2003) *Il commercio librario nell'Italia del Rinascimento*, Milan: FrancoAngeli.
Olivieri, A. (1992) *Riforma ed eresia a Vicenza nel Cinquecento*, Rome: Herder.
Perrenoud, A. (1990) 'La population', in A.-M Piuz and L. Mottu-Weber (eds) *L'économia genevoise, de la Réforme à la fin de l'Ancien Régime XVIe–XVIIIe siècles*, Geneva: Georg-Société d'Histoire et d'Archéologie de Genève, 1990, 41–82.
Polanyi, K. (1980) *Economie primitive, antiche e moderne*, Turin: Einaudi.
Prosperi, A. (2009) *Tribunali della coscienza. Inquisitori, confessori, missionari*, Turin: Einaudi.
Righi, C. (1986) *L'Inquisizione ecclesiastica a Modena nel '700*, in A. Biondi (ed.) *Formazione e controllo dell'opinione pubblica a Modena nel '700*, Modena: Mucchi, 51–95.
Romeo, G. (2009) *L'Inquisizione nell'Italia moderna*, Rome-Bari: Laterza.
Sabbatini, R. (1988) 'Nell'emporio del mondo, "sentina di ogni ribalderia": mercanti lucchesi ad Anversa, in *Città italiane del '500 tra Riforma e Controriforma. Atti del Convegno internazionale di studi: Lucca, 13–15 ottobre 1983*, Lucca: Maria Pacini Fazzi editore, 127–43.
Sabbatini, R. (2012) *Le mura e l'Europa. Aspetti della politica estera della Repubblica di Lucca (1500–1799)*, Milan: FrancoAngeli.
Savoja, M. (1985) 'Aspetti del commercio nello Stato di Milano in epoca spagnola', in Archivio di Stato di Milano, *Aspetti della società lombarda in età spagnola*, Como: New Press, volume 2, 51–108.
Scaramella, P. (2002) *Le lettere della Congregazione del Sant'Ufficio ai tribunali di fede di Napoli 1563–1625*, Trieste-Naples: Edizioni Università di Trieste-Istituto italiano per gli studi filosofici.
Scaramella, P. (2011) 'Mescolanze. Proibizione e pratica dei matrimoni misti nell'Europa della prima età moderna: riflessioni per una ricerca in corso', in D. Dall'Olio, A. Malena and P. Scaramella (eds) *La fede degli italiani. Per Adriano Prosperi*, vol. 1, Pisa: Edizioni della Normale, 403–12.
Scaramellini, G. (2014) '"Et è ormai Chiavenna fatta una Genevretta, et minaccia a Italia". Mercanti e "libertà retica": riformati ed eterodossi sulle vie d'Oltralpe nel XVI secolo', in G. Maifreda (ed.) *Mercanti, eresia e Inquisizione nell'Italia moderna*, special issue of *Storia economica* (1): 43–84.
Schwedt, H. H. (2009) 'Gli inquisitori generali di Siena, 1560–1782' in O. Di Simplicio (ed.) *Le lettere della Congregazione del Sant'Ufficio all'inquisitore di Siena 1581–1721*, Trieste: Edizioni Università di Trieste, IX–LXXVI.
Toaff, R. (1990) *La Nazione ebrea a Livorno e a Pisa (1591–1700)*, Florence: Olschki.
Tonelli, G. (2002) 'Percorsi di integrazione commerciale e finanziaria fra Milano e i Paesi d'Oltralpe nel primo Seicento', in L. Mocarelli (eds) *Tra identità e integrazione. La Lombardia nella macroregione alpina dello sviluppo economico europeo (secoli XVII–XX)*, Milan: FrancoAngeli, 151–94.
Tonelli, G. (2012) *Affari e lussuosa sobrietà. Traffici e stili di vita dei negozianti milanesi nel XVII secolo (1600–1659)*, Milan: FrancoAngeli.
Tonelli, G. (2014) '"Mercanti che hanno negotio grosso" fra Milano e i paesi riformati nel primo Seicento', in G. Maifreda (ed.) *Mercanti, eresia e Inquisizione nell'Italia moderna*, special issue of *Storia economica* (1): 101–142.
Tosi, M. (1968) *La società romana dalla feudalità al patriziato (1816–1853)*, Rome: Edizioni di Storia e letteratura.

Vianello, F. (2004) *Seta fine e panni grossi. Manifatture e commerci nel Vicentino 1570–1700*, Milan: FrancoAngeli.

Visintin, D. (2008) *L'attività dell'inquisitore fra Giulio Missini in Friuli (1645–1653): l'efficienza della normalità*, Trieste: Edizioni Università di Trieste–Circolo culturale Menocchio Montereale Valcellina.

Vismara, P. (2004) *Oltre l'usura. La Chiesa moderna e il prestito a interesse*, Soveria Mannelli: Rubbettino.

Vismara, P. (2010) 'Usura', in A. Prosperi (ed.) *Dizionario storico dell'Inquisizione*, with the collaboration of V. Lavenia, J. Tedeschi, Pisa: Edizioni della Normale, vol. 3.

Epilogue

When, in the waning years of the Roman Inquisition, the rulers of the Catholic Church found themselves in the unaccustomed necessity of justifying the legitimacy of the justice of faith through the nuncio in Vienna, Antonio Eugenio Visconti, they fell back on arguments which no historian of the Holy Office would consider acceptable today. Visconti invoked the rigour of procedure and investigation of the truth; he averred the solidity of an impartial evaluation of the proof, the guarantees of a competent defence for the accused, restraint in the procedures and the punishments applied to the self-accused who – often under legal pressure of the confessors – presented themselves spontaneously ["*sponte comparentes*"]; the moderation of the punishment inflicted upon the condemned; and, finally, the exclusive responsibility of the "secular arm" in the execution of capital sentences. Still, monsignor Visconti did on that occasion offer the Empress Maria Theresa at least one, personal,[1] conviction which would have a fair possibility of acceptance by the scholars cited in this book: the prime object of the Holy Office, he affirmed, was to persecute heterodoxy, inducing individuals to abjure and thus to convert: not – though this too had been done – to punish heretics even to the point of loss of life.

The Inquisition was not a criminal court in the contemporary sense of the term, for the crimes prosecuted had no victims save "Divine Majesty". The Holy Office trials – through implicit threat or the real infliction of torture and death – had as their principal consequence the discouraging of the very creation of heterodox religious ideas, blocking, beyond their circulation, the mental and verbal formulation of ideal alternative systems for the creation of truth. This work was carried out by the inquisitors: not simply through the ordinary procedures and the punishments, but through a tireless work of prevention, surveillance and prohibition (not only *a posteriori* but *a prori* – before anything "happened"), blocking the individual and collective possibility to think in dissent. So the activities of the Inquisition cannot be compared – whether as to procedure or punishment – to that of ordinary criminal courts past or present if not, perhaps, to the special courts instituted to persecute political crimes.

276 *Epilogue*

Grado Giovanni Merlo – though referring specifically to the harsh anti-heretic campaigns of the Middle Ages – outlined an approach that, as my research findings show, is equally apt for the early modern period:

> It would be a mistake to think that the victory of the Roman Church over the heretics in the middle years of the Middle Ages is due simply to the recourse to the instruments of violent coercion [...] The strengthening of repressive rigidity was justified initially where no other roads to reconciliation were discovered – or where such attempts proved inefficacious, and when the heretic presence was judged to be – and presented as – a dangerous and unacceptable violation of the norms which ought to regulate individuals living together in society. Such conviviality [...] could not contemplate the separation of the civil and the religious dimensions, for it was the premise of the eternal individual and collective destiny: it was a conviviality to be ordered towards other-worldly salvation. So it was that the repression of heretics brought with it a pastoral attitude whose end was to conform the behaviour of the faithful to models constructed expressly to that end.[2]

In those countries where the Catholic religion predominated not only did the generalized exercise of the justice of faith become an important presence in the entirw Middle Ages and – with renewed impetus – in the decades and the centuries following the explosion of Lutheranism, but a religious climate of dissuasion of heterodoxy emerged with fundamental characteristics and consequences over the long period which have been – and are still – objects of study and evaluation by generations of scholars. Though the general reader may still be drawn – and at the same time repulsed – by the bloody side of the Inquisition (just as scholars of the past were often spurred to open or covert polemic intent by it), an approach centred upon the choice of apology or denunciation of a sort of "Dark Legend", must itself be firmly consigned to history. Retrospective analyses rigorously limited to quantitative and comparative evaluations of the physical victims of inquisitorial repression are equally inadequate to express the historic complexity of the justice of faith – and, indeed, with the actual state of the sources, they are wholly unreliable.[3] The same may be said of referring to the number of death sentences and the torture, citing dramatic individual episodes as the basis for evaluations of the cruelty or the "leniency" of the Holy Office – or indeed of its greater or lesser influence upon modern Italian history.

Today, it seems rather indispensable to continue to explore the aspects of the justice of faith which pervaded the material and the ideal life of the people, reconstructing the broadest and most complete image of the behaviour of its courts – even in the very moment in which they created and shaped the presuppositions and the operative foundations of the project as a whole – aimed at systematically imposing (but this, contrary to the nuncio Visconti's view, was anything but an extenuating circumstance) "more amendment than punishment".

Opening out our visual to everything that happened in the relations between the Inquisition and society – *before* and *alongside* as well as *during* and *after* the flames and the stake – we can continue to develop our understanding of the degree (and the manner) in which the justice of faith was efficient in converting and forestalling (besides punishing, in a more or less broad number of cases), the spread of heterodoxy of belief, of thought, and of way of life, even unto death. Re-examining from its roots that "schematic representation of the Inquisition as a malign excrescence, a structure of dominion pressed down from outside upon the free development of society", which Adriano Prosperi stigmatized in a seminal reconsideration, we can repopulate what has long been a "no man's land", illuminating a "dense forest of structured realities; a flow of initiatives and social dynamics activated by the operation of the Inquisition – but which, at the same time, also conditioned [that functioning], imposing multiple, place-specific, characteristics upon it".[4]

Turning from the observation of trial procedure in a strict sense to the analysis of the wider and complex design of affirmation and control over a conception of the world – and, I should venture to say, of the very procedure of formulating such conceptions – we can give the economic dimension of the Holy Office's activity its proper importance and depth. Moving in this direction, we will also need to give further thought to the organizational and economic forms of the Roman Holy Office and of its operative peripheral network, whose ability to be efficient was one of the prerequisites of the continuative, capillary, and coordinated action required for the adequate execution of its constant, day-to-day, mission of blocking heterodoxy. It was a mission which, in the complex institutional mosaic of modern peninsula Italian reality, was exercised in a plurality of political and social contexts; in dialogue with multiple subjects and mobilizing diversified and integrated strategies including economic ones. Balance sheets, orders of payment, sales contracts, bank coupons are all apparently opaque objects of study; yet – as I hope this book shows – all of them can contribute notably to explaining how the justice of faith "did business": the procedures followed and, indeed, the very professional identity of the inquisitors of faith themselves.

The long road of economic emancipation which the Italian inquisitorial courts followed, through benefices, pensions and, finally, stable, autonomous incomes – which the first part of this book deals with – still needs to be fully understood and explained. Besides the difficult questions inherent in the relations between Ordinaries and judges of faith – and the crucial problem of the deviation of resources from pastoral engagement to serve the repressive thrust of the early decades of the Counter Reformation – we need to look carefully into the connections between the construction of a solid beneficiary foundation, autonomy and the professionalization of the inquisitorial function. Though from the very beginnings of the Congregation of the Holy Office's campaign the bishops had contributed – more or less adequately – to the operative expenses of the peripheral courts, the achievement of their financial independence probably also implied an increased material (and symbolic) procedural autonomy from diocesan organisms and their controls.

Why did the popes and the Roman Holy Office of the mid-1500s – though aware from the prior Spanish example, of the material and moral risks of a strategy promoting an inquisitorial network entirely based on the economic autonomy of the individual, local, offices and the lack of a predisposed ordinary, fixed, income – follow the same pattern for decades in Italy? It seems difficult to deny that beyond and above the reasons we have already noted in the course of this study (like the resistance of the bishops and the secular princes, which could slow down and complicate the assignment of benefices and ordinary, fixed, incomes) this decision sprang from the considered intent of making the intervention of the justice of faith harsher, more punitive and strongly dissuasive, in the context of what the papacy considered an unprecedented attack upon its spiritual and temporal supremacy.

Besides constituting a source of publicity for the Holy Office – compensating the secrecy of the procedural phases of the justice of faith preceding sentencing – this policy obliged the sixteenth-century inquisitors throughout the Italian peninsula to rely first of all on confiscation of property and monetary penalties to sustain them (as the Spanish and – though with the limitations we have seen – Portuguese contemporaries who had preceded them had done), and served thus as an instrument assuring the Holy Office of strong peripheral roots. The virtuous results of the Inquisition's operative structure in the living heart of the societies and the cultures in the Italian states, though weakened by the potential operative limits and the conflicts of interest would – as we have seen in analysing the ways in which the local courts managed their patrimonies over the long period – persist until suppression.

As the dramatic episodes of the Ancona Jews burnt at the stake in the mid-sixteenth century show, the Roman Inquisition did not lack persecutory excesses – probably due to economic greed. Still – and despite the fact that the fragmentary state of surviving documentary sources imposes, even here, strong methodological caution – from what we know today it does not seem possible to identify within the system of central and peripheral Italian courts of the mid and late sixteenth century a systematic programme of appropriation of the property of individuals involved in inquisitorial trials; nor an integration of ordinary procedure of faith and patrimonial investigations comparable to those which studies of the Spanish situation have ascertained. The societal impact of confiscation was attenuated in Italy not only by the general respect of the Roman procedural practice – which imposed its application only in the event of a death sentence – but by the necessity (unknown in Spain and Portugal) of coming to an agreement on each occasion as to the division of the confiscated patrimony with the relevant secular authorities. For the Holy Office, the dialogue between the local courts and the peninsular governments – including negotiations concerning confiscation – represented at once a formidable instrument of institutional, political, judicial, social and informative communication, and a limit (more or less firm from region to region) to the freedom and independence of intervention, especially on the ground opened by the pronunciation of the sentences *in causa fidei*.

When – chiefly due to the "inquisitor popes" like Paul IV and Pius V who acquired the new, permanent, physical seat of the Congregation – the peripheral courts were supplied with pensions, beneficiary incomes and an articulated system of support able to guarantee the continuity of their operation, the anti-Lutheran emergency was drawing to a close. The new phase in the history of the Roman Inquisition was characterized by the massive process of building up local seats, bureaucratizing the operative functions and enlarging their personnel, and the households and external collaborators completing them.

This organizational evolution can also be read in parallel to the Spanish case, for the Spanish Inquisition, too, was almost contemporaneously assuming a tentacular – and almost definitive – administrative structure. In 1560, Philip II had increased the number of treasurers of the courts of faith and favoured the autonomy of the separate offices in economic matters, suppressing the post of General Accountant ("*contador general*") of the Suprema and retaining the Receiver General with the function of collecting and centralizing the surpluses of local courts on the basis of the budgetary data which they submitted. Further, in 1561, the Supreme Inquisitor, Fernando de Valdés, with his 81-article *Instructions*, imposed a centralized structure under the firm control of the Suprema, guarantor of the financial stability of the courts. All the members of the Suprema – the Inquisitor General, the provincial inquisitors, senior prelates, legal advisors and lawyers – were appointed exclusively by the king.

At the end of the sixteenth and the beginning of the seventeenth century, the three Mediterranean Inquisitions were thus obliged to deal with a structural evolution which brought with it increased fixed costs and a parallel diversification of the areas of competence of trial procedures. While the Spanish Inquisition was partially emancipated from the economic surveillance of the Crown and found an autonomous, stable, functional basis, the Portuguese Inquisition – which had initially suffered from legislative limits impeding it from counting upon a constant flow of confiscations – inaugurated a policy of direct collaboration with the king to guarantee its greater financial stability. The first general code of the Portuguese Inquisition was promulgated in 1552 and it opened, in fact, with instructions for the administration of the budget and the payment of salaries: thereafter, it fixed a ceiling on the amount Lisbon's inquisitors might spend upon a single item; and, in 1554, the Crown succeeded in obtaining from the Apostolic Seat the creation of annual pensions from episcopal income (a coup which was received with much grumbling and protest by the Ordinaries upon whom its costs fell). As Giuseppe Marcocci's innovative studies have shown, in the second half of the sixteenth century all resistance on the part of Portuguese bishops in the matter of inquisitorial jurisdiction over heresy was also silenced, while the application of confiscation was freed of restraints and – between 1567 and 1573 – former limits on the mobility of New Christians and their possibility of leaving the realm, as well as that of selling their property, were reinstated.[5]

Unfortunately, we still cannot completely reconstruct the economic story of the Roman Inquisition over the course of the modern period. The series at our disposition – for the most part regarding the central, Roman, court – seem to suggest a substantial stability in the pattern of income and expense in the latter half of the sixteenth century and in the seventeenth as well. We have only occasional data on the behaviour of the budgets of local courts which, however, the 1749 Table 1.1 seems to suggest, were certainly not very substantial.

The information available on this aspect of the last decades of the sixteenth and the first decades of the seventeenth centuries seems, on the contrary, to indicate a situation in which, with a growing level of accumulation from patrimony and investments, we see a parallel expansion of costs in the maintenance of the inquisitorial household. For the Roman Inquisition, the contribution of the convents – where the various local inquisitors were physically housed and carried out their functions, while remaining situated in the traditional hierarchical structure of the Order concerned – was certainly fundamental. Further research would, however, be necessary to attempt any convincing evaluation as to just what percentage of the financial burden created by the administration of the Holy Office was in reality supported by the convents (and therefore by the Mendicant Orders), and in what measure this participation influenced the efficiency of the prosecution of the justice of faith within the convent walls.

Probably, over the long period, the incentive system typical of the managerial model – a mixture of salaried dependent and entrepreneur – led the inquisitors to feel themselves obliged to reduce the costs of investigations and the prosecution of trials which might be presumed to involve notable expenses weighing on peripheral budgets. A situation which – once the sixteenth-century emergency was over – it is reasonable to suppose did not fail to exercise some sort of influence on the spread of spontaneous presentation and the highly limited recourse to the costly official opening of a case by the inquisitor's office, as well as upon various other aspects of the Roman Inquisition's administration.[6] Still, the local courts of the Roman Inquisition certainly did not grow rich with fines and confiscations. Most of the fixed income in money or in returns deriving from the property of Italian courts of faith, whether central or local, was most probably used to cover the costs of building and operating their ordinary structures, as well as in trials and in the maintenance of those prisoners who were not able to pay their own costs.

Here, too, the economic history of the Roman Inquisition seems to show the same tendencies we find in Spain. Scholars of Spain have formulated some hypotheses as to why its Holy Office, though for various decades it had the possibility of holding on to the wealth furnished by the ample confiscations inflicted on the *conversos*, failed to accumulate large, long-term patrimonies. These hypotheses fall roughly into two large categories and, with opportune adjustments they may be usefully applied to the Italian case.

First of all, from the late 1400s the Spanish Crown – as the pontifical Curia also sometimes did – appropriated an important part of the property deriving from confiscation (which was sold at auction and invested "by order of the Catholic King" – as a 1519 Order signed by King Ferdinand declared). In addition, the Suprema, like the Congregation of the Holy Office in the Roman case, handled the central management of the monetary flow from the individual courts, apportioning and directing it towards the poorer seats, according to procedures formalized by the administrative Reform of 1556 which established a system of transfers ("*consignaciones*"). The individual courts were ordered to send a fixed annual sum of money to the Suprema, or directly to other local, indicated, seats; the sum total of such charge already in the late 1500s exceeded 2,000,000 maravedis and, in the 1600s, with the severe Spanish depression, swelled to more than 3,000,000. Thanks to the recourse to the *consignaciones*, the *hacienda* of the *Consejo* – despite years of deficit – tended to solvency even during the difficult seventeenth and eighteenth centuries, when the progressive economic and social crisis threw the whole contextual Spanish system into a crisis of resources and the monarchy (especially under Philip IV and Olivares) began to demand ever larger "general grants" from the Inquisition, obliging many seats to sell off property both real and financial.[7]

Diversion and redistribution of local resources in favour of the general inquisitorial system are present – as we have seen – in the Roman case as well, but on the order of the Congregation. The Congregation appropriated to itself (or apportioned to courts with passive accounts) any annual surplus local seats might realize. As I have tried to demonstrate, it was a mechanism which has weakened the incentives of individual inquisitors to pursue a systematic policy aimed at securing money or land which, when Rome should become aware of them, would inevitably be transferred elsewhere; indeed, perhaps incentivizing peripheral offices to seek thrifty subsistence rather than profit might have been a tacit objective. The Ministry in Rome also imposed forms of redistributive solidarity on its courts, imposing stipends for poorer seats upon those which were wealthy. The whole structure was aimed at stabilizing a constant minimum "floor" of operational efficiency for the entire Holy Office network, efficient even in cases where local budgets suffered lengthy periods of passivity.

The second group of explanations suggested by studies of the Spanish and Portuguese Inquisitions to justify the relative scarcity of their overall patrimonial accumulation, is the hypothesis that a significant portion of the rich confiscations went to cover the costs of keeping the prisoners and paying the outstanding debts of the culprits, as well as in aid to innocent family members and persons in their employment (expenses which, in Spain, were the obligation of the Inquisition, though the judges of faith did not always honour it). It has been calculated that 36.6 per cent of the property of a royal official executed by the Santander Inquisition in 1760 went to liquidate his outstanding debts; 31.7 per cent was spent supporting relatives who were not materially self-sufficient; and only 31.7 per cent was finally secured by the Inquisition. Faced with these obstacles, as well as the general crisis of agriculture and of seventeenth-century Spanish and Portuguese incomes, the need for a fixed annual income that was as liquid as possible spurred many courts of faith in Spain – and in Italy – to invest in property yielding tributary fees and other financial and credit tools. These sources of income – as the number of laws regarding their management promulgated by the Suprema in the 1600s and 1700s testifies – became the structural bases of local finance in the second half of this institution's life. In 1573, 74 per cent (and in 1576, 80 per cent) of Granada's income came from tributary fees and rents from properties; in 1611, 63.3 per cent of Llerna's income had similar origins. Valencia – the court which perhaps benefited most from the income deriving from the expulsion of the Moriscos decreed in the 1610s – in 1630 had about 17,200,000 maravedis at its disposal: all invested in properties yielding 5 per cent tributes. The attempt made in the first half of the 1500s to provide the local courts with certificates of the public debt to be purchased with financial surplus deriving from the infliction of monetary penalties did not work out.[8]

Bureaucratization, financialization, functional diversification, seem – as this book has discussed at length – to constitute in the Roman case, as well, the three essential traits of the transformation within the Italian inquisitorial system. In this case, a limit to income was certainly constituted by the activities of the secular governments and the episcopal *Mensa* which, in the Italian peninsular context, insisted upon the division of confiscated property or – especially in the case of republics – slowed down or impeded the procedure even when undertaken against Jews. However, in the Italian case – perhaps due to a lesser depression of income from agricultural properties as compared to contemporary Spain – cases of overwhelming prevalence of financial investment over investment in real estate on the part of inquisitorial courts are marginal. The seats engaged in the economic management of fully developed agricultural businesses are fairly numerous. Certainly, the Italian Inquisition, like the Spanish, experienced a growing engagement of its local inquisitors in the field of credit over the seventeenth century. As they took advantage of bank deposits and began granting loans to families and communities, as well as to the Jewish universities and single individuals, these local operators found themselves faced with a series of new situations whose implications invite (and deserve) closer prosopographical analysis. The affirmation of these general Italian tendencies was, most probably, influenced in large measure by the somewhat different nature of the Mediterranean depression in the two peninsulas as, of course, by the varied local secular situations constituted by the multiplicity of civil governments within Italy.

Finally, there is the problem presented by the forms – and the consequences – of the intervention of the Holy Office in the regulation of economic activity, freedom of trade and the mobility of entrepreneurs in early modern Italy. These were factors which made the Inquisition – albeit in a degree and with a geographic and chronological extension still wholly to be defined – an interlocutor in establishing the institutions (and the legal ethos) which presided over the founding of the goods and services "markets".[9] We lack a new, more analytic, look into the history of the Roman Inquisition: one placing it within the processes of cultural transformation which, in late sixteenth and seventeenth-century Europe, presided over the changing intellectual attitudes towards commerce in the contemporary context of religious and spiritual transformation.

If, rather than focusing on its activity of sanction and punishment, we look anew at the historical significance of the Inquisition in its deeper dimension as an instrument of confessional unity and ideological propaganda, the economic side of its history takes on unexpected importance. There are a number of reasons for this: the need to make the collecting of testimonies more efficient and certain (even by foiling private vendettas); the exigency that the judge remain immune to any outside influence and any personal interest; the obligation to avoid defamation of suspected individuals; the will to consent to a more rapid and easy expiation on the part of the culprit; the opportunity of avoiding publicity for the existence – and the practice – of a crime as exceptional as heresy; and the judge's fear of being overwhelmed by the sophisms of the moment in which public discussion should occur.[10]

The economic requirements of their courts, the patrimonial and financial punishments they imposed, the properties and the financial assets they accumulated over time, the ordinary and beneficiary incomes – often torn from the bishops, the abbots, or their own superiors (or bitterly contested with them) – did, however, allow the local inquisitors to break out of convent, or episcopal palace walls; both physically and metaphorically tearing, as well, the veil of secrecy imposed upon the trials and consenting to the visibility necessary for any authentically political institution, together with the sinking of deep and lasting roots at all levels of *Ancien régime* society.

Economic action is necessarily relational action. Buying and selling goods, confiscating them, loaning money and extending credit, renting property, imposing or paying fines and expenses: all of these were the daily business of the judges of faith. They imposed visibility, a capacity for dialogue and, therefore, a fully public projection of the Holy Office in the life of the community in which it found itself, to all intents and purposes, immersed.

The economic dimension of inquisitorial action allowed – indeed made necessary – confrontation and, sometimes, the active collaboration of the inquisitors and their personnel, with a very broad range of interlocutors: secular magistrates and their officials, feud holders, notaries and experts, tenants, day labourers, creditors and debtors, fellow judges of faith, families, friends, enemies and mere acquaintances. Judiciary activity itself was not exempt, for the many moments of a life which might be delved into, or removed, in the course of investigative procedure and trial which necessarily invested "the ordinary business of life", bearing witness to the common existential fabric into which victims and tormenters were equally woven. So the Milan inquisitor might, as he carried out a confiscation, discover that the heretic Bernardo Appiani from Pallanza – a medical doctor with an enthusiasm for theology and the occult sciences (who had escaped from prison in 1571 and been burnt at the stake), was the creditor of the notable sum of 1,964 gold scudi, owed to him by Count Giorgio Costa della Trinità, Captain General of the tragic military expedition against the Waldensian valleys ordered by Emanuel Philibert of Savoy in 1560.[11]

The ordinary business of life can be so unpredictable that it throws the reassuring division between good and evil – set at the heart of the modern West – into crisis.

Notes

1 ASM, *Atti di governo, Culto parte antica*, box 2106, folder "1771/1775","*Copia di memoria sulla necessità, e convenienza di conservare nello Stato di Milano il tribunale dell'Inquisizione*" ("Copy of the memorandum on the necessity and the opportunity of conserving the tribunal of the Inquisition in the State of Milan"), Antonio Eugenio Visconti to Maria Theresa, June 22, 1774.
2 Merlo (2012), p. 113.
3 See the decisive examination of this question in Del Col (2006), pp. 772 ff.
4 Prosperi (1991), p. 35.
5 Marcocci (2004).
6 "Since the use of proceeding *ex officio*", reads a comment to Masini (1730) in early eighteenth century editions, "and through inquisition in trials of faith, without revealing through whom their judges received notice of the crimes and of the culprits, [this procedure] is strongly disliked by the Supreme tribunal of the Holy, Universal Roman Inquisition; therefore the judges of the same [Inquisition], in the presentation which they make at the opening of the Trial, will establish that from whom, or in what manner, the information presented was obtained must always be mentioned" (p. 19).
7 Martínez Millán (1993), pp. 916ff.
8 Kamen (1998), pp. 148–56; Martínez Millán (1993), pp. 908ff.
9 For further discussion of this question, see Maifreda (2014).
10 These themes have been well analysed by Chiffoleau (2006).
11 On this figure and on his brother, Gerolamo, condemned for aiding his escape, see Fumi (1910), pp. 387ff.; Bendiscioli (1957), pp. 283–6; Maselli (1970), p. 356. The credit dated from 1558, the year in which Costa della Trintà participated actively in the defence of Cuneo, held by Count Manfredi di Luserna and under heavy siege by the Duke of Brissac. In 1580, the Extraordinary Magistrate condemned the Costa heirs to pay the debt to the Appiani who had the right to inherit from Bernardo, constraining them, however, to auction off the right to duty fees of the municipal Mill in Pavia (Cfr. ASM, Fc, box 216, folder "1592. Applanorum Pallantiae et alios in causa confiscationis Bernardi Applani", printed sheet *In causa sequestri reddituum Comitiis Coste, ratione confiscationis bonorum Bernardi Applani, haec erunt pro fisco ponderanda* and sentence of the Extraordinary Magistrate, Milan, August 25, 1580).

Bibliography

Bendiscioli, M. (1957) 'Politica, amministrazione e religione nell'età dei Borromei', *Storia di Milano*, vol. 10, *L'età della Riforma cattolica (1559–1630)*, Milan: Fondazione Treccani degli Alfieri per la Storia di Milano, 1–350.

Chiffoleau, J. (2006) '"*Ecclesia de occultis non iudicat*". L'Église, le secret et l'occulte du XIIe au XVe siècle', *Micrologus. Nature, Sciences and Medieval Societies* (13): 359–481.

Del Col, A. (2006) *L'Inquisizione in Italia dal XII al XXI secolo*, Milan: Mondadori.

Fumi, L. (1910) 'L'Inquisizione romana e lo Stato di Milano. Saggio di ricerche nell'Archivio di Stato', *Archivio storico lombardo* (35, 36, 37): 5–124, 145–220, 285–414.

Kamen, H. (1998) *The Spanish Inquisition: A Historical Revision*, New Haven, CT and London: Yale University Press.

Maifreda, G. (2014) (ed.) *Mercanti, eresia e Inquisizione nell'Italia moderna*, special issue of *Storia economica* (1).

Marcocci, G. (2004) *I custodi dell'ortodossia. Inquisizione e Chiesa nel Portogallo del Cinquecento*, Rome: Edizioni di Storia e letteratura.

Martínez Millán, J. (1993) *Estructura de la hacienda de la Inquisición*, in J. P. Villanueva and B. Escandell Bonet (eds) *Historia de la Inquisición en España y Amèrica*, vol. 2, *Las estructuras del Santo Officio*, Madrid: Biblioteca de autores cristianos-Centro de estudios inquisitoriales, 883–1076.

Maselli, D. (1970) 'Per la storia religiosa dello Stato di Milano durante il dominio di Filippo II: l'eresia e la sua repressione dal 1555 al 1584', *Nuova rivista storica* (3–4): 317–73.

Masini, E. (1730) *Sacro arsenale, ovvero pratica dell'uffizio della santa Inquisizione; coll'inserzione di alcune regole fatte dal padre inquisitore Tommaso Meneghini domenicano*, Rome: nella stamperia di S. Michele a Ripa (1st edn 1621).

Merlo, G. G. (2012) *Il cristianesimo medievale in Occidente*, Rome and Bari: Laterza.

Prosperi, A. (1991) 'Per una storia dell'Inquisizione romana' in A. Del Col and G. Paolin (eds) *L'Inquisizione romana in Italia nell'età moderna. Archivi, problemi di metodo e nuove ricerche. Atti del seminario internazionale, Trieste, 18–20 maggio 1988*, Udine: Del Bianco, 27–64.

Index

Italic page numbers indicate tables.

Albertinelli, Carlo 262, 263
Albizzi, Francesco 154
Alexander IV 149
Alexander VII 36
Ancona 103, 157–8
Apostolic Chamber 158–60, 161
autonomy of courts, financial 3–4

Bad Faith 214
Balsamo confiscation 189–90, 192–3, 195–203
Barberini, Francesco 62
Beccaria, Cesare 140, 141
Belinchetto 252
Belo, Pietro 155
Benedetti, Marina 89
Benedict XI 149
benefices: assignment of 32–3, 35; control of 41–2
bequests from inquisitors 231
Berengo, Marion 249
Bergamo 34, 72–4
Bichi, Alessandro 59
bishops 15–16; competition with inquisitors 32–9, 41; control of resources of 41–2
blasphemy, monetary penalties for 95–6
Bologna 34, 233, 234, 256
Boncompagni, Francesco 60
book-keeping, inquisitors' view of 89
Borromeo, Carlo, Cardinal 37–8, 162
Boselli, Giovan Battista 254–5
Brescia 34
Bruchman, Pandolfo 142, 262–3
Bruno, Giordano 184
business and trade, impact of Inquisition on: businessmen, role of 247; circulation of individuals and merchandise 248–9; confiscations 252; continued surveillance of 258–60; emigration to Geneva 249–50; foreign operators, presence of 252–8; foreign trade, impact on 141–2; German merchants 247; heresy as contagious disease 249; informers 266; Kraków 250; Lyons 250; marketplaces panicking the Inquisition 250; Milan 258–60; Nuremburg, Italian merchants in 261–2; Reformed Dutch 247; Reformed ideas, spread of 249–50, 252; residence in mixed religion countries 257, 261–6; searching of goods 249, 258; secular authorities 265; self-discipline of merchants 265–6; social networks of merchants 251–2; Swiss merchants 257–8; Torregiani merchants 261–2; travel abroad 251, 258; Venice, Republic of 247–9

Cantimori, Delio 247
Capece Galeota, Fabio 185
Capodistria, inquisitor of 40
Carafa, Gian Pietro 32
Casale Monferrato Inquisition 23–4
Castiglione confiscation 207–15
Castro, Alfonso de 150–1
Cenci family 158
Centini, Giacinto 160, 161
centralization 15, 19, 40, 41, 120
Centurione, Agostino 251
Chabod, Federico 264
Clement VIII 37, 40, 257, 265
Clement X 120

code manual of Sixtus V 104–6
Como 207–15
Conca estate 24, 26, 236
confiscation of goods and property: 'A Note on Some of the Many Examples Which May Be Furnished of Punishments and Confiscations Regarding the Holy Office' 161; Apostolic Chamber 158–60, 161; attempted assassination of Urban VIII 160–1; Balsamo confiscation 189–90, 192–3, 195–203; broadening of recourse to 160–1; business and trade, impact of Inquisition on 252; as cancellation of the past 140–52; Castiglione confiscation 207–15; collaborations in 181; confusion about ownership 75; conscience 151; credit, system of 170–2; *Cum secundum leges* 149–50; custodians, situation of during 191–3; from the day of the committed error 152–6; *Description* of the patrimony 191–2; development of system for 147–52; as enhancing value of Holy Office 145; eye-witness testimony 194–203; failure to accumulate long-term patrimonies 280–2; Ferrara Inquisition 167–9, 170; Ferrari confiscation 205–6; financial and mercantile world, impact on 141–2; foreign trade, impact on 141–2; Good/Bad Faith 214–15; impact on economics and mission 6; as improving inquisitors' position and importance 169–70; and income of courts 139; as inquisitorial income 142–4; intervention by Congregation of the Holy Office 146; as investigative tool 194–205; legal sources 147–8; link with inquisitorial process 145; medium/long-term effects 169–70; Milan 187–8; moral and philosophical implications of 141; Naples 184–5; nature of 150; path dependence 170; pervasiveness of the Inquisition as result of 180–1; as phase within Inquisitorial continuum 181; politics, intertwining with Inquisition 163–7; Portuguese Inquisition 140; post-mortem 149; as pre-emininent function of the Inquisition 146; previously sold to others 211–15; princes, power of 161–7; protection of family patrimony 190; public officials as inquisitors 205–15; *Quod super nonnulis* 149; rediscovery of 147; retroactivity of 152–6, 208; secular/ecclesiastical authorities, division among 148–9, 156–61; secular/ecclesiastical controversies 144–5; sentencing, waiting for 151; social and fiduciary framework as disturbed by 141; as social control 140; society/Inquisition relations 191; Spanish Inquisition 116–19, 120, 139–40, 142, 184; State institutions/inquisitors relations 207–8; study of 139; tripartite division of confiscated goods 187–9, 192–3; Vaaz family 181–4; *Vergentis in senium* 148. *See also* penalties, monetary

Confraternity of San Pietro Martire 69

Congregation of the Holy Office: conversion campaigns, donations for 62–3; ethos, development of common 111–13; events leading to creation of 18–19; expenditure 28; financial reputation, protection of 112–13; gathering and investment of money, rules for 111; gifts to inquisitors 57, 58–61, 237; income of 24, *24*, 28, *29–30*; intervention in confiscations 146; *Licet ab initio* 19, 146; as part of inquisitorial structure 4; recommendations about monetary penalties 89–90; role in organizational structure 14; salaries and gratuities 93; secrecy 32; social, geographic and religious interventions 63–4

conscience 151

consistorialization of benefices 33

convents: assistance provided to inquisitors 108–9; economic initiatives by 68–9; and inquisitors, relations between 66–72, 104–10; regulation and control of, increase in 107–8; transfer of Inquisition funds to 108

conversion campaigns, donations for 62–3, 65

Cornaro, Federico 72

Corteni, Pietro 196–7

courts: advantages of being interlocutor 233–4; confiscation of property 139; economic contexts for 27; expenditure 65, 66; familiars, increase in 234–6; financial autonomy of 3–4;

288 Index

fixed income, assignment of 29, 29–30, 31–2; inadequacy of financial conditions 57; income of 21–7, 22, 23; increase resources, requirement to 3; informal support to 61–5, 66; mission/economics, joining of 3–4, 5; monitoring of economic decisions 4–5; needs of, and monetary penalties 97–9; receipts and expenses of 78, 79–80, 80; reimbursement of expenditure, failure of 44–5; responsibilization of 111–12; risky financing of 39–46; solidarity among 53–6; stabilization of 227; unclear business administration of 72–4
credit, inquisitor's 74–5, 76–8, 79–80, 80–1
credit system 170–2, 229–31
Cremona Inquisition 188, 192, 204–5, 232
Crocesignati 234–6
Cum secundum leges 149–50
custodians, situation of during confiscation 191–3

De poteste legis poenalis (Castro) 150–1
Decrees of Derogation 96
Description of the patrimony 191–2
districts 16
Divine Majesty 153–4
Dominican 'families' 103–4
Donati, Claudio 43
Donghi, Giovanni Stefano, Cardinal 36

economics of the Roman Inquisition: complexity of 27; importance of 277; income of peripheral courts 21–7, 22, 23; institutional/political confrontation, role in 21; management as fragmentary 121–7; monitoring of local decisions 4–5; studying, reasons for 1–7. *See also* business and trade, impact of Inquisition on; confiscation of goods and property; expenditure; incentive system; income; inquisitors; penalties, monetary
emigration to Geneva 249–50
England and Genoa, relations between 265
entrepreneurial activities of inquisitors 70–1
Eretici italiani del Cinquecento (Cantimori) 247

Estense Holy Office 167–9
ethos, development of common 111–13
Ex tuae circumspectionis literis 184
excommunication 150–1
exile 146–7
expenditure: Congregation of the Holy Office 28; courts 65, 66, 78, 79–80, 80; expansion of in modern period 280; Holy Office 237; mixture of items in accounts 237–9; postal expenses 102; reimbursement, failure of 44–5; Siena Inquisition 241–2; Spanish Inquisition 119–20
extraordinary income 23–4
eye-witness testimony 194–203

Faenza court 170
Falangonio, Giovanni Vincenzo 157–8
Faleri, Girolamo Antonio 80–1
familiars, increase in 234–6
Ferrara Inquisition 167–9, 170
Ferrari confiscation 205–6
Figliodoni, Danesio 204–5
financial accounts, receipt and filing of in Rome 102–3
financial control as fragmentary 121–7
financial information, reasons for studying 1–7
financial investments, property and land conversions into 229–31
financial performance: and judicial activity 239–40, 241–2, 243–6. *See also* confiscation of goods and property; expenditure; income; penalties, monetary
fines, faith. *See* penalties, monetary
Firpo, Massimo 32
fixed income: assignment of 29, 29–30, 31–2; Naples 59
Florence 253
foreign business operators, presence of 252–8, 260. *See also* business and trade, impact of Inquisition on
foreign collaborators 62
foreign dynasties, diffidence regarding 183
foreign trade, impact on 141–2. *See also* business and trade, impact of Inquisition on
Franciscan 'families' 103–4
Frigo, Daniela 163–4

Gabrielli, Pietro 159
Galassi, Pelegrino 45

Gattelli, Angelo 1–2
Gaudiniero, Enrico 253–4
Geneva, emigration to 249–50
Genoa 157, 265
German merchants 247
Ghislieri, Michele 34–5
Giberti, Gian Matteo 41
gifts to inquisitors 57, 58–61, 237
Giudobaldo II della Rovere 162
Giugni, Claudio 66–8
Gonzaga, Carlo 98–9
Gonzaga, Guglielmo 162
Good/Bad Faith 214–15
Gottarelli, Serafino 74–5
grants to inquisitors 57, 58–61, 124–5
Gregory VII 15
Gregory XIII 34, 35
Guazzini, Sebastiano 153
Gubbio 35–6

Hercules II d'Este 161–2
heresy as contagious disease 249
Holy Office: confiscation as enhancing value of 145; expenditure 237; financial autonomy of courts 3–4; historic roots 15; income 236–7; increase in numbers of helpers 227–8, 234–6
Houses of the Catechumans and the Neophytes 65
housing for inquisitorial activities 90–4

Imola, Bishop of 36
In coena Domini 40
incentive system: Bergamo, unclear business administration of 72–4; confusion about property ownership 75; and costs of investigation and trials 280; credit, inquisitor's 74–5, 76–8, 79–80, 80–1; financially onerous cases, avoidance of 77–8; individually answerable, inquisitors as 76–7; prompt recovery of credit 78, 80–1; receipts and expenses of courts 78, 79–80, 80; voluntary presentations 77–8
income: aristocratic families, transactions with 231; bequests from inquisitors 231; communities' financial dependence on courts 232; complexity of 27; confiscation of goods and property as 142–4; conflicts of interest 231–2; Congregation of the Holy Office 24, *24*, 28, *29–30*; courts 78, *79–80*, *80*; economic contexts for 27; fixed, assignment of 29, *29–30*, 31–2; Holy Office 236–7; and jurisdiction of courts 28; lack of regular, reasons for 122–7; mixture of items in accounts 237–9; peripheral courts 21–7, *22*, *23*; from property 229; property conversion into financial investments 229–31; Siena Inquisition *241–2*; solidarity among inquisitors 53–6; Spanish Inquisition 116–19; taxation, rights of 232; variations in 243; water, right to draw 232
informal support to inquisitors 61–5, 66
informers 266
Innocent III 15
Innocent IV 16
Innocent XI 42
inquisitors: actions of collaborators, responsibility for 111–12; as administrators, development into 228; appointment of 16; bequests from 231; book-keeping, inquisitors' view of 89; competition with bishops 32–9, 41; convents, assistance provided by 108–9; and convents, relations between 66–72, 104–10; credit, inquisitor's 70–80, 74–5, 76–8, 80–1; distribution of 55; entrepreneurial activities 70–1; as entrepreneurs 5; financial accounts, Rome as requiring 102–3; financially onerous cases, avoidance of 77–8; friars as, responsibilities of 112; gathering and invesment of money 111; gifts/grants from the Congregation 57, 124/5, 237; inadequacy of financial conditions 57; income from property 229; as individually answerable for management 76–7; judicial authorities, links with 194–205; land management by 229; local relationships and networks 170; position and importance, confiscation as improving 169–70; princes, alliances and support with 163–7; property purchases 228–9; public officials as 205–15; solidarity among 53–6; transfer of Inquisition funds to convents 108; vicars, appointment of for 105; voluntary presentations 77–8
institutes, conversion, donations for 65
investigative tool, confiscation as

290 *Index*

194–205
judges of faith. *See* inquisitors
judicial activity, financial performance and 239–40, *241–2*, 243–6
judicial authorities, links with inquisitors 194–205
Julius III 184
jurisdiction of the Inquisition: and income 28; offenders under 14; Spanish/Portuguese comparison 114
Justinian *Codex* 146–7

Kamen, Henry 115, 119, 142
Kaunitz, Wenzel Anton von 19, 20–1
Kraków 250

land: conversion into financial investments 229–31; management by inquisitors 229. *See also* confiscation of goods and property; penalties, monetary; property and land
Lavenia, Vincenzo 139
law, development of 99–1–1
lay confraternities 234–6
Lea, Henry Charles 114, 116
lending activity of the Inquisition 170–1. *See also* credit system
Leo X 115
Licet ab initio 19, 146
Listier, Richard 62
Livorno 252–3
loans, property and land conversions into 229–31. *See also* credit system
local relationships and networks 170
Locati, Umberto 153, 163
Lucca, Republic of 17, 156–7, 264–5
Lyons 250

Maggi Inquisition 204–5
Mantua 34
manuals, inquisitorial 16–17
Marcocci, Giuseppe 279–80
Mendoza, Juan Hurtado de 207–8
merchants. *See* business and trade, impact of Inquisition on
Merlo, Grado Giovanni 276
Michelozzi, Giovan Battista 264
Milan 17, 37–8, 91–2, 102–3, 144–5, 187–8, 229, 236, 258–60
Minor Conventuals 103
missionary activity 61
Modena 90–1, 234, 256
monasteries. *See* convents

Moneglia, Agostino 97–8
monetary penalties. *See* penalties, monetary
Monter, William 139–40
moral and philosophical implications of confiscation 141
Morone, Giovanni 41
mortgages 170–1. *See also* credit system
Most Accurate Index Compiled upon the Final Section of the Arsenal of the Holy Office 155
Multorum querela 16

Naples 58–61, 184–5, 253–4
Neopolitan Inquisition 58–61
Nicolò da Brettinoro 72–3
Nocera Inferiore-Sarno, Bishop of 58–9
'Note on Some of the Many Examples Which May Be Furnished of Punishments and Confiscations Regarding the Holy Office, A' 161
Notes for the Administration of the Holy Inquisition of Rome 100–1
Novara Inquisition 232
Nuremburg, Italian merchants in 261–2

Olmo, Matteo dell' 69–70
open system, management as 236–46
oral testimony 194–203
Orano, Giuseppe 21
ordinary income 23
organizational structure 4–5, 14–18; centralization 40; evolution of 279–80; plague, impact of 44; war, impact of 44
Ottoboni, Pietro 42–3

Padua 34
Pallavicini, Orazio 265
Panciatichi, Bartolomeo 251251
Paolini, Lorenzo 87
Páramo, Ludovico da 153
patrimonies. *See* confiscation of goods and property
Paul III 18–19, 117–18
Paul IV 32, 119
Pellegrini da Como, Domenico Francesco 155–6
Pellizzari, Gian Antonio 249
Pellizzari, Giovan Andrea 206
Pellizzari, Nicolò 249
Peña, Francisco 152
penalties, monetary: amount of, Rome as determiner of 96; blasphemy 95–

6; book-keeping, inquisitors' view of 89; collector and distributor, Rome as 96; Decrees of Derogation 96; development of new 93; Gonzaga, Carlo, trial of 98–9; housing for inquisitorial activities 90–4; as innovation 87; as inquisitors' responsibility, risk of 89; investigations into abuse of 88–9; as long-lasting practice 95; Naples 59; needs of the court 97–9; new objects of persecution, emergence of 92; penal sentences commuted to 96; recommendations from Holy Office 89–90; regulation of by Rome 95, 101; secular organizations, sharing with 94; Spanish Inquisition 116–19; versatility and flexibility of 94–5; wealth of the accused 97–9. *See also* confiscation of goods and property
pensions, episcopal 42
peripheral courts: abolition of peripheral seats 19–20; expenditure 65, 66; familiars, increase in 234–6; income of 21–7, 22, 23; informal support to 61–5, 66; needs of, and monetary penalties 97–9; receipts and expenses of 78, 79–80, 80; reimbursement of expenditure, failure of 44–5; responsibilization of 111–12; risky financing of 39–46; solidarity among 53–6; stabilization of 227; unclear business administration of 72–4
personal aid to inquisitors 58–62
pervasiveness of the Inquisition: as result of confiscation 180–1; Vaaz family 181–4
Philip II, King of Spain 38, 184
philosophical implications of confiscation 141
Piacenza 162–3, 166–7
Pisa 35
Pius IV 24
Pius V 24, 34–5
plague, impact of 44
politics: intertwining with Inquisition 163–7; and personal interests 183
Portuguese Inquisition 114, 116, 118, 119, 140, 279, 281–2
postal expenses 102
Pozzobonelli, Galeazzo 198–200
Pozzobonelli, Giuliano 200–1
princes, and confiscation of goods and property 161–7

procedural code of Sixtus V 104–6
Prodi, Paolo 208
Prodomino, Antonio 63
property and land: conversion into financial investments 229–31; development of by Inquisition 229; income from 229; purchases by the Inquisition 228–9. *See also* confiscation of goods and property; penalties, monetary
public officials as inquisitors 205–15
punishment: excommunication 150–1; exile 146–7. *See also* confiscation of goods and property; penalties, monetary

Quod super nonnullis 149

Ranuccio I Farnese 163, 164
Rebiba, Scipione 202
Reformed Dutch 247
residence: abroad by Italian merchants 261–6; in mixed religion countries 202–3, 257
responsibilization of courts 111–12
retroactivity of confiscation 152–6, 208
Rimini Inquisition 228
Roman Inquisition: aim of 276; body of law, development of 99–1–1; continuance of policies, reasons for 278; deeper historical significance of 283; districts 16; ethos, development of common 111–13; evasion of financial support for 35–6; evolution of organizational structure 279–80; financial control as fragmentary 121–7; Franciscan and Dominican 'families' 103–4; further research 277–8, 280; income of peripheral courts 21–7, 22, 23; innovations introduced by Paul IV 32; justification for near the end 276; long-term effects of 276; medieval, transformation of 19; offenders under 14; open system, management as 236–46; organizational structure 4–5, 14–18; peripheral seats, abolition of 19–20; plague, impact of 44; priorities and problems at turn of 17th century 101; researching 276; Spanish/Portuguese Inquisitions compared 114–21; stabilization of courts 227, 279; stable procedures, establishment of 101–2; suppression of

courts in Milan 19–20; war, impact of 44
Romeo, Giovanni 14–15, 124
Ruinagia, Alessio 163

salaries in the Congregation of the Holy Office 93
Sarpi, Paolo 154
Savoy, Duchy of 165–6, 255–6
Sbriccoli, Mario 153–4
Schöbingen brothers 254–5
secular/ecclesiastical authorities: business and trade, impact of Inquisition on 265; controversies regarding confiscation 144–5; division of confiscated goods 94, 148–9, 156–61; foreign business operators, presence of 254–7; interdependence, and confiscation 183–7; judicial authorities, links with inquisitors 194–205; residence abroad by merchants 265; tripartite division of confiscated goods 187–9, 192–3
self-accusations 77–8, 150–1
self-discipline of merchants 265–6
Sicily 17
Siena 143–4
Siena Inquisition 240, *241–2*, 243–6
Silvola, Antonio 75
Sixtus V 35, 40, 104–6, 257–8
social networks of merchants 251–2
solidarity among inquisitors 53–6
Sozzini, Fausto 143–4
Spanish Inquisition 114–21, 139–40, 142, 184, 279, 280–2
Speciano, Cesare 261–2
state institutions/inquisitors relations 207–8
Stoppani, Givanni Pietro 64
Swiss merchants 257–8

taxation: exemption from, Holy Office's 232; Naples 59–60; rights of 232
Torregiani merchants 261–2
Tortona 35
Tractus de confiscatione bonorum (Guazzini) 153
trade, impact of Inquisition on. *See* business and trade, impact of Inquisition on
travel abroad: impact of 251; mixed religion countries 202–3; regulation of 258; residence abroad by merchants 261–6
tributes 170–1
tripartite division of confiscated goods 187–9
trustees, appointment of 102

Ugolini, Zanchino 153
Urban VI 159
Urban VIII 160–1, 255

Vaaz family 181–4
Varahona, Juan de 204–5
Vasto, Marquis of 18
Venice, Republic of 35, 37, 157, 247–9
Vercelli, Bishop of 35
Vergentis in senium 148
vicariates 28–9
vicars, appointment of 105
Visconti, Antonio Eugenio 20, 276
Vitoria, Francisco de 151
Vizzani, Carlo Maria 125–6
voluntary presentations 77–8, 150–1

war, impact of 44
water, right to draw 232
wealth of the accused 97–9
witchcraft 164–5
witness testimony 194–203